THE GREAT IRISH FAMINE

A History in Four Lives

The Author

Born in Dublin, Enda Delaney is currently Reader in Modern History at the University of Edinburgh. In 2010 he was the recipient of a prestigious UK Economic and Social Research Council Mid-Career Fellowship, awarded on the basis of a proven track record of excellence in research and 'exceptional all round scholarly ability'. He has written extensively on the history of modern Ireland and its diaspora, including three scholarly books and three jointly-edited volumes.

THE GREAT IRISH FAMINE

A History in Four Lives

ENDA DELANEY

Gill Books

For my daughters
Katie and Emma

Gill Books
Hume Avenue, Park West, Dublin 12
www.gillbooks.ie

Gill Books is an imprint of M.H. Gill & Co.

© Enda Delaney 2012, 2014
First published in hard cover 2012 under the title *The Curse of Reason*
This paperback edition first published 2014
978 07171 6010 5

Typography design by Make Communication
Print origination by Síofra Murphy
Printed by TJ International, Cornwall

The paper used in this book comes from the wood pulp of managed forests. For every tree felled, at least one tree is planted, thereby renewing natural resources.

A CIP catalogue record for this book is available from the British Library.

5 4

Praise for *The Great Irish Famine*

'A subtle, probing and vivid reflection of the impact made by the Famine on four different lives, which is also a fascinating experiment in biography and micro-history. Enda Delaney's focus delineates the national catastrophe as seen by figures from the Catholic-nationalist establishment, the counter-culture of revolutionary agitation, the world of the small landlord, and the myopic official mind in Dublin Castle; the result is a genuinely original and illuminating perspective on a subject too often dealt with by means of second-hand narrative and unexamined clichés.' *Roy Foster, Professor of Irish History, Oxford University*

'… a sophisticated and significant addition to the historiography of the Famine', *Christopher Cusack, Times Literary Supplement*

'In a highly original account of a hugely traumatic series of events, Enda Delaney takes a novel approach by interweaving 50 years of history with the lives of four important actors. The result is an at times gripping narrative.' *The Times Higher Education Supplement*

'Delaney offers an insightful, readable overview of this overwhelming disaster … highly recommended.' *Choice, America's Library Association publication*

'Delaney's approach to the story is innovative … (it will be found) in the hands of those who appreciate first-rate history … a very impressive book.' *Breandán Mac Suibhne, Dublin Review of Books*

'… an extraordinarily important subject … focusing on four fascinating characters', *Ryan Tubridy*

CONTENTS

PREFACE

The Great Famine of 1845–1852 was the defining event in the history of modern Ireland. Proportionately one of the most lethal famines in global history, the consequences were shocking: at least one million people died, and double that number fled the country within a decade.

The work of a whole generation of scholars since the 1980s has laid bare the brutal realities of the late 1840s in a raft of detailed and pioneering studies. My heavy debt to this body of scholarship will be evident from the notes. This book does not present detailed findings based on consulting large amounts of new evidence or hitherto unknown archival documents, as the relevant material has been extensively worked through by other people. On certain essential points it does incorporate original research on contemporary sources; nevertheless the objective is to draw on the existing scholarship, much of it not accessible to a broader audience, and present a distinctive interpretation. This is therefore a narrative history, with an interpretative dimension. It gives equal weight to the social, economic and political aspects of the crisis. My purpose in writing the book is to further our understanding and deepen our knowledge of those most horrific years in the complex and fascinating history of modern Ireland.

ACKNOWLEDGEMENTS

Writing a book of this type by necessity involves drawing on the expertise of others. For detailed guidance on particular points I am indebted to Breandán Mac Suibhne and Ciarán Reilly. Owen Dudley Edwards, with characteristic generosity, read draft chapters at various stages of evolution, offered encouragement and spotted numerous errors of both fact and interpretation, despite retaining a healthy degree of scepticism about the project as a whole. Other colleagues with Irish interests at Edinburgh were equally supportive, in particular Alvin Jackson. Students who took my special subject on the Great Irish Famine in 2009/10 provided a stimulating audience for many of the ideas developed here; and my thanks go especially to two gifted young scholars, Andrew Phemister and Thomas Dolan. Beyond our group of Irish historians good friends, including Frank Cogliano, Ewen Cameron, Fabian Hilfrich and especially Donald Bloxham, have encouraged me to think about these issues in broader contexts. Don Akenson, Tom Devine and Joe Lee offered support at a critical juncture. Vincent Comerford, Sean Connolly, Marianne Elliott, Roy Foster, Liam Kennedy, Kevin Kenny, Don MacRaild and Cormac Ó Gráda, while not being involved directly with this book (and therefore free of any blame of guilt by association!), have shown me many kindnesses and supported my work in different ways over the years. Within my family circle my brother-in-law Gary Healy read some early drafts and offered helpful suggestions. The death of my father (and keenest reader) shortly before the book was completed was a great loss: he, like my late mother, was one of the sharpest intellects I have ever encountered.

At Gill & Macmillan, Fergal Tobin was very enthusiastic about the book and offered wise comments on an earlier draft. To have a publisher with such impressive knowledge of the subject is a rarity these days. Deirdre Rennison Kunz saw it through publication with endless courtesy and patience, Jen Patton sourced the illustrations, Deborah Marsh looked after administrative matters, and Teresa Daly and Ciara O'Connor were very helpful when it came to publicity and marketing.

This book would never have seen the light of day without the support of two people. Ivan Mulcahy first spotted its potential, and his remarkable enthusiasm for the subject brought the project from being simply an inchoate idea to the completion of the first draft, for which I am deeply grateful. His passion for accessible yet scholarly history-writing was an inspiration throughout. My wife, Kathryn, has lived with this book for far too long and created the practical conditions whereby it could be written, making many sacrifices along the way. In the meantime, our lives were immeasurably enriched by the arrival of two little girls to whom this book is dedicated with deep love and affection.

PROLOGUE
The land of the dead

An engraving of Bridget O'Donnell and her children that appeared in the *Illustrated London News* in December 1849 put names and faces on the victims of Ireland's Great Famine. It remains one of the most widely recognised images of the crisis: a woman in rags, with sunken face and limbs emaciated, beside two young children. According to an accompanying news story, her husband had held a little less than five acres in the townland of Garraunnatooha in the parish of Kilmacduane, near Kilrush, Co. Clare, but the family had been evicted for falling behind in the payment of rent. They had purchased oats for seed from Marcus Keane, who owned the land, and they had sown the crop and harvested it. As soon as the corn was stacked, a neighbour named Blake had taken the corn and stored it, on the instructions of one Dan Sheedy, presumably a henchman acting for Keane. Sheedy then arrived with a group of men to eject the family and level the cabin. Bridget, pregnant and suffering from fever, remained inside, until neighbours rescued her. A week later she gave birth to a stillborn child and received the last rites from her priest, the Rev. Michael Meehan. Another child, aged thirteen, died three weeks later. Sheedy and Blake sold the corn at the market in nearby Kilrush.[1] What happened to Bridget O'Donnell thereafter has never been established.

Marcus Keane was a notorious agent who represented absentee landlords in Co. Clare, such as Francis Conyngham, second Marquess Conyngham, but was himself the owner of a small estate. In addition to the O'Donnells he had evicted twelve other families in Garraunnatooha, leaving some sixty people homeless.[2] He was described in 1846 by a state functionary as a 'gentleman of high character'; the *Limerick Reporter* later said of him that he was 'unhappy when not exterminating',[3] and one historian has described him as the 'exterminator general'.[4] Keane earned this notoriety through the large-scale evictions he oversaw throughout Co. Clare, especially in the Kilrush Poor Law Union from 1847 onwards.[5] The Poor Law inspector for the union, Captain Arthur Kennedy, drew the attention of senior officials in London to his systematic removal of smallholders during 1848 and 1849.[6] Ultimately a parliamentary committee chaired by the radical MP George Poulett Scrope examined the whole issue of the shocking events that had taken place in the Kilrush Union during the previous three years.

The reporter from the *Illustrated London News* who recorded Bridget O'Donnell's story had been despatched to west Clare to investigate the mass evictions in late 1849. On entering a village he felt he was transplanted to 'the land of the dead'.

> It is a specimen of the dilapidation I behold all around. There is nothing but devastation, while the soil is of the finest description, capable of yielding as much as any land in the empire. Here, at Tullig, and other places, the ruthless destroyer, as if he delighted in seeing the monuments of his skill, has left the walls of the houses standing, while he has unroofed them and taken away all shelter from the people. They look like the tombs of a departed race, rather than the recent abodes of a yet living people, and I felt actually relieved at seeing one or two half-clad spectres gliding about, as an evidence that I was not in the land of the dead.[7]

The orders to clear estates of smallholders came from landlords or from agents acting for them. After the necessary legal processes were completed they were executed by gangs of men known as 'wreckers'. From similar poor backgrounds to those of the evicted tenants, these were hardened young men. 'Rough-looking peasants', they were known for drinking heavily before they got down to wrecking.[8]

When the legal processes of eviction and levelling had been done, the wreckers set about removing the evicted tenants from the public roads near their old homes, along which many often set up makeshift shelters. After one eviction, on 22 October 1850, recounted by the English philanthropist Lord Sidney Godolphin Osborne in a letter to the *Times* (London), a family threw up a scalp (a makeshift shelter made of sods) on the roadside. When the husband was away his wife visited a nearby neighbour about a hundred yards distant. A girl called out that the scalp was on fire, and the woman ran back to save her child, but it was too late. The distraught mother arrived in time to witness her child being 'taken out of the scalp on a shovel, all burnt to death, by a man named Michael Griffin'. She knew that the tragedy was no accident: 'I am sure that the scalp was set on fire by some person or persons, for it could not otherwise take fire'.[9]

Brutal evictions, occasionally with lethal consequences, were but one symptom of the complete disintegration of Irish society by the late 1840s; the exodus of a quarter of a million people in one year, 1851, was another. The complete failure of the potato crop in 1846 and 1848, with partial failures in other years, was the result of a destructive blight that destroyed the food that at least a third of the people of Ireland relied on for survival. First and foremost, it was this unprecedented environmental disaster that created widespread hunger.

This book describes how Ireland descended into chaos in the middle of the nineteenth century. Yet the country was politically integrated in the United Kingdom, the most advanced industrial economy in the world. It lays special emphasis on the conditions on the eve of the famine, before the blight struck in September 1845, as this served to expose the existing weaknesses in Ireland's political, economic and social structure. Particular attention is paid to the role of the British state in responding to hunger in Ireland. Rather than just creating a need to feed the poor, the outbreak of famine was seen by influential British politicians and officials as presenting a unique opportunity to implement far-reaching changes in Irish society. For some of an evangelical bent this was a divinely ordained moment for bringing about root-and-branch reform in the organisation of the rural economy; for others, reason and logic, together with Divine Providence, demanded that an archaic peasant culture be eradicated and replaced with a capitalist form of agriculture. The fatal decisions that led to hundreds of thousands of people being placed on the edge of starvation were taken by these 'enlightened' men in the context of an ideological policy that lauded the transformative power of the state. Legislative measures such as the introduction of the Poor Relief (Ireland) Act (1838) were the work of rational improvers who sought to impose an orderly structure on what was considered an uncivilised society.

What was self-consciously 'progressive' social engineering had a cruel outcome. People would undergo great suffering, many would die or be forced into the workhouse or emigration, but at the end of this painful process a stronger and more rational society would gradually emerge. The application of these principles had horrific, almost unimaginable consequences for the Irish poor.

The British government cannot be singled out for the inadequate, and at times inhumane, response to the famine. Many of those who made up the upper and middle classes, both Catholics and Protestants, landlords, farmers and merchants, stood by as millions of poor people simply vanished from the landscape. The Great Irish Famine had winners as well as victims, as self-interest overrode basic humanitarian concern for the vulnerable and powerless.

This book chronicles the tragic sequence of events that unfolded during the late 1840s and early 1850s by placing a strong emphasis on the experiences and contrasting viewpoints of four contemporaries.

Elizabeth Smith, *née* Grant (1797–1885), came to Ireland through sheer chance when her husband inherited an estate in west Co. Wicklow in 1830 and remained in the country for the rest of her long life. She was a perceptive observer of Irish life in her volumes of diaries, occasionally acerbic and adopting the high moral tone typical of her social class. She could also be very sympathetic to the plight of the poor in her locality of Baltiboys, near Blessington. In her lifetime she was anonymous: only after her niece Lady Strachey published her memoirs in 1898 did she come to public notice.

John MacHale (1791–1881), Catholic Archbishop of Tuam, was one of the most popular figures in nineteenth-century Ireland. Hated by some British politicians and his many Irish enemies, clerical and lay, he was loved by his devoted flock for his popular radicalism and concern for the poor. He was the classic patriot-bishop, known as the Patriarch of the West or, as Daniel O'Connell dubbed him, the 'Lion of the West' or the 'Lion of the Fold of Judah'.

Sir Charles E. Trevelyan (1807–86) was assistant secretary to the Treasury, the most senior official who oversaw relief efforts in Ireland. A reforming and conscientious public servant with strong religious convictions, he often privileged principles over common sense in his decisions. As the person associated to this day with British parsimony during Ireland's Great Famine, he remains a controversial figure.

The final figure is John Mitchel (1815–75), the famous nineteenth-century nationalist writer whose passion and radical views on the shortcomings of the British government of Ireland helped create a deep sense of grievance among the Irish diaspora, especially in the United States. His most famous judgement may be: 'The Almighty, indeed, sent the potato blight. But the English created the Famine.'

Each of these characters brings a unique viewpoint, influenced by who they were, what they witnessed, and what they stood for. Human failings are evident in the actions and personalities of each of them, whether this be Trevelyan's unflinching commitment to administrative rectitude over and above all other considerations, Smith's instinctive abhorrence of Catholicism,

MacHale's disputatious nature, or the ferocity of Mitchel's hatred of everything English. Retelling the well-known events of the Great Irish Famine through the lives and experiences of these four very different individuals allows for an intimate view on these tragic years.

Our story opens in Co. Mayo in the late 1790s.

PART I

Before the Famine

Chapter 1 ～

ENCOUNTERS

DEATH OF A PRIEST

Piercing wails reverberated through the steep ravine known as the Windy Gap and were heard miles away. A procession wound its way gingerly along the mountain path. At its head, a small group carried a corpse. The news spread rapidly among the inhabitants of Addergoole. Hundreds marked the route as the much-loved priest was brought home, back to his chapel and final resting place. At the foot of Nephin, a place of immense natural beauty where the tall mountain peak runs down to meet Lough Conn, he was buried.

The origin of this tragedy was in the turmoil of the 1798 Rebellion. French forces led by General Jean Humbert arrived in August 1798 at Killala Bay, on the coast of Co. Mayo. They made quick progress inland, with the intention of joining Irish rebels who were engaged in the uprising against the Crown in the north and east. The French camped in Lahardaun, the village within the parish of Addergoole. The parish priest, Andrew Conroy, had been educated in France and spoke French. A number of the officers called at his home, and local legend has it that he gave directions to the invading force on how to reach Castlebar through the Windy Gap, thus avoiding the normal route along the Foxford road. No-one knows how much assistance he gave, and contemporary accounts present widely divergent versions. Sir Richard Musgrave, in his partisan history of the 1798 Rebellion, charged Conroy with entertaining the French, making food available to them and stopping a messenger from passing word to the British forces that the French were advancing towards Castlebar.

The small French force, together with Irish volunteers, achieved a victory at Castlebar on 27 August 1798 in the battle that became known as the 'Races of Castlebar', because of the speed of the retreat of the exhausted Crown forces. A vital factor was that the French and Irish approached the town through the Windy Gap, which the British forces did not believe was passable by an army with artillery and so had left undefended. It was just about traversable for a lightly equipped force, and Conroy certainly knew this. After first pretending to take the Foxford road, the French doubled back and marched through the night over the mountain track.

In the wake of the failed uprising Denis Browne, the chief magistrate of the county and a prominent member of the local Protestant ascendancy, rounded up all the county's inhabitants believed to have assisted the French. They were to be treated as traitors and shown no mercy, and his arbitrary justice dispensed to the local people who joined the French earned him the nickname of 'Denis the Rope'. Browne's house in Claremorris, along with those of other prominent Mayo government supporters, was sacked by Irish rebels during the uprising. Father Conroy's actions in assisting the invading army were judged treasonous and he was arraigned before a court-martial in Castlebar, presided over by the vengeful Browne. Loyal parishioners made the long trek into the town to testify in support of their priest. For them he was a hero, not a traitor. Conroy was swiftly convicted and sentenced to death by hanging. Within an hour he was taken outside the courthouse, and his devoted flock watched in horror as 'the man of God was hung like a dog before their eyes'.[1] The 'hanging tree' in the Mall in Castlebar became a spot of local reverence until it was uprooted in a storm 120 years later.[2]

A young lad had supposedly been sent by Conroy to muster support for the French among the local Catholic families. At the church this young boy, aged seven, now kissed the cold lifeless hand of the dead priest. He was shocked by the facial contortions caused by the hanging, and the lasting image of Conroy's twisted face was inscribed on his memory for life. This boy was John MacHale, future Archbishop of Tuam.

His sister recounted the effect of Conroy's execution in fostering MacHale's early resolve to challenge the existing order:

… It is said that he then vowed in his heart, that if the Almighty gave him life, ability, and position, he would expose the misdeeds of those who ruled Ireland, and denounce the laws which permitted such foul crimes to go unpunished.[3]

MacHale made vocal and persistent attacks on British rule in Ireland for more than half a century. The protection of the Catholic faith, above all of its priests, was his prime concern, but he also sought to promote the cause of Ireland in his frequent political interventions.

A SENSE OF DUTY

Asymmetrical power relations also dominated Britain's other major colonial environment in the nineteenth century, the jewel in the crown of the British Empire: India. Generations of able, and not so able, young men left Britain and Ireland for the Subcontinent to serve as civil servants and military officers. Careers were made and lost in the service of the East India Company, which had begun as a trading operation but was to have overall responsibility for the government of India until 1858.

Sir Edward Colebrooke was Resident of Delhi, the principal representative of the Company in the city. In his late sixties and after nearly fifty years' service, in 1829 he was unceremoniously dismissed from his post. He was accused of corruption by his own first assistant, a callow youth aged twenty-two, in Colebrook's words 'a Boy just escaped from school'.[4] After a six-month prosecution the case against Colebrook was upheld and his ignominious fall from grace confirmed.

The precocious assistant was Charles E. Trevelyan. He was the epitome of a new breed of imperial civil servant: bright, ambitious, learned, proficient in Persian and Hindi, with a strong sense of public duty and unshakeable confidence in his own judgements. The son of a clergyman, he was born at Taunton, Somerset, in 1807. The Trevelyans were a well-connected gentry family, originally Cornish, with estates in Nettlecombe, Somerset and Northumberland, though his parents had little independent wealth and had to provide for a large family of nine children.

The young Charles was educated at the local school in Taunton, then a boarding school in Devon, before going to the famous Charterhouse School in London, where he displayed a remarkable aptitude for classical languages. On leaving there at the age of seventeen he entered Haileybury, the East India Company's training college in Hertfordshire, destined for a career as a writer (clerk) in the Indian imperial civil service. His time there was marked by distinction: he won numerous prizes in classics, history, political economy and Sanskrit. Among his teachers was the Rev. Thomas Malthus, the famous author of *An Essay on the Principle of Population* (1798), a text often cited in contemporary debates about the natural 'check' that famines would exert on population growth. 'Pop' or 'Old Pop', as Malthus was known to his devoted students, taught history and political economy at Haileybury until his death in 1834.

Generations of Indian administrators were educated at Haileybury. Political economy—the study of the economic life of the state—was central to how British officials in India interpreted the world around them. The problems they faced, the solutions they formulated and their understanding of the role of government were all grounded in the principles of classical political economy. The standard text was Adam Smith's canonical work, *An Inquiry into the Nature and Causes of the Wealth of Nations* (1776), and for history the writings of the famous Scottish historian William Robertson. Both were to have a lasting influence on the young Trevelyan—Smith with his emphasis on free trade, the limited role of the state and good governance. For Trevelyan, *The Wealth of Nations* was the 'Bible of Economical Science', as he later told a relative. Robertson's works articulated a global vision of the improvement of all nations through Christianity, Western 'civilisation' and the adoption of Enlightenment values that chimed with the young Trevelyan's evangelical world view.[5]

In 1827, a year after he graduated from Haileybury, Trevelyan set off for India to complete his studies of Persian and Hindi at Fort William College in Calcutta (now Kolkata), where he quickly mastered both languages. Within a year he was appointed an assistant to Sir Charles Theophilus Metcalfe, Resident of Delhi. He proved an able and talented administrator and earned the respect of his superiors. Metcalfe was transferred from Delhi shortly after Trevelyan's posting, and Sir Edward Colebrooke was appointed Resident. Disgusted by his superior's actions in taking bribes and allowing others to do so, including his wife and underlings, Trevelyan covertly gathered evidence against him. In May 1829 he publicly accused Colebrooke of corruption and reported the matter to the central government in Calcutta, leading to his appointment as prosecutor before a commission of inquiry. After a laborious time building a solid case against Colebrooke, the government ruled in Trevelyan's favour in December 1829. His actions were commended, and it was noted that he had 'ably, and honourably, and manfully, discharged his duty as a public servant', and that 'by his zealous and unremitting exertions in the performance of a most painful and invidious task, [he] has justly entitled himself to the warmest approbation of Govt.'

His pleasure was obvious when he wrote to his mother that, 'if I had penned it myself, I would not have said one word more or less'.[6]

This incident made Trevelyan's career, and his abilities were brought to the notice of a wider public in India and beyond. His challenge to the vested interests of the *ancien régime* of British officials in India marked him out as a courageous, determined and punctilious official whose actions were driven by a deeply held if sometimes over-earnest sense of public duty. It would be wrong to see him as merely work-obsessed. Until he was more or less excluded by the Colebrookes, as a young Company official he took an active part in the social life of Delhi led by the Resident's wife, Lady Louisa Colebrooke. Contemporaries recounted his love of riding and hunting and indeed his remarkable capacity to consume copious amounts of alcohol during his time in Delhi. But it was work that dominated his life. His concern extended to Delhi's physical environment, and he planned—and partly financed from his salary—a new suburb for the city's middle classes on three hundred acres, which was known as Trevelyanganj.[7] His ambitions were realised in 1831: at the tender age of twenty-four he was appointed deputy secretary in the Political Department of the government of India in Calcutta, working under the direction of the reformist governor-general, Lord William Bentinck. Trevelyan was a young man in a hurry.

FROM THE HIGHLANDS TO BOMBAY
At more or less the same time Elizabeth (Eliza) Grant, now thirty-one years old, arrived in India in February 1828 after her father accepted a position as a judge. His appointment was a favour secured by a family friend, Charles Grant, later Lord Glenelg. A former MP and lawyer, the recently knighted John Grant needed a lifeline: he was drowning in debt, and his many creditors were steadily catching up with him. He first sought unsuccessfully to carve out a career as an advocate in both London and Edinburgh and then made an attempt at politics, with equally unsuccessful endeavours to gain a parliamentary seat, first in Inverness-shire and then in Elginshire.[8] He then sought an English constituency. Securing a seat in the unreformed House of Commons was then a very expensive business, with the mandatory bribes to gain the support of the tiny unrepresentative electorate. Grant squandered his large inheritance in pursuit of the 'thoroughly rotten borough' of Great Grimsby, Lincolnshire, to which he was duly elected in 1812 but at great financial cost to himself and his family. In the words of his devoted daughter, 'Great Grimsby was gained—at what cost the ruin of a family could certify'.[9]

He lost this seat in 1818 and was 'appointed' in 1819 to another rotten borough, that of Tavistock, Devon, by the Duke of Bedford, to keep the position warm until his son, Lord William Russell, was old enough to take it up, which he duly did in 1826. So ended a political career marked by a singular lack of achievement. Grant was no fool, however: he was later described as 'one of those brilliant men who are not born to succeed'.[10]

Grant's political ambitions had disastrous consequences for his family. He had inherited the Highland estate of Rothiemurchus, near Aviemore in Morayshire, in 1790, and could have earned a comfortable living as its laird. The Grants of Rothiemurchus were a powerful Highland dynasty, descended from the sixteenth-century chief of Clan Grant, James Grant. But his extravagant life-style and reckless spending resulted in mounting debts. By 1824 Grant owed £65,000. He was bankrupt but was protected by his position as a member of Parliament; as Elizabeth observed, his forced retirement from politics meant that 'without this shield his person was not safe'.[11] An entail prevented him from selling Rothiemurchus, or his creditors from seizing it. In 1827 the estate was taken over by a trust administered by his creditors.

Elizabeth, his eldest daughter, was acutely aware of the family's precarious financial position. The men in Elizabeth's life, her father and brother William, were profligate individuals who wasted money, lived well beyond their means and never repaid loans given by friends or family members. Her own approach to money was exactly the reverse; her diaries show how conscious she was of the need to live within her means. Throughout her life she prudently and carefully managed the family finances.

Elizabeth loved growing up at Rothiemurchus, along with her two sisters and two brothers. Many of her childhood and teenage years were spent there, punctuated by spells in Edinburgh and London. The estate itself was spectacular, one of the most beautiful sites in the Scottish Highlands, an enchanting landscape of lochs, glens, mountains, wildlife and rolling forests. Elizabeth's childhood was centred on the Doune, the mansion that was the family home and the centre of all its activities. Those years were happy ones. Unlike her stern and reproachful mother, who suffered from a 'resident sick headache' and often became frustrated, Sir John Grant was adored by his children, notwithstanding his obvious failings.

On 28 September 1827 the Grants left Portsmouth on the *Mountstuart Elphinstone*, bound for Bombay (now Mumbai). In the words of her sister Mary, they were 'done with home'.

It was an ignominious departure. The family's departure for India was marked by persistent harrying from their many creditors, emboldened by her father's recent fall from political power. On the journey from the Highlands to the port of Leith their carriage was seized by a coachmaker in Perth who was owed money; to redeem it Elizabeth had to hand over £40 that she had received for her writings. After they arrived in London, clandestine moves between the homes of friends and relatives were necessary to avoid other creditors. Her father and brothers, who had earlier fled to the Continent, joined the ship from a small boat out at sea. The family, now reunited, set off on the six-month voyage around the Cape of Good Hope to Bombay.

PASSION AND PLEASURE

Sitting in his cell in Kilmainham Jail, twenty-one-year-old John Mitchel reflected upon his predicament. He had been brought back to Ireland and incarcerated after being arrested at Chester. His crime was one of passion. He had first met the sixteen-year-old daughter of a new neighbour in Newry in the spring of 1836 and was 'fascinated by her beauty'.[12] Over the next few months the couple fell in love, spending almost every waking moment with each other, and secretly became engaged in the autumn of that year.

When the girl's father announced that the family was leaving for a long period in France, Mitchel was determined to act. As a biographer was to write, 'he was naturally impetuous and headstrong, even in matters where his passions were much less deeply involved. He at once made up his mind that the parting should not take place.' Mitchel asked his lover to marry him, and she accepted his proposal. They decided to elope to England, where they would be married. Both families were alerted when the couple left Ireland on the Warrenpoint ferry to Liverpool; the girl's father quickly followed, discovered them in Chester, brought the couple back to Ireland and had the young man charged with abduction, a charge later dropped. He confined his daughter to an isolated part of the county until he was ready to leave for France.

Not to be thwarted, her determined fiancé sought her out and obtained a marriage licence, and the couple were eventually married in February 1837 at Drumcree parish church, near Portadown, Co. Armagh.

The bride was Jane (Jenny) Verner, daughter of Captain James Verner (1777–1847), a member of a prominent Armagh gentry family. The Verners were scions of the Protestant and Orange landed class in Ulster, with James's brother, Sir William, member of Parliament for Armagh, 1832–68, and Deputy Grand Master of the Orange Order in Ireland.[13] Her mother, Mary Ward, was the daughter of a coachman working on the Verner estate in Loughgall, Co. Armagh. Jenny's parentage is a matter of some doubt: when James died, his brother William denied that James was ever married to Mary Ward, or indeed that Jenny was his daughter. Nevertheless she was raised as such and sent to Miss Bryden's School for Young Ladies in Newry, and it was on her daily walk to school that she first met her future husband.

Mitchel was working as an apprentice in a solicitor's office in Newry. The son of a Presbyterian minister, the Rev. John Mitchel, he was born near Dungiven, Co. Derry, in 1815. In 1823 his father became minister of Newry Presbyterian Church, and John attended the Classical School run by a Dr David Henderson, after a brief unsuccessful stint at another local school. He had a capacious intellect: by the age of seven he had mastered Latin grammar and was a star pupil at the school. With Henderson's encouragement he matriculated at Trinity College, Dublin, in 1831, at the age of sixteen. It was envisaged that he would follow his father into the ministry after completing his degree. He travelled up and down to Dublin for examinations, spending as little time there as he could, forged few friendships, and did not win any prizes or achieve honours in his degree examinations, which he duly completed in 1836. Despite his obvious abilities, Mitchel did not prosper at university. His focus was on his home life in Newry, especially his mother, rather than that of Trinity. More importantly, it became clear in his preparation to be a minister that his initial enthusiasm for a life of scripture and theology had waned. He had doubts about the teachings of the Presbyterian church and declared that he did not want to become a minister, to his father's great disappointment.

He was devoted to both his parents, who were very different people. His mother, Mary Haslett, a native of Dungiven, was a formidable woman with a first-rate intellect, though she could be impulsive and impatient—traits her son inherited. She was a 'Presbyterian parson's widow of the best Scotch type', in the words of Thomas Carlyle, the Victorian man of letters, who met her when she was in her early sixties.[14] Small in stature, she was described by one of her children as 'vivacious, hazel-eyed, apprehensive and energetic'. Her political outlook was essentially that of the tradition of late eighteenth-century Ulster Presbyterian radicalism, and her father had been a United Irishman.[15]

The Rev. John Mitchel, of Scottish Covenanter descent, was educated at the University of Glasgow and by all accounts was a conscientious minister, who cared for the poor of his locality, regardless of religious denomination. In the 1820s Mitchel senior was centrally involved in the bitter doctrinal controversies that led to a schism in the Synod of Ulster. During the impassioned debates he wrote a number of tracts that favoured Unitarianism, and his young son helped him by identifying relevant passages of scripture to be employed in support of his argument. He was in essence a liberal, broad-minded and tolerant individual who was a central figure in leading the 'New Light' Presbyterians out of the Synod of Ulster to form the Remonstrant Synod in 1830.[16]

Dromalane House, perched on a hill above the town of Newry, where the Mitchels lived, was a busy household. John had one younger brother and four sisters. Learning, reading, arguments and animated debates characterised the day-to-day routine of the Mitchel family, and John would often give his siblings classes on a range of subjects. Despite the conviviality of this environment, he liked his own company and would often walk for hours around the surrounding hills, following streams or exploring new routes. He had a passion for the natural beauty of this drumlin landscape and derived particular pleasure, and indeed a sense of inner peace, from the idyllic vistas he encountered.

But Mitchel needed to carve out a career for himself. His parents arranged for him to take up a position as a clerk in Derry in 1834, where his uncle was a director of the local bank. He hated every moment of this job—the routine, the lack of free time for reading, the sheer monotony of the life of a bank clerk—and complained at length to his father. It was 'unintermitting slavery'. His father agreed that a career in banking did not suit him, and he returned home to Newry.

On his way to Derry he visited friends in Belfast and met a woman six years older than himself. He was smitten with her and saw her frequently when he came back to Newry in the late summer of 1834. Secretly they became engaged, but when his parents found out they forbade any further contact, as did the woman's parents on learning of the opposition of the Mitchels.

The effect of this involuntary separation on the sensitive nineteen-year-old was profound. He withdrew from family life, went walking for hours, sometimes returning only the following morning, and refused to answer any questions about his whereabouts. He tried to contact the woman; his letters were returned unopened. Eventually, in desperation, he set off walking to Belfast to see her, a distance of over thirty miles, without telling anyone he was leaving, and disappeared without a trace for two days. After this unsuccessful attempt to see his lover he was brought back to Newry. He became seriously ill in the early months of 1835 and experienced what was to all intents and purposes a breakdown of sorts.

Some months passed, Mitchel was considered by his parents to have fully recovered, and the question of a career arose again. A solicitor friend of his father's agreed to take him on as an apprentice, and in early 1836 he began his training in John Quinn's office in Newry. After the dramatic events of the previous year a state of moderate equilibrium was restored and, in the delicate words of his nineteenth-century biographer, 'time at length, and the feeling that his love-dream was irrevocably over, gradually restored his health of mind and body'. Mitchel then encountered the young Jenny Verner on her way to school. This chance meeting was to completely change both their lives.

THE RISE OF HIEROPHILOS

Born in 1791, the fifth son of Patrick MacHale, an innkeeper, small farmer and linen trader at Tobernaveen, Tirawley, Co. Mayo—one of the most impoverished western regions—John MacHale was raised in a comfortable home in the district known as Glen Nephin.[17] His home was on the slopes of Nephin, a 'lordly mountain' in the words of the writer Caesar Otway, who visited the area in the late 1830s.[18] John was a sickly and feeble baby, requiring constant nursing. Even though it was an Irish-speaking community, the boy also learnt English. He attended the local 'hedge school' at the nearby village of Lahardaun. These were makeshift classes run by self-taught masters who often held their lessons outside in summer weather, hence the label. At the age of twelve young MacHale was sent to the 'classical academy' in Castlebar run by Patrick Stanton, which prepared boys for university through the study of Greek and Latin. His mother, to whom he was devoted, died when he was only thirteen, leaving a chasm in his life. He resumed his studies and soon came to the attention of the Bishop of Killala, Dominic Bellew, who nominated MacHale for a bursary to study at St Patrick's College, Maynooth, the national seminary for Catholic priests. By deciding to train for the priesthood, MacHale was fulfilling one of his mother's wishes.

With his older brother he made the long journey by horseback across the country and in September 1807 formally entered Maynooth. MacHale was an able scholar, and over the seven-year period required as training for the priesthood he excelled in the courses he took in philosophy and theology. He often came back home in the long summer holidays, the return of the brilliant scholar being a local event.[19] In 1814 he was ordained a priest and appointed as a lecturer to assist an ailing professor, the Frenchman Louis Delahogue. In 1820 he was elected to the chair of dogmatic theology in succession to Delahogue at the tender age of twenty-nine.

MacHale was a natural teacher and readily identified with his students. His having been born and raised in Ireland marked him out as different from the older generation of Maynooth professors, who were mainly French, or Irish but educated at one of the Irish colleges on the Continent. One of his former students testified to MacHale's patriotism: 'Your belief in that peculiar and distinguishing characteristic of your countrymen—an Irishman is a lamb when stroked, a lion when provoked—have contributed, by awakening the national feeling, to cast an air of sacredness about your character …'.[20]

MacHale was no mere monkish scholar. He would walk from Maynooth to Dublin in the same day—a round trip of more than thirty miles—and his physical appearance was striking. His frame, while slender, was muscular and remarkably strong.[21] By his late twenties he was already making his mark as a scholar, teacher and leader. He gradually evolved from being a well-respected figure within the cloistered environment of Maynooth to become a public figure, a person who over his lifetime generated affection and vitriol in equal measure.

MacHale first earned public notice when he wrote a series of public letters under the pen-name 'Hierophilos' in the 1820s. His topics were variations on the same theme. He attacked the proselytising activities of the Bible Societies towards Catholics. He also criticised the sectarian role of the Kildare Place Society, an initiative under Protestant control to provide education for the poor. He drew attention to the intolerance of the established Anglican Church of Ireland, and the general neglect of the country by the British government.

Some of Hierophilos's letters were addressed to the English people to expose the inequities of British rule.[22] Others were written to prominent British politicians, such as George Canning, foreign secretary and future prime minister, on the necessity of Catholic emancipation and the granting of equal rights to Catholics with those enjoyed by Protestants. Their tone— fierce, truculent and uncompromising—caused controversy in both Britain and Ireland, yet in 1825 he was appointed coadjutor (successor) to the Bishop of Killala and given the titular post of Bishop of Maronia. He was consecrated in the chapel of St Patrick's College, Maynooth, on 5 June 1825, becoming the first Catholic bishop in more than three hundred years to have been fully educated in Ireland.

MacHale embarked on his new pastoral duties with enthusiasm. The elderly Bishop of Killala, Peter Waldron, had neglected the organisation of the church in the poor diocese. MacHale set about an intensive programme of visits. In 1827, after a fund-raising effort, including an appeal to English

Catholics, the foundation stone for a cathedral was laid in Ballina (though the building was completed only in the 1830s). He remained politically involved and plotted to ensure that Dominick Browne, sitting MP for Mayo and a cousin of the magistrate who had presided over the case against his beloved parish priest in 1798, did not stand in the 1826 general election. As the Brownes were a powerful political dynasty, this event was hugely symbolic, so much so that it was recorded in a popular verse:

Where long a servile alien band,
The satraps of the cruel Browne,
Despoiled and robbed the fated land
Till bold Maronia pulled them down.[23]

MacHale's victory was short-lived, however: Browne was elected once more in 1830 and re-elected until 1836, when he was given a peerage.

In November 1826 MacHale was obliged to appear before the commissioners inquiring into St Patrick's College, Maynooth. They were critical of his political statements while a professor there, in particular his comments on the position of the established church in Ireland. Political comment of any kind was specifically precluded by the college's statutes. MacHale denied he had broken any rules, as he had written under a pen name. In three days of interrogation, much of which seemed designed to ensnare him on theological and doctrinal matters, MacHale defended his actions with characteristic vigour. It was a bravura performance by the thirty-five-year-old bishop in which he demonstrated his considerable oratorical and intellectual sparring skills, memorably pointing out that if he had 'freely expressed himself on the abuses of that country [England]', he did so 'only using the privileges of a British citizen'.[24]

In September 1831 MacHale set off for Rome on a pilgrimage that lasted more than a year, travelling through Britain, France and Italy and recording his impressions of the places he visited in a series of letters published in the *Freeman's Journal*, a popular Dublin newspaper of the day. In London he witnessed the coronation of King William IV in Westminster Abbey, reporting that despite its obvious splendour it was 'nothing more than a mere worldly pageant'.[25] In Rome he made important connections, notably with Pope Gregory XVI. This was a relationship that would stand to him in due course. He left Rome in September 1832, returning to Ireland through Austria, Switzerland and Germany and finally arriving back in December of that year.

1834 was an important year for MacHale. In May the Bishop of Killala, Peter Waldron, died at the age of eighty-two. A month earlier the Archbishop of Tuam, Oliver Kelly, had also passed away. MacHale was immediately elevated to the position of Bishop of Killala, but his was also one of the names put forward to Rome to replace Kelly as Archbishop of Tuam. When the government became aware of the possibility of MacHale securing the vacant position, British ministers lobbied hard to prevent this. Such was his reputation that the prime minister, Lord Melbourne, declared: 'Anybody but him'.[26] The prospect of one of the four Catholic archbishoprics in Ireland being held by a vocal critic of government policy galvanised diplomats into action. The foreign secretary, Lord Palmerston, engaged in a campaign of subterfuge at Rome to block the appointment, ostensibly on the grounds of MacHale's political views. Pope Gregory sought the advice of the Archbishop of Dublin, Daniel Murray, who was critical of the tone of MacHale's writings but confirmed that he was not a rabble-rouser and was 'not connected with any civil disturbances or with any counsel according to which the civil power could be endangered'.[27] The pope was growing weary of British influence on Irish appointments and wished to assert his independence of mind. He read some of MacHale's writings described by his opponents as seditious and deemed them not be.

On 1 August 1834 MacHale was named Archbishop of Tuam. When the news filtered back to Ireland it was greeted enthusiastically, with bonfires in Tuam and widespread jubilation. It became widely known that the government opposed his appointment. In a congratulatory letter the nationalist leader Daniel O'Connell heralded MacHale's appointment as demonstrating the independence of Rome over British attempts to control appointments and stating that MacHale had proved himself 'too honest an Irishman not to be obnoxious to the British administration'.[28]

In his 'brief' or letter of appointment Pope Gregory reminded MacHale that 'we do not doubt that you will maintain in every transaction of your rule singular prudence, moderation of spirit, and the greatest care for peace and beneficial quiet'.[29] This advice was completely disregarded by MacHale. When he attended a banquet in his honour on his arrival in Tuam on 13 October a toast was made to the repeal of the union between Ireland and Britain. On learning of this, Pope Gregory was not pleased but could do little. MacHale was a fiercely independent mind, and no external authority, even God's representative on earth, would temper his political outlook.

LIFE IN NEWRY

After his marriage to Jenny Verner in February 1837, John Mitchel settled down and completed his training as a solicitor. His parents welcomed his new wife into their family as if she were their own daughter. This was especially important as Jenny was now estranged from the Verner family. Their first son, John, was born in January 1838. The Mitchels had a happy domestic life in Newry, and as they lived close to his parental home they saw his family almost every day. Mitchel had the two things he desired most of all: a happy domestic life and the support of his parents and siblings.

Beyond his family and legal work, Mitchel was also involved in a local literary society. He read widely and often read aloud to his family. His favourite writer was the Scottish savant Thomas Carlyle, whom he regarded as the greatest living authority and the 'salt of the earth'. He described Carlyle's recently published monumental work *The French Revolution: A History* (1837) as 'the profoundest book, and the most eloquent and fascinating history, that English literature ever produced'.[30] For Mitchel the only book that came anywhere close to it was Edward Gibbon's *Decline and Fall of the Roman Empire* (1776–88). These books had a special appeal for him: engaging in their prose style, authoritative and wide in scope. He later sought to emulate this writing in his own work.

Far from the metropolitan centres of Dublin and London, Mitchel created his own world of letters through his reading and discussions with family and friends. Chief among these was his lifelong confidant John Martin. Martin had attended Dr Henderson's School in Newry with him. They became close friends and remained so, and in the 1860s Martin married Mitchel's sister Henrietta. He had also studied at Trinity College, albeit with greater distinction than Mitchel, and then decided to pursue a course in medicine. He gave up his medical studies in 1835 on inheriting his uncle's small estate at Loughorne, Co. Down, about five miles from Newry, where he lived the life of a gentleman-farmer. He was known later as 'honest John'; his sweetness of nature and consideration for others contrasted with Mitchel, whose choice of him for a friend is significant in itself. Martin had the leisure time to read widely, and for Mitchel these intellectual pursuits acted as a counterpoise to the drudgery of his legal work.

Signs of Mitchel's future public role were not as obvious in the late 1830s. However, with Martin he helped organise a public dinner for Daniel O'Connell's visit to Newry in 1839. The event went off peacefully despite an expectation of violence, given the Orange tradition in the town. That year also marked the onset of asthma, a lifelong affliction for Mitchel, who had regular attacks from then on, some severe, on occasion even life-threatening.

Mitchel's father died in February 1839, an event that raised feelings of intense remorse. Despite his father's stated wish that Mitchel should follow him into the ministry, he had taken another course. Mitchel's personal life— in particular the elopement to marry Jenny—had caused a great deal of anxiety for his parents. When a parishioner and friend of his father called to pay his respects he commented that the Rev. Mitchel had retained much of his original hair colour; the response from his son was telling: 'I put more grey hairs on that head than time ever did'.[31] He rarely spoke about his father, even after the passage of many years.

In June 1839 Mitchel had completed his legal training and went into partnership with Samuel Fraser in Newry. The following summer the Mitchels left Newry and moved to Banbridge, a growing town ten miles north, to establish a branch office of the legal firm. The life of a provincial solicitor was now his destiny.

ON THE RIGHT SIDE IN EVERY QUESTION

By moving to Calcutta in 1831 to become deputy secretary in the Political Department of the government, Charles Trevelyan was now at the apex of British rule in India. His important new role ensured that he was a participant in the social life associated with the circle of the governor-general. In December 1834 he married Hannah Macaulay, sister of Thomas Babington Macaulay, who had arrived with him in March.

Macaulay would be the legal member of the new Supreme Council for India in June 1834. He was devoted to his younger sisters, Margaret and Hannah, for whom his love bordered on the obsessive. He craved their company, adoration and constant affection. His father, Zachary Macaulay, a leading campaigner for the abolition of slavery, was a stern and critical parent, concealing his pride in the prodigy he loved. Outwardly Macaulay displayed great self-confidence, even arrogance, yet he was deeply insecure, craving continuous affirmation of his genius from family members and his few close friends. His sisters adored their famous brother but apparently, unlike him, realised that their eventual marriage rather than setting up home with him was inevitable. Hannah accompanied him to India in 1834, mainly to act as his crutch.[32] Macaulay was dismayed about her impending marriage to Trevelyan. His long letter to his sister Margaret provides one of the few accounts of the young Trevelyan, now twenty-seven.

As to his person, nobody can think him handsome; and Nancy [a pet name for Hannah], I suppose in order to anticipate the verdict of others, pronounces him ugly. He has however a very good figure, and looks like a gentleman everywhere, but particularly on horse-back. He is very active and athletic, and is renowned as a great master in the most exciting and perilous of field-sports, the spearing of wild boars ... Trevelyan's face has a most characteristic expression of ardour and impetuosity which make his countenance very interesting to me, and, if she would own up to it, Nancy too. Birth is a thing that I care nothing about; but his family is one of the oldest and best in England.

And, like Macaulay, Trevelyan's ancestors were Celtic. He was a good match for Hannah: reliable, on the rise in his career, trustworthy, diligent and, not least, from a distinguished lineage, an important consideration despite Macaulay's dismissal of it. Yet he had weaknesses. His learning was limited, his manners were 'odd', and his 'religious feelings are ardent'. This quality Trevelyan shared with Macaulay's father; Thomas found it virtuous but narrowing. Macaulay lamented Trevelyan's insularity and the fact that he 'had no great tact or knowledge of the world'.

Before the marriage it was agreed that Macaulay would live with them. This was portrayed as a financial arrangement, though it had more to do with reconciling Macaulay to Hannah's new life. Her marriage was a 'great blow' to him, though not as bad as the death of Margaret from scarlet fever in August 1834, the news of which threatened his reason. For her part, Hannah tried to soften the blow, and her brother settled in to the domesticity she and her new husband offered.

The Trevelyans lived a quiet life in Calcutta, with Charles working long hours and then relaxing in the evening before retiring early, as his day began at 4 a.m. Occasional dinner parties and public events only interrupted the routine described by Macaulay as monotonous. Trevelyan was immersed in his work for the Indian government and produced a number of important reports during this time, as did Macaulay, who nevertheless saw his Indian sojourn as enforced exile more than his brother-in-law.

Trevelyan now had the ear of Lord William Bentinck, the reforming governor-general, who acted as his patron and friend, enabling him to have influence well beyond his official status. Bentinck told Macaulay that Trevelyan was the 'ablest young man in the service, and [the] most noble-minded man he had ever seen'.[33] Bentinck also recognised his weakness when he was later to say of his protégé: 'That man is almost always on the right side in every question: and it is well that he is so: for he gives a most confounded deal of trouble when he happens to take the wrong one'.[34]

The Macaulay-Trevelyan household was enlivened by the birth of a daughter, Margaret, in October 1835. Her uncle doted on 'Baba', and she was a 'source of great and almost painful pleasure' to him.[35] She filled a little of the terrible void from the death of his sister. Macaulay affectionately recorded each minute stage in her development in long letters to his other sisters and continued to adore her in later life. A second daughter, Hannah, was born in March 1837; she died three months later, a crushing blow for her devoted parents and for her equally devoted uncle.[36] By 1837 Macaulay could return to England, as Trevelyan would take his leave of absence at the same time, enabling the family to travel back as a group. Unlike Trevelyan, Macaulay resigned his position and would never again return to India. They sailed on the *Lord Hungerford* in late January and landed in England on 1 June 1837.

SPLENDID EXILE

For Macaulay, India was exile, but for other British people it could offer a glimpse of redemption. The Grants arrived on 8 February 1828 after a long and monotonous voyage. On their entering the spectacular port of Bombay, first impressions were very positive, and Elizabeth Grant, standing on the deck, declared that 'if this be exile, it is splendid exile'.[37] They were greeted with due pomp and ceremony: as a judge, Sir John Grant was a '*burra sahib*', a 'big man'. When he took his oath of office his daughter proudly reported that the cannon was fired from the Fort, the symbol of British rule built around Bombay Castle overlooking the bay.

The Grants lived well at their house, known as the Retreat—a 'palace', according to Elizabeth—with a retinue of servants who waited on their every whim. After the intense week of introductions, when established residents called on the newcomers, she had a more relaxed life, riding early in the morning, then a leisurely breakfast before receiving visitors or calling on friends and spending the remainder of the day reading or writing. Colonial life in Bombay was an endless schedule of dinner parties, balls and events for dignitaries passing through on the way to postings in other parts of India. Highlights were the grand balls—'the prettiest assemblies possible'—held at Government House in Parel, a short distance outside Bombay, hosted by Sir John Malcolm. Malcolm had a distinguished military and diplomatic career before his appointment as governor of the city in 1827. His personal life was less successful: his wife did not accompany him to India, which left his married daughter, Lady Campbell, to act as hostess. In Elizabeth's words, 'she did the honours for a while, but, poor thing, went mad and had to be sent home. She died within a year or two, never recovering her senses'. Life in the colonies could take its toll.

Malcolm was born in Dumfriesshire and, like many of the representatives of the East India Company, came from the ranks of the Scottish upper middle and landed classes. He spoke highly of the Grants and enjoyed their company, until a very public dispute with Grant about his legal duties soured relations.[38] Much of the Grants' social circle was dominated by the 'Scotch', either working as civilians or serving in the military. Elizabeth noted ruefully that 'most of those in high places [in Bombay] we had known at home in their less prosperous days', an ironic comment given that the posting to India was a lifeline for her own family. A whole ensemble of cousins was also in Bombay, and Elizabeth frequently spent time with them.

This sense of a familiar world helped ease the transition for Elizabeth to a completely different life. Her reading on India did little to prepare her. 'I remember being struck with surprise that all accounts of India that had ever fallen in my way were so meagre, when materials new and strange were in such abundance'. Gone were the certitudes of Rothiemurchus, Edinburgh and London. Everything struck her as exotic. These differences were most obvious in her observations on the 'natives' and their unorthodox practices. One particular source of discomfort to her was the Parsi burial ground that sat high on the hill between the Retreat and the sea. In Parsi tradition the corpse was left out in the open to be devoured by vultures. Her first encounter with the monsoon was a terrifying experience yet 'one of the grandest phenomena in nature'. As the monsoon approached in June or July, temperatures remained stable but the humidity was intolerable. Its actual onset was marked by a fierce thunderstorm, high winds and driving rain, leaving Elizabeth and her mother as 'pale as two spectres'. She was relieved when it finally departed in September.

The domestic life of the Grant household was enlivened by the arrival of a granddaughter in November 1828. Elizabeth's younger sister, Mary, had married an Irish official of the East India Company, Charles Gardiner, whom she had met on the voyage to India. The wedding was a grand ceremony in Bombay Cathedral shortly after they had arrived. Gardiner, who had been left a large estate, appeared an eminently suitable marriage prospect. Closely observing her sister at the wedding ceremony, however, Elizabeth had her doubts about the extent to which she was truly in love with this man. But she had her own concerns on this front. Now just over thirty, she looked ten years younger. Her family were busy identifying suitable candidates when her uncle's friend Colonel Henry (Hal) Smith arrived in Bombay and called on the Grants. Smith was an Irish officer in the East India Company's army and 'a sad Orangeman', but after the first meeting Elizabeth said that he was the 'most gentlemanly man I have seen in India'. Critically, her father was keen on Smith, not least after he heard about his bachelor brother's estate in Ireland. Her mother, on the other hand, dismissively described him as 'no great catch, just a soldier'. Elizabeth herself later reflected: 'Who could have thought a marriage thus systematically arranged could have turned out so well'. After a long period of courtship they were married in the cathedral at a ceremony attended by all the local notables.

Just before the marriage, news arrived of the death of Smith's brother and his inheritance of the Baltiboys estate in Co. Wicklow. The original intention was for the newly-weds to remain in India for at least three years, but Hal Smith's recurrent asthma attacks put paid to this, and his doctor advised him to return to Europe. He left the East India Company as an invalid and was given a pension.[39]

The couple set sail from Bombay in November 1830. The scene was a sad one. Elizabeth's father and mother came on board the ship to say their final goodbyes. Her father lingered on behind his wife, hugged his eldest daughter, said nothing, then left. That was the last time she would ever see him.

CONNECTIONS

Elizabeth's connection with Ireland was forged by chance through her choice of a husband in India. That she became the wife of a landlord in Co. Wicklow, where she was destined to remain for the rest of her long life, was an accident of fate. She knew little about the country before she arrived in 1831 and even less about the strange life of an Irish landlord, disconnected from the tenants by class, religion and politics.

From the earliest experience of the death of his local priest, John MacHale was almost pre-ordained to occupy a public role in his Anglophobic defence of his Catholic faith and the poor of the west of Ireland. In another time he might well have remained a distinguished if contentious scholar and churchman, closeted within the institutional confines of Maynooth or a comfortable episcopal palace. Though he was often dismissed as a mere contrarian, MacHale's actions were driven by his steadfast desire to challenge injustice, whatever form it might take. For him this did not mean making compromises, holding his tongue, or fudging matters of principle. He had the fortitude that religious certainty gave.

John Mitchel had not. In his early life he was a troubled soul, aimless and wandering, a perennial concern for his anxious parents. His life was plagued with false starts, difficulties and anxiety, until he met Jenny Verner. There were few omens of Mitchel's future political prominence in his early life. After marrying he was content to settle down to the life of a country solicitor and raise a family.

Mitchel's near-contemporary Charles Trevelyan was on an altogether different path. By the age of thirty he was one of the shining stars of the Indian civil service, a young man destined for great achievement and honours. India was his 'first love'.[40] He confidently expected to return immediately after his leave of absence; but his return was delayed for two decades, during which Trevelyan's dealings with Ireland earned him his controversial place in history.

Chapter 2 ⌒

| LAND AND PEOPLE

JUDGEMENT DAY

Sunday 6 January 1839 was a cold day, with sporadic rain and snow showers, standard weather for that time of year. In the afternoon a light breeze developed and it became unusually warm, with temperatures rising by more than 10°F (12°C) in only six hours. During the evening the wind became much stronger, and by midnight westerly gales buffeted the country. In the early hours of Monday morning these gales turned into a fierce hurricane, at its height between two and four o'clock and battering the country until sunrise. The storm was the worst experienced in Ireland in five hundred years, immortalised in collective memory for over a century as the 'Night of the Big Wind'.

The Famine census commissioner, William R. Wilde, Dublin surgeon and future father of Oscar, chronicled that it was 'a storm, surpassing, in violence, duration, and extent of damage produced, any within the memory of the existing generation, before or since that period'.[1] John O'Donovan, the Irish scholar then travelling the length of the country working for the Ordnance Survey, recounted the scene in his hotel in Glendalough, Co. Wicklow. He felt the building rocking from side to side 'as if it were a ship', and at two o'clock in the morning he was thrown from his bed by a sudden gust of wind that shot through the window. Only with the assistance of his travelling companion was he eventually able to close the shutters and take refuge with the other guests downstairs.[2]

Newspapers recounted the destruction around the country in the days following the hurricane. According to the *Dublin Evening Mail*, Dublin was like 'a sacked city—houses burned, others unroofed, and a few levelled with the ground'.[3] Belfast was also a scene of desolation, with debris strewn everywhere. Many other towns suffered a similar fate, and widespread devastation was evident over the length and breadth of the country.

The worst-affected people, as always with natural disasters, were the poor. The flimsy cabins they inhabited were swept away effortlessly by the hurricane. Fires broke out as sparks from the turf smouldering in the hearths ignited thatched roofs. 'Tens of thousands of their wretched cabins have been swept away or unroofed—and many ... have become a prey to the flames'.[4] Reports of the night sky lit up with flames added a mystical dimension to accounts.

The sheer force of the wind was confirmed by the damage done to trees: one estimate was that more than three million trees were destroyed that night, leaving many woodlands denuded. A landowner with an estate containing 70,000 trees in Co. Mayo on the Atlantic seaboard said afterwards that 'my estate is now as bare as the palm of my hand'.[5] Flooding occurred as rivers broke their banks. The winds also carried seabirds, sea salt and even fish long distances inland, reinforcing the sense that the natural order was overturned in those two dramatic hours. At sea, vessels were wrecked, others grounded, and off Liverpool, the worst-affected region in Britain, many people died at sea.

Given the ferocity of the storm, the relatively low loss of life was remarkable. How many perished no-one knows for certain, but at least one hundred died, and perhaps even double than number if those lost at sea and people who subsequently died from injuries sustained are included.[6]

The 'Night of the Big Wind' was deeply etched in the popular memory. Into the twentieth century stories abounded of old people who recalled the destruction and panic that fateful night. When in 1908 the old-age pension was introduced in Ireland for people over seventy, claimants cited living through the storm as evidence in declarations of their age, as civil birth registration began only in 1864. It became such a widespread and unreliable claim that it was quickly disregarded by the more eagle-eyed officials scrutinising the applications.[7]

Modern science offers a meteorological explanation for this freak weather event. A very deep depression came in quickly from the Atlantic towards Ireland and Britain during the night, centred on the Hebrides off the north-west coast of Scotland, with unusually low pressures, generating the very strong westerly gales that caused so much destruction.[8] The winds are estimated to have been in the region of 86 to 104 miles per hour, with hurricane-force gales in the middle of the night. One of the reasons for the relatively low number of deaths was that the storm hit during the time when people were sleeping and under shelter indoors.

In popular culture the happening was interpreted in an altogether different and supernatural way. In Ventry, Co. Kerry, the inhabitants viewed the 'Big Wind' as retribution invoked by the local priest on those who had 'forsaken their faith'. That the storm occurred on the feast of the Epiphany (the twelfth day of Christmas, or Little Christmas, as it was known in Ireland), was portentous, as that day in the religious calendar was traditionally associated with the dead. On the Epiphany 'the dead walk, and on every tile of the house a soul is sitting, waiting for your prayers to take it out of purgatory'.[9] Added to this was the day of the week. In Irish folk culture Monday was the Day of Judgement, and such mysterious phenomena as dead fish found miles inland, birds dropping from the sky and the deafening noise of the gales generated fears that the Almighty was expressing his displeasure.[10] Such millennial interpretations were codified by the poet Mícheál Burke in 'The Night of the Big Wind, or the End of the World', apparently written the day after the event and running to some twenty-five verses, versions of which could still be recited in the late 1950s.

Supernatural interpretations of natural disasters were a common feature of the Irish Catholic mental world in the early nineteenth century. Some years earlier the fears caused by an outbreak of cholera in 1832, in which 25,000 people perished, led to widespread panic for six days in June and the rapid nationwide circulation of the 'blessed turf', pieces of which had been anointed by priests and, it was vouched, would protect one against the disease, with the ultimate objective of complete distribution among the Catholic population.[11] Whether it be the havoc created by a natural disaster such as the 'Big Wind' in 1839, the dreadful visitation of cholera or the arrival of potato blight some years later in September 1845, only the celestial power of the Almighty could explain such events.

RURAL UNREST

The other event that dominated press coverage in January 1839 was a human one: the murder of Hector John Toler, second Earl of Norbury, at his residence, Durrow Abbey, in Co. Offaly. While he was out inspecting some trees with his steward on New Year's Day he was shot in the back by an assassin; he died two days later. The murder attracted widespread publicity in the Irish and British press, not least because Lord Norbury was known as a kindly landlord. This was seen as a particularly callous act.

The background is murky. Lord Norbury, it appears, paid the ultimate price for the efforts of his land agent, George Garvey, to extend his demesne by removing tenants from their holdings, often dealing harshly with them. A number who had been served with ejectment notices took the stopping of these evictions into their own hands. Garvey was well aware of the risks: it emerged at the subsequent trial of those charged with the murder that he had taken the sensible precaution of wearing a steel vest to protect himself. Local people knew this, and so the landlord rather than the agent became the target.

Two of Lord Norbury's tenants were tried for the murder in July 1844 at the King's County (Co. Offaly) Assizes, one for committing the murder, the other as an accessory. To everybody's surprise, not least the Crown law officers and the defendants themselves, both men were acquitted by the jury after it deliberated for only twenty minutes.[12] No-one was ever subsequently arrested for the murder.

The 1830s were an anxious time for landlords. About a third were absentees who rarely if ever set foot on Irish soil, preferring to leave the day-to-day management of their estates to agents. For the majority who did reside in Ireland there was the ever-present threat of intimidation

Violence directed against landlords, agents or farmers had many causes, including rack-renting (charging an extortionate rent), evictions, or taking a holding that was seen as by right that of another tenant. Indeed any form of dispute between landlord and tenant, agent and tenant, or farmers and labourers might eventuate in violence. Numerous oath-bound secret societies, such as the Whiteboys, Rightboys and Defenders—often lumped together in government reports as 'Ribbonmen'—developed from the middle of the eighteenth century onwards to defend the traditional rights of the tenant. Breaches of the unwritten code resulted in retribution, which took many forms. The tactics could vary from threatening letters and the mutilation of farm animals to violent attacks and ultimately murder.[13]

The amount and frequency of rural unrest was taken as evidence by British politicians and officials of the 'distressed' state of the country and the age-old propensity of 'the Celt' to resort to lethal violence to settle disputes. Every decade since the 1760s had witnessed a serious outbreak of rural unrest. George Cornewall Lewis conducted a comprehensive analysis of the causes of unrest in rural Ireland, based largely on his years in Ireland working for various government inquiries in the early 1830s. Published in 1836, it remains the most insightful contemporary account.

Lewis rejected racial stereotypes of the Catholic Irish as innately prone to violence, underlined the limited successes of coercion in bringing peace to the countryside, and argued that the solution lay in addressing the issue of widespread poverty. This would involve transforming cottiers who lived on smallholdings into labourers who would be paid a regular wage by farmers, who would be 'a class of capitalist cultivators'. For all this to occur, however, it was necessary to introduce a legal right to Poor Law relief, as it would 'give the Irish peasant an alternative besides the possession of land and starvation, and this for the sake of facilitating the transition from small to large farms, from the rude to the systematic mode of cultivation'.[14] Such commercialisation of agriculture would fundamentally alter social and economic relationships in rural Ireland.

The response of successive governments was predictable. Emergency legislation was introduced as British governments met Irish unrest with coercion, including the suspension of such constitutional rights as *habeas corpus*. Repressive measures were introduced in response to agrarian crimes orchestrated by secret societies. The Local Disturbances etc. (Ireland) Act (1833), introduced by Earl Grey's Whig ministry and commonly called the Coercion Act, allowed for extensive powers, including the proclamation of martial law; and despite Daniel O'Connell's efforts to amend its most repulsive aspects as it worked its way through the House of Commons it was a draconian piece of legislation.

The issue of tithes—a 10 per cent tax paid by tenants on all agricultural produce to support the established Church of Ireland—was a long-standing grievance for nationalists, not least because the Catholic poor contributed disproportionately to the support of a privileged minority church. This was the most blatant injustice in early nineteenth-century Ireland. The financial fortunes of the two churches could not have been sharper, as Sydney Smith, canon of St Paul's, London, and famous wit, noted.

The revenue of the Irish Roman Catholic Church is made of half-pence, potatoes, rags, bones, and fragments of old clothes, and those Irish old clothes. They worship often in hovels, or in the open air, from the want of any place of worship. Their religion is the religion of three-fourths of the population! Not far off, in a well-windowed and well-roofed house, is a well-paid Protestant clergyman, preaching to stools and hassocks, and crying in the wilderness; near him the clerk, near him the sexton, near him the sexton's wife—furious against the errors of Popery ...[15]

From the winter of 1830 onwards a campaign of civil disobedience developed with the non-payment of tithes by tenants, supported by the Catholic middle classes, the clergy and O'Connell. The enforcement of tithe claims through the seizing of produce or cattle involving the constabulary and the military produced scenes of violent disorder in the early 1830s, immortalised as 'battles', such as that at Carrickshock, Co. Kilkenny, in December 1831, when twelve policemen and three members of the crowd lost their lives. In another shocking incident in December 1834 a large force of police and army arrived to collect the tithes owed by a widow to Archdeacon Ryder in Gortroe, Co. Cork. She lived near the hamlet of Rathcormac, and more than 150 local people had barricaded themselves into her farmyard. In the chaos that ensued the soldiers opened fire, killing twelve men and injuring forty-two others, all for an unpaid debt of £2.[16] The event lived on in popular memory as the 'massacre of Rathcormac'. After this bloodbath soldiers were not employed in enforcing tithe claims, for fear of similar slaughter.[17]

By 1834 both the Catholic Church and O'Connell sought to achieve a compromise, fearing the widespread disorder that the 'tithe war' was fuelling, and eventually by 1838 a compromise to reduce tithe payments was worked out by converting them into rental charges paid by the landowner rather than the tenant.

LANDLORDS AND TENANTS

Rural Ireland had an incredibly complex social structure, not captured by the simple distinction between landlord and tenant.[18] Landlords numbered roughly ten thousand, or less than 1 per cent of the country's inhabitants, and received £12 million annually in rent. Political and economic power was concentrated in this tiny elite. Often vilified by nationalists for their callousness—accusations that were sometimes wholly justified—they, like any other social group, were a mixed bag: 'some were good and some were bad; some cared and some did not; some knew their people and others did not'.[19] The great magnates, such as Earl Fitzwilliam, the Duke of Leinster, the Earl of Leitrim and the Marquess of Downshire, had extensive estates that stretched over many counties. The majority, however, had relatively modest holdings of a few hundred acres and a demesne house on the estate with its staff of servants.

Whereas ownership of the land was concentrated in relatively few hands, occupation of the land was much more diverse. Landlords often rented holdings to middlemen, who then sublet these to tenant-farmers. Many of these middleman were prosperous middle-class Catholics. The days of the middleman were numbered, however. The Napoleonic wars were a boom time for Irish agriculture as prices rose to meet the growing demand in Britain, and increasingly landlords took direct control of their estates when the leases to middlemen ran out, cutting them out of the transaction to increase their own income.[20]

'Strong farmers', with holdings of more than thirty acres, were essentially market-oriented enterprises, although the quality and site of the land determined the extent to which a good living could be had. Beneath them, smallholders had a less attractive position, with approximately ten acres, sometimes employing labourers but mostly relying on family members to work the holding. These categories were often fluid, depending on the region and the quality of the land.

The most numerous group, accounting for roughly three-quarters of the rural population, were cottiers and landless labourers. Cottiers rented small plots of potato land from farmers for one season in return for their labour or a share of the crop, and sometimes they had a separate arrangement for renting a cabin.

The group in the most precarious position—essentially the rural proletariat—were landless labourers who had no formal arrangement with a farmer. They lived on a tightrope: dependent on farmers for employment, and equally dependent for access to a small plot of rented land, called a conacre, from which they could provide food for their family and, with a good harvest, sell some produce. Labourers were often exploited by farmers who charged high rents for the much-sought-after conacre, received very low wages, and spent many months without work, especially in areas where opportunities for employment were uncertain.

In 1845 farmers were outnumbered by smallholders, cottiers and labourers by more than two to one.[21] The Devon Commission on the land question, which conducted its inquiries in the early 1840s, observed that the plight of the Irish labourer was an unenviable one.

A reference to the evidence of most of the witnesses will show that the agricultural labourer of Ireland continues to suffer the greatest privations and hardships—that he continues to depend on casual and precarious employment for assistance—that he is still badly housed, badly fed, badly clothed, and badly paid for his labour ... We cannot forbear expressing our strong sense of the patient endurance which the labouring classes have generally exhibited under sufferings greater, we believe, than any other country in Europe have to sustain.[22]

Ironically, the fault lines in early nineteenth-century Ireland were less between landlords and tenants, as is widely assumed, than between those who held land and those who did not: farmers and labourers. The relationship between farmers and labourers was an exploitative one. Witnesses before the Devon Commission testified to the oppression of labourers by farmers: they were as 'dependent as slaves' and 'more wretched than the Fellahs of Egypt or the blacks of Cuba'.[23] Most of the tensions in rural Ireland concerned access to land, as land meant survival.

At the very bottom of the social hierarchy were beggars and vagrants, who had neither land nor access to land but were transients, moving between districts, relying on charity. As J. E. Bicheno noted, this group relied almost exclusively on the poor for charity, as the 'most compassionate class will always be the poor themselves'.[24] The oppressive nature of this social system was encapsulated by one contemporary: 'Every class in this country oppresses the class below it, until you come to the most wretched class ... There is no exaction practised by their superiors that they do not practise upon those below them.'[25]

AGE OF IMPROVEMENT

Into this complex and ever-changing world came Elizabeth Smith. When she first arrived in Baltiboys, Co. Wicklow, in October 1831 to inspect the estate her husband had inherited she was disconcerted by what she found. A group of people gathered to welcome the new landlord and his Scottish wife. Elizabeth presumed that they were beggars, 'dirty ragged queer looking men doffing their remnants of hats with much civility'. But '"Them's the tenants" said the only man amongst them with a whole coat'.[26] Smith's tenants had been without a resident landlord for more than a quarter of a century and were naturally curious to see their new lord and master and his exotic Scottish wife, both of whom had just returned from India.

The arrival of a resident landlord heralded change in Baltiboys. The Smiths set about making improvements to the homes of the tenants as well as introducing new crops, such as turnips, and embarking on land drainage projects. Among the tenants there existed a two-tier system. Large tenants, such as the Darker brothers, John and Thomas, and Thomas and Hugh Kelly, accounted for roughly half the estate. The Darker brothers were ideal tenants, according to Elizabeth, and Tom Darker was the steward of the estate: 'northerners, protestants, well educated, industrious, they are a credit to the country'.[27] The other group was that of smallholders with tiny plots of land; former tenants, such as the Widow Quinn, who no longer had any land but was left with a house; and sub-tenants, who rented land from one of the tenants, a practice that the Smiths wished to eradicate.[28]

The new landlords embarked on a corrosive process, consolidating the size of the farms by clearing poor smallholders and giving this land to existing 'good' tenants, such as the transfer of the land of George Kearns to Thomas Kelly. Doing it quietly over time, 'without annoying anyone—or even causing a murmur', in Elizabeth's words, they seized opportunities when they presented themselves as leases ran out, and provided compensation to enable the evicted tenants to emigrate to North America.[29] While she was at pains to show how humane they were in removing smallholders—by the standards of less considerate landlords they certainly handled this with sensitivity— regardless of how the tenants were treated there is no doubt about the inherent brutality of pushing poor families off the land. Many of the tenants had little prospect of getting another holding locally, and with neither the resources nor the inclination to cross the Atlantic they were essentially forced off their ancestral homesteads, some ending up homeless or reliant on Poor Law relief. In nineteenth-century Ireland the eviction of tenants also fed into the bitter memories of Catholic dispossession, a theme that had its origins in the Cromwellian settlement of the 1650s, when the lands of Irish Catholic elites were confiscated and granted to loyal British settlers.

Elizabeth's knowledge of rural society was derived from the many years spent in the Scottish Highlands, a not dissimilar environment to parts of Ireland. But Co. Wicklow was different from the Highlands, or indeed the west of Ireland, in that, like most of Leinster, it was a prosperous agricultural region. What she brought with her was an unflinching emphasis on 'improvement': making the estate more profitable, trying to make the life of the tenants better, and enhancing holdings through drainage, reclamation and consolidation.[30] In November 1842 when the tenants paid up punctually on the gale day (one of the two days per year when rents were customarily paid, the other being in May) she derived satisfaction from their clean and well-dressed appearance but especially from the impression that 'most of them' were 'bit [bitten] with spirit of improvement'.[31]

This was the 'age of improvement'. Classical political economy stressed the role of individual self-help in promoting prosperity, a constant theme in Elizabeth's reflections on what was needed in Ireland. In this respect she reflected educated opinion of the time. Inspired by Enlightenment rational thought and advances in scientific thinking, colonial policy throughout the empire set out to 'improve' societies through education, more efficient techniques of production, the introduction of capitalism, and removing vestiges of the pre-modern world.

High-minded notions of improvement can have vastly different interpretations. Elizabeth often became frustrated with what she perceived as the lack of initiative and exertion on the part of her tenants. While the consolidation of smallholdings into larger ones seemed entirely rational from the viewpoint of the landlord, removing tenants, many of whom had long-standing connections with a particular piece of land, was contravening well-established social codes. Improving landlords were often targeted for retributive violence, negligent or profligate ones rarely so, as they had little interest in their estates or their tenants, apart from the collection of rent. The atmosphere persuaded many landlords in the 1830s and early 1840s that inertia was the most sensible policy to pursue.

Near Clonmel, Co. Tipperary, whenever the Earl of Donoughmore removed a tenant he did not re-let the land but instead allowed it to remain idle. After the passage of time he hoped he could eventually find a tenant. When he had attempted to do so previously the replacement tenant was attacked and had to be protected. In another instance a 'respectable' farmer who had taken over the holding of an evicted tenant was murdered; apparently all the local people knew the perpetrators, but the culprits were never charged. A liberal-minded Scottish visitor in 1835 was aghast that the Donoughmores lived in a state of virtual siege at Knocklofty House, with pistols left ready for use at night and the agent's house fortified like a military garrison.[32] It was hardly the idyllic picture of a rural retreat. Cos. Tipperary, Offaly, Leitrim and Roscommon were the most 'disturbed' counties in the 1830s.

Tenants likewise had little incentive to improve their holdings. Unlike England and Scotland, under Irish land law there was no legal right to compensation for the increased value of the land paid to the tenant after the lease had expired, and landlords could simply charge a higher rent for a more profitable holding. This was rightly seen as the main obstacle to the improvement of agriculture in Ireland. The fact that an ever-increasing number were tenants at will, or on annual leases, heightened insecurity and made any form of initiative in improving the land even more unattractive. There were, of course, exceptions: conscientious landlords who in co-operation with tenants set about making the land more productive, or tenants who knew that their lease would be continued and were therefore willing to invest in the holding. The spread of commercial farming in Leinster and Munster, with the emphasis on efficiency and economies of scale, created larger holdings, run essentially as businesses through the supply of food to the British market.

Not much is known about the first decade of Elizabeth Smith's life in Ireland. Most of her time was concerned with rebuilding Baltiboys House, constructed in the seventeenth century, now in ruins. Her niece, Lady Strachey, claimed that the house had been destroyed in the 1798 Rebellion and that the landlord 'had left the country in disgust'. The truth was more mundane. Indeed it was occupied by Crown forces in 1798 and had suffered much damage; nevertheless Hal Smith's brother had little interest in his property, moved abroad, and had the roof removed to pay his debts. Elizabeth's sister Jane, who came to Baltiboys the following year, lamented that the house was 'in a very curious state of abandonment'. The Smiths rented a cottage nearby while the new house was being built, which took more than ten years to complete. The installation of the landlord brought employment to the locality, as the building work required labour.

Elizabeth and her young family moved into their new home in 1837, although the building work continued for a couple of years. By this time she had just turned forty and had two young children: Janey, born in England in July 1831, and Annie, born two years later in Ireland, who were later joined by her son, Jack, born in 1838. Another daughter, Elizabeth, had died of whooping cough at the age of three months.

The newly rebuilt Baltiboys House was a medium-sized gentry house situated where the River Liffey and King's River meet and set back into a hill. A long tree-lined avenue led to the house, which was in typical Regency style, with a two-storey main building and two smaller blocks. Inside, it contained the usual arrangement for a gentleman's house: a drawing-room, a morning room, a large dining-room and a library, with a 'curved Regency staircase' leading to the bedrooms upstairs. Situated in a place of great natural beauty, it looked down the sloping fields towards the Liffey, and many of the rooms had a wonderful view of the landscape. In an adjoining block, the nursery and schoolroom above the stables looked over the large courtyard.[33] The heart of the house was the basement, in which a huge kitchen ran the full length of the building and which also housed the servants' quarters, along with a scullery, pantry, laundry and various other rooms. It was a most 'convenient mansion'.[34]

THE STATE OF IRELAND

Visitors to nineteenth-century Ireland were immediately struck by a paradox: it was a country of magnificent beauty, yet signs of destitution were ubiquitous. 'Misery' was the description most often applied to the lives of the poor who inhabited the rural landscape. This was nicely captured in the title of one account, *Miseries and Beauties of Ireland* (1837), by an English Quaker, Jonathan Binns, from a well-known Lancashire draper family with strong radical connections. Binns was in Ireland working as an assistant commissioner on the inquiry into the establishment of an Irish Poor Law, and he toured the country, reporting in great detail on every locality he visited. His purpose was more than simply producing a travelogue. Unlike many of the other, more superficial accounts, his diagnosis was sensitive to the peculiarities of the Irish situation in the 1830s. He observed the Irish poor 'in a state of continual starvation'. For him, agricultural improvement was the answer to the country's many problems, but he also emphasised the political aspects.

Ireland presents to those who contemplate her peculiar position, a striking and fearfully disgraceful anomaly. Possessing a singularly fertile soil, capable of abundantly repaying the labour bestowed upon it, she also possesses a population depressed by more than ordinary destitution, and dishonoured by a long catalogue of more than ordinary crimes.

Referring to more recent history, be believed that while the Act of Union promised 'an equality of civil rights', until such time as this actually occurred 'Ireland never will, and never ought to be a contented country'.[35] Political and economic equality were all part of the same equation.

The extent of poverty shocked outsiders, particularly those who visited the impoverished western districts along the rugged Atlantic coast. The conditions of the poor seemed to defy all standard classifications of human existence. Thomas Reid, a surgeon and well-known prison reformer, born in Co. Tyrone, toured the country in 1822 and reflected on a journey he had taken on foot from Killorglin to Cahersiveen in Co. Kerry: 'I think it physically impossible for human beings to exist in a worse plight than are most of those I saw … today'.[36]

For Gustave de Beaumont, the French travelling companion of Alexis de Tocqueville in the 1830s, the living conditions were more degrading than anything he had witnessed on his extensive travels. 'I have seen the Indian in his forests, the Negro in his chains, and, reflecting upon their pitiable condition, I believed that I had seen the last degree of human misery: I knew nothing then of poor Ireland's lot'.[37]

'For until he has seen the West', concluded the German traveller J. G. Kohl, who toured the country in the early 1840s, 'he can have no conception that human beings can live more miserably and poorly'.[38]

Travellers were shocked by the horrific scenes they encountered on visiting the poorer parts of the country. For many this was the overriding impression. Accounts of being greeted by crowds of poor 'wretches', barely clothed in rags and living in hovels, abound in the voluminous writings of American, British and European observers who came to Ireland in the first few decades of the nineteenth century.[39] Other accounts from the 1830s and 1840s are full of descriptions of grinding poverty.

Appearances, however, can be deceptive. These texts need careful reading, as they often reveal more about the sensibilities of the observer than about the situation they encountered. The most obvious indications were the ragged clothing and poor housing; but middling farmers and landless labourers often dressed in similar clothes, and the conflation of all the social classes into the convenient category of 'the poor' was far from uncommon.[40] The existence of a vigorous agricultural economy in pre-Famine Ireland, as shown by the thousands of fairs that took place, also provides some evidence of rural prosperity, albeit very unevenly spread.

Poverty was associated in the popular imagination with the west of Ireland, but it was not confined to such counties as Kerry, Clare, Galway, Mayo and Donegal. Henry Inglis, a well-known Scottish travel writer, described the architectural splendour of the great Georgian streets and squares of Dublin in the mid-1830s, but after a short walk he was in the Liberties, where the city's poor mostly lived. He concluded that 'in walking through the streets of Dublin, strange and striking contrasts are presented between grandeur and poverty'. After a short stay he travelled to nearby Co. Wicklow. While he noted the beauties of Enniskerry, the Glen of the Downs, Glendalough and Powerscourt Waterfall, all favourites on the tourist's itinerary, his first experience of the mud cabins of the poor was a shocking one. While staying at Avoca he ventured out into the adjacent mountain and glens and discovered people living in desperate conditions, and he found little 'to bear out the assertions of some of my Dublin friends, to whom Wicklow ought to have been familiar,—that I should find all the labourers employed, and all tolerably comfortable'.[41]

When it came to Ulster, on the other hand, and especially the industrial city of Belfast, British visitors found much that was reassuring. The novelist W. M. Thackeray on his tour in 1842 described Belfast in his inimitable way as 'hearty, thriving, and prosperous, as if it had money in its pockets and roast-beef for dinner'.[42] Inglis, for example, noted the neat organisation of farms and towns, refreshingly familiar, more akin to his native Scotland. 'Prosperous' and 'industrious' were the words most frequently used to describe Ulster. Samuel Carter Hall and Anna Maria Hall on their arrival in Belfast proclaimed that 'the clean and bustling appearance of Belfast is decidedly unnational. That it is in Ireland, but not of it, is a remark often on the lips of visitors from the south or west.'[43]

Underlying such comments was the widely held view that the Protestant Irish had the moral character and enterprising outlook essential to economic well-being, unlike the Catholics, who had innate tendencies towards indolence and improvidence.

It was often wrongly assumed that Ireland could be written off as simply a poor country. In fact by almost every measure of economic activity, such as average income, trade, consumption patterns, development of banking and communications, steady if unspectacular progress was evident in the 1830s and early 1840s.[44] Ireland's destiny was to supply produce to the British market, mainly agricultural but also linen, and this generated considerable wealth. What was true, however, was that Ireland contained a large and ever-increasing number of poor people. Wealth was concentrated in few hands, those who benefited from the concentration on exports or served the growing domestic market, such as farmers, merchants, traders, shopkeepers and others involved in commercial and industrial activities. The Drummond Commission acknowledged as much in 1837 in its consideration of the benefit of the introduction of railways to Ireland.

The present social aspect and condition of Ireland is an anomaly in itself. Whilst the country is making a visible and steady progress in improvement, and signs of increasing wealth present themselves on all sides, the labouring population, constituting a majority of the community, derive no proportionate benefit from the growing prosperity around them. In many places their condition is even worse than it has been.[45]

It was this deep social inequality that ensured that wealth was unevenly distributed, and if anything the plight of the rural poor was becoming worse.

FAMINE IN THE MIDST OF PLENTY

In a remote outpost of the United Kingdom a young mother died from a hunger-related disease in 1831. The tragedy was compounded by the revelation that when neighbours arrived with food, her ailing husband noticed that she had passed away only when the lips of their baby were covered with blood rather than breast milk.[46]

That the poor went hungry was altogether unexceptional in the early nineteenth-century world. The death of this anonymous woman was of no special public interest, except that she was a citizen of the world's richest state. In a public letter to Earl Grey, the new Whig prime minister, published in April 1831, Bishop John MacHale described this harrowing scene in which this mother of three young children had died. It would be easy to accuse MacHale of sensationalising what was essentially a terrible personal tragedy. Yet his motivation in publicising the case was his immutable opposition to all forms of injustice—economic, political and religious. Hunger in Ireland combined all three.

Throughout his lifetime MacHale gave voice to the poor and the powerless. He earned the devotion of his flock through his tireless championing of their plight, both in public and in private. He was one of the few bishops to preach in Irish, the language of the poor in the west of Ireland. Unlike his fellow-bishops in the comfortable dioceses in other parts of Ireland, he daily witnessed dehumanising poverty, as some of the poorest districts in the country were in Co. Mayo. Catholic priests, in addition to their spiritual roles, performed other duties and acted as leaders for the poor and intermediaries with officialdom, writing to politicians and administrators in Dublin Castle or to relief committees but, most importantly, drawing attention to the plight of their flock.[47] The onset of famine in the west of Ireland in 1830–31 brought MacHale, then Coadjutor Bishop of Killala, back once again into the public sphere.

The potato crop had partially failed in the autumn of 1830, leaving thousands of smallholders and landless labourers on the verge of starvation. The situation the following year was even worse, and in Cos. Mayo and Galway more than half a million people were in need of aid, most of which was provided by charities.[48] Never one for half-measures, in typical fashion MacHale wrote four long public letters to the prime minister between April and August 1831, chronicling in graphic detail the extent of suffering and outlining what he believed to be the solutions to the problem of Irish poverty: disestablishment of the Church of Ireland, removal of tithe payments, reform of the system of land tenure, and ultimately repeal of the Act of Union. He travelled to London as part of the deputation from Co. Mayo to meet the prime minister. Irish Catholics, led by O'Connell, had expectations that Grey's Whig ministry, in power from November 1830, would, unlike the previous Tory governments that had governed more or less for the previous three decades, eventually bring about reforms in Ireland.

Grey listened politely to the deputation, gave some vague undertakings, but did not take any action.

The core of the problems that affected Ireland was the land system, according to MacHale. That oats could continue to be exported during a time of severe shortage for the poor was a scandal, and he concluded that 'ours was a famine in the midst of plenty'.[49] Its essential inequality, together with the rapaciousness of the landlords and agents, lay at the heart of the injustices. 'What is there to prevent the people from starving if they have no law to keep as much as will appease hunger, and if the proprietors have no heart to feel for their misery'.[50]

Famine conditions were nothing new in Ireland. In 1851 William Wilde prepared his famous table entitled 'Cosmical phenomena, epizootics, famines and pestilences in Ireland', which ran to nearly three hundred pages, describing every event of this kind since the pre-Christian period.[51] It makes for macabre reading and underlines the fragile balance between life and death, between humans and nature, in Ireland from time immemorial. In 1740/41 an Arctic frost of unprecedented duration destroyed the potato crop and between 310,000 and 480,000 people perished; and these are only estimates, as few reliable records exist of this terrible tragedy that has been overshadowed by the events of the 1840s.[52] Throughout the second half of the eighteenth century partial failures of the potato crop occurred in 1765, 1770 and 1795. The early nineteenth century also witnessed famines or near-famines caused by the failure of the potato crop in 1800–01, 1816–19, 1822 and 1830–31. Such disasters were caused by bad weather; some, like the crisis of 1816–19, were Europe-wide events, others unique to districts such as the west of Ireland, as in 1830–31.[53] Public works schemes and local relief committees were established to help the poor, avoiding large numbers of deaths. Local charity assisted by state relief prevented the wholesale loss of life, but some people died from famine-related diseases in 1822 and again in 1831.[54] Few people die from direct starvation during a famine: the diseases caused by malnutrition kill most victims.

'A VILE WATERY BULB'

At the centre of this story was the humble potato, which had a long and complex history in Ireland since its introduction at the end of the sixteenth century. Originally used to supplement other foods, by the eighteenth century it had become the main food of the growing ranks of the poor. With the commercialisation of Irish agriculture in the eighteenth century, good land became a valuable commodity. This meant in effect that cereal crops dominated the most productive and sought-after land, as they produced the best financial return when sold, whereas the potato was grown to eat.

At first a number of varieties were grown, but the 'lumper' came to dominate in the early decades of the nineteenth century. Described as 'a vile watery bulb, in which there is neither flavour nor nourishment', it produced a good crop even on very poor soil, which accounts for its widespread adoption.[55] It was widely condemned by contemporary observers as tasteless and barely fit for animals and denounced during the 1840s as being particularly vulnerable to disease. In fact even better varieties, such as the 'cup' and the 'apple', were equally susceptible to blight, as became apparent later.

The further down the social hierarchy one went the less likely that other foods were eaten in addition to the potato. Oatmeal, milk and fish did feature in the reports of contemporaries as eaten by poor people; but there is no doubting the pre-eminence of the potato. The Irish poor ate huge quantities of them, roughly 10 to 12 pounds per day. A family with three or four growing children would need 40 pounds of potatoes per day. Modern research has shown that this daily consumption would have been extremely nutritious and provided all the essential elements of a healthy diet.[56]

Whether the potato fuelled the staggering rise in population is a moot point. Ireland had the highest rate of population growth in western Europe, and reliable estimates suggest that the number of people in the country trebled between 1750 and 1820, from 2½ million to almost 7 million. We cannot be sure of the exact numbers before the first reliable census, which was undertaken in 1821. Certainly the widespread growing of the potato enabled people to survive on relatively small resources; but the most persuasive explanation is the near-universal preference for early marriage and the high level of fertility after marriage, which resulted in what was effectually a population explosion. In other words, the poorest and most numerous section of Irish society married young—occasionally very young, in their teens—and had large families, which were supported by a reliance on the potato as the main food.

In the 1820s and 1830s population growth slowed down; yet by the early 1840s the population was over 8 million, more than four times what it was estimated to be in the 1680s.

Contemporaries were well aware of the potential dangers of unrestrained population growth. Malthusian interpretations were common at the time, and have retained a lasting appeal to the present day. What Malthus argued in his famous *Essay on Population* (1798) was that famine would act as a 'positive check' on unrestrained population growth, given the inevitable pressure it places on food supply.

> Famine seems to be the last, the most dreadful resource of nature. The power of population is so superior to the power in the earth to produce subsistence for man, that premature death must in some shape or other visit the human race. The vices of mankind are active and able ministers of depopulation. They are the precursors in the great army of destruction; and often finish the dreadful work themselves. But should they fail in this war of extermination, sickly seasons, epidemics, pestilence, and plague, advance in terrific array, and sweep off their thousands and ten thousands. Should success be still incomplete, gigantic inevitable famine stalks in the rear, and with one mighty blow levels the population with the food of the world.[57]

According to Malthusian logic, Ireland was poor because it was over-populated. The population would keep growing, thereby increasing the levels of poverty, until a disaster struck, and then it would ultimately be punished for its 'demographic profligacy'.[58] In the words of Thomas Carlyle, writing in 1839:

> This cannot last, Heaven disowns it, Earth is against it; Ireland will be burnt into a black unpeopled field of ashes rather than this should last ... The time has come when the Irish population must either be improved a little, or else exterminated.[59]

Nevertheless Malthus in his prophecy, inspired by the Old Testament, was not referring to Ireland, and when he did write about Irish overpopulation a decade later he predicted a slow, gradual adjustment rather than a violent shock.[60] The signs of this adjustment were evident in the early decades of the nineteenth century: the population increased at a slower rate—though in poorer counties this was less apparent—and emigration to North America and Britain was gathering pace. An ingenious test of the Malthusian model applied to Ireland does not support the much-assumed link between poverty and overpopulation.[61] Where the vulnerability existed was in the reliance on one crop as the main source of food for roughly a third of the people—the poorest third. Even then the role of the potato was that in most years it gave an abundant harvest that provided a good, healthy diet for growing families. Certainly the potato, like any other crop, was prone to failure, yet on the whole it was a remarkably reliable source of food for Ireland's poor before the mid-1840s.

ON THE EDGE

The uncertain foundations on which Irish society was built were evident to most contemporaries: a propertied class with little interest in the plight of its tenants, a land system that was based on inequality, and large-scale rural unrest and violence that reached a peak at particular points, such as the 'tithe war' in the early 1830s. A succession of British governments refused to interfere with property rights, as political power in Britain rested on the landed classes. Politicians defended the landed interest, as 'the sanctity of property was the bedrock of civilisation'.[62] Ireland's future prosperity lay in the hands of the landlords, who would bring about the changes in the rural economy that were essential to growth. The constant challenges to the rights of landlords merely showed that the Irish were 'uncivilised' and that there was a strong moral justification for coercion.[63] Industrialisation had made little headway outside the north-east of Ulster, and most of the people relied on agriculture to survive. Apart from Belfast, and to a lesser extent Cork and Dublin, Ireland did not possess the great manufacturing cities that acted as such a magnet for displaced rural workers in Britain. Global capitalism also shaped Ireland's destiny to be a supplier of food to these cities of urban, industrial Britain.

Lastly, there was the plight of the poor who depended on the potato to survive: powerless, marginalised and extremely vulnerable. Three million people teetered on the brink of hunger. Critics advocated the greater commercialisation of Irish agriculture, so creating a class of capitalist farmers, with ranks of paid labourers, who would act to improve the country, casting away the serried ranks of smallholders and labourers with their tiny plots of land.

The singular logic of capitalist agriculture may well have appeared rational to contemporaries, but small farmers and labourers would violently resist any such clearances or evictions. Access to land, even a tiny holding, was critical for survival. Only in catastrophic circumstances would this deep bond between the land and the people ever be broken.

Chapter 3 ～

| POLITICS AND POWER

AT THE TREASURY

John Mitchel famously declared that Ireland during the Famine was 'a nation perishing of political economy,' a view that was articulated in the *Nation* as well as by other contemporaries, such as John MacHale.[1] After the disaster of the late 1840s this became the conventional wisdom in nationalist critiques of the British government's role in Ireland under the Union. Yet economic liberalism, with its heavily circumscribed role for the state and its reliance on individual self-help, often described as the principle of *laissez-faire*, was the ideology widely acknowledged by the majority of enlightened thinkers in both Britain and Ireland as promoting progress and growth. Certainly it had its opponents, such as Thomas Carlyle, but they were a few lonely voices. Daniel O'Connell in the 1830s was 'a doctrinaire free trader and the keen enemy of all constraints on trade or the supply of labour', forging links with the Anti-Corn-Law League in Britain and strongly supporting the repeal of the Corn Laws.[2] It must also be said that O'Connell's economic ideas were eclectic, drawn from a wide range of influences, including his devout Catholicism.[3]

Classical political economy stressed the belief that the prosperity of a nation was due to individuals, who, by virtue of human nature, would seek to improve their own circumstances. Individual self-interest corresponded to national well-being. It was also widely perceived that free trade contributed to Britain's world economic and political dominance. Non-interference in the market by the state was a core element of this belief, as it was considered the most efficient mechanism for the distribution of goods, with the law of supply and demand to regulate prices. States, therefore, should not control prices, provide incentives to import food, or prohibit exports.[4]

Over the course of the nineteenth century these principles, derived from the writings of classical political economists, shaped policy in Britain, Ireland and such colonies as India. Historically, Britain's imperial expansion had as much to do with trade and commerce as with political and territorial gains.

After his leave of absence ended, Charles Trevelyan, with Hannah and their two young children, was due to return to his position in India in September 1840. A son and heir, George Otto Trevelyan—later to become a famous Liberal politician—arrived shortly after they came back to England in 1838. Another daughter, Alice, was born in 1843. Destiny, or more accurately Trevelyan's powerful brother-in-law Macaulay, now a member of Parliament for Edinburgh and elevated to Lord Melbourne's cabinet as secretary of war, intervened to keep the Trevelyan family in England.

Macaulay was devastated at the thoughts of separation from his beloved sister Hannah and her children; she recounted afterwards that 'his misery at the prospect of our return to India was the most painful and hourly trial'. It seems probable that Macaulay persuaded James Stephen, the senior official at the Colonial Office, to suggest Trevelyan for the vacant role of assistant secretary to the Treasury. The letter of January 1840 from Francis Baring, chancellor of the exchequer, offering Trevelyan the post of the most senior administrative official in the Treasury came out of the blue. He took up his new post later that month. This effectually gave him administrative control over much of the state's finances.

Within political circles it was widely presumed that Macaulay had secured the job for Trevelyan, with one contemporary, J. A. Stuart, noting privately that he had obtained 'the best thing going for his brother in law, who was never heard of before'.[5] It was an irony that the person who did so much to introduce competition and merit into entry to the British civil service in the 1850s, as joint author of the Northcote-Trevelyan Report in 1854, was himself appointed through the representations of a well-placed relative. Eight years later Trevelyan recorded his gratitude to Stephen: 'I owe to your good opinion & good word the comfortable settlement of myself and family in this country, and all the advantages consequent thereon'.[6]

The annual salary of £2,000 enabled the Trevelyans to move to Clapham in Surrey, then a growing suburb of London, where Hannah had spent her early years. Much has been made of Trevelyan's connections with the

'Clapham Sect', the cluster of progressive families with evangelical views, such as the Wilberforces, prominent in the campaign to abolish slavery. Trevelyan certainly shared this Anglican evangelical outlook, and frequent visitors to his home, such as Macaulay, were prominent members of the 'intellectual aristocracy' of nineteenth-century Britain, a group of writers, politicians and thinkers who had close family connections, including the Trevelyans.[7] In his politics he was firmly a Liberal, but as a civil servant he had to work with all ministers, regardless of party affiliation.

Trevelyan was a workaholic, travelling to his office in London six days each week and keeping very long hours. The demands of the post were considerable. Of his immediate predecessors, two had died in office; the last incumbent had been forced to retire at the age of forty-six on the grounds of serious illness caused by overwork.[8] Trevelyan expected as much of his subordinates as he did of himself. The work load was relentless. His role was essentially that of anticipating and fulfilling the wishes of the chancellor of the exchequer; the days of powerful civil servants formulating and shaping government policy were to come later.

Even Trevelyan was not beyond exercising patronage, and despite his almost unimpeachable propriety and 'rigid integrity', in Macaulay's words, he used his position to lobby for sinecures for relatives, which he was able to do because of his position at the centre of power and influence.[9]

REVOLUTION

1843 was a momentous year in Irish history. The sense that Ireland was teetering on the brink of revolution was widespread among the British ruling classes. Trevelyan arrived at this conclusion after visiting Ireland for six weeks in late 1843. He came in search of an elusive ancestral estate in the north of Ireland and to deal with a pressing family matter. He toured the country but failed to identify the estate.

The family matter was a sensitive one. Sir Walter Trevelyan, the sixth baronet, had no children, and so the heir to the Trevelyan estates in England was Alfred Wilson Trevelyan, the son of Walter's dead younger brother, Charles's cousin. Alfred was being raised by his widowed mother and her parents in Co. Limerick. Charles and Walter Trevelyan were concerned about his education, as it was believed that the proper schooling for a prospective landlord was at an English public school, such as Eton, followed by university at Cambridge or Oxford. In any event, Charles visited Alfred's family to persuade his mother and grandparents that he should be sent to Eton. (As it happened, this plan fell through and Alfred went to school in Limerick and then to Trinity College, Dublin—an altogether inferior education!)

Trevelyan was in Ireland during a time of great upheaval, in his words during 'a crisis of no ordinary importance'. He attended some of O'Connell's monster meetings in Dublin. He was clearly impressed by the sheer depth of feeling about repeal as well as by O'Connell's powerful oratory, even if he was no more than a 'demagogue', but was perturbed by the sense of popular uprising that was in the air. On his return he had an interview with the prime minister, Sir Robert Peel, and the home secretary, Sir James Graham, who had responsibility for law and order in Ireland, at which he reported on his findings. Unusually, but characteristically, he then published two letters in the *Morning Chronicle*, under the pseudonym Philalethes ('lover of truth'), in which he described his impressions, both of which were later reprinted in the *Times*.[10] His tone was alarmist, predicting a revolution inspired by O'Connell's rhetoric and fomented by the Catholic priests. O'Connell was in 'the hands of the priests', and he 'has evoked a spirit which is too strong for him'.

He also recounted some hair-raising conversations with Irish 'peasants' that were bound to strike fear into English middle-class hearts, fed on a diet of Irish violence that centred on 'blood', 'murder', sedition and rebellion, an uprising that would involve widespread loss of life. He noted that the Catholic poor were amiable but also 'very ignorant' and 'very excitable', labouring as they were under 'a miserable state of delusion', incited to violence by the priests—a common theme in British discussions about the malevolence of Catholic 'priestcraft'. He then described how such a rebellion could be easily defeated by the sheer might of British military power.

Peel was indignant at Trevelyan's publishing these letters, even under a pen-name. He wrote to Graham in exasperation about his breach of confidence, saying that Trevelyan 'must be a consummate fool'.[11] After he was rebuked by Graham, Trevelyan published the second letter, though Graham may have tacitly wanted the accounts to be made public, as they supported his hard-line position on coercion in Ireland.

Trevelyan was no fool, whatever Peel may have thought. His action was classic Trevelyan: conscientious to the point of recklessness, an unwavering belief in his own judgement, and the calculated use of publicity to apply pressure on his political masters. It was also symbolic of the complexities of the man that his time in Ireland initiated a lifelong passion for collecting and learning by heart Repeal poetry and ballads, and from then onwards Irish correspondents sent him broadsheet ballads. When he took up his post as governor of Madras in 1859 he wrote to his wife in London to request that his books of Irish poetry and ballads be sent to him.[12] This was an odd pastime for a public servant working at the heart of the British establishment, but to be an agent of the destruction of a culture for political and economic imperatives was not entirely inconsistent with a nostalgic appreciation of its inherent beauty.

KICKS AND KINDNESS

The origins of the crisis in the early 1840s can be traced to the campaign for Catholic emancipation, led by the great nationalist leader Daniel O'Connell. Even after emancipation was achieved, in 1829, and Catholics could now sit in Parliament and hold high government offices and judicial posts, there remained a lasting if sporadic interest throughout the nineteenth century. Ireland tended to come into sharp focus during times of intense upheaval, and to disappear almost as quickly in times of relative calm.

The demand for fair government was the main battleground between Irish nationalists, under O'Connell's leadership, and British politicians. By the 1830s the legislative and financial provisions of the Act of Union were firmly established. The system of governance was a half-way house, with a separate administration in Dublin Castle, run by an under-secretary; the chief secretary, a politician based in London, responsible to the British government for the various arms of the government of Ireland; and the lord lieutenant or viceroy, usually a peer, occasionally with an Irish peerage.

The 'Castle' was associated in many minds with 'the unsympathetic authority of an external power'.[13] Ireland was governed not as a colony, like Britain's other possessions, nor as a fully integrated political entity within the United Kingdom, but as a political dependency.[14] With the abolition of the Irish Parliament, Irish MPs took their seats in the British House of Commons, yet the exercise of power was determined by the policy of the government. Ireland had a political voice in London, unlike other dependencies, a voice that became increasingly louder in the 1830s and 1840s.

One of the arguments put forward for Union was that Ireland would prosper as an integrated component of the United Kingdom, as had Scotland after its union with England in 1707. In the early years, just as the war with France had spurred on the political union, so too did the continuance of this conflict divert the gaze of British ministers away from Ireland until the Battle of Waterloo in 1815. The much-vaunted incorporation never came to pass. If anything, the two countries seemed to drift further apart. Ireland never achieved full integration within the United Kingdom. The country's economy was struggling, poverty was widespread and, most importantly, it was ruled in an entirely different way from England and Scotland. This was partly to do with attitudes towards Ireland but was also a consequence of the nature of the system of governance. Unlike England, local government by landowners was never a practical option in Ireland, as the landed classes were too widely dispersed and too thin on the ground to form an effective cadre of leaders. Dublin Castle retained strong authoritarian control over most aspects of day-to-day government, even if ultimately the main decisions on policy were made in London. And when the spectre of parliamentary reform emerged in Britain in the 1830s, stimulated by the much more real threat of the O'Connell movement, Irish Protestants preferred strong central government control to the prospect of having to share power locally with middle-class Irish Catholics.

The essential difference was that after 1801 these were now British as well as Irish concerns. These problems, which were not new in any respect, were identified, debated and discussed at length in scores of parliamentary inquiries and royal commissions about virtually every aspect of life, particularly the perennial subjects of rural poverty and underemployment. In the forty years after the Union numerous official investigations were conducted into Irish affairs, producing reports of which a considerable number ran to more than a thousand pages. The 'condition' or 'state' of the country was debated also with extraordinary regularity by writers on classical political economy, as Irish poverty constituted a direct challenge to an ideology centred on the power of the state to improve social and economic life.[15] Irish matters occupied an increasing proportion of parliamentary time, much to the irritation of many British politicians, who saw themselves as primarily concerned with global issues.

Yet parliamentary debates or extensive social and economic surveys did not necessarily mean that beliefs about conditions were either well informed or based on any degree of accurate knowledge. Information and understanding are two different things: as John MacHale once remarked, the ardent strictures of political economists and other commentators were far removed from the realities of life in Ireland.

The gilded saloons [salons] of London are not the appropriate lecture-halls for studying the wretchedness of an Irish cabin ... Faces sparkling with mirth are not the fittest mirror for reflecting the sunken eye and gaunt visage of despair; a taste palled with the satiety of feast and revels cannot well judge the acuteness of the pangs of hunger ... It requires a heart as well as eyes to be affected by the wants of others.[16]

An anonymous writer claimed in 1835 that the average Englishman knew 'more of Siberia or Caffreland [southern Africa] than they do of their next door neighbours'.[17] Within educated circles, where knowledge of Ireland was communicated through writings of varying insight, the Irish 'national character' was described as friendly, hospitable and gregarious but debased by its laziness, Catholicism and violent behaviour.[18] For British politicians, as with the middle classes, an impenetrable barrier of ignorance, ill-informed judgements and sheer prejudice militated against Ireland's effective incorporation in the Union during its early decades. Sydney Smith quipped in 1807 that 'the moment the very name of Ireland is mentioned, the English seem to bid adieu to common feeling, common prudence, and common sense, and to act with the barbarity of tyrants, and the fatuity of idiots'.[19]

British politicians of differing political outlooks were certain, however, about one thing: normal standards of good governance and responsibility were simply not applicable in Ireland. Government policy oscillated between coercion and conciliation or, in the memorable words of one commentator, 'a quick alternation of kicks and kindness'.[20] In the first half of the nineteenth century the balance was firmly on the side of kicks. Ireland was governed for only five years under ordinary law during the first fifty years of the Union. Coercive legislation was introduced as successive British governments met Irish unrest with severe repression. At critical times, such as the 1830s, repressive measures were put on the statute book in response to a specific threat, such as agrarian crime and rural violence. If there was ever any doubt about the ability of the authorities to enforce order, a constabulary force of roughly ten thousand men, together with twenty thousand soldiers stationed in the country, meant that Ireland was one of the most heavily policed societies in Europe. 'Special' Irish circumstances demanded that the military were often called out to assist the police in maintaining public order.

But the extent and frequency of such measures was also influenced by the widely shared view within the British governing elite that Ireland was altogether different when it came to governance. The Celt had a natural predisposition towards conspiratorial violence and understood only one language: force. A young Robert Peel, then chief secretary of Ireland, wrote in 1816 that 'an honest despotic Government would be by far the fittest government for Ireland', although he realised that accountability to

Parliament made this impossible.[21] The much-vaunted values of the unwritten British constitution did not apply to Ireland. More than any other grievance, this fuelled nationalist sentiment.

The hypocrisy was obvious: British statesmen preached values of representative parliamentary government on behalf of people 'with a stake in the country', that is, those that mattered, and the immutable rights of citizens yet were always falling short of implementing such lofty principles when it came to Ireland, almost instinctively resorting to coercion and the overwhelming use of power when any threat emerged, as it did in 1843, 'Repeal Year'.

REPEAL AND O'CONNELL

Daniel O'Connell turned his attention back to his campaign for the repeal of the Union in the early 1840s with the founding of the Loyal National Repeal Association in August 1840. As he had anticipated, the Whigs—O'Connell's natural allies—lost power in the general election of 1841 and the Tories, under Sir Robert Peel, came into office. Only twenty repeal MPs were returned, less than half the number who had gained seats in 1832. The days of securing concessions through the parliamentary alliance with the Whigs were over.

There was considerable disillusionment among younger nationalists about what the alliance had actually obtained for Ireland in the 1830s. The Liberator had delivered Catholic emancipation in 1829 through a mass movement that placed enormous pressure on the government, and he again returned to this tactic. Large-scale political mobilisation supported by effective local organisations established the traction for the repeal movement. In 1843 the famous monster meetings took place around the country, with hundreds of thousands attending.

The climax in the campaign was to be the monster meeting at Clontarf, on the outskirts of Dublin, on 8 October. Peel's government, fearing that the meeting would descend into large-scale violence, sent extra military forces to Ireland. There was a growing resolution to face down O'Connell, and the excuse was provided by the careless use of military language in the notice for the meeting. This gave the Dublin Castle administration the legal justification for issuing a proclamation prohibiting the meeting, which it duly did the night before. O'Connell complied with the proclamation, in line with his hostility to violence, rooted as much in his training and practice as a lawyer as in any theoretical conviction and fearing widespread bloodshed if the crowds clashed with the military. The Repeal Association acted quickly to prevent people converging on Dublin.

O'Connell and his principal supporters were arrested two days later on charges of sedition and were tried the following year. He was imprisoned for a year in May 1844, but the conviction was quashed in September by the House of Lords. O'Connell's 'crime' was that the very success of the political mobilisation he organised for the repeal of the Union was, from the British viewpoint, the challenge it posed to imperial power.[22] His reputation was enhanced by the show trial and imprisonment, and he emerged victorious on his release from Richmond Jail in Dublin in September; but the Liberator was humiliated, and aged by his martyrdom.

The two men had a long history. At the tender age of twenty-four Peel was appointed chief secretary for Ireland in 1812. This job was especially attractive to 'a young politician with ambitions to satisfy and a reputation to make'.[23] Peel's time in office was a success and helped to consolidate his emerging political career, though his time in Ireland left a deep and lasting impression— so much so that he never returned to the country after his resignation in 1818. Nevertheless he retained an interest in Ireland, keeping up extensive reading on it, a preoccupation that became obvious when he became prime minister for the second and final time in August 1841.

His spell as chief secretary was not without incident. A young barrister and emerging champion of Catholic rights, Daniel O'Connell, had described Peel on his appointment in 1812 as 'a raw youth squeezed out of the workings of I know not what factory in England'.[24] In 1815 Peel became involved in a very public dispute with O'Connell caused by 'ludicrous blunderings and misunderstandings', which very nearly ended in a deadly duel in Ostend, only for the timely intervention of the authorities as O'Connell passed through England.[25]

Thus began a lifetime of mutual hostility. O'Connell had coined the memorable epithet 'Orange Peel' to encapsulate his adversary's political sympathies.[26] Such deep enmities did not lessen with time. On his death bed in delirium in Genoa in May 1847, O'Connell 'shouted defiance of a phantasmagoric Peel and exulted that repeal was safely in the box'.[27] Peel thought he had called his bluff, that O'Connell had blinked first in the face of the overwhelming power of the state and had exposed the limitations of constitutional nationalism. There was no bluff: O'Connell neither advocated nor intended violence.

Peel's facing down of O'Connell's campaign for repeal was driven by wider considerations than personal animus. Within the British governing elite there was a real fear of revolution, fuelled by events on the Continent. Any form of mass agitation, either from British radicals or from Irish nationalists, was a danger to the state. Ireland, it seemed, would descend into anarchy. It certainly had all the ingredients for a revolution: a surrogate class in the Irish landlords who were widely distrusted and even more widely despised, the politicisation of the Catholic population through O'Connellite nationalism, and millions of poor and disfranchised people. Added to this was the growing threat of the Chartist movement in England, a mass organisation advocating radical political reform, led by O'Connell's former follower Feargus O'Connor.

Despite the public protestations that the Union was the successful means of incorporating Ireland in the United Kingdom, the evidence over the previous four decades suggested exactly the opposite. The formidable alliance of O'Connellite nationalism with the growing power of the Irish Catholic Church converged in a gathering momentum for repeal, placing the Union in jeopardy, fuelling demands for home rule and an Irish parliament in Dublin. That the government had to resort to the threat of coercion in 1843 demonstrated the weight attached to maintaining the Union at all costs. This was not simply about the constitutional relationship between Britain and Ireland: it was essentially an imperial issue, as it questioned the legitimacy of British rule in its many colonial possessions.

Another observer, albeit from an entirely different political viewpoint, Frederick Engels, reporting from Manchester in June 1843, noted that despite all his posturing and the mobilisation of the masses what O'Connell truly wanted was the defeat of Peel's Tories and the reinstatement of the Whig government. O'Connell was disingenuous in using 'the impoverished, oppressed Irish people to embarrass the Tory ministers and to help his middle-class friends get back into office'.[28] Engels noted the potential for revolution in Ireland: 'Give me two hundred thousand Irishmen and I could overthrow the entire British monarchy'. O'Connell's nationalism was unlikely to effect any real change, as true democracy posed a challenge to his own position and that of his class.

> If the people were set free even for a moment, Daniel O'Connell and his moneyed aristocrats would soon find themselves in the wilderness, where O'Connell himself would like to drive the Tories. This is the reason for O'Connell's close association with the Catholic clergy; that is why he exhorts the Irish to be on their guard against the dangerous socialists; this is why he rejects the assistance offered by the Chartists … Consequently, the only thing he will achieve is the political education of the Irish people, and this is ultimately for no one more dangerous than for himself.[29]

Engels was correct in one important respect. O'Connell was no social revolutionary, and even in the midst of the crisis in September 1843 he was urging a well-placed Whig politician that Lord John Russell, the leader of the opposition, should publicly offer a programme of reforms to prove that he was 'a high-minded, high-gifted statesman, capable of leading his friends into all the advantages to be derived from conciliating the Irish nation and strengthening the British empire'. As his correspondent Lord Campbell noted, this showed that, 'in the midst of apparent fury, [O'Connell] was very peaceably inclined, and would have been glad of a pretext for relaxing from Repeal agitation'.[30]

O'Connell's faith in parliamentary politics was unshakeable. His subordination of social reform to political gains was an obvious shortcoming, especially the lack of interest he showed in land reform, explained by his own landlord background and that of his principal supporters.[31] In this he resembled almost all other commentators on Ireland.

A HAPPY ENGLISH CHILD

British politicians perceived education as the principal mechanism for successfully incorporating Ireland in the United Kingdom. State involvement in schooling was a vexed issue. Education, controlled and financed by the British state, was seen as the way to bring about moral, social and economic improvement and the means by which the majority population might be freed from the shackles of Catholic dominance. Popish error would be combated by the teaching of the basic principles of 'civilisation'.

Elizabeth Smith founded a national school in 1834 and devoted much of her free time to encouraging the local children to attend it.[32] Her Catholic tenants seemed to epitomise all that was reprehensible about the indolent Celts, who seemed resigned to a lifetime in dehumanising poverty, a view shared by many contemporary commentators. In education lay the solution to improving conditions in Ireland. The process of establishing the school was not without its difficulties, as she was later to recount:

> I remember that there was a great deal of trouble in setting up the School—a sign of progress much wanted—none of the men and few of the women could read—none of the women could sew—method equally unknown in the home. Poor creatures they had been neglected for more than a generation.[33]

A Protestant landlord involved in sponsoring a school for Catholic children, even with the best of paternalist intentions, was viewed with deep suspicion. The Catholic parish priest of nearby Blackditches, Arthur Germaine, jointly sponsored the school with Elizabeth Smith, but he did very little to assist her in encouraging children to attend regularly. Behind the scenes he was promoting the local hedge school. Like many Catholic priests, Germaine feared that the state schools would become mechanisms for Protestant proselytising and seek to convert Catholic children rather than educate them. Such was the extent of denominational suspicion in mid-nineteenth-century Ireland that even on the provision of elementary education, which all sides acknowledged was badly needed, confessional divisions quickly emerged.

Up to the 1830s elementary education was provided by a hotchpotch of private individuals and charitable foundations and by schools run by Catholic religious orders, such as the Christian Brothers, whose first school was opened in Waterford in 1802. The hedge schools may have provided schooling for between 300,000 and 400,000 children in the mid-1820s, paid for by the parents, sometimes from very modest incomes.[34] The Society for Promoting the Education of the Poor in Ireland (commonly called the Kildare Place Society), founded in 1811, established schools for the poor throughout the country from 1816 onwards on a non-sectarian basis and received generous grants from the government. At first the schools received support from Catholic politicians and bishops, but Daniel O'Connell withdrew from its board of managers in 1820. The Catholic bishops became increasingly critical of its policy of reading the Bible 'without note or comment,' with reports of proselytism in some of its schools. John MacHale would be one of the most vocal critics of the Kildare Place Society from the early 1820s.

As part of a general package of reforms, Grey's government devised a state-financed national system of education. This was established in 1831, with local committees running and part-financing the construction of each school. Elizabeth Smith's school was one of the thousands set up under this new scheme.

The Irish national education system was the most far-reaching experiment in social engineering ever undertaken in Ireland or Britain. Instituted some forty years before an equivalent system emerged in England, it was designed to counter the potential educational influence of the Catholic Church and to improve standards of literary and thereby dispel 'ignorance'.

'Ignorance' included Irishness. A verse placed on a notice that hung in every school simplified the ideals of the National Board of Education:

I thank the goodness and the grace
That on my birth have smiled,
And made me in these Christian days
A happy English child.[35]

The Catholic bishops were at first supportive of the new national schools, believing the system to be the best available compromise in the circumstances. In 1838 MacHale broke ranks and launched a withering attack on the schools, and implicitly on the bishops who supported them. His public letter to Lord John Russell, the home secretary, asserted the sole prerogative of the 'Catholic bishops, and Catholic bishops alone', to select the textbooks for Catholic children, rather than any state agency or board.[36]

MacHale's concerns embraced the religious composition of the National Board of Education, which included a number of Protestants. This set in train a long-lasting and bitter controversy within the Catholic hierarchy. Daniel Murray, the elderly Archbishop of Dublin, and William Crolly, Archbishop of Armagh, along with many other bishops, supported the schools; MacHale and his followers vehemently opposed the involvement of the state in Catholic education. Predictably, MacHale turned to Pope Gregory XVI for support for his position, and at first it appeared that Rome would endorse his view, but eventually the supporters of the national schools were able to secure a compromise. This formula, issued from Rome in January 1841, left each bishop free to decide whether the national schools should be approved of within his diocese.[37]

Meanwhile MacHale took steps to remove Catholic involvement in the national schools in his Archdiocese of Tuam. By 1840, of the original hundred national schools established there only twelve remained open, mostly run by Protestant groups.[38] Despite the efforts of MacHale to encourage Catholic religious orders to make up this deficiency, it proved impossible to replace the state-financed national schools with a Catholic system, effectually forcing poor Catholics in the west to either send their children to Protestant missionary schools or, more likely, condemning them to a lifetime without the benefits of basic education.[39] Inadvertently, as long as this boycott continued MacHale also created the conditions under which Protestant missions operating in Connacht flourished, in particular in Connemara and Achill Island. MacHale was all too aware of the threat to the Catholic faith that such proselytism posed in Tuam.

ON THE EDUCATION OF THE PEOPLE

Education was also a vexed issue in India, where it was also closely tied up with imperial objectives. Ever since he made his life there, Charles Trevelyan saw education as the principal method of fostering Western values, one of his pet projects being the application of the Roman alphabet to Oriental languages. Like most of his educated contemporaries, Trevelyan divided the world into higher and less-developed civilisations, with the latter learning from the former, which inevitably was the western European Christian tradition. When posted to Delhi he was appointed to the committee of Delhi College in July 1828, and he played an important role in formulating a new policy for the college, based on Western scholarship learnt through English. The language of the reports produced by the committee bears all the hallmarks of Trevelyan's thinking, with the emphasis placed on the improvement of morals and the 'amelioration of the human race, and … the real and lasting glory of our nation'.[40]

After he moved to Calcutta in 1831 Trevelyan was heavily involved in the vexed debates surrounding Indian education in the 1830s, in which his brother-in-law Macaulay played a pivotal role in determining future British policy in India. The differences essentially hinged around two competing visions for Indian education but also raised broader ideological questions about the nature of colonial rule. The Orientalists wanted to maintain the emphasis on the classical Indian languages of Sanskrit, Persian and Arabic, whereas the Anglicists wished to substitute English or, less desirably, the vernacular languages, such as Hindi or Bengali, in the education system.

There were wider issues at stake. Lord William Bentinck was a reformist governor-general who during his time sought to 'govern India for the benefit of the Indians', though, as Trevelyan was to say in 1852, 'the laws of God are so happily adjusted that, in benefiting the natives, we also benefit ourselves'.[41]

These tensions came to a head in January 1835 when the General Committee of Public Instruction, the body charged with administering public funds for education in India, was unable to reach a compromise and asked the Supreme Council of India, headed by Bentinck, to settle the question once and for all. Trevelyan had been appointed to the committee in 1833 and had launched a series of withering public attacks on the Orientalists, using periodicals to make his arguments heard. In January 1834 he described what he saw as the demise of the Orientalist dominance:

Orientalism has, at length, ceased to be considered the exclusive test of merit, and the public mind has completely awoke to the fact that the shortest and most effectual way of communicating knowledge to the people of this country is by educating the youth in English literature, and, where this is impracticable, by providing them with translations of books on European science in their own languages.[42]

In his view, what was needed was teaching in living languages, such as English and the Indian vernaculars.

We do not want a Babel of dead languages, but the living languages of the English and Indians. We do not want an ocean of words, but an influx of ideas.[43]

Macaulay was president of the committee, and his famous 'Minute on Education in India', drafted in February 1835, set out the terms for the general policy in British India. He was notoriously dismissive of classical Eastern learning and argued that state funds should be used to promote English as the gateway to European civilisation.

I am quite ready to take the oriental learning at the valuation of the Orientalists themselves. I have never found one among them who could deny that a single shelf of a good European library was worth the whole native literature of India and Arabia. The intrinsic superiority of the Western literature is indeed fully admitted by those members of the Committee who support the Oriental plan of education ... The question now before us is simply whether, when it is in our power to teach this language, we shall teach languages in which, by universal confession, there are no books on any subject which deserve to be compared to our own, whether, when we can teach European science, we shall teach systems which, by universal confession, wherever they differ from those of Europe differ for the worse, and whether, when we can patronize sound Philosophy and true History, we shall countenance, at the public expense, medical doctrines which would disgrace an English Farrier— Astronomy which would move laughter in girls at an English boarding school—History, abounding with kings thirty feet high, and reigns thirty thousand years long—and Geography made of seas of treacle and seas of butter ...[44]

Behind the scenes Trevelyan had worked hard to achieve this victory. Characteristically, while on leave in England four years later he published a long account of this controversy in which he argued that English language and literature was 'best adapted for the improvement of India', and that the desire for Western learning came from educated Indians, which in the case of the aspiring Bengali middle classes was certainly true.[45] There was also the practical consideration that instruction in English would create a pool of middle-class Indians who could work in government and reduce the need for, and the cost of, British-born administrators.

Aside from these very pragmatic concerns, Trevelyan had more lofty motives, inspired by his evangelicalism. He wrote privately to Bentinck in April 1833, describing a proposal to introduce an ambitious universal system of national education that would bring about 'the moral and intellectual regeneration of the people of India'. He could think of nothing better than spending the remainder of his life establishing and overseeing this system. Its purpose would be to bring about the establishment of 'our language, our learning, and ultimately our religion in India', he wrote a year later. And the potential benefits would not be confined to the Subcontinent, as Providence 'was evidently concentrating her means of improvement here in order that, setting out from India a base of operation, these may afterwards be applied with greater effect to the surrounding nations'.[46]

Trevelyan's evangelical aspirations were not, nevertheless, reflected in the famous minute, as Macaulay did not advocate a universal system of education, or emphasise the potential benefits to Christianity of using English. In fact the official position of the British government in India was strict neutrality on religious grounds. As Macaulay acknowledged, instituting such a system was not immediately practicable, and his emphasis was on forming 'a class who may be interpreters between us and the millions whom we govern,—a class of persons Indian in blood and colour, but English in tastes, in opinions, in morals, and in intellect'.[47]

Trevelyan was deeply influenced by the Rev. Alexander Duff, an energetic twenty-four-year-old evangelical Scottish Presbyterian missionary who had opened a school in Calcutta in 1830, the General Assembly Institution, which taught Western arts and sciences through English as well as the central teachings of Christianity.[48] The two young men had met shortly after Trevelyan was transferred to Calcutta, and there was a meeting of minds about the importance of bringing Christianity to India, and how this could be achieved. English must be used 'as the medium of all Christianizing and civilizing'.[49]

Duff was an advocate of the 'filter down' approach, which assumed that if the Indian elite was educated in English this would 'be the instrument of the eventual transformation of Indian society and its conversion to Christianity'.[50] Trevelyan greatly admired Duff's zeal and sense of purpose and later said that his missionary efforts in India earned him 'a high place among the benefactors of mankind'.[51] In the event, Duff had left before the victory was secured in 1835, as ill-health had forced him to travel back to Scotland.

This sequence of events presents a unique insight into Trevelyan's world view and how, above all else, his religious convictions shaped his manoeuvrings behind the scenes to achieve his objectives. Undoubtedly his concerns about the use of English in the education system were sincere, yet the overriding motivation was to bring about a Christianised India and, if possible, to extend this throughout Asia. Moral regeneration in India was to be achieved through the widespread adoption of the civilising mission of Christianity. His unshakeable self-belief, bordering on arrogance, his tenacity if not underhand tactics in employing public opinion to achieve his own ends and discredit his opponents, as well as the effective lobbying of powerful allies, such as his brother-in-law, were to become painfully evident in the late 1840s when Ireland rather than India was, in Trevelyan's view, in need of regeneration.

'HE HAD DIED FOR IRELAND'

When the new ministry headed by Lord Melbourne came to power in 1835 the opportunity arose for a fresh view on how Ireland might be governed. Many Whig politicians, including Lord Melbourne, recognised the failings of previous policies and sought a rapprochement with nationalists, led by Daniel O'Connell, in return for support for his minority ministry. Under the Lichfield House compact of February 1835 O'Connell agreed to suspend his recently inaugurated campaign for repeal of the Union and to support the Whigs, in return for 'justice for Ireland'. For O'Connellites the implication was that this would involve weakening the power of the Protestant ascendancy.[52]

The first step was the installation in Dublin Castle of an administration more sympathetic to the Irish situation. Constantine Phipps, Earl of Mulgrave, was appointed lord lieutenant, a role to which he brought considerable skill by winning the support of middle-class Catholics through what was essentially a charm offensive. O'Connell declared on his arrival in May 1835 that he was 'an excellent man' and that 'there cannot be better'; his colleague Lord John Russell wryly remarked that Ireland was 'a strange country, but Lord Mulgrave seems to have found a way of governing it'.[53]

The second was the appointment as chief secretary of George Howard, Viscount Morpeth, who had a genuine commitment to achieving reform in Ireland.

The final member of the triumvirate was a young Scottish military engineer and administrator, Thomas Drummond, who has been rightly described as 'the greatest Irish public servant of the nineteenth century'.[54] Drummond's background included an involvement for five years in the surveying of Ireland for the Ordnance Survey, established in 1824. During this time he was credited with two inventions that greatly improved surveying techniques. He was appointed under-secretary at Dublin Castle in July 1835, effectually the chief administrative official. Unlike most previous holders of this post, Drummond came to it with extensive knowledge of conditions in Ireland, and a Scottish Presbyterian outlook that saw religious equality as the key to good government.

Drummond, with the support of his political superiors, Mulgrave and Morpeth, set about a programme of comprehensive reforms, concentrating on law and order, the administration of justice and challenging the dominant role of the ascendancy and the Orange Order.[55] The first stage in this process was reform of the police, through the establishment of the Irish Constabulary and the Dublin Metropolitan Police in 1836. The aim was to make policing impartial, fair and respected by Catholics. Secondly, he set out to achieve the same impartiality in the administration of justice through changes in the appointment of magistrates, and an increasing number of Catholics were nominated as judges. Finally, he took on two powerful interests: the Protestant landed ascendancy and the Orange Order. He had extensive knowledge of the conditions of the poor in Ireland and little sympathy for landlords who did not at least try to improve the lot of tenants. After the murder of a landlord, Austin Cooper, in April 1838, the Tipperary magistrates, including a number of prominent peers, petitioned Lord Mulgrave to introduce coercive legislation. Drummond's oft-quoted reply a month later to the Earl of Donoughmore, the lord lieutenant for the county, challenged the assertion that juries were intimidated and robustly defended the government's record in maintaining order. He asserted that agrarian crime was caused by the land system and explained that such actions were often driven by the eviction of cottiers, who were acting in the interests of 'self-preservation ... in vindication of what they falsely assume to be their rights'. But, he continued, landowners could not demand that their own rights be respected without taking equal account of their responsibilities.

> Property has its duties as well as its rights; to the neglect of those duties in times past is mainly to be ascribed that diseased state of society in which such crimes take their rise; and it is not in the enactment or enforcement of statutes of extraordinary severity, but chiefly in the better and more faithful performance of those duties, and the more enlightened and humane exercise of those rights, that a permanent remedy for such disorders is sought.[56]

Drummond's impertinence in reminding landowners of their duties ensured that he remained a target for vilification by the ascendancy class. The opportunity for a direct assault on the administration's policies arose six months later, after the murder of Lord Norbury in January 1839. The murder, as we have seen, received extensive newspaper publicity. The *Times* in an editorial singled out Drummond's 'insolence' and his association of rural crime with the actions of landowners as a particularly reprehensible action on the part of the Irish government.[57]

In Parliament a group of Tory MPs and peers led efforts to have the conduct of the Melbourne ministry on law and order investigated. In April 1839 a select committee was appointed by the House of Lords. Instigated by the Earl of Roden, an Ulster landowner, 'ultra' Tory and leading figure in the Orange Order, it was to investigate the state of Ireland 'in respect of crime and outrage, which have rendered life and property insecure in that part of the empire'.[58]

Against the advice of friends, as he was ill, Drummond appeared before the committee in June 1839 and was questioned for seven days. His performance served to enhance his reputation as he remained 'cool and firm' under fire when facing hostile questions from his detractors. In the words of a sympathetic biographer, 'he proved that by justice and fair play, the Irish people might be made loyal to the English connection'.[59]

Drummond's health suffered from overwork and the demands of his post. He kept extremely long hours, with little time left for his wife and young family. Friends had urged him to resign his post for the sake of his health. Despite breaks in 1838 and 1840, during which he regained his strength, he had lost weight and suffered from recurrent illnesses, such as influenza. In April 1840 he became seriously ill and his doctor was called to the Under-

Secretary's Lodge in the Phoenix Park. The diagnosis was grim: he had 'internal erysipelas'. Drummond died four days later, on 15 April, aged forty-two. On his deathbed, when asked if he would prefer to be buried in Scotland or Ireland he replied: 'In Ireland, the land of my adoption. I have loved her well and served her faithfully, and lost my life in her service.'

According to the *Freeman's Journal*, his death was a 'national calamity'.[60] He was buried at Mount Jerome Cemetery, Harold's Cross, Dublin, after a funeral service attended by hundreds of public figures, including O'Connell. As his friend Sir Thomas Larcom lamented, 'he had died for Ireland'.[61]

ORANGEISM AND POWER

Drummond's achievements were many and varied, not least his bringing of a sense of equality to the governance of Ireland by involving Catholics, facing down the entrenched ascendancy interests, and reforming the administration of policing and the legal system.[62] Many of these administrative reforms had their antecedents in the Whig government's Irish policies of the early 1830s, and Drummond was essentially continuing a process that had begun earlier. What was novel, however, was his direct challenge to the pervasive influence of the Orange Order in the exercise of justice.

The attitude of Tory politicians towards Orangeism was ambivalent: Peel, for instance, endorsed the ideological outlook of the order but was suspicious of its secretive oath-bound organisation and its reputation for violent disorder.[63] On the ground, however, Irish Tories, including prominent landowners, supported the order, in no small part because of fears of diminishing Protestant power generated by the granting of Catholic emancipation in 1829.

In Ulster the administration of justice through local magistrates and justices of the peace was dominated by the gentry and landlords, many of whom were either members of the loyal orders or had open Orange sympathies. In Co. Armagh, where animosities often descended into sectarian violence, well-documented cases of the blatant maladministration of justice in favour of Orangemen were numerous. Magistrates could hinder investigations or, failing that, pass lenient sentences on those convicted; in many instances the jury were also Orangemen, unlikely to convict a brother.[64] As one Catholic barrister remarked in 1835, 'between Protestant and Catholic, justice is positively denied to the Catholic'.[65]

Drummond, as under-secretary, actively challenged the worst excesses of magistrates' partiality in the administration of justice. He appointed stipendiary magistrates, often drawn from outside the region, paid by and directly accountable to Dublin Castle, to counter the influence of the voluntary local magistrates.[66] Even though the Orange Order had been banned in 1825 it continued to grow in strength into the 1830s. In 1836 the order voluntarily disbanded after parliamentary investigations brought to light its activities in the British army, the magistracy and other public bodies and rumours of an incredible plot to assassinate the heir to the throne, Princess Victoria, and replace her with the king's brother, the Duke of Cumberland, who happened to be Imperial Grand Master of the order.[67] But it continued to operate at the local level. In a famous case Drummond challenged Colonel William Verner, MP for Armagh and deputy lieutenant of Co. Tyrone, to say whether he had been present at a toast to the Battle of the Diamond at an election dinner in August 1837. When Verner refused to 'dignify' the inquiry with a response, feigning not to understand the reference to the event (though he was Deputy Grand Master of Ireland), he was dismissed. This led to a very public controversy, including a debate in the House of Commons.[68] The Verner family were prominent Orange grandees, and Drummond's actions provoked fury and accusations that the administration of Ireland was being conducted to favour Catholics.[69]

John Mitchel would have watched this case closely, not least because the person concerned was his wife's uncle. After moving to establish a legal practice in Banbridge, Mitchel became centrally involved in local sectarian disputes that were a feature of life in mid-Ulster. It was an Orange town, and the aftermath of the annual Twelfth of July parades was usually violence. Mitchel often acted for Catholics who were being prosecuted in the local courts. Most of the magistrates were Orangemen, who had little sympathy for Ulster Catholics.

It was through this public role that Mitchel first came to know Charles Gavan Duffy, a native of Co. Monaghan who was editor of the *Belfast Vindicator*, a popular newspaper that expressed the grievances of the city's Catholics, who were excluded from its governance. Mitchel met Duffy in Belfast in 1841. Duffy recounted later than he was impressed by the 'vigour and liberality of his opinions, as well as by his culture and suavity'. His description of the young Mitchel, then in his mid-twenties, is a rare glimpse into his demeanour and personality.

He was rather above the middle size, well-made and with a face which was thoughtful and comely, though pensive blue eyes and masses of soft brown hair, a stray ringlet of which he had the habit of twining round his finger while he spoke, gave it, perhaps too feminine a cast ... he was silent and retiring, slow to speak and apt to deliver his opinion in a form which would be abrupt and dogmatic if it were not relieved by a pleasant smile.[70]

When Duffy started his new weekly newspaper, the *Nation*, in October 1842, Mitchel and his long-time friend John Martin subscribed. With its mixture of cultural nationalism and political comment it appealed to Mitchel, who predicted—rightly, as it happened—that it would do 'very well'. By 1843 it had an average weekly circulation of more than ten thousand, the largest of any newspaper in Ireland.[71]

There is no escaping the sense of an inner conflict within Mitchel at this time. His growing family—by 1844 he had four young children—meant that he could not avoid his responsibilities to his practice. He took these very seriously, preparing documents and attending court to represent his clients, though he derived very little satisfaction from his legal work, finding it monotonous and draining. By all accounts he was a devoted husband and good father, spending time playing with his young children when not working. Yet his life lacked the intellectual nourishment and spark that he seemed to crave. He read widely, borrowing books from the local minister, an old friend of his father, and engaging in discussions with his friends, either in person or by correspondence.

Ironically for someone who was later to emerge as a strong supporter of slavery in the United States, what drove Mitchel was his deep sense of justice. And injustice was all around him, fuelled by religious and political animosities very obvious in his daily observation of the treatment of Catholics in the Ulster courts. His growing radicalism is evident in his letters to his long-time friend John Martin throughout the 'Repeal Year' of 1843. When discussing O'Connell's campaign he joked with Martin that if he were to put his thoughts on paper he might well be arrested for treason. His frustration with O'Connell's strategy, and equally the response of Peel's government, was leading him towards more drastic solutions.

Indeed, I am tired of loud agitation: loud seditious rhetoric on the one side, and stern, contemptuous denial and fixed bayonets on the other ... If Ireland be not ready to achieve the repeal with a strong hand, she ought to make herself ready without delay; and if she be worthy of the place she seeks among the nations, she will *do* that.[72]

The final event that propelled Mitchel from support for O'Connellite nationalism into engagement in national politics was the trial of O'Connell and others, including Duffy, on charges of conspiracy in January 1844. While on business he went to the court hearings in Dublin. In the wake of O'Connell's being handed a prison sentence in late May, the following month he attended his first repeal meeting, in Tullylish, Co. Down. (He had joined the Repeal Association the previous year.) He confided to Martin afterwards that 'I think I see a growing interest about repeal amongst Protestants'—in retrospect an unduly sanguine assessment.[73]

Mitchel had moved from being a supportive, if detached, observer of the repeal movement to a position of active involvement. From 1845 his life would be devoted to the cause of Irish nationalism as his legal career came to a premature end when he and his family left Ulster.

PRISONS OF THE POOR

From the late 1830s, imposing gothic-style buildings sprang up in the length and breadth of Ireland. These were the workhouses, built to provide an industrial-scale response to Irish poverty, the other major issue of the 1830s and early 1840s. By then there was widespread recognition that Irish poverty was in need of urgent attention.

In 1833 the Whig government established a commission of inquiry, chaired by the Church of Ireland Archbishop of Dublin, Richard Whately, to investigate the conditions of the poor. It set about the gargantuan task of collecting information, taking evidence from witnesses at local hearings and distributing nearly eight thousand questionnaires to respondents. When it finally reported, in 1836, it recommended a radical programme to bring about a 'national improvement', with an emphasis on public works, agriculture and the promotion of state-sponsored emigration of the poor. The commissioners rejected a workhouse system along the lines of the one that had been introduced in England and Wales in 1834. Ireland was different in one crucial respect: the able-bodied poor were 'eager for work', but as employment was not readily available 'they are therefore, and not from any fault of their own, in permanent want'.[74] It was estimated that 2½ to 3 million people were potentially in need of assistance. The final report of the commission, published in 1836, along with the ancillary volumes of information and evidence, remains to this day the most valuable survey of the poor in Ireland immediately before the disaster of the Great Irish Famine.

On its publication the report was ignored by the government, which blanched at the interventionist nature of the recommendations and feared the costs and the controversy that these wholesale schemes would incur. One official, George Cornewall Lewis, who had worked for the commission, charting the condition of the Irish poor who had made their way to Britain, wrote a devastating critique of the recommendations. The government's preference was for a workhouse system modelled closely on the English one. The home secretary, Lord John Russell, instructed an English Poor Law commissioner, George Nicholls, to travel to Ireland and prepare a report, which he duly did in a matter of weeks. His short stay did not prevent him formulating views about the Irish peasantry, their intemperance and general lack of interest in self-improvement.

> During my progress through the country, it was impossible not to notice the depression of feeling, morally and personally, of the Irish peasantry, and this to an extent which a stranger could not witness without very painful emotions. It shows itself in their mode of living, in their habitations, in their dress, in the dress of their children, and in their general economy and conduct. They seem to feel no pride, no emulation; to be heedless of the present, and reckless of the future.[75]

Nicholls recommended the introduction of the workhouse system, financed by rates (property taxes) paid by landowners and tenants, with several important divergences from the English model: there would be no legal right to relief, and assistance would be given only within the confines of the workhouse. He also made it clear that a famine was 'a contingency altogether above the powers of a Poor Law to provide for', advice that was completely neglected a decade later.[76] In 1838 the Poor Law was established, and over the following years Poor Law unions (i.e. unions of parishes) were mapped out, boards of guardians elected by the ratepayers, and workhouses constructed according to a standardised pattern. By the end of 1841, 127 of the planned 130 workhouses were complete.

At the heart of the workhouse system was the principle of 'less eligibility': that the standard of living within the workhouse should be less than that of the poorest people outside. This was to discourage anyone but those in dire need from seeking assistance, making the resort to relief punitive. In this inhumane respect the Poor Law was successful. Whole families were required to enter the workhouse, with men, women, girls and boys divided into separate quarters, separating children from their parents. Clothes were removed and new arrivals made to wear a demeaning uniform. The diet was oatmeal, potatoes and milk, distributed in carefully rationed portions for breakfast and dinner. Monotonous routine and strict discipline were paramount, with the inmates spending their days removing oakum from old ropes, which was used as caulk in warships. Any deviation from the rules could be severely punished by the master of the workhouse. Inmates were free to discharge themselves at any time, and many did, preferring to take their chances in the uncertain outside world than to be subjected to this dehumanising life.

Contrary to the expectation that there would be an overwhelming demand for relief under the Poor Law, only the most desperate resigned themselves to this terrible fate. It was a matter of great shame for individuals and families to enter the workhouse. Elizabeth Smith commented that 'many a decent family suffer bitterly and won't complain', and that the poor of Baltiboys would rather die than enter the workhouse at Naas.[77] The German writer Johann Kohl found in 1842 that it was the last resort of the defeated.

> The Irishman would rather wander through the entire world seeking employment, than endure the discipline of a workhouse, so long as he is in possession of his health and strength. Imprisonment, and confinement of every kind, is to the Irishman more irksome than to the Englishman. Consequently, even though he were much better off in a workhouse than he could be at home, he would never enter one except in case of the most extreme distress; and he will be sure to remain in it not a single moment longer than this distress continues.[78]

Each Poor Law union was run by a board of guardians, two-thirds of whom were elected from the ranks of the ratepayers; the other third were members *ex officio*, such as justices of the peace. The guardians oversaw the running of the workhouse and the Poor Law union more generally, and were answerable to the ratepayers for all expenditure. The system was financed by local rates levied in equal proportions on those who owned the land and the occupiers. There is little doubt that landowners, especially large ones, dominated the boards of guardians, as they had multiple votes and could exercise influence over larger farmers and tenants.

The annual elections of Poor Law guardians could bring underlying sectarian and political tensions to the fore, as they did in Baltiboys. Poor Law guardians exercised considerable power, and the annual elections were a glimpse of what limited democracy might look like in Ireland. Landlords assumed that customary deference towards wealth and status would ensure their election, whereas tenants had their own ideas about who might best represent the interests of the occupiers of the land. Hal Smith was nominated in April 1841. The local Catholic priests favoured another candidate, a Mr Riley (or Reilly), and campaigned vigorously, and successfully, for his election. The tactics of the clergy apparently included denouncing Colonel Smith from the altar, refusing to baptise the child of a ratepayer who voted for the landlord, and explicit threats to individual ratepayers who did not vote for the 'candidate of the true faith'.[79] Elizabeth's reflections on the role of priests in this minor fracas were expressed when, on hearing anecdotal reports that the power of the Catholic clergy over their flock in the locality was on the wane, she wrote:

> I think nay I feel sure that if we protestants did our duty, if we acted up to our principles, if the landlords visited and assisted and became acquainted with their tenantry and our clergy laboured with zeal in their vocation, there would be few papists in this country in twenty years.[80]

THE FATE OF IRELAND

The central objection of Irish nationalists was not British rule in Ireland. Republican demands for self-determination and independence truly emerged only with Fenianism in the 1860s. The legitimacy of the Crown was rarely questioned, and vocal nationalists, such as O'Connell and MacHale, did not advocate severing the constitutional link with Britain. The principal grievance was the way in which Britain ruled Ireland. Nationalists argued that a parliament in Dublin would provide better government for Ireland, with policies that were more in tune with Irish circumstances.

On almost every pressing issue since the introduction of the Union in 1801 scant allowance was made for the unique conditions that existed in Ireland, with the notable exception of Thomas Drummond's time in Dublin Castle. Unlike its powerful neighbour, Ireland was primarily an agricultural country, lacking the heavy industries that dominated the British economic landscape. Inappropriate British solutions were imposed on Ireland. Such measures certainly would have generated massive opposition if their introduction was contemplated in England or Scotland, yet they were somehow seen as acceptable in Ireland.

It was not only the principles underlying policies that raised the ire of nationalists but their implementation. When MacHale complained bitterly and very publicly about the composition of the Board of National Education in 1838 it was not that he opposed elementary education for the poor— although that was the effect of his intervention: his chief objections were to the form it would take, the content of the curriculum and, most importantly, who ultimately exercised control over the schools.

> Alas, it seems to be the fate of Ireland that no plan can be devised for her improvement, whether it regards education or the relief of the poor, that is not to be conducted by individuals opposed to us by religious and national antipathies.[81]

These fault lines in mid-nineteenth-century Ireland were to prove catastrophic after the potato blight arrived in September 1845. The government in London had limited knowledge of conditions in Ireland and was blinkered in its world view by an ideological commitment to the central tenets of classical political economy and the pre-eminence of the market, far more appropriate to Britain than to Ireland. Where the state did display its muscular character was in the area of law and order, challenging popular protest, brutally suppressing rural unrest and supporting the entrenched interests of property and the established Church of Ireland.

Irish nationalism, which, under O'Connell's dominant leadership, had sought to achieve reform, was to fracture into opposing camps in 1846, with radicals such as John Mitchel and other Young Irelanders losing patience with constitutional means for achieving justice for Ireland, and with no real alternative outside romantic rhetoric.

PART II

That coming storm

Chapter 4 ∿

SPECTRE OF FAMINE

Early in 1845, to all appearances, there was going to be a fine crop as the potatoes grew well and were far advanced for the time of year … A dense fog came in from the sea and lasted three to four days. When the fog cleared away the potato stalks withered away in a couple of nights. The fields became black and, in a week's time, not a stalk remained.[1]

'THE BLESSING OF PROVIDENCE'

The voices of the people most affected by the Great Irish Famine are largely silent. Their reactions, views and understanding of the uncertain world around them rarely feature in the historical record. This account from folklore captures the sudden destruction of the Irish potato harvest in 1845 and equally the mysterious origins of the devastation. But it was taken down in the 1940s by a collector working for the Irish Folklore Commission from a man then in his late sixties, born decades after the event. A story that was handed down from generation to generation, it shows how the extraordinary outbreak of the famine retained its place in popular memory nearly a century later.

The culprit was a fungus, *Phytophthora infestans*, that first appeared in Europe in June 1845. Two years previously it had substantially damaged crops along the eastern seaboard of the United States, moving inland into the midwestern states and parts of Canada in 1843 and 1844. Exactly how the blight crossed the Atlantic remains something of a botanical mystery. One feasible explanation is that seed potatoes ordered by Belgian farmers from the United States carried the fungus to Europe.[2]

After arriving in Flanders, over the summer it spread with alacrity, radiating outwards from Belgium into France, the Netherlands, southern Germany, the north of Italy and Switzerland until its appearance in the Isle of Wight, off the south coast of England, at the beginning of August 1845.

A few days later the wholesale wasting of the potato crop in Kent was reported by a farmer. The failure of the crop in England was undoubtedly a matter for concern; but in Ireland it would spell widespread hunger, as 3 to 4 million people depended on it.

Early indications of the year's potato harvest were reassuring. In late spring the *Limerick Chronicle* expressed the natural expectation that 'should it please Providence to continue the same favourable prosperity, the next harvest will be one of the earliest and most abundant remembered in this country'.[3] The *Freeman's Journal* likewise observed in July that 'the poor man's property, the potato crop, was never before so large and at the same time so abundant'. It continued—ominously, as it turned out—to declare that 'the near approach of an abundant harvest, may, therefore be looked upon, with the blessing of Providence, as almost certain'.[4]

A disease attacking potatoes in Britain would not necessarily have consequences for Ireland. However, isolated reports of the blight emerged in early September. John Lindley, editor of the *Gardeners' Chronicle*, the leading English horticultural journal of the time, could not conceal his alarm at this ominous development. A brilliant botanist and not a person predisposed towards sensationalism, he stopped the press of the *Gardeners' Chronicle* on 13 September 1845 to announce the dreadful news.

> We stop the press, with very great regret, to announce that the potato Murrain has unequivocally declared itself in Ireland. The crops about Dublin are suddenly perishing. The conversion of potatoes into flour … becomes then a process of the first national importance; for where will Ireland be, in the event of a universal potato rot?[5]

Because of the late harvesting of the potato, the full scale of the disaster came to light only in the early weeks of October 1845, when the devastating effects of a widespread failure were discussed in the newspapers. Within three months the blight was transformed from a vague concern in faraway lands to a ghastly local reality. Andrew Kettle, the future Land Leaguer, then a schoolboy, said later that 'the blight came on like a thief in the night in the autumn of 1845'.[6] After appearing on the east coast it spread steadily across the country during October and November. Its progress was tracked locally— and clandestinely, to prevent panic—by members of the Irish Constabulary. The blight hit hardest in the east of the country, the worst-affected areas being Cos. Antrim, Down, Monaghan, Meath, Dublin and Waterford, but it also hit the south-west and parts of Cos. Galway and Roscommon. Only about a third of the potatoes were destroyed in late 1845; much of the plentiful early crop had already been lifted before the outbreak of the disease.[7] This explains why the hardship was not as widespread as anticipated in the winter of 1845. Many of these counties were also more affluent than their western counterparts, where reliance on the potato for food was greatest.[8]

'A PLACE OF SUCH GOOD ORDER'

Within a matter of weeks of Elizabeth and Hal Smith's return to Ireland in July 1845 the crisis unfolded. The family spent two years living in France, first at Pau in the Pyrenees, where Elizabeth's sister Mary was living, and then Avranches in Normandy.[9] The main reason for leaving Ireland was to save money, which could be used to improve the estate. To reduce their outgoings, Baltiboys House was let. A secondary consideration was Elizabeth's health. As Hal too was often ill, essentially an invalid by now, the burden of running the estate fell on Elizabeth. This had taken its toll on her. Before she left she described how the previous winters affected her general health.

> The last three winters, have, however, made a sad change in me, the first passed as accidental derangement, the second staggered *me*, the third frightened *Hal*, and I am sure not causelessly ... It would be worse than folly to try a fourth; so no sentimental nonsense shall overset me, feeling our removal right, I will make it agreeable, so *couleur de rose* must brighten all.[10]

When her doctor, George Robinson, came to visit her in Avranches in April 1845 he identified an extensive list of causes of her illness.

> He examined me very particularly and finds the complaint to be in the womb and the best surgical advice necessary, the lower bowels are apathetick, something wrong with the duodenum, the liver torpid in a degree, considerable irritation everywhere, the nervous system deranged, the heart affected by sympathy, no organick disease anywhere. It is a state of very miserable ill health without any hope of speedy recovery ... For three or four years I must make up my mind to be a regular invalid, living by rule, a most disagreeable rule, for between medicines and lotions and frictions and bathing and minutes of exercise and hours of repose these years are to pass away, in the hope of what, comfortable *old age*.[11]

The decision to return to Ireland was therefore taken in the belief that Elizabeth would have a more comfortable daily life there. In any event she was glad to get back, staying a couple of nights in 'dear old Dublin' before travelling down to rural Wicklow. The sheer splendour of the countryside in full midsummer bloom was her first impression after the long exile: 'Baltiboys looks beautiful', she recorded with deep pride, 'quite sheltered, flourishing trees, clean fields, good fences,—it is quite pleasant to return to a place of such good order'.[12] Within days the usual routine was established: attending to the business of the estate, overseeing the national school, calculating the household finances—always a stressful activity, given the relative impoverishment of the Smiths—hiring a new governess for the three children, and generally busying herself with planned improvements financed by the savings accrued while in France. With Elizabeth now in her late forties, the combination of these arduous responsibilities was beginning to take a toll on her energy. She was getting older and was 'able for little of the business of life'.[13]

Unusually for a nineteenth-century Irish landlord, Elizabeth Smith knew most of the tenants on the estate personally. On her return she acquainted herself with the news that she had missed while away. She learnt of marriages, babies and deaths, including the passing of one woman, Judy Byrne, who had died shortly after childbirth, leaving three young children.

At the farm of Tom Kelly she noticed a modest transformation. Kelly was one of the Smiths' largest tenants, with a holding of 120 acres, and he employed seven labourers. Elizabeth was continually frustrated with his lack of initiative when it came to improving his lands but had great hopes that he would eventually turn the farm around. She was pleasantly surprised by what she now encountered. It was 'flourishing', clean and contained 'half a dozen as fine lively children as ever were seen'. Kelly was given additional land, previously held by George Kearns. The latter was 'almost a fool—simple as a child and really almost as innocent, evil not in him nor good either'. Elizabeth could be compassionate and cold-blooded in almost equal measure. Kearns epitomised all that was wrong with the Irish smallholder: he was indolent and lacking in initiative. A visit to his home, 'a really wretched cabin,' confirmed Elizabeth's judgement that this man held out no promise. His wife told her that they 'were beginning to thrive', which led her to conclude sardonically, 'I hope so for they seem to want it'.

As always, tensions were not far beneath the surface. Tom Darker, the Smiths' steward, was the subject of a local whispering campaign.[14] Darker, a

Northern Protestant, was given land in the early 1840s that three small Catholic tenants had leased. As steward he had to deal with the difficult business of ejecting tenants, making him the focus of anger. Despite the legal position, it proved difficult to dislodge one of them, the 'obdurate' Patrick Quin, who still occupied the land and was in arrears with his rent. The Smiths had decided to evict him the previous year, although Elizabeth knew then that 'with his vindictive disposition this will be a disagreeable business'.[15] And indeed it was. What she referred to as a 'delicate investigation' involved one local man testifying to the gossip he had heard about Darker's dishonesty. A public confrontation with his accusers resulted in a 'triumphant refutation after which there was a shaking of hands'.

But it was not simply public confrontations over land in Baltiboys that confounded Elizabeth Smith. Factions or disputes between the local people were rife in Baltiboys, as in most districts in rural Ireland, many of which were presented to the landlord for unofficial arbitration. She put this down to the irascible nature of the Irish character.

> If the abominable spirit of faction which is now agitating the place could by any means be calmed, our life here would be all sunshine, but with such excitable natures the people are ill to manage, both parties being violent, prejudiced, vindictive, jealous and so on to the end of the catalogue of follies, the fruits of ignorance.

She frequently lamented what she perceived as the irrational and impulsive character traits of the Celt. This stereotype was shared by many commentators, fuelled by images of agrarian violence, who concluded that if only the Irish were more Anglo-Saxon in constitution the country would be a much better place.

When it came to national politics, her strictures were just as severe. The repeal movement was simple rabble-rousing and O'Connell a 'mischief maker', misleading the 'mob' by creating expectations that could never be realised. The resurgence of the Orange Order in 1845 merely reinforced her suspicion that the politics of party were simply the politics of ignorance, even if it was led by a sometime near neighbour, the new Lord Downshire, the fourth marquess, who inherited the title in April 1845 on the death of his father. The 'prejudicial intolerance' of Orangemen 'places their characters very low in the scale of intellect,' and reading their arguments 'fatigues the mind almost to sickness'.

By late October, Elizabeth was concerned about the reports coming from England and from other parts of Ireland describing the failure of the potato crop. There was no sign of it yet in Baltiboys. In early November, however, the disease was discovered on the estate. In one large field planted with potatoes half the crop was destroyed by blight. This galvanised the Smiths into action.

THE REMEDY OF SCIENCE
In early 1845 the Earl of Rosse's magnificent new telescope at Birr Castle in Parsonstown, Co. Offaly, began observing the night sky. The longest telescope in the world for over half a century, at almost 60 feet, with a 6-foot aperture, it was known as the 'Leviathan of Parsonstown' and quickly became a tourist attraction. This monument to scientific progress received wide international press coverage after Lord Rosse reported his most famous finding in June 1845: the discovery of the spiral structure of the whirlpool nebula Messier 51.[16] On reading the newspaper report that Lord Rosse's telescope had discovered that the moon had no atmosphere and was therefore not inhabited, Elizabeth wittily concluded: 'If only useful to *us*, we must be of more importance than we supposed'.[17] Such advances contributed to the widespread sense that nature could be tamed by human ingenuity. The potato blight confounded these expectations when the force of nature proved omnipotent.

Charles Trevelyan later remarked that 'every remedy which science or experience could dictate was had recourse to, but the potato equally melted away under the opposite modes of treatment'.[18] The prime minister, Sir Robert Peel, turned to three experts of the day in mid-October, including Lyon Playfair, a well-connected but not yet famous chemist, and invited them to spend the weekend at his country home, Drayton Manor, near Tamworth in Staffordshire.[19] There the group mulled over the situation and inspected a sample of diseased potatoes from the locality. It was impressed upon Peel that urgent action was required.

Playfair and John Lindley were asked by Peel to go to Ireland without delay. They were charged with estimating the extent of the damage, devising a procedure for preserving the stock of healthy potatoes and, lastly, formulating proposals for any uses that could be made of the diseased crop. In Peel's view the pair were well suited to this task, as neither had any connection with Ireland; 'being free from the contagion of undue local apprehensions, they would be enabled to form a dispassionate judgement as to the real character and extent of the evil to be apprehended'.[20]

A constant refrain in British politicians' assessment of conditions in Ireland was that there was an innate tendency towards exaggeration. Robert Kane, the distinguished Irish chemist recently appointed president of Queen's College, Cork, was also a member of this scientific commission.[21] Kane had already begun conducting experiments under the auspices of the Royal Agricultural Improvement Society of Ireland. Within days Playfair wrote to Peel to tell him that 'we are confident that the reports are underrated rather than exaggerated'.[22] The commission estimated in its report of November 1845 that approximately half the crop was lost, an estimate that proved unduly pessimistic.[23] It also circulated a plethora of detailed instructions on the building of adequately ventilated storage pits, on the presumption that the disease was associated with dampness, and a set of very complicated guidelines for making use of diseased potatoes, all of which ultimately proved fruitless against the ravages of the blight that winter. The complexity of a number of these proposals served only to create confusion among smallholders.[24]

Nationalist opinion was sceptical about the value of much of the advice provided by the commission, not least because it did not recognise the realities facing those who planted and harvested the potato crop. According to the *Freeman's Journal*, 'the present commissioners have satisfactorily proved that they know nothing whatever about the causes of or the remedies for the disease'.[25] This was a harsh but essentially correct judgement. John Mitchel was later to say that 'these learned men, amongst them, prepared so valuable and large a book that, if it had been eatable, the famine had been stayed'.[26] Mitchel was not going to let the details get in the way of his rhetoric. The reports were admirably concise; but his comment captures the general sentiment about the efficacy of the commission.

Experts in many countries had investigated the blight after its first appearance in Europe but met with little success. The disease spread by means of airborne spores, and the blight enveloped large areas of land with astonishing speed. Eye-witnesses reported complete fields that turned black overnight. Wet but warm weather was the ideal condition for the production of spores. The blight was parasitic, squeezing the life of the plant with brutal efficiency. Though the precise relationship was not established definitively, contemporaries did at least realise that the disease was associated in some way with the weather. After the potatoes were lifted and stored, spores could still infect the good crops, turning them into rotten, withered stalks within days.

Most scientists concluded that the blight was caused by this unusually damp weather, which resulted in a form of wet rot. Inquiries about the origins of the disease were inconclusive and came up with a range of explanations, some grounded in evidence, others simply based on hunches. The newspapers published detailed items on the progress of the disease through Europe. Such publicity provided frequent opportunities for more speculation. This ranged from the practical (such as the type of manure used) to the bizarre (this was divine wrath at the introduction of Catholic emancipation in 1829). The recent lightning was also blamed for 'blasting the crop', and even a purported defeat of the Connacht fairies by their northern counterparts, who subsequently destroyed the potatoes, was put forward by people living in that province.[27] Solutions came from all quarters, from agriculturalists and botanists and from concerned letter-writers to newspapers. It seemed that almost everyone had a cure.[28] Among scientists, however, Lindley's influential opinion that the wet weather was the chief cause was the consensus among European experts.

A few solitary voices challenged this explanation, albeit unsuccessfully. Some botanists advanced a fungal cause for the disease, yet they were in the minority at that time. An Anglican clergyman in Northamptonshire, the Rev. Miles Berkeley, a botanist of considerable repute with an expertise in fungi, noticed a minute growth on the leaves and tubers of the potato plants in his parish. After corresponding with a French authority on fungi in August 1845 and observing the blight around his own house he wrote in the *Gardeners' Chronicle* in September 1845 that the disease was caused by the growth of the fungus.[29] He was correct. The fungus was the cause of the disease, rather than a consequence of a depleted plant, as was widely thought. What Berkeley could not do, however, was provide incontrovertible evidence to prove his hypothesis. Only later was it gradually accepted that the blight was caused by a fungus.[30]

In the midst of all these debates there was what appears to have been a missed opportunity to combat the disease. A Limerick landlord and former mayor of the city, Garrett Hugh Fitzgerald, conducted private experiments using copper sulphate on diseased potatoes and recognised that the blight was a parasitic fungus. He had not devised a method for combating the blight, yet he was thinking along the right lines.[31] He communicated these preliminary findings to the government in Dublin, and they were reproduced in the *Gardener's Chronicle*, along with other suggestions. The difficulty was that Fitzgerald suggested steeping seed potatoes in copper sulphate; this was tried in the Botanic Gardens in Dublin but did not work.[32] Nearly forty years later the French chemist Pierre Millardet discovered that spraying the crop with a copper sulphate solution—the 'Bordeaux mixture'—controlled late blight.[33]

Even if scientists had correctly diagnosed the cause in the 1840s, identifying the origins of the blight and quickly coming up with an effective antidote were completely different matters.

BLACK POTATOES

The wonders of scientific reasoning had little purchase among those most affected by the blight: the landless labourers and smallholders who depended on the potato for survival. Its arrival and the destruction that unfolded in its wake took on mysterious and inexplicable tendencies. The aggressive and unpredictable spread of the blight astounded contemporaries. An eye-witness described a scene that was repeated on countless occasions around the country:

> Suddenly ... the withering breath of a simoon seemed to sweep over the land, blasting all in its path. I myself saw whole tracts of potato growth changed, in one night, from smiling luxuriance to a shrivelled and blackened waste.[34]

Panic ensued. The disease was also explained by the abnormal weather. In some accounts it occurred after a violent thunderstorm; in folklore accounts, stories of a dark sky, followed by a thick fog, heralded the first outbreak of the disease. It was as though a malign supernatural presence roamed the fields and attacked the crop. The impact defied logic. Some fields were left untouched, whereas others in the same locality were devastated.[35] With no ready explanation, people were understandably terrified and were fearful for the future.

> Sometimes there was but slight alarm at first, for potato disease in a less virulent form was no stranger. In other districts panic spread quickly as whole fields were laid waste in a few hours: people who had gone to bed, leaving fields green as holly, awoke to find them black as soot or to see a brown swath of decay spreading rapidly over a whole field and from field to field.[36]

Ominously, the weather changed quite suddenly: there were extreme conditions, with storms and high winds combined with lingering mists punctuated by 'periods of vast and terrible stillness'.[37] This stillness was juxtaposed with the violence of the silent disease.

Most contemporaries saw divine intervention in all aspects of everyday life and viewed the potato blight as a 'visitation of God'. One thing that united disparate people in the middle of the nineteenth century was an unshakeable belief in God as the all-powerful supernatural presence, who dispensed mercy and wrath in almost equal measure. For evangelical Protestant politicians such as Sir James Graham, the home secretary, divine providence was at work with the appearance of the blight. Its capacity for destruction also underlined the limitations of even the most powerful of states to determine the natural course of events, as Graham confided, in Old Testament terms, to Peel in mid-October 1845.

> It is awful how the Almighty humbles the pride of nations. The sword, the pestilence, and famine are the instruments of his displeasure; the canker-worm and the locust are his armies, he gives the word: a single crop is blighted; and we see a nation prostrate, stretching out its hands for bread. These are solemn warnings, and they fill me with reverence; they proclaim a voice not to be mistaken, that 'doubtless there is a God, who judgeth the Earth.'[38]

Such providentialist views were extremely influential. Devout Christians reflected on the biblical resonances of the mysterious appearance of the blight and the message it conveyed about the need for moral and spiritual reform. The blight was divinely ordered and would ultimately be for the good of human beings.[39] Some evangelicals with strong anti-Catholic and millenarian tendencies declared that the Almighty's displeasure had been incurred by the greater toleration of Catholicism in general and the recent increased endowment of the Catholic seminary at Maynooth in June 1845 in particular.[40]

That such extraordinary views were expressed shows the depth and ferocity of this strain of anti-Catholicism in Victorian Britain. Anti-Catholicism was a central component of British national identity in the middle of the nineteenth century, ranging from street-level 'no popery' agitation, which reached its peak in the early 1850s, to long-held suspicions about the aspirations of Rome in influencing British affairs.[41] Issues such as the endowment of Maynooth brought to the fore this visceral element of a sense of nationhood that was never far beneath the surface. The revival of the Catholic Church in England and Wales and the conversion of prominent Anglicans, such as John Henry Newman in October 1845, added to the perception of a resurgent threat.

When the Catholic hierarchy was restored in England and Wales a few years later, in 1850, this was seen as 'papal aggression' and set in train a public furore, partly stirred up by the *Times* and eventually resulting in the passing of the Ecclesiastical Titles Act (1851), prohibiting anyone but Anglican bishops using titles of established dioceses.[42]

Providentialist interpretations were not, however, confined to evangelical Protestants. Many Catholics at first saw the blight as a 'divine punishment for their own shortcomings', especially for wasting food in times of plenty, heavy drinking and base sinfulness.[43] This theme of God's retribution features prominently in folklore accounts. 'Old people said it was God's will to have the Famine come, for people abused fine food when they had it plenty', according to one man interviewed in Co. Cork nearly a hundred years later.[44] From a farmer in Co. Westmeath came stories of potatoes dumped before the blight, and the salutary lesson that was learnt once it arrived: 'Afterwards it was said that the famine was a just retribution from God for the great waste of food. A local saying which may refer to this is "A wilful waste makes a woeful want".'[45] Other legends attributed the arrival of the blight to the breaking of the pledge to abstain from alcohol associated with Father Theobald Mathew's mass temperance movement in the early 1840s, as a popular ballad reminded its listeners:

> The pledge we've violated
> Blest Father Mathew gave us,
> And that brought desolation
> To our poor country.[46]

That the power of the Almighty would be invoked to explain the arrival of the blight is entirely consistent with the mid-nineteenth-century world view in which God's supernatural presence determined the natural order. Notwithstanding the different emphases, Catholics and Protestants alike saw the hand of Providence regulating the day-to-day lives of all believers. Specifically, what they had in mind was the Book of Exodus, with plague visited on the Egyptians for keeping the Israelites in servitude.

'GODLESS COLLEGES'
Archbishop John MacHale was also concerned about incurring the Almighty's displeasure, but for altogether different reasons. The British government proposed establishing non-denominational seats of learning, what MacHale

termed 'infidel colleges'. He believed such secular institutions would destroy the Catholic faith in Ireland.

A system of non-denominational university education was first mooted by Peel as part of a broader package of reforms in 1844. The dualism of British policy in Ireland once again emerged: conciliation would be intermixed with sharp doses of coercion when a particular threat arose. After the coercion of 1843, in a conciliatory move Peel sought to fragment support for the campaign for the repeal of the Union by introducing reforms destined to appeal to the Catholic middle class.[47] By the mid-1840s, after an earlier rift in 1837, MacHale was once again a strong supporter of O'Connell and an outspoken critic of Conservative government policy. Using all his usual techniques, MacHale resisted the encroachments of the state on matters that he believed were essentially the preserve of the church and on which he was uniquely qualified to speak: the spiritual and moral welfare of the Irish Catholic population.

The Charitable Donations and Bequests (Ireland) Bill, introduced by Peel in 1844, seemed an innocuous matter, unlikely to spark off the bitter controversy that eventually involved Pope Gregory xvi. This measure reformed the law on donations and bequests and reconstituted what had previously been a supervisory board dominated by Protestants to allow for Catholics to become members. This was a genuine reform. MacHale, with the support of O'Connell, objected to certain elements of the legislation, seeing these measures as interference by the government in the internal affairs of the Irish Catholic Church. With characteristic thunder MacHale declared that the bill would associate Catholics 'with the old and inveterate enemies of our faith ... detached from their brethren and acting against the interests of their religion, dependent on the crown, fearful of its displeasure, and fawning on its caresses'.[48] Eventually, after the bill was passed into law in August 1844, amid a great deal of public controversy three Catholic bishops—Daniel Murray, William Crolly and Cornelius Denvir of Down and Connor—accepted places on the commission. O'Connell and the Repeal Association were weakened by this division among the Catholic bishops, and the dispute over this act set the tone for future confrontations between MacHale and his fellow-bishops over the degree of co-operation with the government.

Peel's next reform was to increase the annual grant to St Patrick's College, Maynooth, which was trebled in 1845 and made a recurrent charge on the exchequer, with a large sum provided for improving the dilapidated buildings. The mere name of Maynooth instilled fear in the minds of some Protestants.

For the *Times* 'it is a name and a thing above all others odious and suspicious to England'.[49] When the bill was announced in February 1845 the 'endowment of popery' generated considerable opposition, both in Parliament and in a virulent outburst of anti-Catholicism in British public debate.[50] Peel weathered this storm but as leader of a deeply divided party. The crisis now unfolding in Ireland would test the considerable political skill of Peel over the next couple of months.

When the potato crop failed, the prices of other foodstuffs, as widely expected, rose and were quickly beyond the reach of the poor. Concerns about the availability of food were a perennial worry for the European ruling classes. After all, shortages caused riots that initiated revolutions, and food disturbances were the major form of social unrest in eighteenth-century and early nineteenth-century Europe. Peel, for instance, repeatedly fretted in private about the effect of bad weather on the year's harvest. He knew all too well the potential consequences of a shortage in food that would ratchet up prices: riots, social unrest and popular discontent.

The question in late 1845 was, would the Irish poor, whose existence wholly depended on the potato, be left to fend for themselves? Heavy expectations were placed on the shoulders of Peel and his ministry with the prospect of famine looming in Ireland. A financial implication of the Union was that the vast resources at the disposal of the British exchequer would naturally flow to a constituent part of the United Kingdom that was in dire need. Whatever concerns existed about exaggeration of the extent of the failure, few doubted the potential scale of the catastrophe. While the disaster deepened on one side of the Irish Sea, the emphasis on the other side shifted to the British government to see what, if anything, it would do. Black potatoes in Ireland were transformed into a British political crisis.

We know with extraordinary detail the quality and nature of the information that reached London. Volume after volume of official papers were published at the time. Many of these were the work of Charles Trevelyan, who, as the most senior administrator at the Treasury, had his hands firmly clasped around the purse-strings of the British exchequer. A famous satirical pen-picture by Anthony Trollope of Sir Gregory Hardlines in his novel on the British civil service, *The Three Clerks* (1857), captures the character of a punctilious and reforming civil servant with a strong sense of public duty. Hardlines, of the Office of Weights and Measures, 'wore on his forehead a broad phylactery [amulet], stamped with the mark of Crown property', devoted to his elaborate systems with no sense of the human factor.[51]

Whatever criticisms can be made of Trevelyan's moralistic outlook, or indeed of his actions, no-one could question his work ethic. A huge volume of correspondence arrived at the Treasury each day. Trevelyan gave priority to letters from Ireland, as he 'laid it down as a rule, so far as depends upon me & those acting under me, that everything related to Ireland is to be answered by return of post'.[52] He was a hard taskmaster, demanding as much of others as he did of himself. When the head of the Relief Commission in Ireland, Sir Randolph Routh, complained that 'I cannot write more, as I am an invalid today and intend to remain quiet to recruit', Trevelyan replied: 'I hope to hear tomorrow that you have got rid of your indisposition—we have not time to be ill nowadays.'[53]

WAR WITH THE CLERGY
For Elizabeth Smith, self-help and moral improvement were the key to Ireland's greater prosperity. Through exhortation and example, the Smiths were keen to improve their estates and, in doing so, the unhappy lot of the poorer tenants and landless labourers.

Just as there were good and bad tenants, so it was with Irish landlords. Others in Elizabeth's social world, such as her near neighbour Joseph Leeson, fourth Earl of Milltown, in Russborough House, were indifferent to the estate and its tenants. Russborough was one of Ireland's finest stately houses, built in the Palladian style in the middle of the eighteenth century. But Lord Milltown had squandered this inheritance, had three children outside marriage (whom he absurdly named Fitzleeson) and was addicted to gambling on horses, caring little about his estates or tenants—an example of the worst excesses of the Irish aristocratic class. He was precisely the sort of individual that Elizabeth despised, with his sense of entitlement and carefree life. A couple of years earlier a meeting with Lord Milltown had provoked her to reflect on his character:

What a life, feverish excitement or despair leading to everything that is bad, by slow but sure degrees eradicating all that is good. I never see him without a mixed feeling of sorrow and pity and shame that is really painful, for nature though she inflicted one very dreadful infirmity on him gifted him with many admirable qualities, fine talents, good understanding, amiable temper, very handsome countenance, and rank and wealth and zealous friends. A bad education and disreputable society and an ill assorted marriage have altogether made him to be shunned instead of courted, and he is himself most unhappy.[54]

Soon after returning from France, Hal Smith paid an evening visit to Russborough with his daughters, where they encountered the Duke of Leinster, Ireland's leading peer, whose ancestral home was the magnificent Carton House at Maynooth. Elizabeth, using the information provided by her husband, observed that the dinner was a drawn-out affair and was followed by postprandial games that she judged to be frivolous, reflecting her Scottish pragmatism. A liberal and enlightened figure, the duke was 'good natured', his wife 'noisy', their son pleasant enough and their daughter simply 'ugly'.

Elizabeth's most urgent concern was her beloved national school. The Catholic parish priest, the Rev. Arthur Germaine, did as little as possible to assist her in her untiring efforts to encourage children to attend regularly. Like many Irish Catholics, he feared that the state schools would become a mechanism for Protestant proselytising and would seek to convert Catholic children while educating them. In frustration, in October 1845 Elizabeth wrote to Daniel Murray, the gentle and infirm Catholic Archbishop of Dublin, to complain about the priest's indifference. Archbishop Murray was the most prominent Catholic supporter of the national schools and a strong advocate of education for the poor. But this was a risky strategy, as Murray could either support his cleric or adopt an indifferent attitude, which would effectually sound the death knell for Elizabeth's school. Her action led to a denunciation of the school from the altar of the local Catholic church before Germaine was eventually summoned to Dublin to see the aged prelate. Afterwards, Smith observed, he 'returned quite amiable, wrote me the kindest possible note, and we are to walk through the parish here—after hand in hand doing good and peace ensuing! If he will be but quiet I shall be quite content.'

Apart from these minor incursions the life of the Smiths in 1845 went on much as usual, and the blight was just one of the many things on Elizabeth's mind: visits to Dublin, overseeing the local school, attending dinner parties at Russborough House and reading entertaining newspaper accounts of the antics of the British aristocracy, including the elopement of Lady Adela Villiers, the seventeen-year-old daughter of the Earl of Jersey, who mysteriously disappeared in November 1845 only to turn up a week later after marrying an army captain in Gretna Green.[55]

The 'war with the clergy' preoccupied Elizabeth throughout October and November 1845. Her concerns about the future of the national school seemed trivial, moreover, as the potato crop failed in Baltiboys. Hal was spurred into action as local landlords devised plans for dealing with the likely consequences of relieving widespread hunger in west Wicklow. She had ambivalent views on the relief efforts, believing that self-help was essential.

> Relieve them I can't, instruct them I can't, but I can try, every little helps, and many littles make a muckle. Energy is so wanting among these Celtick races there is no inspiring them to help themselves, and there is no other help really availing. Mental force seems to be wanting, it will require a generation or two to reproduce any in beings so degraded. How absurd in me to feel angry with creatures so deficient yet their folly is so lamentable it is very hard to bear patiently all the evil it produces.

For her this was merely further evidence of what she had long ago concluded: the Catholic Irish were morally deficient, relying on others to help them.

What Elizabeth lamented was the struggle of the poor to buy food with rising prices and the limited means available to them. She was frustrated with the passivity that relied on the will of God, and the absence of an ethos of improvement. After attempting to explain to some of the local people how the crop should be treated to remove the disease (in fact a futile procedure) she fulminated that they seemed resigned to 'sit down with folded hands to bear the Will of God, in other words relief from the benevolent without any exertion on their part'.

Such prejudices about the fatalistic outlook of Irish Catholics were a constant feature of the debate about how best to provide for the poor in this time of acute crisis. Elizabeth's views were echoed by T. C. Foster, a barrister commissioned by the *Times* to travel around the country and produce a series of articles about the conditions he encountered, as he had done for Wales and the Scottish Highlands. He was a well-intentioned if opinionated observer. Described by O'Connell as 'the gutter commissioner'—O'Connell had a bitter history with this newspaper—he subsequently clashed with O'Connell over the state of the tenants on his estate at Derrynane, Co. Kerry, whom he described as being 'worse off than any tenantry in Ireland'.[56] Writing in the *Times* from Cork in November 1845, he outlined a number of sensible schemes to avert a food shortage, including helping the poor to buy oatmeal at cost price. He then turned his attention to the character of the Irish people.

> I am as firmly convinced as that I am now writing to you, such is the general apathy, want of exertion, and feeling of fatality amongst the

people—such their general distrust of everybody and suspicion of every project—such the disunion among the higher classes, with similar apathetic indifference, that unless the government steps forward to carry out, to order or *enforce* these or similar plans for the national welfare, *not any one of them will be generally adopted, and nothing will be done . . .* The government . . . have been *warned—let* them act promptly, decisively, and at once, and not depend on the people helping themselves; for such is the character of the people, that *they will do nothing till starvation faces them*.[57]

Leaving aside the pertinent question of the availability of resources with which the poor might help themselves, such views, whichever way they were precisely calibrated, resounded with a governing elite in London that had precious little faith in the capacity of Irish landlords to demonstrate leadership and even less in the Catholic populace. Irish Catholicism was widely perceived as encouraging fatalism and apathy and letting events take their course, whatever the consequences might be. Such stereotypes in normal times were dangerous, but when they emerged at a moment when the state was required to intervene to help the poor they could have fatal consequences.

YOUNG AND OLD IRELAND

September 1845 was a turning-point for John Mitchel. His life was irrevocably changed by a decision to give up his comfortable life as a busy solicitor to earn a precarious livelihood as a writer. As one admirer noted, he 'ceased to be merely a private individual and became a part of history'.[58] After the tragic death in September 1845 of the great romantic patriot Thomas Davis from scarlet fever at the tender age of thirty-one, Mitchel moved his family from Banbridge to Dublin. He was appalled when Davis died; Davis was the 'friend who first filled our souls with the passion of a great ambition and lofty purpose'.[59] In Dublin he took up residence just off Upper Leeson Street. When Thomas Carlyle visited Mitchel he described it as a 'frugally elegant small house and table', and 'simplicity and frugality, combined with neatness and elegance, were the leading features of Mitchel's home'.[60]

Mitchel had taken up a full-time post as leader-writer at the *Nation*. Even though the Young Ireland movement was part of O'Connell's much larger Repeal Association, it differed with the Liberator on a number of issues, especially the use of physical force and the degree of deference to be accorded to the Catholic Church. At this time Mitchel was publicly more or less an unknown quantity. His creative energies were completely consumed by writing for the *Nation*. Already a writer with talent, he perfected his powerful raw rhetorical style during these formative years.

Notwithstanding the subsequent confusion, Mitchel was never the editor of this newspaper, and Charles Gavan Duffy retained overall editorial control. Duffy's first wife, Emily, had died two weeks after the death of his friend Davis in September 1845, leaving him to care for two small children, and left Mitchel in charge of the day-to-day running of the paper.[61] From the outset, as a leader-writer Mitchel set out the radical and revolutionary thoughts, albeit cautiously at first, that were to become the hallmark of his writing.

Mitchel was a man of contrasts. A figure renowned for his public denunciations of the British government of Ireland, in his private life he enjoyed nothing more than the company of his five children. Even his method of working was far from orthodox. He would sit in deep contemplation for hours, sometimes surrounded by his young children, oblivious to their antics, 'twirling one of the locks on his forehead round his finger', and then, without warning, start writing furiously, often not breaking for hours. And there were no breaks for reflection, as 'he seemed to have arranged it all, and to have nothing to do but to write it out as quickly as possible'.[62] The result was typically an enervating critique, written with a passion and style that owed much to his early immersion in disputatious theological tracts.

From October 1845 the impending famine began to feature regularly in articles written by Mitchel and others in the *Nation*. He warned landlords of the inherent dangers of seeking to collect rents in the shadow of such a disaster.[63] By early November he was reminding his readers how hunger was an agent of revolution.

> In the history of mankind there has been no such powerful agent, no such irresistible force to sway, this way or that, the fate of nations as dearness and scarcity of food. Heavy social and political wrongs have often been borne patiently and long, when a food panic, a serious derangement of the money-market, has suddenly convulsed the whole frame of society; and the agony of one season of famine and disease has given birth to revolutions which might otherwise be postponed for a generation.[64]

Mitchel was one of the first people to recognise the revolutionary potential of the catastrophe and its capacity to foster discontent. Given his later role as the figure who formulated and expressed the most vocal denunciation of

British policy in Ireland during the late 1840s, there is more than a touch of wish-fulfilment in this early observation.

In another article, published later that month, Mitchel caused great controversy by suggesting that the Irish railway network could be sabotaged in an uprising. This was written in response to a suggestion in the *Morning Herald*, an English Tory paper, that the new Irish railways would be a valuable mechanism for coercion.[65] Mitchel turned the table on it and described how railway tracks could be removed and used to make weapons, and how troops travelling by train could be ambushed, and he observed that railways might be used equally effectively for subversion as for coercion.[66]

Educated opinion in Britain was incensed with this public act of treachery. O'Connell was no less so, as the article mentioned that Repeal wardens, who were local organisers of the Repeal Association, could take the lead in this subversive activity. O'Connell had defined his career by the rejection of violence and was 'aghast' at this suggestion and as a lawyer was well aware that a prosecution could be instigated. The Liberator stormed into the offices of the *Nation* to complain about the reference to the Repeal wardens, secured a commitment to withdraw the comment in the next issue, and publicly dissociated the Repeal Association from Mitchel's article at its next meeting.[67]

A few weeks later the prosecution for sedition of Duffy, as proprietor of the *Nation*, was initiated by the solicitor-general. It was widely assumed in Young Ireland circles that O'Connell's denunciation had paved the way for the legal action.[68] It provided O'Connell with the justification he needed for distancing the Repeal Association from the *Nation*. Mitchel and Duffy for their part were convinced that O'Connell intended to crush the paper, as its radical voice intensely irritated the Liberator.

Davis had kept O'Connell and the *Nation* from a total break, but now Mitchel's views were increasingly radical. Along with many of the Young Irelanders, he was completely disillusioned with the slow progress of constitutional nationalism under O'Connell's stewardship. The stage was set for a very public confrontation between the Young Irelanders and 'Old' Ireland, in the person of O'Connell and his loyal lieutenants.

A QUESTION OF SURVIVAL

The internecine tensions within Irish nationalism mattered little to those most at risk, confronted by the spectre of famine. What did matter to them was the prospect of hungry months during the coming winter—in other words, survival. Such was the nature of the tortured relationship between Ireland

and Britain that swift government intervention to supply food directly to the poor at cost price to make up the shortfall in the potato crop would be far from straightforward. Relief measures became entangled in ideological conflicts about the government's role in the economy and the basic responsibilities of a state towards its citizens.

This was the background to one of the most decisive moments in the history of global trade, when Peel decided in October 1845 that the crisis in Ireland necessitated the repeal of the Corn Laws. Though the Irish situation was the immediate pretext, there had been a long-running campaign in Britain, centred on the Anti-Corn-Law League, which had been founded in Manchester in 1838, with Richard Cobden and John Bright as its most prominent leaders. There was widespread support for reform within Britain, especially from the middle classes in the commercial and industrial centres of the north of England, to bring an end to protection for British agricultural producers. Peel's commitment to free trade, however, was of much longer standing. The removal of tariffs on the importing of corn was 'a policy designed to meet British rather than Irish interests', despite what he might have said at the time and in subsequent years.[69]

Chapter 5 ∽

PEEL'S BRIMSTONE

Ireland, Ireland! That Cloud in the West, that coming storm, the minister of God's retribution upon cruel and inveterate and but half-atoned injustice! Ireland forces upon us these great social and great religious questions— God grant that we may have courage—to look them in the face and to work through them. (W. E. Gladstone)[1]

THAT CLOUD IN THE WEST

Writing to his wife from Germany in October 1845, William Gladstone feared the upheaval that the potato blight would bring about.[2] It seemed to Gladstone, the British politician and future prime minister whose career was increasingly dominated by the Irish question, that the tempest was beginning to gather pace. It was Peel, however, who now had to endure the full force of this unfolding calamity in Ireland. The genesis of this crisis, however, was not in the elevated sphere of party politics in London, or in the popular agitation for repeal of the Union, led by his inveterate enemy Daniel O'Connell: it was the more powerful, and uncontrollable, force of nature.

Peel was consumed with the heavy responsibilities of governing a vast expanse of imperial possessions around the globe. At that time one in four of the world's population was ruled from London. Ten months later, by the end of June 1846, he had resigned from office. His government was defeated, and his actions had split the Conservative Party down the middle. Relief for Ireland and the removal of protectionist duties on the importing of corn became intertwined in a toxic cocktail that ended his prime-ministerial career.

Though Peel was ultimately responsible, the politician most immediately concerned was Sir James Graham, the home secretary. A close confidant of the prime minister, he was Peel's staunchest supporter within the cabinet.

After first receiving reassuring reports in early September from various sources, Graham contemplated the much bleaker prospect of the wholesale devastation of the crop. By mid-October he was requesting that Peel give this matter his urgent attention. He concluded solemnly with 'the fatal certainty that a famine in that quarter of the United Kingdom will be a great crisis in our national affairs.'[3] But the likelihood of famine was already on Peel's mind. He had been closely monitoring the unfolding situation from reports by various observers since the news of the blight's arrival in Ireland. Coincidentally, he had written the same day to Graham, warning him of the potential problems ahead.

> The accounts of the state of the potato crop in Ireland are becoming very alarming. There is a tendency to exaggeration and inaccuracy in Irish reports, that delay in acting upon them is always desirable. But I foresee the necessity that may be imposed upon us at an early period of considering whether there is not that well-grounded apprehension of actual scarcity that justifies and compels the adoption of every means of relief.[4]

On 17 October, Peel received confirmation of his worst fears from the lord lieutenant of Ireland, Lord Heytesbury, the Crown's official representative in Ireland. The failure was more or less widespread throughout the country and limited stock was available from the previous year; even more alarming was the news that the price of cereal crops on the market was already rising.

Nationalist opinion was less than reassured about the government's response. This was based on the reasonable supposition that nothing much seemed to be happening since blight was first reported in mid-September. A committee of Dublin Corporation met to consider the situation, and after that a public meeting was held on 31 October. Out of this emerged the Mansion House Committee, established under the chairmanship of Ireland's leading aristocrat, the Duke of Leinster. Daniel O'Connell suggested that representations should be made to the government. A deputation was constituted to seek a meeting with Lord Heytesbury, including such luminaries as the Duke of Leinster, Lord Cloncurry and the Lord Mayor of Dublin, John L. Arabin, and, of course, the Liberator himself. These were important figures in the Irish establishment and not mere rabble-rousers. O'Connell formulated a set of proposals for urgent action: the immediate cessation of distilling and brewing (because they used corn); a prohibition on the export of food to other countries (with the odd exception of Britain); the importing of food without tariffs; and the setting up of public works, to be paid for by taxing absentee landlords.

This meeting took place on 3 November at the Viceregal Lodge, the lord lieutenant's residence in the Phoenix Park. The deputation was most 'coldly received', and after the Lord Mayor of Dublin read the resolutions, Lord Heytesbury responded with a prepared non-committal reply. He stated that the effects of the potato blight were receiving the 'most anxious attention of the government' and that the scientific commission composed of the experts sent over from England had yet to report and assured the deputation that the government was only too well aware of the potential problems.[5] He undertook to forward these proposals to the cabinet, which he duly did. He then unceremoniously ushered the group out. One anonymous member of the deputation recounted that while the greeting on arrival was cordial it was a 'momentary audience', and that the reaction 'was evidently a far more *sincere* one on our departure'.[6]

The reaction to this seeming indifference was a thundering indictment of the chilly response the deputation's recommendations had received. According to the leading article in the *Freeman's Journal* the next day, the message was clear and unequivocal.

> They may starve! Such in spirit, if not the words, was the reply given yesterday by the English Viceroy, to the memorial of the deputation, who, in the name of Lords and Commons of Ireland, prayed that the food of this kingdom be preserved, lest the people thereof perish.[7]

Lord Heytesbury's cold reaction was insensitive. Inadvertently, he seemed to suggest that the authorities were sceptical about the true extent of the damage to the crop. His attitude, apparently, was driven by other political considerations. Firstly, Peel did not want to be seen to be giving any credence to an initiative sponsored by O'Connell, even if the Mansion House Committee was avowedly non-partisan.[8] More pressing was the knowledge that Peel had summoned an emergency cabinet meeting on 31 October and the lord lieutenant could not anticipate any decisions taken there, especially on the crucial issue of government interference in the food market.

Whatever the manoeuvres behind the scenes that could not be revealed, Lord Heytesbury created the impression that the authorities were bereft of plans for dealing with the inevitable food shortage that would result. Such inertia could have serious consequences, as the *Freeman's Journal* warned the two prominent leaders of the Mansion House Committee, the Duke of Leinster and Lord Cloncurry.

> Sir Robert Peel *is unhappily afflicted with the gout,* and eight millions of Irishmen must await his recovery! Everything is dependent upon him— no Irishman is anything. Is this a system that you can countenance? My Lords, you are now doing your duty to your country like Irishmen and Christians—see that you fail not in the whole duty you owe your country, *for you have much to lose.*[9]

Peel was no doubt moved by this touching concern for his painful affliction, but he was more concerned with formulating his detailed plans. The first step was to secure the approval of his deeply divided cabinet. Given the vested interests it contained, representing landed and agricultural interests, that would be no straightforward task.

'A GREAT CAUSE'

By late 1845 John Mitchel was completely consumed with his work on the *Nation.* Surrounded by a coterie of equally committed idealistic men in the Young Ireland movement, such as John Blake Dillon and Thomas Francis Meagher, he thrived in the cut and thrust of vigorous debate. He later described being 'absorbed and engrossed and possessed by a great cause' in those intense years.[10] The home of the Mitchels in Dublin was frequently a venue for the informal entertaining of figures from the Young Ireland set. Each week a supper was held in alternate houses, during which pressing political issues were discussed, or there was simply the mutual enjoyment of conviviality and company. It was a bohemian set of writers and intellectuals. This was precisely the sort of interaction Mitchel had craved while in Banbridge. Nevertheless, even his friends observed that there 'was a fund of seriousness in his character, and he never suffered himself to be drawn from the matter in hand'.[11]

Charles Gavan Duffy's frequent absences from the *Nation* left Mitchel considerable latitude to shape the editorial tone of the paper, and this he did with characteristic radicalism. At this time he wrote most of the political articles and referred to himself as the 'ostensible editor'; Duffy, with whom he later had a bitter and acrimonious debate, described him as the 'assistant editor'.[12] Duffy recognised Mitchel's obvious talents as a writer, although he believed that his fatal weakness was his faulty judgement.

One faculty that he wanted at that time, and during all his career, a faculty without which great results are rarely accomplished, the gift ordinarily called judgement—a capacity of estimating justly the relative momentum of forces, and of discerning the fit occasion, which counts for so much in the conduct of affairs.[13]

Mitchel's lack of discretion led to Duffy's prosecution for seditious libel for the 'railway article', in which Mitchel had advocated the use of the railways for the purpose of rebellion. The case opened in June 1846, with Mitchel as defence solicitor instructing Robert Holmes, an octogenarian veteran of the Irish bar and fellow-Unitarian and a brother-in-law of the revolutionary Robert Emmet, hanged for his role in leading the doomed insurrection of 1803. Holmes's speech, which barely mentioned the specific charge, was by all accounts the show-piece of the trial. The courtroom burst into applause on the conclusion of his detailed exposition of the 'injustice and broken faith of England towards Ireland, and Ireland's degradation'. The presiding Chief Justice said it was 'the grandest exposition of oratory ever delivered in a court of justice'.[14] It also had the desired effect: after endless hours of deliberation the jury were unable to agree a unanimous verdict and were discharged. This was a great victory for Mitchel and the Young Irelanders, bringing public attention to their activities.

Mitchel travelled to London in May 1846 as a member of the deputation to visit William Smith O'Brien, the Irish MP who was imprisoned for contempt in the 'cellar' of the Houses of Parliament for refusing to serve on any select committees that did not relate to Ireland. The deputation was organised by the '82 Club, a quasi-military organisation composed of Young Irelanders. O'Connell was the nominal president, mainly so that he could keep a watchful eye on its activities. The sight of the Young Irelanders bedecked in their green-and-gold uniforms must have startled onlookers in London. The only other call Mitchel made while in London was to visit his hero Thomas Carlyle, the 'Sage of Chelsea'.

Carlyle's writings were fervently admired by Mitchel, Davis and Duffy.[15] Mitchel had anonymously reviewed his edition of Cromwell's letters and speeches in the *Nation* in January 1846, and while he was critical of the Irish sections he observed that the Scottish savant was the person 'at whose feet we have studied long and hard'.[16] Carlyle wrote to Duffy to thank him, not knowing that Mitchel was the author. Mitchel visited Carlyle's house and they spent an evening together. The encounter was a mixed one, as Mitchel told his friend John Martin.

He kept most of the talk to himself; and I scarcely agreed with him in any single thing he said the whole night, and told him my mind occasionally broadly enough. His views on Irish questions are strangely and wickedly unjust, and his notion of might and right generally are altogether atheistical.[17]

This unsettling evening did nothing to moderate Mitchel's adoration for Carlyle, with whom he shared many opinions about the perils of liberalism, especially that which took the form of Daniel O'Connell and his Whig allies, as well as O'Connell's public denunciation of slavery.[18]

REPEAL OF THE CORN LAWS
By October 1846 Sir Robert Peel faced a range of related problems: the failure of the potato crop, the contentious question of the level of protection for British and Irish agriculture that the issue of food imports raised, and the constant potential for widespread political unrest in Ireland. For one cartoonist these elements made up a single nightmare tormenting the prime minister, with his old foe O'Connell looming in the background.[19] Peel decided that he must repeal the Corn Laws and remove all vestiges of agricultural protection, much to the chagrin of the strong protectionist lobby among the Tories. Writing to Lord Heytesbury in mid-October, he concluded that 'the remedy is the removal of all impediments to the import of all kinds of human food—that is, the total and absolute repeal for ever of all duties on all articles of subsistence'.[20]

Much ink has been spilt on the immediate circumstance surrounding Peel's proposals to repeal the Corn Laws. At the time, it was presented as an expedient measure in the face of widespread destruction of the potato crop in Ireland. Peel saw the combination of the blight and repeal of the Corn Laws as providing an unparalleled opportunity to bring about a far-reaching economic and social reformation of Irish society, in particular to improve its backward agricultural methods and to diminish the excessive reliance of the rural poor on the unpredictable potato as the main foodstuff. As Sir Randolph Routh indicated, the aim was to wean the Irish from the potato, 'which is one of the causes that impede the civilisation of the country'.[21] His primary concern, however, was with bringing about a reform he long wished to implement, and Ireland was simply the proximate cause for his actions.[22]

At this emergency cabinet meeting Peel laid out his plan to authorise the lord lieutenant to establish a Relief Commission to oversee public works and, if need be, to purchase and distribute additional food. This would of necessity involve either a suspension or ultimately a repeal of import duties on foodstuffs.

After two days of meetings it became clear that senior figures within the cabinet, in particular Lord Stanley and the Duke of Buccleuch, could not countenance the removal of tariffs, a rift that became increasingly divisive over the coming weeks. In early December, under severe pressure, Peel offered his resignation to Queen Victoria. Lord John Russell, leader of the Whig opposition in the House of Commons, who had publicly committed himself to the repeal of the Corn Laws in his famous Edinburgh Letter, was invited by the queen to form a government. Despite extensive negotiations in what were called the 'ten long days', he failed to do so. Peel was once again called upon to head a ministry, which he duly did from late December, though painfully aware of the fissures both within his own party and within the Parliament more generally.

Meanwhile, on his own initiative, Peel had ordered maize (also called Indian corn) to the value of £100,000 to be shipped to Ireland from the United States and to be stored until the 'hungry months' of June and July. Maize was used because it attracted such a heavy import duty that it was not heavily consumed in either Britain or Ireland, and 'private merchants, therefore, could not complain of interference with a trade that did not exist'.[23] The transaction was conducted in the utmost secrecy by an American agent for the London merchants, Baring Brothers. The intention was never that this secret supply could feed a substantial section of the Irish poor—it was only a drop in the ocean of what would be required to replace the potato—but that the authorities could intervene in the market when prices began to rise by selling the maize at cost price.

Peel established the Relief Commission (at first called the Scarcity Commission) in mid-November to oversee the distribution of this food.[24] The practicalities were to be undertaken by the Commissariat, a civilian department of the Treasury that supplied the army when it was on campaign or garrisoned overseas and therefore had extensive experience in the transport of food and other supplies. Through a network of food depots the Commissariat would make the corn available to local relief committees. All this appeared a reasoned response to the unfolding situation.

By January 1846 the main elements of Peel's policy were established. In a famous speech to the House of Commons on 27 January 1846 that lasted three-and-a-half hours he described his proposal to gradually remove protectionist tariffs on imports of corn.[25] Over the coming months a bitter debate raged among the Tories, between the landed gentry and commercial interests. As Elizabeth Smith observed, Peel managed to offend all sorts of interests, including the Anti-Corn-Law League, which had campaigned for the immediate removal of duties to make food cheaper for the working class. 'Tories are outrageous [*sic*], the topbooted gentry furious, the [Anti-Corn-Law] League not satisfied, nor the Repealers'.[26] Eventually the measure was passed in June 1846, with support from the Liberals and the Radicals, leaving deep divisions in the Conservative Party. The following year would see the beginning of the protracted process whereby all tariffs were eventually removed, creating the conditions for free trade.

THE AWFUL VISITATION OF FAMINE

In his Lenten pastoral letter of March 1846 John MacHale described 'the awful visitation of Famine, with which the Almighty threatens to punish the sins of his people'. He reminded his flock of the mysterious workings of what was essentially an Old Testament God:

> No matter how scientific men may be occupied in tracing the causes and explaining the symptoms of the disease—we are taught by wisdom from a higher source that every such calamity is a portion of that vengeance which God has in store, and occasionally discharges, on account of the infraction of His holy laws.[27]

The faithful needed to atone for past sins during Lent through fasting, humility and prayer. MacHale continued to say that when entire nations face such a calamity 'they are usually indicted for some great national transgression'. Ironically, such providentialist views had much in common with those of Trevelyan and other moralists. The particular transgression MacHale had in mind was the spread of liberalism and secularism and more specifically the threat posed to the Catholic faith in Ireland by the 'infidel colleges'. He warned against the 'apostasy' of accepting the colleges, with their secular ethos and potential for proselytising activities, and even delineated the dire consequences for individuals who accepted work in the building of these institutions.

To present-day sensibilities MacHale's strictures seem wrong-headed and distasteful, especially at a time when the early effects of the food shortage were beginning to bite on the poor. Urging people to fast during Lent as famine threatened was unnecessary at best. Yet for Christians, of all denominations, only through penance and atonement could God's favour be gained. But this was all part of a wider campaign. MacHale fought a long battle to have the colleges condemned as unfit places for Catholics to be educated, with the support of the future Archbishop of Dublin, Paul Cullen, who later became his bitter enemy. Daniel Murray, then Archbishop of Dublin, along with a number of other bishops, was supportive of Peel's proposals.

The Queen's Colleges at Belfast, Cork and Galway opened their doors in 1849. Condemnations of the colleges came from Rome in 1847 and again in 1848, and Catholics were advised not to attend them after the matter was finally agreed by the bishops at the national synod in Tuam in 1850. What might have seemed a genuine reform on the part of Peel's government ended up mired in controversy and division, and MacHale was naturally at the forefront of the group that opposed Irish Catholics attending the colleges.[28] For him, education was Catholic education: no compromises, no watering down, and most certainly no dilution of this immutable principle.

The association of the impending famine with the 'godless' colleges by MacHale tells us much about the mid-nineteenth-century world view. In a speech in the House of Commons two weeks earlier Daniel O'Connell said that this 'calamity is a dispensation of Providence, and we [members of Parliament] should bow to the will of an all-dispensing power whilst we fulfil the duties of charitable Christians and endeavour to mitigate the evils that may arise'.[29] O'Connell made a critical distinction between the potato disease, which was divinely ordained, and the potential effects, which human beings could materially alter. The separation of the secular and the spiritual did not exist, and political, economic and religious sensibilities were inextricably linked. If famine occurred, this was God's design, and those of faith should seek to mitigate its worst effects through seeking mercy and dispensing charity to those most in need.

Characteristically, MacHale, who effectually combined the roles of a sacred and a secular leader, urged his followers to 'use all legitimate means' to call on the government to prohibit the export of food from Ireland. Prayer and good intentions alone would not deliver the Irish poor through this time of crisis: urgent action by humans was required.

A FEARFUL FAMINE

The shortage of food at a reasonable price was beginning to take its toll. In an impassioned speech to the House of Commons in February 1846 O'Connell outlined the historical background to Irish poverty. Now quite ill, his concern was more immediate. He read out harrowing accounts from around the country of the increasing spiral of destitution. All this required urgent government action.

> I have shown you our distress. I have shown that there are no agricultural labourers, no peasantry in Europe, so badly off, suffering such privations as do the great body of the Irish people ... There are five millions of people always on the verge of starvation ... They are in the utmost danger of a fearful famine, with all its concomitant horrors.[30]

Private reports from officials in Ireland sent to Trevelyan in March 1846 showed the acute hardship that was experienced in the south-west of the country, where supplies were exhausted as stored potatoes succumbed to the disease; these people had no other option but to 'go to market for their immediate wants'.[31] Accounts of destitution and starvation were widely publicised in the press from places as diverse as Cos. Clare, Limerick and Tipperary as well as Belfast in the early months of 1846.[32]

Each year from the end of May until the early crop of potatoes was harvested in August there was what was termed the 'hungry gap', as stored supplies from the previous year were exhausted. This year the shortfall was a great deal more severe, as the poor had only a limited reserve to draw on. The other recourse was to buy food locally. Prices inevitably went up in a time of scarcity, but this quickly became an option only for the few who had savings or other resources on which to draw. Those most affected at first were itinerant beggars, who relied on the good will of others to survive. It was the poorer classes who had always helped beggars, being acutely aware that there was a thin line between having little and having nothing.[33] The other groups most at risk were landless labourers, cottiers and small farmers. The importing of food by the government had the effect of moderating prices, as was intended by Peel.

In Baltiboys Elizabeth and Hal Smith were busy collecting funds for the relief of the poor, as required of the local committees. In March, Elizabeth observed that the merchants were raising the price of food. She saw the role of landlords as countering such exploitation. She described the plight of the labourer struggling to pay for food, despite the prices.

> With potatoes at their present price it would take 9/– [nine shillings] a week to buy sufficient of them for the labourer's family; he can earn at best

but 6/– and there are all his other necessaries, house rent, clothes, fuel, milk. The Managers who buy up the flour and meal and sell it out in the very small quantities the labourers can only buy, nearly double the cost price on the price on the poor purchaser, and if they give them credit, charge usurious interest beside—a system that ruins hundreds—a system every landlord or master is bound to check as far as in him lies.[34]

The plight of the poor she witnessed every day was causing her sleepless nights. In early April snow fell and there were very cold conditions. Hal Smith purchased supplies of potatoes and meal and sold them at low prices to people on the estate. As the weeks passed the situation of the poor worsened considerably, and the most vulnerable were the first affected. A visit to the home of the Delanys illustrated this. They were tenants on the neighbouring estate of John Hornidge, who wanted to evict them. Hal Smith had thatched their 'miserable cabin' the previous winter. The old couple were in a dire situation: immobile, ill and emaciated, with only a young son who worked as a labourer to pay the rent. It was a shocking experience for Elizabeth, as they were 'underfed, under-clothed, under-housed, crushed body and soul by the extreme of poverty'. Even the Kearns family, who she hoped were improving their situation, were in desperate circumstances. Rather than coming to pay the rent, Mrs Kearns pleaded with the Smiths for food, as she had only one day's supply left. When a couple of weeks later her husband asked the Smiths for help, he was given meal at a low price, on undertaking that if his farm had not improved by November 'he will at once give up his ground and turn with our help to something that will answer better'.

When it came to helping the poor, Elizabeth could display endless humanity. She heard reports that another of Hornidge's tenants was in a grave condition. Edward Shannon was an elderly cottier with two acres of land. After his rent was deducted he had two shillings a week with which to feed a family of six children. They were reduced to one meal a day when his store of potatoes was exhausted. A relative sent some meal, but the children were clearly suffering. Elizabeth gave them money to buy milk and meal and the next day had broth sent over to their home.

In among this misery Elizabeth had another world, an exclusively Protestant social world of tea with Lady Milltown (whose manner and affectations irritated her to the point of loathing), of conversations with her doctor, George Robinson, with Tom Darker and other neighbours, such as the Hornidges, well-established landlords. These worlds could collide. The highlight of the Smiths' social calendar was the local ball in June, which was the source of great excitement for her daughters, not least because of the prospect of a long night of dancing. This year it was 'knocked on the head' when the rector, the Rev. William Ogle Moore, wrote to the committee reminding his brethren that it was inappropriate to have such an ostentatious display of wealth given the 'misery of the poor'. The committee agreed, rather reluctantly by all accounts, to postpone the ball. Yet the deteriorating position of the poor was never far away. Elizabeth went with a party to have a picnic on a nearby hill, and it was an evening of dancing and general merriment. The local people who helped were enjoying the leftovers of meat and other luxuries when her attention was drawn to a frightened little boy who had collected the scraps of bread that were shaken out of the table-cloth. He had piled up the crusts 'with one hand and holding bare bones to his mouth with the other—the impersonation of famine'.

'WITH EVERY GRAIN OF THAT CORN GOES A HEAVY CURSE'

For John Mitchel the immediate cause of hunger in Ireland was the policy of the British government, and the only solution was the end of 'English rule'. In the *Nation* he emphasised the injustice of exports in a time of food shortage and pinpointed precisely where the blame should lie for this policy.

> The Irish people, always half-starved, are expecting absolute famine day-by-day; they know they are doomed to months of a weed-diet next summer; that 'hungry ruin has them in the wind'—and they ascribe it, *unanimously*, not so much to the wrath of Heaven as to the greedy and cruel policy of England … They behold their own wretched food melting in rottenness off the face of the earth; and they see the heavy-laden ships, freighted with the yellow corn their own hands have sown and reaped, spreading all sail *for England*; they see it, and with every grain of that corn goes a heavy curse.[35]

The continued exporting of food, whatever the dictates of the market and the need to maintain a free-trade economy, was damning evidence for Mitchel of the moral failure of the British government of Ireland. This was an issue that came up repeatedly during the crisis: whether food should be exported. Mitchel later cited these food exports to demonstrate that there was an official policy of exterminating the Irish poor. In fact in the years after 1846 considerably more food was imported than exported, and even stopping exports would have done little to meet the huge shortage of food created by the failure of the potato crop.[36] Retaining this food within the country was largely of symbolic rather than practical value. It was widely assumed that any effort to interfere with the market and prevent middling and large farmers from exporting their goods at the higher prices they could secure would cause a breakdown in the commercial and agricultural economy.

Mitchel's views were later echoed by William Smith O'Brien. He declared in the House of Commons in April 1846 that in Ireland 'the people are starving in the midst of plenty, and that every tide carries from the Irish ports corn sufficient for the maintenance of thousands of the Irish people'.[37] Belgium introduced temporary measures to stop food leaving the country in 1845, and a number of other European countries contemplated a similar prohibition.[38] Other countries, however, such as the Netherlands and Denmark, maintained free trade, whereas France adopted a policy of discouraging exports. When an official in Ireland suggested to Charles Trevelyan in September 1845 a prohibition on exports, he sternly responded that this was 'a false and short-sighted policy [that] would lead to worse results and seriously retard the progress of general improvement'.[39] Free trade was to be maintained, whatever the consequences might be for the Irish poor. Any interference in the market would lead, it was assumed, to a complete collapse of 'normal' trade.

Peaceful protests demanding food occasionally descended into wholesale riots during the spring as people forcibly seized supplies in April 1846.[40] A major concern for officials in London was the possibility of widespread insurrection in Ireland, a recurring concern that was intensified by reports of food riots in a number of south Tipperary towns, a part of the country already notorious for agrarian violence.[41] In Clonmel the barges leaving for Waterford did so under a heavy escort by what was virtually a small army in a show of force by the authorities. A Commissariat official based in Waterford described the scene for Trevelyan: 'The barges leave Clonmel once a week for this place, with the export supplies under convoy which, last Tuesday, consisted of 2 guns, 50 cavalry and 80 infantry escorting them on the banks of the Suir as far as Carrick'.[42] Trade and the proper functioning of the market were to be protected at all costs. And, as William Smith O'Brien noted, the British response in the face of impending famine was to send soldiers rather than food.

Agrarian violence also increased as landlords and agents were targeted by secret organisations. In February 1846 the government introduced a new 'Coercion Bill'—the Protection of Life (Ireland) Bill—which would give the lord lieutenant wide-ranging powers to impose a form of martial law, with curfews and the power to arrest people on the basis of suspicion rather than evidence. Widely publicised evictions, such as that of three hundred tenants to make way for a grazing farm from the Gerrard estate in Ballinlass, Co. Galway, on 13 March 1846, fuelled agrarian unrest. These tenants were not in arrears with their rent, and the scenes of houses being demolished with the assistance of soldiers and police, after which the tenants were driven out, shocked many contemporaries, especially those in Britain who believed that Irish landlords were irresponsible.[43] Lord Londonderry, an Ulster landlord with extensive estates, expressed his disgust at these horrific scenes and wondered aloud if such events explained the upsurge in agrarian violence.[44] And, as Daniel O'Connell laconically noted, the names on the list of those killed at Aliwal and Sobraon in two famous battles fighting against the odds for the empire in India closely resembled 'the names of the cottagers dispossessed by Mrs. Gerrard'.[45]

RELIEF OPERATIONS

The first chairman of the Relief Commission, Edward Lucas, was replaced in February 1846 by Sir Randolph Routh, the Scottish head of the Commissariat in Ireland, who had unrivalled experience of the logistical demands of feeding large numbers of people quickly. Routh was schooled in the thinking that he should 'save a farthing wherever a farthing could be saved', a commendable maxim in normal circumstances but a very inhumane attitude in the face of the prospect of widespread starvation.[46] He believed that the commission should do everything possible to encourage self-reliance, or else 'the people would rest on their oars and throw the whole labour on the government'.[47]

Back in Ireland the machinery of relief was taking shape, under Trevelyan's close supervision. From early 1846 he drafted a whole raft of instructions and guidelines for relief officials in Ireland. He was in nearly daily contact with Routh and the other Commissariat officers who were directly under his control, with nearly a hundred letters despatched between November 1845 and June 1846. By February the process of establishing a network of food depots was well under way and local relief committees were formed throughout the country, usually comprising landowners, clergy, Poor Law guardians and other notables. The intention was to store the maize at local depots for sale to local relief committees. The local committees would be able to buy the corn by obtaining subscriptions from landowners or government donations and to sell it to the poor at cost price. Only in the most exceptional cases was food to be given away without charge. Even though the importing of this additional source of food was kept secret, news leaked out in February after cargoes began to arrive in Cork Harbour.[48]

Trevelyan had two considerations guiding his actions. The first imperative was to avoid mass starvation. The second was that the government's new role as a provider of cheap food was an extraordinary measure in extraordinary circumstances; the Irish poor should be self-reliant and not become dependent on the government.

> Besides, the greatest improvement of all which could take place in Ireland would be to teach the people to depend on themselves for developing the resources of the country, instead of having recourse to the assistance of the government on every occasion.[49]

The teachings of classical political economy required that private enterprise should be 'the chief resource for the subsistence of the people', though he added that 'the people must not, *under any circumstances*, be allowed to starve'.[50] In principle, such aspirations were very much in line with contemporary thinking about the limited role of the state in economic life. In practice, it misunderstood the fundamentals of the rural economy in Ireland, where the poor if left to the ravages of the market would simply not survive. In some regions the market for food simply did not exist.

Throughout the famine Trevelyan had a wide range of correspondents who knew Ireland well, the best-known being the temperance campaigner Father Theobald Mathew, who frequently wrote to him to describe the local conditions he encountered.

The first public meeting of a local relief committee was held on 10 January 1846 at Kilkee, Co. Clare. It was an inauspicious start. The gathering descended into chaos after rival meetings were organised and disputes between a local Catholic parish priest, the Rev. Michael Comyn, and the landed gentry, a melting-pot of bitter acrimony that was later stilled. The landowners were not prepared to make money available to the committee, as it was dominated by 'mad speculators' such as Comyn. Routh confided to Trevelyan that no local money was forthcoming to support the work of the local committee, and this might necessitate a reconsideration of the role of the local landowners in financing these extraordinary relief efforts.[51] This was an early indication of a problem that would bedevil relief efforts for the duration of the famine: the landed elite were all too willing to delegate to the state their financial and moral responsibility to the Irish poor. In due course British public opinion would come to blame the landlords for widespread poverty in the country.

A further problem also emerged in which Trevelyan was deeply embroiled. The lines of demarcation between Dublin Castle and London were never clear. The lord lieutenant and chief secretary were directly responsible for the executive government of Ireland, but the prime minister and home secretary formulated overall policy from London. Sir James Graham often issued instructions directly to particular individuals, and the Relief Commission was under his control. Much of the squabbling about money and its use for particular activities was broadly reflective of the confused lines of command between Dublin Castle and London. Lord Heytesbury was frustrated by Trevelyan in particular, as the Treasury controlled the purse strings, and Trevelyan had the final say on all expenditure.

When Lord Lincoln arrived as chief secretary to replace Sir Thomas Fremantle in February 1846 these difficulties intensified. Lincoln, with the support of Graham, in a thinly veiled criticism of Trevelyan complained to the prime minister two months later that Treasury controls were delaying the relief effort. This charge was vigorously rejected by Trevelyan's political master, the chancellor of the exchequer, Henry Goulburn, who loyally defended his most senior civil servant.[52] This intricate politicking had little impact, fortuitously, on the course of events but it does illustrate the extent of misunderstanding and confusion and even the degree of suspicion between London and Dublin. This was to foreshadow the difficulties that emerged in coming years between officials based in Ireland and those in the metropolis.

Peel's government saw the provision of public employment as an essential element of relief policy, as the poor needed to earn cash that would enable them to buy food sold by the local committees. This was a tried and trusted method of introducing money into a rural world where transactions were based on exchanges of land and labour. Routh explained the system to Trevelyan in May 1846:

> I believe in ordinary years, from that con-acre system, there is no such thing literally as wages; labour is an affair of barter which these people are obliged to give to the farmer as part payment of their holding, and when they have accomplished this, if the season is a good one, and they have plenty of potatoes, they do not care about labour at all, and often refused employment if offered to them. This life of indolence is enough to demoralise any nation.[53]

A number of legislative initiatives were passed by Parliament in January 1846 that it was hoped would have a long-term benefit to the Irish economy, such as the building of piers, harbours and drainage projects. Road improvements, however, dominated the public employment schemes. The Board of Works—a grossly understaffed organisation—was charged with approving and controlling these schemes, financed equally by a government grant and a loan to be repaid by a charge on local landowners. Trevelyan had concerns about the Board of Works and felt that this was 'an inefficient and wasteful means of relief', a private view he continued to hold despite its divergence from government policy.[54]

This system was widely criticised at the time.[55] At its core, the complicated method of financing such public employment schemes meant that landlords were able to avoid paying a contribution towards the improvements, mainly road works, completed around the country. This left the exchequer with a large bill, to be met ultimately from the public purse. When it came to deciding who was allowed to work on the schemes, the procedure was open to widespread abuse. Tickets for obtaining employment on the relief works were often distributed in a haphazard way by the local committees, causing uproar in the press. As Routh told Trevelyan, from London the rules and procedures all seemed very easy to adhere to, but local committees were besieged by people looking for work. It was not necessarily those most in need who were given priority in the allocation of tickets. Logistically the system was cumbersome, to say the least, with applications going back and forth between local committees and government departments, and stretched officials were under great pressure to make decisions.

The cost was also substantial, roughly £600,000 in the first half of 1846. Notwithstanding these shortcomings, as a mechanism for supporting the poor through making cash available for work the schemes were very successful in providing a substantial number with the means to buy food. By the summer of 1846 about 700,000 people were supported by the public employment schemes, roughly one in ten of the total population.[56]

The news that the government had purchased maize created a heightened sense of expectation by March 1846. At one point it was rumoured that it had imported enough to feed four million people daily for four months. Cork and Limerick were selected as central distribution points, and steamers were used to transport the supplies around to the depots on the west coast, where the hardship would be greatest. Problems soon developed: the harbours on the west coast were not of a sufficient size to accommodate the steamers, leading

Routh to conclude that 'it is annoying that all these harbours are so insignificant. It shows Providence never intended Ireland to be a great nation.'[57] The corn also needed to be milled, and this required special processes to be undertaken by local mills.

The imported corn was never intended to be anything other than a stop-gap to deflate prices and prevent unscrupulous merchants from profiteering at the expense of the poor. As the home secretary, Sir James Graham, stated in the House of Commons, the aim was to ensure that through 'judicious management of this supply the markets would be so regulated as to prevent an exorbitant price for native produce'.[58] It had the effect of forcing speculators to make their produce available for sale at a reasonable price, and they were angry about the loss of higher profits. Even the knowledge that the government had supplies in storage dampened down prices. A Commissariat official in Co. Offaly told Trevelyan about small-time dealers who, 'living as wretchedly to all appearances as the rest of the community', used spare cash to buy potatoes or meal.[59] They held their supplies in store, expecting prices to rise when conditions worsened. Knowing that the government had supplies forced them to sell at lower prices. This was exactly the desired effect of the measures adopted.

Trevelyan and his officials were anxious to delay the opening of the food depots till as late as possible, but this proved difficult, as the price of potatoes soared on the open market and public pressure mounted to make the emergency supplies available. The first depots in Cork, Clonmel and Longford opened in late March 1846. The scene at the Cork depots was chaotic and showed the degree of desperation that had set in.

On Saturday last, the government sales of Indian corn and meal commenced in Cork. Immediately on the depots being opened, the crowds of poor persons who gathered round them were so turbulently inclined as to require the immediate interference of the police, who remained there throughout the day.[60]

By mid-May the depots were opened throughout the country and the supply of maize at cost price began in earnest.

Maize, or Indian corn—called 'yellow meal' in Ireland—was not entirely new, as records show that it was imported in the early years of the nineteenth century. For the most part, however, the Irish poor were unfamiliar with the particular requirements of cooking this type of corn. It was nicknamed 'Peel's brimstone' because of its bright yellow colour but also because, if inadequately ground, eating it could lead to serious digestive problems. According to one modern dietary expert, low-quality corn that was not ground properly 'was both sharp and irritating, it could pierce the intestinal wall, and eaten by a starving people produced agonizing pain'.[61] Understandably, at first there was widespread hesitation about consuming 'Peel's brimstone'. Experiments in workhouses were less than reassuring, as even the poor inmates refused to eat the Indian meal.[62] Trevelyan later recounted that in part this was 'arising from the absurd notion that it had the effect of turning those who ate it black'.[63] Instructions for cooking the meal in a form of porridge were issued by the Relief Commission after various experiments, including a set of tests undertaken by Trevelyan on his own family.[64]

The depots sold the meal at cost price, roughly 1 penny per pound, to local committees. Throughout May and June the demand for the corn was intense, leading to a rapid depletion of stocks by the end of June. In early July officials in Ireland were discussing with Trevelyan the possibility of additional orders to replenish the depots, and discussions centred on a provisional date on which the government's emergency operations would cease or the food depots continue. But the political environment changed: Peel was forced to resign in late June and a new Whig ministry, led by Lord John Russell, was now in power. In the event the date set for the closure of the depots was 15 August 1846.

When the government ceased its operations, merchants and traders would be the main source of food, as private enterprise was central to the balanced operation of the market in a free-trade environment. Trevelyan and his ministerial superiors were clear on one point: the role of the government was not to make an open-ended commitment to feeding the Irish poor, as to do so would, in Peel's words, 'lose the support of the Irish gentry, the Irish clergy and the Irish farmer'.[65] Trevelyan, Routh and other senior officials received numerous complaints from Irish corn dealers that the government depots were undercutting the market rate. As Routh knew well, their primary concern was not with feeding the poor but with accumulating profit.

> The whole country is swarmed with dealers, who have been hoarding Corn to exact upon it an injurious price, and it is not fair to call those exactions the market price for an article introduced expressly for its cheapness & recommended under that advantage to the use of the Poor.[66]

And traders were part of a much larger economic system. Farmers sold their produce at markets, seeking the highest rates from the dealers.

The prevailing orthodoxy that Trevelyan expressed so bluntly was that if the government interfered with the market, normal trade would be 'paralysed', a view that was widely shared among officials and politicians.[67] Under no circumstances should the state be left responsible for feeding the poor and so creating a dependent population. As if to remind them of their duties, in April 1846 Trevelyan sent his officials extracts from Edmund Burke's *Thoughts and Details on Scarcity* (1795), in which the perils of state intervention in a time of scarcity were described. A number responded that, while such principles were sound, the actual situation in Ireland was really very different.[68] An unwavering commitment to these ideologies was to leave the Irish poor at the mercy of the market. And, as history has shown on numerous occasions, absolute scarcity of food rarely causes a famine. In the words of the Indian Nobel laureate Amartya Sen, starvation 'is the characteristic of some people not *having* enough to eat. It is not the characteristic of there *being* not enough to eat.'[69]

'SIR ROBERT HAS BEEN OUR JOSEPH'

Scarcity brought out the most selfish characteristics of some individuals. The hoarding of food by farmers and merchants in anticipation of rising prices was frequently commented upon in early 1846. However, the government's purchase of large amounts of maize served to undermine the most rampant speculation, an aspect that led to much satisfaction on the part of officials; by interfering with the perfect equilibrium of the market, many lives were saved.

Trevelyan and others had concerns about such 'exceptional' actions, not least because of the potential 'disquietude' it created. As the summer approached, merchants sought reassurances about the intended role of the government. Trevelyan outlined the situation to Routh: that in future any purchases would be made within the United Kingdom, allowing the dealers to turn a profit.[70]

Peel's government fell not on the repeal of the Corn Laws but, ironically, on a measure to introduce coercion in Ireland to deal with agrarian violence. The effectiveness of the response of his ministry and the partial nature of the failure created a false sense of security that the government could cope with a widespread lack of food. Trevelyan was later to describe it as a 'probationary season of distress'.[71] Death from famine-related starvation was averted.

Archbishop Murray of Dublin later likened Peel to Joseph in Egypt, relieving famine in his native Israel: 'Hitherto, Sir Robert has been our Joseph'.[72] Peel left office in late June 1846 and a Whig ministry came to power. Lord John Russell, unlike Peel, was faced with the prospect of a complete failure of the crop in the summer of 1846. The limitations of the new government's policy in Ireland were then brutally exposed.

PART III

Into the abyss

Chapter 6 ～

A STARVING NATION

James H. Tuke, an English Quaker, toured the most isolated regions of Co. Donegal in December 1846 with another young Quaker, William E. Forster. What he recorded there was shocking. Normal life had collapsed; starvation was widespread; people were dying in horrific circumstances from famine and fever. The old and the young, always the first to fall victim to hunger-related diseases, were suffering disproportionately. In Dunfanaghy, families survived on a single meal of cabbage, supplemented by seaweed. Nothing prepared Tuke, however, for what he witnessed at the workhouse in Glenties.

> We visited the poor-house at Glenties, which is in a dreadful state: the people were in fact half-starved and only half-clothed. The day before, they had but one meal of oatmeal and water; and at the time of our visit had not sufficient food in the house for the day's supply … some were leaving the house, preferring to die in their own hovels rather than in the poor-house. The rooms were hardly bearable for filth. The living and the dying were stretched side by side beneath the same miserable covering! No wonder that disease and pestilence were filling the infirmary, and that the pale, haggard countenances of the poor boys and girls told of sufferings which was impossible to contemplate, without the deepest commiseration and pity.[1]

Another Quaker who visited Carrick-on-Shannon also noticed the effects of severe hunger on the children, whose 'faces look wan and haggard with hunger, and seeming like old men and women'.[2] The children in the workhouse had skeletal frames with protruding bones, as the limbs had wasted away.

Throughout the country there emerged similar harrowing accounts. Skibbereen, Co. Cork, became synonymous with horrific suffering. In late October 1846 Denis M'Kennedy, a labourer working on the Board of Works scheme, dropped dead on the roadside. At the inquest it was revealed that he was owed two weeks' wages and had not eaten properly for days. The doctor who completed the post-mortem examination testified that he had never seen a body so attenuated from lack of food. The jury returned a verdict of death by starvation 'owing to the gross negligence of the Board of Works'.[3]

The plight of the poor in Skibbereen received widespread publicity. A Cork merchant and magistrate, Nicholas Cummins, visited the area to investigate the conditions himself. He described what he encountered in the townland of South Reen in a public letter to the Duke of Wellington, urging him to petition the queen for help. On his arrival in the district it was devoid of people, but the explanation became apparent quickly.

> I entered some of the hovels to ascertain the cause and the scenes that presented themselves were such as no tongue or pen can convey the slightest idea of. In the first six famished and ghastly skeletons, to all appearances dead, were huddled in a corner on some filthy straw, their sole covering what seemed a ragged horsecloth, their wretched legs hanging about, naked above the knees. I approached with horror, and found by a low moaning they were alive—they were in fever, four children, a woman, and what had once been a man. It is impossible to go through the detail. Suffice it to say, that in a few minutes I was surrounded by at least 200 of such phantoms, such frightful spectres as no words can describe. By far the greater number were delirious, either from famine or from fever. Their demoniac yells are still ringing in my ears, and their horrible images are fixed upon my brain.[4]

Both Skibbereen and north-west Donegal were areas of extreme poverty in which reliance on the potato crop was greatest among the smallholders and landless labourers who constituted the local populations. Such districts would be the hardest hit by the famine.

In early July 1846 it was widely thought that the response of Peel's government to the failure of the potato crop was very effective and saved many lives. By the end of that year widespread hunger, starvation and disease led to many thousands of deaths. How this came to pass is a tale of the shortcomings of the official relief operations and the collapse of the basic structures of a society. But it was also a consequence of the sheer scale of the disaster that unfolded in late 1846.

After a heat wave in the early summer, which stemmed the blight, from mid-June the weather was very wet—ideal conditions for the spread of the fungus. The reports of the early potato harvest were deeply alarming. The disease had returned but this time on a catastrophic scale. Reports were emerging that most of the potatoes were destroyed in the ground. Estimates reckon that the potato crop that year was roughly a tenth of the normal harvest.[5] It was a disaster of unimaginable proportions: a total failure of the crop. The blight's reappearance also changed the terms of the new government's response. No longer was this an exceptional emergency: official measures now sought to bring about a wholesale transformation in the lives of those who depended on the potato, with devastating consequences.

THE SPLIT

Relations between the Repeal Association and the small group of Young Irelanders declined rapidly over the first few months of 1846. Disputes arose over the extent to which O'Connell should support the Whigs; it was widely anticipated that they would form the next government. This would demand that O'Connell relax the agitation for repeal of the Union; but disagreements also emerged about wider issues, such as the use of violence and the extent to which the Catholic Church should influence the Repeal Association. The Young Ireland members also supported the 'godless' colleges. This led to a venting of pent-up frustration with O'Connell's conservative leadership.[6]

What became known as the 'moral force resolutions' proposed by O'Connell were concerned with a matter of abstract principle: none of them, Young Ireland included, seriously contemplated using physical force to change Ireland's status within the Union, even if the rhetoric of the *Nation* did seem to suggest otherwise. What O'Connell wanted to ensure was that there was no opposition within the ranks as he negotiated with the Whigs. For the Young Irelanders, nationality was a set of principles not open for negotiation, whereas the Liberator seemed willing to reach a pragmatic agreement with the incoming ministry. The benefits for O'Connell and his lieutenants were obvious, as patronage would naturally flow from an alliance with the Liberals; the benefits for the cause of repeal and the good governance of Ireland were less obvious.

At a general meeting of the Repeal Association at Conciliation Hall, the association's premises at Burgh Quay, Dublin, on 13 July, O'Connell engineered a showdown with the Young Irelanders over the question of the use of physical force. Even though the division was on physical force, the subtext was—as Charles Gavan Duffy later said—'to draw a line between Old and Young Ireland'.[7] Mitchel, with other Young Irelanders, such as Thomas Francis Meagher, made passionate speeches. For his part he declared that the conflict within the Repeal Association was not really about the use of violence but the prospect of an alliance with the Liberals. 'It was plain to all the world the cause of the dissension in the Hall was not physical force; nobody was in the least afraid of physical force, but many were mortally afraid of Whiggery and place-begging'.[8] In a raw and personal speech he set out why he had joined the Repeal Association

> I entered it with a serious determination to do what in me lay to help what I fondly believed might become a great national movement for the liberation of Ireland; and a man who is in earnest by anything he sets about, is not easily driven from his purposes by discouragement or disgust. Besides (and I hope it will not be deemed presumptuous to say so), I am one of the Saxon Irishmen of the north, and you want that race of Irishmen in your ranks more than any others: you cannot well afford to drive even one away from you, however humble and uninfluential. And let me tell you, friends, this is our country as well as yours.[9]

The controversy rumbled on until the next general meeting in late July 1846. Mitchel and Meagher were required to unequivocally repudiate violent action, which they refused to do. Along with the other Young Irelanders they left the Repeal Association on 28 July, led by William Smith O'Brien MP, after it became clear that no agreement was possible. Despite some efforts at a *rapprochement* in December 1846 it was clear that neither side would give way. Mitchel was not displeased with this outcome, as he confided to John Martin.[10]

The secession was a momentous turning-point in the history of Irish nationalism. At the time, O'Connell presented it as a victory for his leadership over an embarrassing and disruptive splinter group made up of 'juvenile members'. He carried with him the support of many Catholic Church leaders, crucial for the success of any large-scale political movement in nineteenth-century Ireland. According to the *Times*, 'Old Ireland has beaten its young rival. The priests have done it.'[11] But O'Connell's policy of seeking what seemed minor concessions from the new government seemed increasingly misplaced in the face of the widespread social disaster that was unfolding. Co-operation with the government yielded few benefits for the repeal movement at this time.

Meanwhile Thomas Carlyle travelled to Ireland in early September and spent two days in Dublin. He attended a Repeal Association meeting in Conciliation Hall with Mitchel. He saw no reason to change his view of the Liberator: 'One day saw Conciliation Hall, and the last glimpse of O'Connell, chief quack of the then world—first time I had ever heard the lying scoundrel speak—a most melancholy scene to me altogether'.[12] He described the experience as having been 'the utmost limit of human platitude'.[13] Carlyle also recorded his thoughts on the young radical Mitchel: 'a fine elastic-spirited young fellow with superior natural talent, whom I grieved to see rushing on destruction, palpable by "attack of windmills" but on whom all my dissuasions were thrown away'.[14] By all accounts there was a most lively encounter at Mitchel's home, and there were some 'angry altercations with him'. Mitchel wrote to Martin to tell him that Carlyle had visited him, and

> for two evenings we heard him prophesying (by 'we' I mean Young Irelanders generally) to our infinite contentment ... For a sight of him for once in a man's life is worth a considerable journey.[15]

This was the life that Mitchel thrived on: entertaining other writers and thinkers, with the tremendous bonus of having Sartor Resartus, Thomas Carlyle, for dinner for two successive nights. Carlyle was clearly impressed by Mitchel, even if the younger man failed to take heed of any of his advice. Mitchel, like Carlyle, had mixed views on the value of democratic government and notions of the equality of all human beings. Both were prominent supporters of black slavery. Reflecting in his later years, Mitchel's brother questioned his commitment to democracy.

> It would, I believe, be a complete mistake to regard John Mitchel as specifically a democrat. Freedom he valued, individual liberty, equality before the law; but he was no doctrinaire, and cared little as to forms of government. Whether he regarded democracy as a good thing in itself, or only as a *pis aller* [last resource], I cannot say.[16]

'LIKE A FAMINE OF THE THIRTEENTH CENTURY'

Lord John Russell became prime minister on 30 June 1846. There were great hopes that O'Connell's renewed alliance with the Whigs would bring about genuine and long-lasting reforms in Ireland. All the early indications were positive. Russell had long experience of Ireland, having had an interest in the country since the early 1820s, and Irish affairs occupied a considerable portion of his time as home secretary in the 1830s. In a speech to the House of Commons on 16 July, after only two weeks in office, he explained that the aim of the new government was to address the social and economic conditions that created misery and destitution in Ireland. No doubt these lofty sentiments were sincerely held, but it was the immediate crisis that determined the government's actions from the second half of 1846 onwards.

The scale of the destruction overwhelmed the Russell ministry in its early months. In the words of the prime minister, it was 'like a famine of the thirteenth century acting upon a population of the nineteenth century'.[17] To add to his problems, two of the leading members of his cabinet, Lord Palmerston and Lord Lansdowne, were Irish landlords with their own views on what was the best course of action.

For Charles Trevelyan the change of government meant business as usual. He commanded the respect of the new ministers, especially Charles Wood, chancellor of the exchequer, who valued his understanding of the intricacies of the relief operation in Ireland. Trevelyan's political disposition was more in tune with the Whigs, and in late July he wrote an assessment of the relief policies adopted by the Conservatives the previous year for consideration by the cabinet. This time the basic mechanism for providing relief was to be employment through public works—the distribution of food was a secondary concern. This was echoed by Russell when he told the House of Commons that 'we do not propose to interfere with the regular mode by which Indian corn and other kinds of grain' were imported into Ireland.[18] Trevelyan had long had concerns about the government operating in the market and argued that as far as food was concerned 'this may safely be left to the foresight and enterprise of private merchants'.[19] An exception was made, however, for the west of Ireland, where poor communications would hinder the normal functioning of such trade. Food depots were to be established to serve the parts of the country west of a line drawn from Derry to Cork, but they would open only when private supplies were exhausted.

The crisis of the late 1840s was a Europe-wide one, as the potato failed throughout the Continent as well as in Britain and Ireland in what was the 'last' European subsistence crisis.[20] During the hungry forties other large states, such as France, Prussia and the Netherlands, were also strongly committed to free trade, though the increase in prices soon provoked debates about the relative merits of free trade and protectionist policies. In the Netherlands the government sought to encourage imports but on the whole was prepared to let the market take its course and believed that 'the country's only hope of salvation was free trade'.[21] The Prussian authorities purchased supplies of rye, financed public works and introduced temporary tariffs on grain exports and also generally followed the free-trade model. The French state was at first more interventionist, importing large amounts of wheat from Russia and reducing transport charges; imports of food increased tenfold in 1846 and 1847.[22]

Politicians in London kept a close eye on how Continental governments dealt with the food shortage. This was not simply instructive, as the demand for food was acute throughout Europe in late 1846, and Britain vied with other countries to purchase food on the international market.[23]

The situation in Belgium was different. The devastation of the potato crop in Flanders in 1845 was on a scale equal to that of Ireland, with up to 95 per cent of the crop destroyed.[24] After the destruction of the harvest in 1845 the Belgian government removed all tariffs on food imports, temporarily banned exports of food, embarked on large-scale purchases of food from other countries and subsidised local authorities. For committed free-traders this was an 'absurd' policy, as the state, they held, should not occupy such a central role in the supply and distribution of food.[25] Whereas most other European governments remained committed to free trade, the essential difference was that, unlike Ireland, a network of local and municipal bodies strove to mitigate the worst effects of the high prices and implemented a panoply of more flexible measures.[26] Driven by well-founded fears of social unrest—food riots occurred in Prussia, the Netherlands, France and Belgium—and drawing on long-established traditions of communal charity, local elites established such measures as distributing food at low prices and organising employment to assist the poor.[27] Financed from charitable donations, and sometimes receiving limited aid from central governments, these local bodies, known in France and Belgium as *bureaux de bienfaisance* (charity offices), provided poor relief. Municipal authorities established public works to ensure that mass starvation on the scale that threatened in Ireland would not occur; in Berlin, for instance, six thousand people worked on municipal schemes in the summer of 1848.[28]

In Ireland it was expected that the local elite would play a crucial role in relief, which they did to some extent as members of committees and grand juries (county authorities elected by ratepayers) and as Poor Law guardians. The traditions of local and municipal government on the Continent were much stronger; also, the Continental authorities were better funded, especially in urban areas, and able to cope with the demands placed on them, whereas in Ireland local bodies were reliant on the rates levied on farmers and landlords and struggled to cope with even relatively low levels of demand for relief.

The centralisation of the Irish administration was based on Dublin Castle, which in turn was subject to close control by London, with little scope for local initiative. Trevelyan also insisted that committees adhere strictly to the principles of the universal policies formulated by the Treasury, and they had relatively little autonomy. The religious and political divisions between the elite, mostly but not exclusively Protestant, and the Catholic populace served to exacerbate these shortcomings.

An act was passed by Parliament in August that empowered the Board of Works to take control of all public employment schemes. A core element of the revised public works was that loans were advanced by the Treasury on condition that they would later be recouped by local poor rates paid by landowners and large farmers. Even though the decisions were to be taken centrally, the cost would be local and met largely by Irish landlords. In theory the centralisation of all applications for schemes seemed a justifiable counterbalance to the inevitable preference for pet projects. Each application was vetted by hard-pressed officials in Dublin, and the whole process took a very long time. Schemes eligible for grants were mainly for the construction of roads and bridges, as the public works were not designed, at least in the beginning, to be 'reproductive': the aim was simply to give the poor the means to purchase food. From his desk at the Treasury, Trevelyan controlled the operation of the revised programme of public works with extraordinary thoroughness, drafting guidelines, writing to officials in Dublin and generally keeping an iron grip on the whole operation. He set out the rules and regulations in a minute sent to all the relevant officials; there was little scope for refining these to suit local circumstances. Uniformity was the ostensible objective, as Trevelyan explained to the chief administrator of the Board, Colonel Harry Jones, but the underlying consideration was the control of public expenditure.[29]

When devising the rules, Trevelyan had inserted a number of stipulations that were later to prove disastrous. Firstly, the level of wages was to be lower than those prevailing in the locality, to encourage people to seek employment elsewhere. Secondly, anyone who could find work in agriculture was not to be employed, though how this could be determined was left vague. Labourers were to be paid by the task rather than by the day, a shocking requirement in a time of near-starvation. Trevelyan later justified such strict conditions by saying that they were designed to 'confine the Relief Works to the destitute, and to enforce a reasonable quantum of work'.[30]

The public works, therefore, were a 'destitution' test, designed to support only the most needy—and indeed the most desperate—who had no other option but to submit to this punitive regime. The widely shared fear of Trevelyan and his political masters was that the Irish poor would become dependent on such support, now in its second year. For him a relief system 'must contain a penal and repulsive element, in order to prevent its leading to the disorganisation of society'.[31] Sir Robert Peel, on whose support Russell's government depended, observed in August 1846 that the continuation of these activities 'stamps a character of permanency on a relief which was *only tolerated* from the hope of its being casual and temporary'.[32] Peel's choice of words is revealing. British 'toleration' of aid for Ireland during a time of starvation was conditional on it being heavily circumscribed.

Underlying these measures was an ideological agenda, what has been perceptively described as the 'moralist' strain within British liberalism.[33] In short, the problems that existed in Ireland were due to the moral failings of the Catholic Irish: the lack of any exertion towards self-help, 'improvident' living on the potato, and fatalism. Trevelyan and others, while naturally regretting the short-term suffering of the Irish poor, saw the famine as a divinely ordained opportunity to bring about a 'social revolution in Ireland', to quote Charles Wood. A society as dysfunctional as Ireland's required root-and-branch transformation to eradicate its social evils. The encouragement of self-help, prudent living and a diet based not on potatoes but on cereals was the desired outcome. As Trevelyan was later to say dismissively, 'but what hope is there for a nation which lives on potatoes?'[34]

This judgement would never have endeared Trevelyan to an Irish audience but it partly explains the policy measures that were adopted after June 1846. If the famine was, in Wood's opinion, 'a calamity sent by Providence', it was the duty of God-fearing people to bring about changes in the organisation of society. 'God grant that we might rightly perform our part and not turn into a curse what was intended for a blessing', Trevelyan wrote to the Liberal politician and Irish landlord Thomas Spring Rice, Lord Monteagle, in

October 1846.[35] It would be misleading to suggest that these opinions were shared by all the members of the cabinet, yet they were strongly held by the people best positioned to shape official policy in Ireland, Charles Wood and his principal official, Charles Trevelyan.

Russell was no moralist, rather a pragmatist struggling to keep ahead of the dramatically deteriorating circumstances in Ireland. Nevertheless his long-term objective was to bring about a wholesale transformation of Irish society: smallholders effectually forced into becoming paid labourers, a Catholic middle class that would constitute a secure and prudent body of tenant-farmers, and insolvent landlords replaced by wealthy Irish middle-class capitalists. In short, Ireland would emerge as a paler version of the apparently harmonious English countryside.[36]

This combination of appeals to reason and doing the work of the Almighty was a powerful cocktail, likely to appeal to British educated opinion, which saw the complete failure of the 1846 harvest as a watershed. Wood and Trevelyan ensured that their views in particular won wide exposure in the *Times*, the most influential public organ of the day.[37] Limited relief was to be provided to the poor to meet the most severe consequences of the food shortage but in such a manner as to encourage self-help, a term that was employed with extraordinary regularity in a time of famine and starvation. The understanding was that these circumstances would not be allowed to continue, as the devastation brought about by the failure had its own unshakeable logic.

PUBLIC WORKS

The public works took much longer than anticipated to become operational, but eventually, by October 1846, a number of applications were approved and work could theoretically begin on the projects. The rules and regulations so carefully designed in London by Trevelyan and others slowed down the whole scheme, almost to a standstill. When labourers working on existing schemes in Cos. Mayo and Roscommon learnt that their wages were to be cut in September 1846, strikes and riots broke out.[38] Adverse criticism appeared in newspapers as frustrations were vented about the delays, some even with accusations of deliberate delaying on the part of the staff of the Board of Works.

The system was an administrative monstrosity. A flood of applications came to the Board of Works from the presentment sessions (extraordinary meetings of ratepayers) around the country. Each one was scrutinised by the

Treasury before approval was given. If the project was approved, the Board of Works, through its local officers, supervised the actual works, including selecting those people most in need of employment from lists supplied by relief committees. In Clones, Co. Monaghan, it took nearly two months for the public works schemes to become fully operational.[39] In west Clare some schemes were started in early November without even receiving formal approval from the Board of Works.[40] This degree of control exercised by Trevelyan placed extraordinary demands on his time. He left his family and took lodgings near his office in order 'to give up the whole of my time to the public'.[41] By November 1846 he was working long hours, seven days a week, and apologising to a dinner host for the discourtesy of apparently falling asleep after an exhausting day at work.[42]

Apart from the delays in setting up the administrative machinery, cracks soon began to appear in the system. One example from Co. Clare, where at its peak the works supported more than a quarter of the population, illustrates the difficulties. Edmond Wynne, a former army officer, was the temporary inspector for the Board of Works, appointed in October 1846.[43] His role involved administering all the relief works in the county, where widespread destitution resulted in numerous deaths. Apart from the sheer scale of the need for public employment, he saw his principal duty as regulating the expenditure of local relief committees and grand juries, working, as they were, on the understandable assumption that in due course the loans provided would be written off by the Treasury. Wynne encountered extensive local vested interests, keen to ensure that particular tenants were selected for employment. He was especially critical of the relief committees' jobbery and patronage: the committees were made up of 'half-gentry, bankrupts in fortune, and in character, to whom the patronage of the situation appears of the greatest importance'.[44] He regularly flouted the rules of the Board of Works, recognising that strict adherence was not practical: for instance, if he was to sign all the tickets for employment, as he was required to do, he would do nothing else. In his pursuit of equity he alienated many of the landlords, gentry and priests who composed the local relief committees. In one remarkable incident in which he suspected that favouritism was at work he brought a poor man before a relief committee in Killane that had refused to help him,

> a man half starved, and considerably more than half naked, bare head, bare
> legs and arms, nothing to cover him but the skeletons of an old pair of

breeches and waistcoat … [who] seized me by my coat with the grasp of death.

His action, however, did not bring about the intended result, as there were 'heartless men'.[45]

This disheartening account also underlines the attitude of some opportunist landlords. When it came to distributing employment on relief schemes some landlords, especially the resident ones with smaller estates, who were often prominent members of the local relief committees, sought to ensure that their tenants were given preference. In part this was due to paternalistic concerns and the natural disposition towards 'our people', as Elizabeth Smith was wont to call her tenants, but also the more pressing concern that these tenants would subsequently be able to make a contribution towards the rent. This was the fear that most concerned Trevelyan: the system of public works would be used to promote jobbery and favouritism and neglect those most in need.

Payment by task rather than a daily rate proved completely unsuitable in the midst of famine. Many of the labourers were simply too weak to complete a full day's manual work, and reports came back to London describing how this system was wholly inappropriate to the situations in which the officials were daily operating. Eventually this was abandoned and a daily rate paid.

Staffing the schemes presented innumerable problems for the Board of Works in an operation that would ultimately employ twelve thousand officials. It was not a sought-after job: apart from travelling around the particular region, officials faced intimidation and abuse from almost every quarter, including landlords, magistrates and what was often described as the 'mob'. Resignations were common; 'some resign from inability to support the strain, some from intimidation, some have resigned the moment they joined and found the prospect before them', the Commissioners noted in a report in November 1846.[46] One English civil engineer, William Henry Smith, who was involved in supervising works in late 1846, recorded the difficulties of administering such a complex system. He remarked that the 'public works were an expedient got up in a hurry, and a sorry expedient they were'.[47] Like many contemporaries, he feared the consequences of a flight from the land that the public works created, as labourers opted for the cash payments available on the public works.

The operation of the public works opened up differences between the administration in Dublin and the Treasury in London. Lord Bessborough, the new lord lieutenant, who had a large estate in Co. Kilkenny, and his chief secretary, Henry Labouchere, perceived that Wood and more especially Trevelyan had a limited understanding of the conditions in Ireland. Trevelyan's strict adherence to his moralist principles about inculcating self-help and the punitive nature of the public works made co-operation difficult both for the poor and for Irish landlords. Prominent Irish landlords such as Lord Monteagle were also critical of the 'unproductive' character of the schemes when the improvement of holdings seemed so essential. Lord Bessborough achieved a minor victory over the Treasury when the cabinet agreed that public schemes could include drainage works on landed estates, to be paid for with a Treasury loan. The 'Labouchere letter' of 4 October 1846, which set out the new policy, was hailed in the press as a great success for Lord Bessborough; in fact it was a pyrrhic victory: relatively few drainage projects on individual estates were initiated under this scheme, largely because of the complexity of the regulations and the requirement that landlords accept full financial responsibility, an outcome that generated mild satisfaction on Trevelyan's part.[48]

The 'Labouchere letter' opened up a gulf of bad feeling between Dublin and London. A couple of weeks later Richard Griffith, a senior official at the Board of Works in Dublin, issued circular no. 38, which stated that payment would be made for work on family farms. The idea was to give some form of payment for drainage and subsoiling work on their own holdings to meet the widespread concern that smallholders had deserted the land for the public works. Russell was horrified, sensing a possible outcry in Britain: it would be argued that people were being paid by the exchequer for working their own land. Trevelyan acted quickly and decisively to suppress it, issuing a stark rebuke to the Commissioners of Public Works. Despite the best intentions of the Dublin administration, there was no room for doubt that the Treasury exercised complete control over public expenditure.[49]

In November the public works descended into chaos. Hard-pressed officials could barely keep up with authorising places let alone supervise the actual work. As prices rose, the payments received no longer enabled those employed to buy food. It was reckoned by one official that the daily payment of 8 to 10 pence barely covered a meal for a family of six.[50] Touching reports emerged of labourers who gave over this meagre allowance to feed other family members, neglecting their own requirements. In Clones one man with a family of six neglected himself '*in toto* until he died of actual starvation on Thursday last!'[51] Along with insufficient wages, delays in paying wages added to the problems. Labourers often had to get into debt with local gombeen-men, shopkeepers and other traders who sold goods on credit with high rates of interest, simply to survive. In Skibbereen more than forty thousand pawn tickets were issued in the winter months of 1846/7 as the spiral of borrowing and debt worsened.[52]

Throughout November and December the numbers applying for work rose dramatically, placing enormous strains on the system. For instance, in Co. Clare by 8 November nearly 25,000 men were employed on the public works—roughly a third of the able-bodied male population—and many thousands more could not get a ticket. By December public works were supporting half a million people in the country as a whole; when dependants are taken into account this equates to roughly 2½ million people receiving relief of some kind, albeit at the lowest level possible.[53] Perhaps double that number were in desperate need.

The public works initiated by the Liberals and closely supervised by Trevelyan and his subordinate officers were a failure. Great hardship and many deaths were caused both by the core principles governing this form of relief and by the logistical demands it made on officials of the Board of Works, many of whom tried in vain to make an unworkable system work. By the end of December it was obvious to officials throughout Ireland that the public works scheme was failing to meet the basic aim of providing the poor with sufficient money to purchase food. The number of people dying rose rapidly in these winter months. Trevelyan later admitted that while during previous food shortages this type of relief had worked, by early 1847 the public works 'had completely broken down under the pressure of this widespread calamity'.[54]

SCENES OF STARVATION

The Rev. Fossey Tackaberry, a Methodist preacher from Co. Wexford, described the conditions he witnessed in Co. Sligo. He visited the families most in need and reported that some were living on one meal of boiled cabbage per day. The worst off were those who squatted on little patches of land without paying rent and who moved on when compelled to do so. Acceptance of the inevitability of dying was widespread.

> You would be surprised at the number of persons who have made up their minds to stay within doors and die,—die of want! And no one seeking out in order to relieve these sons and daughters of destitution. True, they are, for the most part, Romanists; but are they to be let die?[55]

Such impressions of fatalism were no doubt influenced by Tackaberry's evangelical antipathy towards Catholicism. The terrible hardships endured did not weaken religious piety among the poor: 'We have no appearance of a turning to God as the result of all this,—no, not the least sign of it. Indeed Popery, under the rod, waxes worse and worse.'[56] Tackaberry later apparently contracted typhus fever from a boy, Patrick Feeney, whom he rescued after finding him on the verge of death, and he died in June 1847.

It would be wrong to conclude that as conditions worsened in the second half of 1846 those most affected simply accepted their fate with passivity and resignation. Popular protests, such as food riots, strikes on public works schemes, large meetings outside the presentment sessions and deputations to the homes of landlords and other prominent figures demonstrate that this was far from being the case. Counties such as Tipperary, which had a long tradition of agrarian unrest, featured prominently in reports of disorder, but so did parts of north Munster, including Cos. Clare and Limerick. In some cases overseers and other supervisory staff on public work schemes were intimidated or occasionally physically attacked, including the shooting of one man in early December 1846 at Clarecastle, Co. Clare.[57]

From the autumn of 1846 onwards orchestrated attempts to prevent the exporting of food descended into disturbances, sometimes involving hundreds of people. By exporting food, farmers and merchants were violating the principles of the moral economy, in other words acting in a way that was likely to increase the price locally. The purpose was to ensure that all food was kept at a reasonable price and hence available for purchase. In Youghal, Co. Cork, in late September a large crowd attempted to prevent a ship full of oats for export from leaving, and soldiers were called on to disperse the crowd.[58] A couple of days later in Dungarvan, Co. Waterford, a group of hungry labourers issued threats to merchants and shopkeepers not to export corn to England. After two of their leaders were taken into custody the crowd refused to disperse. Despite a Catholic priest intervening, stones were thrown at the military and the soldiers opened fire, killing two men and injuring many others.[59] In total twenty shots were discharged at an unarmed group of people. One of the 'ringleaders', Patrick Power, who was sentenced to twelve months' imprisonment with hard labour, told the court that before the riot he had been living on nothing but cabbage for the previous four days.[60] Another fifty people arrested, having pleaded guilty, were bound over to keep the peace. These were the actions of the desperate.

Such was the determination that the market be maintained that considerable military might was drafted in to assist the Irish Constabulary.

Soldiers often travelled with convoys of food, and Trevelyan ordered military escorts for boats carrying oats on rivers. Bridges were demolished to prevent carts bringing oats or wheat to markets. Crops were taken from fields. In the countryside, police and military protected food depots and even the harvest itself.

The stakes were high. What the authorities referred to as 'mob' rule could potentially threaten both the social order and the market if thousands of poor people decided to take matters into their own hands. For government officials, magistrates, landlords and strong farmers the fear of a descent into anarchy was ever present. The Crown's prosecuting counsel at the Dungarvan trial summed up this perception:

> There was never a time that the public peace should be so strictly kept as on the present—on its perfect observance depend the lives of the destitute poor but … if insubordination and mob law are suffered to intimidate and influence the labours of the authorities, and the well disposed, there would be nothing but anarchy and bloodshed in the country; the poor would be left to themselves, and famine and starvation would most assuredly stalk throughout the land.[61]

Apart from the implicit threat there was a straightforward way to alleviate these frustrations: provide people with the food at low prices. A leading article in the *Freeman's Journal* commended the government on this clemency, urged the poor to follow the advice of their priests and warned 'of the evil consequences of the slightest infraction of the law at the present time'.[62] At the same time it reminded the government that such events could occur when the poor had no food and lost hope that they would get any form of public employment. When the *Pictorial Times* depicted the food riots in October the accompanying commentary concluded that 'a liberal measure of relief, with full stores of cheap grain to distribute at low prices, would contrast beneficially for the English character, with the rapacity evinced by the Irish agitators'.[63]

Catholic priests acted as a critical intermediary between their flock and the authorities, often serving to calm down what potentially could turn into inflammatory situations. Here the church and the state had the same aim of keeping the peace, albeit for different reasons. Riots were likely to reinforce existing British prejudices about the violent predilections of the Catholic Irish. And it was impossible to tell where outbreaks of disorder might eventually lead, as revolutions in Continental Europe had shown. There are numerous accounts of priests intervening to prevent violence, such as by removing notices calling for public meetings and persuading crowds that attacking food exports served no purpose. In Coolock, on the outskirts of Dublin, a group of labourers congregated calling for food and there were ominous signs of trouble in the air; a Catholic curate managed to defuse the situation and they dispersed quietly.[64] Another young priest, the Rev. Thomas O'Carroll, watched as his parish priest persuaded a large crowd of more than two hundred labourers to go home in Clonoulty, Co. Tipperary, in September 1846. He reflected on the irony of this: the image of the Catholic priest inciting violence was very different from the reality.

> It is well for those folk who take such a delight in calumniating the Catholic priesthood that we still retain so much influence over the people—it is generally exerted for their protection and I have known several instances where the lives of oppressive landlords have been saved by our interference.[65]

The Catholic clergy were obliged to maintain public order. By placing their trust in the government to initiate measures for relief they were reflecting the views of Daniel O'Connell.

Plunder, when food was seized using either intimidation or force, was the crime that stoked the most atavistic fear of widespread social disorder. Large numbers of poor starving people rampaging through the streets of towns in search of food were a nightmare scenario for the authorities, and indeed for the fearful middle classes. After a crowd went around the bread shops in Clones in mid-October 1846 the local justice of the peace wrote to the chief secretary in Dublin Castle, warning him that the poor were in a dire situation and that their demands 'are now so pressing as [to] actually endanger the peace of the country and to compromise the lives of the better order of society'.[66] In Belfast in mid-December a crowd of more than two hundred men who had been laid off from working on the construction of the Belfast–Ballymena railway attacked bakers' shops in the city, demanding bread. After obtaining some bread at one bakery they continued to other shops, where a number of the leaders were arrested during a confrontation with the police.[67] More often than not such events were officially described as 'plundering provisions'. But the real aim was not necessarily stealing food as such—though sometimes this did occur—but, most importantly, 'to regulate the price and distribution of food'.[68] Achieving these aims involved of necessity conflict with strong farmers, merchants and others who controlled the trade. One official reported from Limerick that a large quantity of grain was coming into the city, 'but, alas, it is, at present, quite out of the reach of the labouring man and cottier'.[69] Large crowds attacked convoys carrying oats from Co. Clare into Limerick in early October. Millers and shopkeepers were also threatened and 'encouraged' to lower the price of oatmeal. In an incident later that month near O'Brien's Bridge on the Clare-Limerick border a crowd of three to four hundred labourers took control of a convoy of corn en route to Limerick to be exported. Even though it had a military escort they made it turn back.[70] The widespread view among those who had little was that the export of corn was raising the price within Ireland, making the wages earned on the public works of negligible benefit for purchasing food. If a ban on grain exports had been introduced in late 1846 it is by no means a certainty that this would have made food more accessible to the poor; nevertheless the sight of convoys of food heading for ports to be exported when the poor were starving was understandably going to cause conflict.

Underlying these protests was the perception that commercially oriented farmers were benefiting from higher prices and displaying little sympathy for the poor. Given the existing tensions between farmers and labourers, what is remarkable is that, apart from a few isolated incidents, more conflict did not occur. A series of attacks on horses transporting corn in south-east Clare broke out in September 1846, but this was only for a brief period. The local police reported that labourers and small farmers had 'formed a combination to intimidate by such acts the rich farmers from disposing of their corn'.[71]

Much has subsequently been written on the issue of food exports during 1846. For Russell and Trevelyan, a prohibition in late 1846 would have been unthinkable, given their ideological objections to interfering in the market. After all, Russell in his famous Edinburgh letter had committed himself to free trade. Even Daniel O'Connell did not favour a ban on exports to Britain. The people most affected by a closing of the ports would be Irish farmers, traders and merchants, the principal links in the supply chain of grain to Britain, who had strong vested interests in maintaining trade and were seen as vital components in developing the Irish economy. Given the complete failure in 1846, even if grain exports had been retained in Ireland more than ten times more food was needed to meet the shortfall. Nevertheless, during the period of acute hardship between the failure of the potato crop in August and the end of the year, when imports of maize began to arrive in large quantities from the United States, a prohibition on exports would have dampened down the price of food, which had risen dramatically in September and October.[72]

When Routh commented to Trevelyan in late September about the level of the export of oats, saying it was a 'most serious evil,' the response was a strong rebuke:

> We beg of you not to countenance in any way the idea of prohibiting exportation. The discouragement and feeling of insecurity to the [grain] trade from such a proceeding would prevent its doing any *immediate* good; and there cannot be a doubt that it would inflict a permanent injury on the country.[73]

This was textbook classical political economy yet made little sense in the context of a starving population.

Another official in Ireland described the profiteering by corn dealers and millers. One large corn factor in Limerick was charging high prices for both oatmeal and maize, and when he managed to obtain an undertaking to reduce the prices in November he felt that there was a strong reluctance to do. Farmers invariably profited from these high prices also. But for Trevelyan the economic future of the country lay in the hands of such corn dealers, who deserved both sympathy and encouragement.

> How senseless and suicidal ... is the clamour, which not only heaps odium on the profession of the corn-dealer, but makes it positively insecure, and gives a supposed sanction and justification to the outrages which are being committed. So far from any new persons being encouraged into the trade, the existing dealers are barely able to hold their own, and the country will suffer from the manner in which they have considered themselves obliged to contract their operations, owing to the prevailing feeling of insecurity.[74]

This was faith in free trade and the market economy taken to its most illogical conclusion, where dogma rode roughshod over basic humanitarian concerns.

A GREAT DESTINY

As the crop failure became evident in the summer of 1846, Archbishop John MacHale toured the worst-affected districts in his diocese. He wrote a long public letter to Russell on 1 August 1846 that demanded more extensive and more useful public works. The example of the public works was used to bring out a much wider implication of the current crisis: if Ireland had a home rule parliament such measures would have been speedily introduced, unlike the tardy response from London. This was one of the first explicit statements by a Catholic archbishop that linked famine relief to repeal of the Union.

> The trying ordeal out of which our people are now passing with such patience, notwithstanding the extreme privations which they still endure, has had the effect of imprinting more deeply on their souls the necessity of a domestic legislature. Fear not, however, that they meditate for that purpose either violence or insurrection. No, the weapons of their warfare are peaceful, constitutional, and preserving remonstrance.[75]

As well as making an obvious political point, MacHale was implicitly condemning the Young Ireland group, especially its revolutionary demeanour but also its support for the 'infidel colleges'. In doing so he was voicing his strong support for O'Connellite nationalism in the immediate wake of the secession. If MacHale feared the actions of British Liberal politicians, he equally feared romantic Irish revolutionaries with their overt commitment to religious pluralism. 'Mischievous men' who articulated 'dangerous dogmas' was how he characterised the Young Irelanders, a number of whom were Protestants and hence open to suspicion on two counts: faith and ideology.

Throughout the autumn of 1846 and into the winter MacHale was involved in helping the poor of his archdiocese. By mid-December, when it became clear that the relief polices adopted by the Liberals were failing miserably, he wrote another long public letter to Russell. This time he reminded him of the great expectations that his government had created on its coming to power in June by promising to tackle Irish poverty, and how those expectations were dashed in little under six months. He recounted the remarkable details of a meeting between a Catholic priest on Achill Island and Sir Randolph Routh, head of the Commissariat. The unnamed cleric, who happened to be 'as ignorant of the callous lessons of political economy, as he is versed in the warm and practical charity of the Gospel', pleaded with Routh to establish a food depot on the island. Routh rejected this plea, lectured the clergyman on 'free trade and mercantile immunities', and suggested that if he had read the writings of his countryman Edmund Burke on scarcity he would not make such an 'unreasonable' application.[76]

MacHale reminded Russell that it was largely due to the Catholic clergy that the country remained relatively peaceful in the face of inordinate delays in establishing the public works. The irony was that Catholic curates were not permitted to serve on local relief committees, as only parish priests could be members. Yet when it came to persuading the hungry to remain calm, the same curates were called on by magistrates and justices of the peace to dissuade the poor from taking matters into their own hands by preaching patience and restraint. And while MacHale acknowledged that the laws of property were important, 'we value the peace of this country and the lives of the people more'.

Russell did not need a reminder of the fragile state of the country. He was well aware that discontent in Ireland could easily foment large-scale violence. In December 1846, on hearing rumours that arms were being obtained for violent action—false, as they subsequently proved—Russell wrote to Lord Bessborough in Dublin to ask if this were for a specific purpose, sensing that widespread frustration was leading to more alarming developments.[77]

In what proved to be a prophetic challenge, MacHale urged the prime minister in dramatic terms to consider his potential legacy to Ireland.

> Your lordship has now a great destiny to fulfil—the rescuing of an entire people from the jaws of famine; for nothing less than millions from the imperial exchequer can avert the doom that hangs over the Irish nation … Unless you adopt more enlarged measures than throwing the relief of the people on the landlords, who, whatever be their sins, should be corrected and reformed rather than annihilated, your ministry will be memorable in Ireland; and if you are ambitious of a monument, the people's bones, 'slain with the sword of famine,' and piled into cairns more numerous than the ancient pyramids, shall tell posterity the ghastly triumphs of your brief but disastrous administration.[78]

MacHale was drawing attention to one of the central tenets of official policy, which was later to become a central grievance in the nationalist critique of the shortcomings of the relief efforts. Maintaining the rights of private property over and above all other considerations meant that great losses of life occurred in the winter of 1846. It was both unrealistic and inexcusable to expect the Irish landed class to organise and ultimately pay for the relief efforts in the face of such a widespread disaster.

MOUNDS OF GRAVES

One such landlord was Elizabeth Smith. The descent into famine in the second half of 1846 was not so obvious to her after spending a couple of months in Scotland, with time in her beloved Rothiemurchus. Before leaving in July she visited Russborough House to see Lady Milltown, who showed her the 'Paris wardrobe', an extensive collection of expensive clothing. Elizabeth could not understand this obsession with collecting, given that 'the poor woman visits nowhere; none of these things will ever be on hardly as she herself acknowledges'.[79] Such spending was undoubtedly a symptom of her deep unhappiness, largely because of her husband's excessive gambling, mishandling of money and generally boorish behaviour. Another task beckoned, however. Elizabeth brought her eldest daughter, Annie, on a tour of the locality: educating the children about how the poor lived was viewed as a continuing part of their formation, even if the scenes Annie witnessed shocked her.

Elizabeth's visit to Rothiemurchus was a painful one after she had been away for nearly twenty years and had an unsettling effect on her. She noted the changes for the worse to the lives of the Highlanders living without the laird: they consumed too much whisky, fighting was common, and many young women had children outside marriage, with 'hardly a young woman in the country who has not stept aside, as they delicately call her loss of reputation'. It was family relationships that came to the forefront of her mind. Being back made her reflect on her father's squandering of his inheritance and the life-styles of her brothers.

> They will battle on, and they will struggle on, saving, speculating, spending with an extravagance incurable and which will keep them years, if not their lifetime, in the East … I have never felt it pleasant to reflect on the ways of any of them; it is not my affair; the past is gone; if ever any of them want me they shall find me as they left me.

The local people were overjoyed that one of the laird's daughters had returned and went as far as to organise a dance in her honour. She clearly enjoyed being back and interacting with people she had known since her childhood.

The Doune was rented out to the Duke of Bedford, and her visit overlapped with a stay by the duchess, stepmother of the prime minister. They met after a service at the local kirk in what must have been an awkward encounter for Elizabeth, though the duchess was kind and 'very much softened since her Duke's death [in 1839]'. She was determined to see the house so that she could 'take a last lingering look, then try to expect the future though I must ever mourn the past'. Her past even caught up with her on the journey from the Highlands to Edinburgh when they passed Murthly Castle, north of Perth. She had apparently been engaged to John Archibald Drummond-Stewart, who was to become the sixth Stewart Laird of Murthly. The circumstances of the broken engagement are never disclosed; he married another woman in 1832.

She spent the last week of her visit in Edinburgh, seeing the sights and renewing old friendships. Her sister Jane now lived there. After the death of her first husband in 1835 she married Sir James Gibson-Craig of Riccarton, an estate on the outskirts of the city. He was a prominent Scottish Whig politician and stalwart of polite Edinburgh society. As always, Elizabeth had practical concerns: she wanted to meet Robert Chambers, one of the two brothers who ran *Chambers's Edinburgh Journal*, which published a number of her stories, some of which were thinly disguised sketches of the life of an Irish landlord. She also met William Gibson-Craig, the MP for Edinburgh and a junior lord of the Treasury. Just back from London, he told her that his ministerial colleagues were preoccupied with 'devising means to feed the poor potato-less people' in Ireland. No doubt Elizabeth took the opportunity to press on Gibson-Craig her own views about appropriate remedies.[80]

When she returned to Baltiboys in early September the full extent of the impending hunger preoccupied her. The harvest now over, there was little work for labourers and the prices of food were rising steeply; 'here comes the famine', she observed. The local meetings called to organise relief exposed to her the inherent weaknesses of government policy. Good landlords would do as they had done before and help their tenants, and equally would have to pay, through rates, to support the tenants of negligent ones. The Smiths made plans to assist some of their own tenants who would need help, and Hal agreed to sell meal at a low price to those most in need. Elizabeth was critical of the government's policy of not interfering with the market, even as a temporary expedient, as 'capitalists are buying up all the grain to retail really at an exorbitant price'. She also sensed that disputes within the cabinet between Russell and Lord Bessborough on one side and Lord Palmerston on the other merely added to the country's difficulties: 'our wretched peasantry are actually starving while these wiseheads are battling how to relieve them'.

Somewhat reluctantly, Elizabeth travelled to England to visit Oxford with her daughters and attend her niece's wedding in London, although Tom Darker kept in touch by letter. During this interval away from Ireland her views towards the poor hardened and became far less sympathetic, presumably influenced to some degree by the company she kept. When Hal announced that he was considering taking advantage of the loans available under the 'Labouchere letter' to drain his lands she concluded that this 'visitation of providence will thus be the means of prosperity to our nation'. She then considered the smallholders and the poor, and her conclusions were not altogether different from Trevelyan's moralist viewpoint.

> Perhaps it will be a better year for the poor than they have ever known, of essential use in many ways; they must starve or *work*, no bare existing on roots and idleness, their food will be of a better kind, invigorating to *mind* and *body*, they *must* learn decenter habits. Their small holdings will become valueless to them, their children can't be suffered to hang on at home idly when every mouthful has its price well felt. Oh! It may be the dawn of happy days,—God grant it.

A few days later, after reading newspaper reports of events in Ireland, she fulminated against the poor. 'I can't but despise a people so meanspirited, so low-minded, so totally without energy, only I attribute it to the want of animal food'. Being in London and separated from the events in Ireland undoubtedly shaped these objectionable views. In this abstract world she could pontificate on the shortcomings of the Irish poor and how reason demanded that this way of life be eradicated, though when she encountered the subjects of her rants in Baltiboys she displayed much more charity and humanity.

On her return to Ireland in early November she found that the situation had gone from bad to worse. She blamed the government's relief policy and observed that those who were not really in need were employed, harshly judging neighbouring landlords such as the Hornidges for dismissing labourers and sending them to the public works. When it came to the gale day, most of the tenants paid up their rent eventually, apart from the usual recidivists, such as George Kearns, who was deeply in arrears. Elizabeth decided that he 'must go, and at once, for his own sake'. In late November, as the weather turned colder and snow fell, she fretted for the poor who, without adequate food or shelter, were unlikely to survive the winter. Her criticisms of the government became more numerous and more strident. She

questioned the wisdom of not interfering with the markets as the price of
food had risen so rapidly.

> Extraordinary cases require extraordinary treatment. Abstract principles
> are probably correct and in future years may work for good, but having
> never acted on them hitherto we are not prepared to receive them, and one
> shudders at stepping over mounds of graves in the experiment at this time.

By December, Elizabeth concluded that Russell's government was a 'bad
ministry'. The ill-thought-out relief policies were compounded by local
corruption. Hal reported that at the presentment sessions in Blessington a
crowd had gathered awaiting news about new public works, which did not
materialise. Looking down the list of men selected for such employment she
saw farmers' sons, middling farmers and others who 'came craving for the
bread belonging to the poor'. The local workhouse was full, with more than
1,100 inmates, and the poor were starving. On New Year's Eve, looking back
over the year, Elizabeth felt satisfied that none of their tenants were starving,
but it was very near. The demands of the previous year had left her exhausted,
on top of her illness, yet she still had 'work to do'.

CONCLUSION

Widespread suffering throughout the country was evident by December 1846.
No place better exemplified this suffering than Skibbereen, a place that has
become synonymous with famine deaths. The dreadful plight of the poor of
this district was reported extensively in the newspapers, recounting shocking
scenes. The dispensary doctor at the workhouse recorded for the *Cork
Examiner* a typical day in attending to his patients on 2 December 1846. First
there was a Mrs Hegarty, who asked for assistance with burying her husband
and child. When the doctor enquired why he had not seen them she replied
that they were not ill but starving. Then there was a boy who needed ointment
for his mother. She was carrying candles to wake her own mother, who had
died of fever; the neighbours left food and candles but were terrified to enter
the house. The boy's mother was so weak from hunger that she fell over with
the candles while trying to place them near the body and set the thatch on
fire, burning down the cabin. The family were outside in the cold the whole
night, as neighbours refused to offer them shelter, fearing contagion.

By far the most harrowing incident of the day was when the doctor was
walking out to the workhouse at night and came across a woman who had

fallen into the ditch. She was numb with cold. Clasped in her arms, 'which were as rigid as bars of iron, was a dead child, whilst another with its tiny icy fingers was holding a death-grip of its mother's tattered garment'.[81] The following day the woman explained that she had tried to get to the workhouse but collapsed on the road.

A Commissariat officer who arrived in Skibbereen in December came across dead bodies left wasting on the street, or hidden away out of sight in the cabins that had once been their homes. The relief inspector for the Board of Works, Major Hugh Parker, reported that more than two hundred deaths had taken place in the town in the last few weeks, and that he had witnessed a woman begging with a dead child in her arms, and three children lying with their father dead on the roadside. 'Nothing can exceed the deplorable state of this place', he concluded.[82]

Quite rightly, the officials blamed the landlords, who received substantial rental income from the district though seemed unwilling to take the lead in organising local relief efforts. But it was not just the local landlords, many of whom were absentees, who were unmoved by the destitution. Major Parker recounted what to modern sensibilities is a distasteful contradiction: the Saturday market in the town of Skibbereen in late December had plentiful supplies of meat, fish and bread. What often was not understood fully by contemporaries was that there was not an absolute lack of food *per se* in such districts but that the poor had not got the money to buy this food.

The result was widespread death and disease by the winter of 1846. Official relief policy based on the poor having to work to earn money to buy food had failed, and with terrible consequences. The weather considerably increased the suffering: it was one of the worst winters on record, with snow and freezing conditions, which added to the general misery of the poor and vulnerable. By early 1847 Irish society was beginning to fall apart. A new approach was needed.

Chapter 7 ∿

THE FEARFUL REALITY

'POOR DEVILS ONLY'

John Dilworth, an Englishman in Ireland to distribute charitable relief, wrote an impassioned letter in March 1847 in which he described a sepulchral scene. A family named M'Clean left the local workhouse, where fever had taken hold, and returned to their home. The father, mother and a daughter died within a matter of days. Coffins were purchased with Dilworth's assistance to bury the dead. A few days later he returned and found a young man, about twenty, who gestured to an object lying on the floor. Dilworth looked more closely and was horrified by what he found.

> … And oh! what a spectacle! a young man about fourteen or fifteen, on the cold damp floor,—off the rubbish—dead!—without a single vestige of clothing—the eyes sunk—the mouth wide open—the flesh shrivelled up—the bones all visible—so small round the waist, that I could span him with my hand. The corpse had been in that situation for five successive days.[1]

A few days later Dilworth called again to the M'Clean home. The older son was 'now dead upon the floor'. Three surviving children were left, though the local doctor predicted that they too would die soon. A whole family of eight was wiped out in this tragic episode.

Newspapers were filled with such harrowing accounts in early 1847. What makes this particular event different is that it occurred in Lurgan, Co. Armagh, a town at the heart of the prosperous 'linen triangle', where the M'Cleans were a family of Presbyterian weavers. It has often been assumed that Protestant-dominated east Ulster remained insulated from the Great Irish Famine, and that poor Catholics in the south and west had the monopoly on suffering during the dark years of the late 1840s.[2] In fact poverty, rather than religion or geography, was the surest guide to the effects of the famine. Karl Marx was not far from the truth when he declared that the Irish famine 'killed poor devils only'.[3] The fevers that inevitably followed starvation were less particular, however. Such was the scale of the disaster in what became known as Black '47 that virtually every district of the country was affected; but it was the most vulnerable, Protestants and Catholics, who were least equipped to face yet another year of hunger and starvation.

LIFE AND DEATH IN BALTIBOYS

Despite her continuing illness, Elizabeth Smith took it upon herself in January 1847 to catalogue the circumstances of the tenants on her estate. Over a number of days she walked from house to house, meeting families and jotting down her observations in her diaries. Recorded with characteristic vividness, this survey of the tenants underlines the contrasting fortunes of this small community. Her most sympathetic comments were reserved for the old people, a number of whom received direct assistance from the Smiths, in the form of housing. What annoyed Elizabeth most were the tenants who did not exploit their opportunities. Pat Ryan, who had a smallholding of thirteen acres in 'high order', was a hard-working man whose children seemed to want to improve themselves through education. On the other hand Tom Kelly, a large farmer with seven children (and four servants) farming more than 120 acres, was doing well but his practices were antiquated. With a farm of this size Kelly was an independent entity with his own retinue of labourers and servants, something that Elizabeth slightly begrudged.[4]

George Kearns, the *bête noire* of the Smiths, now owed more than two years' rent. His thirty-acre farm was in disarray, though he had managed to hide away enough corn to feed his family of eight until May. By April he had left for the United States, 'begging to the last', in Elizabeth's words. It seems he was more shrewd than she had allowed for. When the Smiths refused to lend the passage money for his cousin—they had already paid the fares for his family and given him £5—he conjured up £7 out of nowhere. Elizabeth was sure he had plenty more money stashed away for his new life. The Smiths were greatly relieved when they left: 'Such a set—'tis worth all they cost to [be] rid of them'.

Elizabeth had her favourites, chief among them the Darker family, two bachelor brothers, John and Tom, and two unnamed spinster sisters, who between them raised five nieces and nephews, 'the children of two brothers who died beggars'. The Darkers between them had more than 160 acres and were the ideal tenants, willing to learn and presumably suitably deferential to the good master and his wife.

The other large to middling farmers included Michael Tyrell, who had nearly a hundred acres and was 'thriving', despite being seventy-six; Jack Byrne, also 'thriving on a good-sized farm of sixty acres'; Garrett Doyle, with roughly forty acres; and Bryan Dempsey, 'a reckless, ruthless, vapouring, "*cute*," model of the bad style of Irishmen'.

Various tradesmen who worked for the Smiths, such as James Carney, and former servants were also given houses. The most vulnerable people were the small farmers, tenants dispossessed of their holdings but allowed to remain in their houses, sub-tenants who rented a house from one of the larger tenants, and squatters who should not have been living on the estate.[5] They relied sometimes on tiny plots of land to grow potatoes and lived in deplorable poverty. The elderly James Cullen and his wife had one acre of land, which they were unable to pay for, and were reliant on soup distributed by the Smiths. Another recipient of the soup was Michael Doyle. He farmed a little more than eight acres and was married to Elizabeth's former nursemaid, Judy Ryan. He had been ill from typhus for several weeks, but they still had oats, which Elizabeth encouraged him to sell at the market so as to buy meal and rice. The living conditions were dreadful.

> She stood to receive us in her cloke [cloak] having but one gown which was washing; all the children nearly naked, the husband very bare; no way of getting up to the house but over a broken wall, or up to the door over the dung hill … Twice I have succeeded in improving this most slatternly Judy, and twice she has fallen back when my watchful eye was removed. I will try again—her and the husband together—rouse them if possible for they want but method to be comfortable.

Another hard case was that of a Mrs Quin, widowed with a large family. Her farm was taken over by Hal Smith, and he forgave seven years' rent. A daughter living with her had married a labourer and they had seven children. Now the family was living in what was previously a cowshed.

> They live in the mother's cowhouse where she had no right to put them and thus settle a whole family of beggars upon us, but we did not look after things then as we have learned to do now. It is the most wretched abode imaginable, without window or fireplace; mud for the floor, neither water nor weather-tight, nor scarce a door, all black with smoke, no furniture scarcely. Yet times are brightening for the nearly naked inmates. A brother in America sent them at Christmas ten pounds which paid their debts, and bought them some meal and fuel, and their eldest son is to go out to this kind uncle in March. They have no business where they are, the man not belonging to Baltiboys, but there they are through our negligence so we must take care of them for the present.

Elizabeth added their names to the 'soup list', entitling them to the broth she distributed. The Smiths now had entered into the provisions trade, supplying food and fuel at cost price to needy tenants. Each day a big cauldron of soup was made and then distributed free to those most in need; the following day the same people were given milk and cheap rice. In early January 1847 twenty-two people were on the soup list, mostly the elderly or those from large poor families. But this number increased as Elizabeth uncovered more cases of severe hardship on her rounds. Both the provisions store and the soup list were partly financed by generous donations from members of the Grant family living outside Ireland. It was a humane and characteristically paternalist initiative by the Smiths to look after 'their' people. It was also an echo of the traditional moral economy, whereby landlords felt a responsibility to lessen the effects of food shortages on their tenants. In her native Scotland landlords were at the forefront of relief efforts during the Great Highland Famine.

Elizabeth had concerns that those most in need were not receiving assistance beyond the estate. Stories abounded of strong farmers sending their families and labourers to the public works and of shopkeepers making huge profits by charging usurious interest on food and other provisions. 'Hucksters', as Elizabeth called them, were making large amounts by essentially forcing the poor to pay well above the market rate for food. At least the Smiths' tenants could buy food from the estate's own provision store.

The stark contrast between the situation of the large farmers and other groups struck Elizabeth. Large farmers could sell their produce at triple the price of a usual year, whereas the small farmer was 'ruined': he had to 'eat his corn, sell his stock, at an unreasonable time because he has no fodder and therefore leave himself penniless for the coming year'. The tradesmen had no work and were reliant on savings, if they had any. The labourer could just about feed a family, but if it was a large one 'they must be very near to starvation'.

This situation—together with other examples of blatant profiteering, self-regarding relief officials who drew sizeable salaries, such as the director-general of the Poor Law Committee for the barony, Captain Brandling, who earned £1,200 per year, the unsympathetic and extravagant landlords who wished merely to dispense with rather than help their tenants, and the poor who seemed curiously resigned to their fate—led Elizabeth to digressions on the Irish character, regardless of rank or station. The Irish people lacked a moral outlook, and 'Irish probity is a curious commodity—about on a par with its industry'. Principles of self-help were also absent, as everyone, from landlords to the starving poor, looked to the government to remedy all problems. Particularly exasperated after being asked to adjudicate in a dispute between a provision dealer and a local person about credit in April 1847, she fulminated on the people who surrounded her:

> I am almost sick of the dishonesty of these poor miserable creatures. In every way, in all classes, lying, cheating, defrauding, concealing—every sort of underhand meanness is practised among them. Here has come to light a tissue of evil as really disgusts one—how can it be otherwise—brought up in sin and sloth for the purpose of struggling through misery we are absurd to expect correct principles from so low a state of morals; patience—one has need to be made of it, to endure life with such surroundings.

When attendance at meetings of the local relief committee dropped off, she resented the fact that her husband, and two of the other smaller landlords, were left carrying the burden. She concluded that the whole Irish race was in need of reformation.

> What people. What melancholy prospects for another generation. Indolence, sulk, irritable dispositions, all to be got the better of in every individual almost, throughout the country before we can hope for any permanent improvement in the race.

Looking to the future, she predicted that the days of the small farmer were near their end. Indebted landlords would be forced to sell their estates; the indolent poor would have to go to the workhouse; and only the strong would survive.

A more immediate concern was the death in May 1847 of a twelve-year-old boy, Andy Ryan, from fever. He was the seventh child out of a family of ten to die. He had gone to the fair in nearby Naas, suffering from malnutrition, and apparently contracted fever; he died soon afterwards. He was one of Elizabeth's favourite pupils at the national school, and she had hoped that one day he would become a teacher. It was not to be. This was a time when the natural order was reversed: parents buried their children rather than *vice versa*.

DEATH OF A PATRIOT

In late May 1847 students at St Jarlath's College, the seminary for the diocese of Tuam, noticed that John MacHale was in a very agitated state, walking alone for hours in the grounds, 'singularly silent and sorrowful'.[6] When they enquired about the cause they were told that MacHale had heard that morning of the death of Daniel O'Connell a week earlier, on 15 May 1847, in Genoa. One former student remembered how stricken with grief MacHale was at this time. He was O'Connell's most prominent clerical supporter, and though they had disagreed on various issues MacHale was acutely aware that O'Connell's passing would raise critical questions about the future of Irish nationalism.

O'Connell spent October 1846 at his estate of Derrynane, Co. Kerry. Like the Smiths and other landlords who felt a responsibility towards the poor, O'Connell had established a provision store, selling food at cost price, and lobbied extensively for local projects. He was shocked by the desperate plight of the poor, and his last few months were devoted to pleading in vain with the Russell government to do more. A weak and dying man, suffering from a brain infection, he set out for Rome at the end of January 1847. In a poignant speech to the House of Commons on 8 February, when he could barely stand and be heard, he called on the members to act with mercy and generosity towards the Irish people, who were

starving in shoals, in hundreds—aye, in thousands and millions. Parliament is bound, then, to act not only liberally but generously—to find out the means of putting a stop to this terrible disaster … She [Ireland] is in your hands—in your power. If you do not save her, she cannot save herself. I solemnly call on you to recollect that I predicted with the sincerest conviction that one-fourth of her population would perish unless Parliament came to their relief.[7]

It was a pitiful sight: the great Liberator shorn of his magnificent oratorical powers, begging for help from the Parliament in which he at one time had played such a dominant role. There was yet another tragic aspect to this speech. O'Connell had done much to galvanise, as a political force, a country that was now laid waste, and there was precious little he could do about it.[8] In 1843 his Repeal Movement threatened the stability of the Union and fed widespread fears of a popular revolution. Four years later, ensuring the basic survival of the same country became his principal concern. In this respect O'Connell and the nation's fate mirrored each other.

MacHale, like O'Connell, was acutely aware of the disastrous reversal in fortune and now perceived the political vacuum that was created by the Liberator's death. He issued a pastoral letter within days of the news, urging the clergy and faithful to pray for the repose of O'Connell's soul. Predictably, he used the opportunity to remind Catholics of the principles that O'Connell stood for and the need for Catholic solidarity in the face of famine and secularist ideologies, a coded reference to his bugbear, the 'godless' colleges in Galway, Cork and Belfast. For MacHale the widespread deaths and hunger were a direct consequence of the Union.

> The evils, the unspeakable evils of the legislative Union are now placed beyond the reach of doubt or controversy. They are attested by the graves of the dead and the skeleton forms of the living, the accusing monuments of that cruel policy which has systematically consigned the people of Ireland to a food as precarious as that of men in a savage state. It has forbidden them, in order to support alien luxury and monopoly, to taste of the abundant harvests and numerous flocks with which the land teems, the produce of their own peaceful and skilful industry.[9]

Such views would enter into the conventional wisdom of nationalist critiques of the Union and become part of the later campaign for home rule in the 1870s and 1880s. If an Irish parliament existed it would adopt policies that would improve the living conditions of the poor. This argument was no doubt a valid one; where the uncertainty arises is whether the same Irish

BRIDGET O'DONNEL AND CHILDREN.

The famous engraving of Bridget O'Donnell and her children, from *Illustrated London News*, 22 December 1849. (© *Mary Evans Picture Library*)

A youthful-looking John MacHale
(1791–1881), Archbishop of Tuam,
c. 1850. (© *Mary Evans Picture Library*)

John Mitchel (1815–1875), c. 1848.
(© *Getty Images*)

An early portrait of Charles Trevelyan (1807–1886) by Eden Ellis, commissioned in 1848 by Commissariat officers to acknowledge his leadership during what he termed the 'Irish crisis'. Note the Famine 'blue books' or parliamentary papers at his feet. (© *National Trust Images*)

Elizabeth Smith, née Grant (1797–1885), in her later years. (*Reproduced by permission of the Trustees of the National Library of Scotland*)

Charlotte Square, Edinburgh, where Elizabeth Smith was born at no. 5, her father's recently completed New Town residence. The impressive house in the centre (no. 6), Bute House, is now the official residence of the First Minister of Scotland. (© *Royal Commission of Ancient and Historical Monuments of Scotland Enterprises*)

The Doune, Rothiemurchus, the ancestral home of the Grants, where Elizabeth Smith spent many happy years. (*Reproduced by permission of the Trustees of the National Library of Scotland*)

Sir Robert Peel (1788–1850), prime minister when the blight first hit in 1845.
(© *Alamy*)

THE MODERN SISYPHUS.

"Sisyphus is said to be doomed for ever to roll to the top of a great mountain a stone, which continually falls down again."

SISYPHUS   SIR R. P—L.   THE STONE   D. O'C—L.   THE FURIES   LORD J. R——L, S——L. &c.

Peel portrayed as a modern Sisyphus by Richard Doyle in *Punch* in 1844, pushing a rock labelled 'Ireland' containing an image of Daniel O'Connell. The caption reads: 'Sisyphus is said to be doomed for ever to roll to the top of a great mountain a stone, which continually falls down again.' (© *Alamy*)

Peel's dilemma, as represented in the *Pictorial Times*, November 1845, combined the question of the corn laws, pressure from English radicals to repeal them, the position of the Irish Catholic clergy, agrarian violence and the looming shadow of Daniel O'Connell in one ghastly nightmare. (© *Mary Evans Picture Library*)

Government sale of Indian meal at Cork, early 1846. (© *Mary Evans Picture Library*)

Lord John Russell, Whig prime minister, 1846–52. (© *Getty Images*)

Food riots in Ireland, April 1846. (© *Mary Evans Picture Library*)

George Frederick William Villiers, Earl of Clarendon, lord lieutenant of Ireland, 1847–52. (© *Alamy*)

The dreaded poorhouse: plan of Carlow workhouse (front view). (© *Mary Evans Picture Library*)

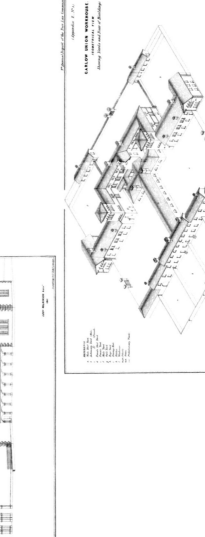

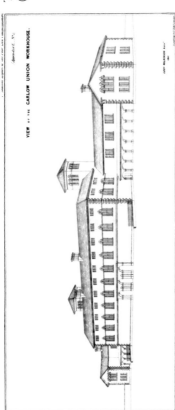

Plan of Carlow workhouse (aerial view). (© *Mary Evans Picture Library*)

ATTACK ON THE POLICE BY THE INSURGENTS UNDER SMITH O'BRIEN.

The 1848 uprising, sometimes described dismissively as the 'Battle of Widow McCormack's Cabbage Patch'. (© *Mary Evans Picture Library*)

The Evicted, an evocative painting by Lady Elizabeth Butler (1880).
(© *National Folklore Collection*, UCD)

'The Day after the Ejectment', from *Illustrated London News*, 16 December
1848. (© *Mary Evans Picture Library*)

Le second monument aux victimes du typhus, à la Grosse Île

The memorial to Irish famine victims at Grosse-Île, near Québec, erected by the Ancient Order of Hibernians and unveiled in 1909. (© *Topfoto*)

DEPARTURE OF THE "NIMROD" AND "ATHLONE" STEAMERS, WITH EMIGRANTS ON BOARD, FOR LIVERPOOL.

'Leaving Ireland': this rather calm depiction belies the sense of panic that was associated with the exodus. (© *Mary Evans Picture Library*)

Embarkation on an emigrant ship. (© *Mary Evans Picture Library*)

LANDING OF QUEEN VICTORIA IN IRELAND.

Sir Patrick Raleigh. "MAY IT PLEASE YOUR MAJESTY TO TREAD ON THE TAIL OF MY COAT."

The landing of Queen Victoria in Ireland, from *Punch*, 1849. (© *Topfoto*)

The terrible consequences as measured by the decline in population and mass emigration. (© *Topfoto*)

Memory of the famine: a republican mural in Belfast. (© *Alamy*)

parliament would have the resources and capacity to deal with a disaster of the magnitude of the Great Famine.

MacHale's views were echoed, albeit with an entirely different purpose, by an unlikely source: the brilliant young Conservative politician and barrister Isaac Butt. At this time Butt was a strong supporter of the Union; later, in the 1870s, he became the leader of the home rule party. His long transformation from an ardent supporter of the Union in the 1830s and defender of the Protestant ascendancy to leading the campaign for home rule was influenced by what he saw as the altered economic and political relationship between Britain and Ireland in the wake of the Famine.[10]

In April 1847 Butt published a lengthy critique of government policy in Ireland, openly critical of the Russell ministry's rigid adherence to *laissez-faire* ideology and especially the use of public works as a means of relief. By their refusing to interfere in the market and to provide food at low prices they were responsible for 'most, if not all, of the suffering in which Ireland is now paying the penalty of the adherence of the present ministry, not to doctrines of political economy, but to an utterly mistaken application of them'.[11] This policy was ill judged, as was the emergence of party politics when it came to formulating policies for Ireland, with some British Conservatives even casting doubt on the extent of the suffering. Butt feared the consequences of mentions of the 'English' treasury in House of Commons debates and newspaper publicity. Surely, he ventured, it was the imperial treasury if the Union was an equal partnership; 'if the Union be not a mockery, there exists no such thing as an English treasury. The exchequer is the exchequer of the United Kingdom.'[12]

With the Union came expectations together with responsibilities. Butt's political outlook, essentially that of an Irish Tory strongly opposed to Repeal, makes such statements all the more noteworthy. He believed that the Union between Britain and Ireland must be one of partnership. He concluded that the experience of the previous year underlined the asymmetrical nature of power within the relationship.

> Irishmen were told indeed that in consenting to a Union which would make them partners with a great and opulent nation, like England, they would have all the advantages that might be expected to flow from such a Union. How are these expectations to be realized, how are the pledges to be fulfilled, if the partnership is only to be one of loss and never of profit to us? If, bearing our share of all imperial burdens—when calamity falls upon us we are to be told that we then recover our separate existence as a

nation, just so far as to disentitle us to the state assistance which any portion of the nation visited with such a calamity had a right to expect from the governing power? If Cornwall had been visited with the scenes that have desolated Cork, would similar arguments have been used? Would men have stood up and denied that Cornwall was entitled to have the whole country share this extraordinary loss?[13]

Here Butt was drawing attention to the most glaring inconsistency in British relief policy after 1846. On the one hand, Ireland was supposed to be an integral part of the wider United Kingdom; yet when it came to allocating a small portion of the huge resources of the British exchequer to assisting the country during a time of irrefutable need, its separateness came to the fore in parliamentary debates and public discussion. Indeed its distinctive conditions were the critical consideration in the formulating of specific policies that would never be contemplated for other parts of the United Kingdom. Butt concluded that if the interests of Ireland were not given greater attention by British politicians the Union was doomed.

Apart from the constitutional implications of the crisis, MacHale had other concerns: the effects of the successive famines on the moral outlook of Irish Catholics. As he correctly diagnosed, the dreadful conditions resulted in the breakdown of the basic principles underpinning any society.

> We need not remind you of the havoc made by such national or rather *political* calamities, not only on the lives, but on the virtue, the morality, and the religion of the people. There are evils which, often recurring, would defy all the influence of an apostle to heal, nay, hardly to mitigate. These would infallibly, and in spite of the efforts of the most zealous clergy, throw any civilized society into a state of disorganization. Such, almost, is the condition of society in our unfortunate country at the present moment. It threatens to fall asunder from that extreme physical privation which is wasting all our vigour.[14]

By mid-1847 there was a sense that Irish society was descending into a spiral of pauperisation, chaos and unending upheaval.

'RESCUE THE FAMISHING FROM DEATH'
Few religious groups stand out more for the sheer humanity of their efforts to help the poor than the Society of Friends.[15] The Quakers formed a Central

Relief Committee in Dublin in November 1846 and were the first private relief initiative to launch a public campaign for aid in Ireland. One of the problems they encountered was the absence of detailed information on the state of the poor, especially in parts of the west. English Quakers, such as R. Barclay Fox, William Forster and William Bennett, visited some of the most remote districts in the winter of 1846/7 and compiled detailed reports.[16] Bennett's account of his six-week tour in March and April, written as letters to his sister, during which he distributed seed and money, laid bare the shocking plight of the poor.

Bennett was less convinced than other religious observers, Catholic and Protestant, about explanations that centred on divine punishment, observing that 'before we can safely arrive at such a conclusion, we must be satisfied that human agency and legislation, individual oppressions, and social relationships have no hand in it'.[17] He emphasised the extent of poverty throughout the country but singled out the terrible conditions in the west.

> In the west it exhibits a people, not in the centre of Africa, the steppes of Asia, the backwoods of America,—not some newly discovered tribes of South Australia, or among the Polynesian Islands,—not Hottentots, Bushmen, or Esquimeaux,—neither Mahomedans nor Pagans,—but some millions of our own Christian nation at home, living in a state and condition low and degraded to a degree unheard of before in any civilized community; driven periodically to the borders of starvation; and now reduced, by a national calamity, to an exigency which all the efforts of benevolence can only mitigate, not control; and under which *absolute thousands* are not merely pining away in misery and wretchedness, but are dying like cattle off the face of the earth, from want and its kindred horrors![18]

Fox toured parts of the south and west in late March and early April 1847, inspecting localities and reporting on the conditions he encountered. He underlined the importance of the Quaker relief efforts in the interval between the end of the public works and the establishment of the soup kitchens, which required a 'prompt and liberal distribution of money'.[19]

The scenes he witnessed in some parts of the west were shocking. At Clifden, Co. Galway, 'a crowd of emaciated and cadaverous beings followed us through the street, crying for food'.[20] Unusually for a Quaker, while identifying a range of causes 'of the deep-rooted misery of Ireland'—including the conflicts between landlord and tenant, the lack of recognition of the duties of property, the 'general want of industry' and the 'want of that stimulus which characterizes the Englishman—a desire to better his condition'—Fox placed particular emphasis on the supposed national character of the Irish people.

> Undoubtedly a main cause of the backwardness of this country in the march of social improvement is to be found in the national character. Strength for endurance combines with weakness for resistance to render the Irish peasant dependent, poor, and reconciled to poverty ... For one class of these evils the pressure of famine will probably bring about its own remedy...[21]

In total, the Quakers received donations of roughly £200,000, with the greater part coming in the form of large consignments of food from the United States, the freight charges being met by the government. The call for immediate aid was met by a generous response, and food to the value of approximately £135,000 was shipped from America, arriving from April 1847 onwards.[22] The remainder was monetary donations received from Britain, the United States, Canada and also Ireland, and not only from Quakers. For a small religious denomination this was a huge amount of relief, which was put to effective use in the areas most in need.

Even though the Quakers were involved in forms of long-term relief, such as distributing seed and clothes and promoting efficient agricultural practices, they will mainly be remembered for the immediate response in establishing the famous soup kitchens from November 1846 onwards in Cork, Clonmel, Limerick, Youghal and Waterford and then throughout the country. Providing soup, or more accurately stirabout, a kind of thin porridge, was an extremely effective direct means of feeding the poor, quickly and without the need for complex arrangements. The Darby brothers of the Coalbrookdale Company in Shropshire, Quaker ironmasters, donated fifty-six large boilers. More than three hundred other boilers were supplied to local committees, along with meal and the other ingredients, such as rice to add body to the liquid, with grants sanctioned by the Central Relief Committee. A nominal charge was made for the soup and a piece of bread, though in practice it was not collected in many instances, especially in the poorer districts of the west.

The soup kitchens were very effective in feeding the poor with pre-cooked food, especially in towns, and saved thousands from starvation. A soup kitchen was established in Charles Street, West, off Ormond Quay, Dublin, which fed the poor of the city and served as a model for other initiatives. When it came to more rural districts the Quakers had few people in the locality and often relied on local agents to distribute grants sanctioned from Dublin.

Shipments from the United States from April 1847, in total nearly a hundred ships carrying almost ten thousand tons of food, were to arrive over the following twelve months. The Irish Relief Committee in New York sent roughly half the food cargoes, purchased with donations from American Quakers and other individuals.

Along with these very practical measures, the publicity generated by the Quakers was significant in drawing attention to the horrific conditions in Ireland. The philanthropic impulse that was characteristic of the Quakers brought widespread international attention to the suffering in Ireland. These Friends formed committees in American cities as well as in London and held public meetings to solicit donations. A meeting held in Washington on 17 February 1847 was addressed by the vice-president of the United States, George Dallas, and fifty members of Congress attended.[23] Seeking donations through emphasising the dreadful conditions of the Irish poor was a remarkably successful strategy.

In sharp contrast to the Protestant evangelical missionaries who operated in Ireland, no accusations of proselytising activities were ever levelled at the Quakers. They distributed food on the basis of simple need, with no regard for the religion of the applicant and no inducement to change denomination. Their work aimed simply to 'rescue the famishing from death', as the secretary of the Central Relief Committee, Jonathan Pim, bluntly described the relief effort.[24]

While the work of the Quakers is the best-known example of private relief, other organisations undertook similar philanthropic efforts. The British Association for the Relief of the Extreme Distress in Ireland and Scotland was established in London by prominent bankers, businessmen and other notables in 1846. Its committee included such luminaries in the world of finance as Thomas Baring of Baring Brothers and Lionel de Rothschild of the banking dynasty. Its public appeal raised £470,000 in donations, mainly from England, with roughly five-sixths going to Ireland and the remainder to the Scottish Highlands, which also experienced a failure of the potato crop in 1846. At the head of the list of subscribers was Queen Victoria, with a donation of £2,000. Her initial donation of £1,000 was doubled when the secretary of the association, Stephen Spring Rice, the son of Lord Monteagle, who served in the Board of Customs, wrote to a government minister to say that 'it wasn't enough'.[25] Other members of the royal family and government ministers, including Russell, made smaller donations.[26]

A story circulated shortly afterwards that a diplomatic incident was avoided when the Sultan of Turkey apparently offered to donate £10,000, five times what the queen had pledged, and to send shiploads of food. Sultan Abdül-Mecid was persuaded to give the lower amount of £1,000 so as not to embarrass the monarch in whose realm the people were starving.[27] Whether this is true or not is another matter, yet the sultan's generous donation attracted much positive newspaper publicity and emphasised the international aspect of Irish famine relief.[28] The queen also issued a public letter, to be read in all Protestant churches in January 1847, calling for donations. A royal proclamation two months later, on 24 March 1847, of a national day of fast throughout the United Kingdom generated another £170,000 for relief.[29] Local committees established in towns and cities in England and Wales also collected funds, which were placed at the disposal of the British Relief Association.

When it came to distributing the funds the association adopted a fairly similar procedure to that of the Society of Friends, using local agents to decide on those areas that were in most severe need. Unlike the Quakers, however, the British Relief Association relied heavily on the Treasury, especially on Trevelyan, for guidance on how the relief should be distributed.[30] Twelve agents worked for the association in Ireland, including the Polish-born explorer of Australia Paul Edmund de Strzelecki, known as 'the Count'.[31] At first Strzelecki had responsibility for Cos. Mayo, Donegal and Sligo, some of the worst-affected areas. His confidential reports to the committee in London chronicled the descent of this region into complete starvation during the spring of 1847. In January he described the conditions and the effect on the outlook of the poor in the districts of Ballina, Foxford, Swinford and Castlebar:

The population seems as if paralyzed, and helpless, more ragged and squalid; here fearfully dejected, there stoically resigned to death; then, again, as if conscious of some greater forthcoming evil, they are deserting their hearths and families. The examination of some individual cases of distress showed most heart-breaking instances of human misery, and of the degree to which that misery can be bought. Of the fate, gloomy and awful, which overhangs the whole population, that of the poor children, and the babies at the breast of their emaciated and enervated mothers, excites the highest feelings of commiseration.[32]

By mid-March profound shock was characteristic of his reports. Writing from Westport, he informs the committee of the unimaginable plight of the poor:

No pen can describe the distress by which I am surrounded. It has actually reached such degree of lamentable extremes, that it becomes above the power of exaggeration and misrepresentation. You now believe anything which you hear and read, because what I actually see surpasses what I ever read of past and present calamities.[33]

A month later he came across five bodies lying in the street in Boyle, Co. Roscommon. This appalling vista 'created no sensation among its inhabitants!'[34] The normal conventions of a civilised society had broken down completely by this time as the dying were left to fend for themselves.

Despite the best efforts of Strzelecki and the other agents, a criticism of the activities of the British Relief Association is that its efforts were too closely modelled on the government's operations. Strzelecki, like the other agents in Ireland, worked closely with Poor Law and government officials to decide where the need was most severe. Originally the committee wished only to distribute food, but monetary donations were advanced in cases of extreme hardship to Poor Law unions that were unable to cope. The principal activity was the distribution of food purchased in London at depots along the western coast of the county, as well as giving seed, clothing and other necessities.

Other smaller charitable groups, based primarily in Dublin, such as the General Central Relief Committee for All Ireland and the Irish Relief Association for the Destitute Peasantry, received monetary donations from the United States, Canada, India, Australia, South Africa and South America.[35] Various regiments of the British army serving in parts of the empire also contributed to these committees. The first major donation, of nearly £14,000, came from India in 1846. Elizabeth Smith's father, Sir John Grant, had organised a meeting in Calcutta in January 1846. An Indian Relief Fund established in Ireland, its trustees including the Duke of Leinster and the Catholic and Protestant Archbishops of Dublin, collected money from throughout India as well as elsewhere.[36]

The relief effort for Ireland in 1846 and 1847 was a truly international one, undoubtedly causing some embarrassment to British politicians, as it seemed to undermine notions of that country's great economic and political power.

One little-known incident that demonstrates the international awareness of the crisis was a bill proposed in the United States Senate by Senator John Crittenden at the end of February 1847 requesting that $500,000 in relief be sent to Ireland. Appealing to his fellow-members, he asked: 'Can you imagine any moral spectacle more sublime than that of one nation holding out that hand which is full of plenty to the suffering people of another country?'[37] The bill passed the Senate and was sent to the House of Representatives, where it was discussed in the Ways and Means Committee, as there were concerns about the constitutionality of sending relief to another country. It was known that the president, James K. Polk, would veto the measure if it passed, as he had concluded that the principal objection 'was the want of constitutional power to appropriate money of the public to charities at home or abroad'.[38] Despite these reservations, Polk reflected in his diary that while Congress had not got the power to use public money for this purpose, 'I have all the sympathy for the oppressed Irish', and he had recently given a donation for Irish famine relief. In the event, the bill did not pass the House of Representatives and he did not need to use his veto.

BEYOND ALL HUMAN POWER

Charles Trevelyan started off 1847 in much the same way that he had ended the previous year, knee-deep in the co-ordination of Irish relief. Reports from all quarters of increasing numbers of deaths around the country between January and February 1847 added to the already considerable pressure on the administrative machinery. Working extremely long hours to deal with the correspondence from Ireland, he despatched his young family to Brighton in February so that he could devote all his energy to his duties.[39]

Trevelyan took great personal pride in his dominant role in Irish famine relief. This was in part a reflection of his judgement of the correctness of the policies being followed but also sheer hubris. In the midst of the famine he meticulously prepared all the correspondence for publication in Blue Books (reports presented to Parliament). Other officials were consulted, the cabinet and the Irish executive vetted drafts, extensive editing was undertaken, and Trevelyan's brother-in-law Macaulay also read drafts. Some politicians and officials did not wish to have their correspondence exposed to public scrutiny. Naturally, Trevelyan believed that the Blue Books were a monument to the rectitude of government policy in which he played such a pivotal part and, unlike others, he sought, sometimes unsuccessfully, to publish the full official record, warts and all.[40] A further consideration was that the Blue Books demonstrated that the relief policy was a judicious use of public money, countering claims of extravagance and misappropriation. It is ironic, then, that this vast cache of letters, memoranda and statistical tables was used so extensively by later historians to expose the shortcomings of the misguided and woefully inadequate official policies. There is also some value in the acerbic remark of the historian of the famine Canon John O'Rourke, who published his account in 1875, in which he stated, echoing Mitchel, that had all the Blue Books 'contained some of the nutritive qualities which go to sustain human life, they would have an appreciable contribution towards feeding the starving Irish people during the Famine'.[41]

Trevelyan was certainly touched by the little incidents that acknowledged his centrality, whether this was the young man who walked up to him in the street and gave him a donation of a sovereign after not putting enough on the church plate at the time of the queen's letter or Lord John Russell forwarding what was apparently a personal donation of £1,240, to be used at Trevelyan's discretion for relief.[42]

After much delay the food depots in the west were opened in January 1847, but ensuring the transport and delivery of adequate supplies occupied a considerable portion of Trevelyan's energy. The reluctance to open the depots was not simply due to Trevelyan's usual caution: the problem was that the depots were virtually empty; and, despite his efforts rather late in the year to secure supplies on the Continent, the fate of the Irish poor rested largely on orders for American maize that would take until at least February to arrive. As usual, he was involved in the minutiae of the arrangements, issuing detailed instructions to Commissariat officials, offering both encouragement and censorious comments as he saw fit, especially to officials, and even concerning himself with ordering boilers for soup kitchens.

Such was the frequency of his contact with Routh, head of the Commissariat, that on one occasion, clearly an exceptional occurrence as far as Routh was concerned, he wrote: 'I have no letter from you today'.[43] He could be blunt with Routh, as they had a close working relationship, forged during those stressful times. He reprimanded him, for instance, for attending social functions in Dublin, which would send out the wrong message about the circumstances of the poor who were suffering and dying. Harshly, he told Routh that there was 'a sort of impropriety in yr. appearing in public on such occasions while the lives of such multitudes of people are dependent on yr. unremitting exertions'.[44] He also reminded him of the delicate balancing act required when it came to relief policies in Ireland: 'We are obliged to show two faces, one to show that we have done enough,—the other to show that we have not done too much'.[45]

Such views were later echoed by Lord Clarendon, who became lord lieutenant after the death of Lord Bessborough in May 1847. 'We shall be equally blamed for keeping them alive or letting them die, and we have only to select between the censure of the economists or the philanthropists', Clarendon confided to Russell after he had been installed for less than two months in the Viceregal Lodge.[46]

What Trevelyan described as the Janus-faced nature of relief policies under the Whigs exposes the ultimately irreconcilable tension at the heart of the British-Irish relationship in the 1840s, which had catastrophic consequences for at least 4 million people in Ireland. In common with his political masters, the chancellor of the exchequer, Sir Charles Wood, and ultimately Russell, Trevelyan had a basic humanitarian concern to do as much as possible to assist the Irish poor, whose main source of food was destroyed; in his own words, the 'evil to be remedied is a *scarcity of food*'.[47] The conflicts arose about how this should be done, who should take the ultimate responsibility for feeding the poor, and whence it should be paid, without causing long-term negative consequences for Ireland and within the United Kingdom more generally. Trevelyan vigorously opposed the distribution of money, fearing both abuse and shooting up the price of food. If both the government and private relief organisations sent supplies, however, 'the evil is acted upon in a direct and effectual manner by increasing the abundance and cheapness of food'.[48]

Trevelyan's role in promoting the work of the British Relief Association allowed him to direct the efforts of the organisation towards the areas most in need of a supply of food. It is clear now that throughout 1847 and into the first half of 1848 he played a vital role both in the establishment of the association and in directing its activities, in tandem with the official machinery. Unlike exchequer resources, which were subject to close public scrutiny, charitable donations were flexible and did not need to meet the rigorous demands of parliamentary supervision. They had the added benefit that, for those ideologically opposed to widespread state intervention, philanthropic activity was firmly based both in scriptural orthodoxy and in the Protestant-evangelical world view.[49] Trevelyan was a prime mover in the promotion of the queen's letter exhorting her subjects to give generously to the British Relief Association, though he was aware of the extent of anti-Irish prejudice, which he thought would be lessened when 'further horrifying accounts are received'.[50]

Within British government circles there were all sorts of views, some informed, others based on simple prejudice, about the correct course of action to be followed. The Tories were split between protectionists, led by Lord George Bentinck, and supporters of the former prime minister, Peel. Bentinck was openly critical of the Whigs' policies, declaring in January 1847 that in the face of such a crisis the rules of political economy no longer applied and that the government should do everything within its power to provide food.[51] In February 1847 he proposed an ambitious scheme of railway construction in Ireland, involving the advance of £16 million in loans, to stimulate employment and economic development, which was defeated by a combination of Whig, Peelite and some of his own protectionist supporters.[52] Bentinck's plan would have required a massive investment of capital by the exchequer, which many thought was more properly the business of private investors. While Peel had divergent views from the Russell ministry on specific points, such as the granting of loans rather than simple expenditure, more broadly he supported the government's policy in Ireland. There is little hard evidence that had he remained in office he would have acted very differently.[53] That said, Peel's achievements usually arose from decision-making prompted by immediate evidence, not long-term convictions.

Within the Whig ministry a divergence of views existed about the appropriate degree of intervention.[54] The moralists, who baulked at interventionist policies, included the chancellor of the exchequer, Wood, the home secretary, Sir George Grey, and the colonial secretary, Earl Grey, all ably supported by Trevelyan.

The chasm between Dublin and London became wider during late 1846 and into 1847 as Lord Bessborough, lord lieutenant until May 1847, and Henry Labouchere, chief secretary for Ireland until July 1847, had an altogether more immediate sense of the calamity and demanded urgent action from London. Prominent Irish Whig landlords, such as Lords Lansdowne (lord president of the council), Palmerston (foreign secretary), Monteagle and Clanricarde, sought to influence Irish policy. These landowners were a powerful if disparate lobby who, in the words of Russell's biographer, acted as a 'stranglehold upon Lord John in his own cabinet'.[55] For his own part there was no doubting that Russell's instinct was to encourage a wholesale transformation of Irish society, but his particular target was negligent Irish landlords.[56]

And beyond the immediate hothouse of Westminster there was the thorny question of British public opinion. How would money devoted to Irish famine relief be viewed by the good citizens of the neighbouring island? Influential moulders of middle-class opinion, such as the *Times*, long held forthright opinions on the proper course of action in relation to Ireland. Reflecting the views of Trevelyan and others, they believed that the blight was a judgement on the inherent evils of Irish society.[57] For the *Times* it was Irish landlords who were most deserving of public censure, as they had neglected their duty to their tenants. Much of the coverage in the *Times* was laced with undertones of anti-Irish and anti-Catholic prejudice, but it did at least accept that relief should be given, though limited and heavily circumscribed.

Thus there was a range of competing concerns for Russell when he announced a new set of policies in January 1847. The public works were to be wound down. As a means of relief they were both ineffective and costly, and an administrative quagmire. From October 1846 the number had risen dramatically as conditions worsened. By December almost half a million people were employed and in March 1847 three-quarters of a million were receiving payments, supporting roughly another 3½ million people.[58] In the spring of 1847, therefore, slightly less than half the population were receiving some kind of assistance through the public works scheme. One of the unforeseen effects of the scheme was that smallholders often neglected the cultivation of their own plots while they were employed elsewhere. Over the harsh winter many of the poor were unable to get employment on the public works, and even when they did get a ticket the reprehensibly low wages were barely sufficient to support an individual, let alone a family, as prices rose. The result was mass deaths. Almost everybody acknowledged that the public works were a complete failure—including Trevelyan, even if he described them as a 'partial failure'—with disastrous consequences.[59]

Public works were to be replaced with outdoor relief (i.e. outside the workhouses) in the form of soup kitchens, based broadly on the lines of those run by the Quakers, which would be established to feed the starving from March 1847. An underlying motive no doubt was that soup kitchens were easily dispensed with when it was considered prudent to do so. Trevelyan had always favoured the direct feeding of the poor and took some pride later in the whole operation: 'Neither ancient nor modern history can furnish a parallel to the fact that upwards of three millions of persons were fed every day in the neighbourhood of their own homes'.[60] An attraction from his point of view was that, unlike the public works, the scope for abuse was limited and only those most in need would obtain food. Nevertheless, when it was assumed that the government would be directly involved in feeding the poor, Trevelyan wrote to Routh in Dublin to point out that 'it is not intended that the government should itself undertake the task of feeding the people through its own officers, but that it should organise the upper and middle classes of society for this purpose'.[61] Relief committees, as well as Poor Law guardians, would take the lead in organising the soup kitchens, with financial assistance from the government where needed. As with the earlier relief measures, the emphasis was on the initiative being taken by the landlords, gentry and other members of relief committees. A new temporary Relief Commission was established, with the inspector-general of fortifications, Sir John Fox Burgoyne, as chairman, which oversaw the operation throughout the country and provided funds to committees and Poor Law unions for the purchase of food when necessary.

The hiatus between the winding down of the public works and the establishment of fully functioning soup kitchens led to more deaths. Board of Works officials were pressured to bring the schemes to an expeditious close to limit the costs, but this was almost impossible to do until such time as the alternative mechanism was operating. The soup kitchens demanded extensive local arrangements and a supply of food for cooking, which took months to organise, as new committees had to be constituted in each district. By May 1847 most of the committees were in operation and three-quarters of a million free rations were issued. In August 1847 more than 3 million people received a daily ration of food.[62]

On the whole, when they were operating fully by the summer of 1847 the soup kitchens were a very successful means of feeding the poor. The large amounts of food imports arriving from February enabled local committees to buy supplies and to distribute daily rations, usually without any charge. As with all universal schemes that existed around the country, there was considerable local discretion about who was entitled to a ration card, and some committees were more stringent than others in the enforcement of regulations.

Nevertheless, even with the obvious success of the soup kitchens, by the spring of 1847 years of malnutrition began to take their toll in another way: famine fever. Actual starvation is rarely the main cause of death during a time of famine.[63] Starvation, which arises from a lack of adequate nutrition, results in a slow and painful death, as muscle wasting occurs and the main organs degenerate, leading to diarrhoea and ultimately heart failure. In children the signs were to be seen in the prematurely aged faces, with sunken eyes that were described so graphically by many observers in the late 1840s.[64] Most victims, however, are killed by infectious diseases, which spread quickly when people are moving about in search of food or relief in unhygienic conditions and exposed to a range of new threats.

What was commonly referred to as fever included relapsing fever and typhus.[65] Changes in what people eat can also cause fatal digestive disorders, especially in a society in which eating potatoes was the norm and they are then forced to consume maize, sometimes with little knowledge about how to prepare it.

Lastly, as victims become weaker through lack of food, basic hygiene is neglected, and 'dirt diseases' spread. The principal killers in Ireland were fever, dysentery and consumption (pulmonary tuberculosis). The outbreak of a cholera epidemic in late 1848 added to the general misery. Contagious diseases rarely respect social class divisions: throughout the famine the middle classes, especially doctors, Catholic and Protestant clergy and any officials who had contact with the poor also succumbed to fever and died.[66]

THE STATE OF IRELAND
Speaking in the House of Commons in a debate on the 'state of Ireland' in late January 1847, Lord John Russell referred to an address signed by the Marquis of Sligo and George H. Moore, two prominent Co. Sligo landlords, that urged people to petition Parliament to make available a supply of food. He poured scorn on the proposal and said he was

> astonished that at a time like this, men of education—men who seek to relieve their countrymen from the difficulties which encompass them, should tell them to demand from Parliament, such steps as may be necessary for an immediate, a constant, and a cheap supply of food.[67]

He outlined what he thought were the limitations placed on the role of any government:

> This is a task which is impossible for us—a task which they ought to tell their countrymen the destitution under which they are suffering has made impossible for man—a task which is beyond all human power; and that all that we can possibly do is in some measure to alleviate the existing distress—somewhat to lighten the dreadful calamity which afflicts them;

and it is their duty to say to these people, 'You are not to imagine that the Government can turn scarcity and even famine into plenty.'[68]

This is a revealing justification of the Whig ministry's policy in Ireland: the responsibility of the state was 'somewhat to lighten the dreadful calamity' rather than to feed the people. This was expected to occur through self-help and charity.

But even this charity was conditional, and by late 1847 sympathy for the plight of the starving in Ireland had waned in Britain. This was explained by the commercial depression that took hold in 1847 but also by feelings of Irish ingratitude as agrarian violence increased and prominent figures, such as MacHale, were more vocal in their critique of the government's efforts.

Chapter 8 ~

PROPERTY AND POVERTY

The Treasury have been quite delighted with the whole conduct of the Highland proprietor in the present crisis— that it was a source of positive pleasure to them to turn from the Irish to the Scotch case—in the former, every thing both with regard to the people and proprietors is sickening and disgusting.[1] *(Charles E. Trevelyan)*

T he potato crop failed in the Scottish Highlands in 1846, causing widespread destitution in some of the poorest regions of the United Kingdom in what became known as the Great Highland Famine. Parts of the western Highlands had a very similar rural economy to that of the west of Ireland, based on the potato and subsistence farming by cottars. Unlike Ireland, though, mass deaths from famine-related causes did not occur. With a combination of measures initiated and organised by Highland landlords and the Free Church of Scotland, a disaster like the one that befell Ireland was averted.

Charles Trevelyan, writing in April 1847 to an agent of John Campbell, Marquis of Breadalbane, a Scottish landlord, was clear about the critical difference in the responses of the elites: the Highland proprietors acted quickly and decisively to avert starvation by taking responsibility for the plight of their tenants, whereas the same could not be said for Irish landlords. A year later he wrote to a relief official in Edinburgh:

There is this important difference in the proprietors and larger class of Farmers, that in Ireland the general disposition of these classes is to do nothing while in Scotland they are disposed to do what is in their power … If Skye were in the west of Ireland, the people would be left to starve in helpless idleness.[2]

No group emerged so badly from the events of the 1840s as the ten thousand or so Irish landlords, who are usually cast as the villains of these tragic years. British politicians, administrators and the press chastised them for their lack of initiative and their indolence; nationalists held them responsible for mass deaths, brutal clearances and evictions; and almost everybody was shocked by the degree of callousness displayed when it came to the well-being of their tenants. Nevertheless the historical record is more complex: some landlords went to extraordinary lengths to assist their tenants, others did little or nothing; and the actions of the great majority lay somewhere in between.

'I DO WHAT I CONSIDERED ONLY MY DUTY'

From the early days of the potato failure, landlords were to occupy a central role in the plethora of official relief measures. A landlord was assumed to have a paternalist concern for tenants that went beyond a simple economic transaction by acting to protect their interests. The members of this elite were political representatives and Poor Law guardians as well as landed proprietors. A significant number of Irish landlords, roughly a third, were absentees. These came in for the fiercest opprobrium, although again the record is more mixed. The expectation was that, within a district, landlords would take on two related responsibilities: organising the relief effort, through taking the lead in establishing and overseeing the activities of local relief committees, and, most importantly, meeting the costs, both as ratepayers within Poor Law unions and subscribers, albeit with matching government funds in some instances. All this appeared straightforward enough in principle; the reality, however, was very different.

The first issue that arose was a lack of will on the part of some landlords to act as leaders of their communities. It was assumed that, as the local elite, they would energetically take the lead in the formation of relief committees; and most did, either personally or through agents. As the relief committees were largely dependent on subscriptions, landlords should contribute generously, setting an example to the larger tenant-farmers and members of the middle classes. They were a pivotal component of the public works schemes initiated by both Peel and Russell. Prominent landlords also took on what can be described as an advocacy function, bringing destitution to the attention of either the administration in Dublin or the government in London. Hundreds of relief committees on which landlords or their representatives sat were established around the country from November 1845 onwards and, despite the extraordinary demand for assistance, worked reasonably well.

Where these committees were not formed or, for one reason or another, failed to function effectively the consequences were disastrous. Such circumstances existed in west Cork in February 1847. A Royal Navy captain delivering a cargo of meal to Skull reported that three-quarters of the inhabitants of the town 'were reduced to mere skeletons.'³ Dr Robert Traill, Church of Ireland rector and chairman of the local relief committee, who was to lose his own life from fever in April 1847, brought the captain around his parish to visit the cabins of the poor and dying. The captain was shocked by what he found: the dead were left unburied in their homes where they had perished, people were dying from malnutrition and fever in almost every cabin, and there were reports of dogs and rats eating corpses. The shaken officer observed that 'never in my life have I seen such wholesale misery, nor could I have thought it so complete'.⁴ Another sailor who went ashore at Skull was horrified at the scenes he witnessed: dead babies lying on their mothers' lifeless bodies, and people who threw themselves 'on their knees before us, holding up their dead infants to our sight'.⁵

The American philanthropist Elihu Burritt visited Skibbereen in February 1847 and described the appearance of the children in nearby Castlehaven.

No words can describe this peculiar appearance of the famished children. Never have I seen such bright, blue, clear eyes looking so steadfastly at nothing. I could almost fancy that the angels of God had been sent to unseal the vision of these little patient, perishing creatures, to the beatitudes of another world; and that they were listening to the whispers of unseen spirits bidding them to 'wait a little longer'.⁶

Another report from the nearby parish of Caheragh was equally horrific. The half-buried bodies of a mother and her children were eaten by dogs, and bodies of people who had died over a fortnight previously were left where they expired. No wonder the rector of Caheragh, the Rev. Francis Webb, asked in a public letter to a newspaper describing the apocalyptic scenes, 'Are we living in a portion of the United Kingdom?'⁷

Trevelyan's immediate response was to write to the Relief Commission in Dublin, instructing that efficient local relief committees be established in Skull and Caheragh.⁸ But these were wasted words. Resident landlords and gentry were few in this district. It was impossible for members of the relief committees, always stretched to their limits, to take the lead in ensuring that the dead were buried and providing food for the living and care for the ill. In west Cork the famine hit particularly hard, and the poor died in their thousands, despite the best efforts of members of several relief committees. It was left primarily to the active clergy, Catholic and Protestant, to help the poor. The sheer scale of the disaster in this district demanded exceptional assistance from the government, which was not forthcoming.[9]

When landlords did take the initiative and assumed responsibility for their tenants and others in the locality, this could make an appreciable difference. A well-known example is that of Sir Robert Gore Booth of Lissadell House, Drumcliff, Co. Sligo, one of the largest landlords in the county. He was a member of the board of guardians of Sligo Poor Law union and chairman of four local relief committees and also chaired the Sligo Grand Jury, which at its presentment sessions decided which public works were to be initiated.[10] He also purchased food for sale at cost price, set up soup kitchens, and assisted the tenants on neighbouring estates, including those of Lord Palmerston, the foreign secretary, at Ahamlish, along the north Sligo coast, who were starving. Lord Palmerston was an improving landlord, who supposedly cared for his tenants, even if the day-to-day care of the estate was left to his Dublin agents, Stewart and Kincaird.

After an initial lethargic response, by January 1847 food imports and soup kitchens came into operation, helping to relieve the destitute on Lord Palmerston's lands.[11] Nevertheless by the spring of 1847 he had concluded that the only permanent solution to the destitution of his tenants was the much more drastic course of assisting them to emigrate to North America.

When they came to public knowledge, Gore Booth was reluctant to publicise his activities. He wrote that 'I do what I considered only my duty, and I have at all times endeavoured to do the same, therefore I do not wish nor care to be vindicated in any way as an Irish landlord'.[12] A Board of Works official described Gore Booth as a saviour to his tenants. Like other caring and humane landlords, he was unstinting in his efforts to help the poor and destitute.

Another conscientious landlord who was prepared to risk everything for his tenants was John Hamilton of St Ernan's, Donegal.[13] Elizabeth and Mary Isabella Oliver Gascoigne, who had inherited their parents' large estate at Kilfinnane, Co. Limerick, and were in the process of building what became Castle Oliver, ensured that the locality had no need for public works. It was reported in March 1847 that they gave employment to the able-bodied and help to the ill, had bread made and distributed locally, employed male labourers on improvements and local women on spinning and weaving.

R. Barclay Fox, who learnt of their activities, observed that they served 'to show what might be done by landlords in their districts'.[14]

Many worked quietly and without fanfare to help their tenants and their locality. An example of such low-key efforts was the activities of a Catholic landed family, the Butlers of Ballyslatteen, near Golden, Co. Tipperary. Richard Butler took the lead in establishing a meal fund and collected subscriptions from the landlords and large tenant-farmers in the district. Golden was a particularly prosperous part of the county, and the funds collected were used to purchase meal for sale at cost price to those most in need.[15] This was precisely the sort of local initiative that the government wished to encourage; whether it occurred or not was up to individuals. For every landlord like Gore Booth or Butler there was another one who lacked basic humanitarian concern for his tenants, such as Colonel Crofton Vandeleur of Kilrush, Co. Clare. Inevitably it was those who completely neglected their tenants, the indolent landlords, or those on the other hand who actively engaged in a systematic policy of large-scale evictions, who attracted most public scrutiny.

This reliance on local elites created a patchwork of relief, with a large degree of variation according to the circumstances in a particular Poor Law union or district. This resulted in some huge disparities in the conditions of the poor, sometimes in the same areas but with different landlords. The apparent indifference of absentee or uninterested landlords could leave the poor on the edge of starvation.[16] Where this principle unravelled was in the remoter regions of the west and north-west, as resident landlords and gentry were thin on the ground. This was a universal problem throughout the country. Agents for the British Relief Association constantly complained about the absence of prominent individuals to take the lead in organising energetic relief committees. In many places the leaders by default became the clergy, the Catholic priests and Protestant ministers.[17]

IRISH PROPERTY AND IRISH POVERTY

Throughout the early years of the famine the Poor Law system, financed wholly by local ratepayers, played a secondary role to the public works, which were the main mechanism for relief. Deep-rooted antipathy against entering the workhouse ensured that only the most desperate submitted to the harsh conditions endured by inmates. By late 1846, however, the numbers admitted began to rise as the painful inadequacies of the public works pushed more and more people into destitution. By February 1847 the workhouses were full.[18] A number of Poor Law unions in the west and south struggled to meet the costs of the extraordinary demand for assistance. Though explicitly prohibited by legislation, faced with crowds of starving people the boards of guardians in some unions gave outdoor relief in the form of basic meals in the harsh winter of 1846/7.

The government sought to keep the temporary relief measures and the permanent Poor Law system separate, fearing that any overlap would result in the exchequer, rather than ratepayers, footing the mounting bill for the workhouses. In reality, where other mechanisms failed or were inadequate the burden fell on the Poor Law union, causing severe crises in the areas hardest hit.

In the set of proposals announced by Russell in January 1847 the Irish Poor Law was to be amended to grant relief to the old, sick, widows and orphans. Outdoor relief was permitted to what were described as the 'able-bodied poor' in certain circumstances, but only when the workhouse was full. Otherwise the test of destitution, that is, admission to the workhouse, would still apply. Ratepayers, including landlords and tenant-farmers, wanted the disincentives to seek relief from the Poor Law union to be strong, not least to keep down the costs. Underlying this reversal of the fear that outdoor relief would create an indolent Irish population were long-standing objectives: the transfer of permanent financial responsibility from the Treasury to the Irish propertied classes and the gradual winding down of what were described as 'temporary' relief measures. The widespread perception was that the amended Poor Law would begin the painful process of the wholesale transformation of Irish society, and there was no other way of doing this 'except through a purgatory of misery and starvation', in the words of Sir Charles Wood, chancellor of the exchequer, writing to Lord Clarendon, the new lord lieutenant, in July 1847.[19]

The Poor Relief (Ireland) Act was passed in June 1847, and a separate Poor Law Commission for Ireland was established a month later.[20] During the debates on the bill in Parliament and in the newspaper coverage in the preceding months Irish landlords were frequently attacked for their negligence. The maxim that 'Irish property must pay for Irish poverty' was constantly invoked to justify making assistance a local rather than a national charge. Landlords were blamed for endemic poverty, or, as the *Times* put it more succinctly in March 1847, they were 'the old original pauper of Ireland'.[21] Press reports of heartless evictions merely added to the general opprobrium heaped on them. They were seen as living extravagantly and beyond their means, resulting in mounting indebtedness as their tenants starved. Landlords had singularly failed to meet their responsibilities, and only legal compulsion would require them to do so. According to the *Times* in April 1847, the Irish landlords were 'a class without social humanity, without legal obligation, without natural shame'.[22]

Even more repulsive to middle-class British sensibilities were the constant demands for assistance from the Treasury to meet the costs of relief in Ireland. One Scottish radical MP, Archibald Hastie, declared in the House of Commons in February 1847 that they were a group of people who 'had done nothing but sit down and howl for English money'.[23] The human consequences of large-scale evictions were beginning to be felt in Britain. Thousands of refugees from famine arrived in Liverpool and other ports from early 1847, often in a deplorable physical state. The municipal authorities in those cities were required to care for the destitute and those in need, as Irish landlords shifted the financial burden of relief to English, Welsh and Scottish ratepayers.[24]

These views chimed with those of Russell and other members of his ministry. Russell's long-standing antipathy towards Irish landlords was well known. Getting the bill through Parliament proved a struggle; as Lord Bessborough, the lord lieutenant, had predicted, it was 'the most difficult subject'.[25] And so it proved. Irish landlords and their supporters, fearing the financial obligations of the outdoor relief and the higher rates this would involve, mounted a rearguard action to have tenants rather than owners liable. They claimed that landlords would be ruined. Lord Lansdowne, a close political ally of Russell who held almost 100,000 acres in Co. Kerry but had last visited his estate in 1840, warned against granting outdoor relief and advocated instead concessions to landlords.[26] Rates were levied equally on landowners and tenants on holdings with a rateable valuation of more than £4; landlords were liable for rates on smaller holders.[27]

William Gregory, heir to the family estate at Coole Park, near Gort, Co. Galway, a Tory MP for Dublin and supporter of Peel, successfully proposed an amendment to the legislation in March 1847. This would require that any person occupying a quarter of an acre of land or more would not be entitled to relief from the Poor Law union. Some members of Parliament, such as the radical George Poulett Scrope, recognised that this would be used to clear small farmers from estates throughout Ireland.[28] When challenged about the wholesale devastation that it would unleash, Gregory's logic was brutal:

Many honourable members insist that the operation of a clause of this kind would destroy all the small farmers. If it could have such an effect, I do not see of what use such small farmers could possibly be.[29]

To receive any relief from the Poor Law union, small farmers would be required to surrender the tiny plots upon which they barely survived. What came to be known as the Gregory clause, or quarter-acre clause, was one of the most draconian measures ever passed by a British Parliament. Together with the requirement that landlords pay the rates for holdings valued at less than £4, it gave them a free hand in systematically clearing estates of smallholders who, by necessity, were in need of some poor relief.

When Canon John O'Rourke wrote his history of the Great Irish Famine in the early 1870s, the usually moderate timbre of his narrative was replaced by unbridled rage when it came to the Gregory clause. 'A more complete engine for the slaughter and expatriation of a people was never designed', was how he described the clause.[30] Gregory would earn his place in Irish history, according to O'Rourke, if for all the wrong reasons: 'Mr. Gregory's words— the words of a liberal, and a pretended friend of the people—and Mr. Gregory's clause are things that should be for ever remembered by the descendants of the slaughtered and expatriated small farmers of Ireland'.[31]

Only a handful of MPs opposed the clause, including Scrope and a pitiful showing of Irish representatives. It is no small irony that the name of the future aged husband of one of the leading lights in the Irish cultural revival at the beginning of the twentieth century, Lady Augusta Gregory, was associated with this inhumane and hugely destructive measure.[32]

The bursting of the railway 'bubble' in 1847 and a run on the reserves of the Bank of England created a severe financial crisis that heightened insecurity, and Ireland's plight had to take second place to a commercial and financial crisis that gripped Britain. Any further government expenditure for famine relief in Ireland would be difficult to secure. When it became clear in October 1847, just as the financial crisis was deepening, that no further money would be available, Lord Clarendon wrote in desperation to Russell to urge him to make allowance for insolvent Poor Law unions: 'Ireland cannot be left to her own resources'.[33]

Russell's antipathy towards Irish landlords was reflected in another set of measures introduced in 1848 and 1849 to deal with insolvent owners and to replace them with a new class of capitalists, mostly from Britain, able and willing to spend money on improving their estates. A revised system introduced under the Encumbered Estates Act (1849) allowed for creditors to petition a court for the sale of estates heavily in debt.[34] Despite what had been anticipated by Russell and others, the influx of British capitalists never materialised. Most of the purchases were made by gentry and landlords who already had properties in Ireland, some to rising Catholic finance capitalists, from pawnbrokers to bankers. Throughout the 1850s hundreds of estates were sold to new owners, many of whom engaged in a systematic programme of evictions in the early 1850s.[35]

'WE WANT NO CHARITY'

As spring turned into summer, Elizabeth Smith was hopeful of a good harvest. In 1847 the harvest was small but sound, and free of blight. On the May gale day most of the rents were paid, but she feared for the future. 'The upper class are well nigh ruined the best of us cannot recover this over-whelming calamity under many years,' she wrote in her diary. For the 'improvident, a large class,' who were 'utterly bankrupt swept from their places, they must be'.[36] Her apprehension about the future even extended to her own family, as she sensed that her only son had succumbed to the 'curse of his race': 'he can neither rouse mind nor body when the fit is on him'.

Along with many other smaller landlords she was concerned about the effect of the new relief policies. Outdoor relief, provided by the Poor Law authorities, would spell the end of the landed classes and ruin the lower orders: 'This out-door relief has put the finishing stroke to the resources of the upper classes, and the immorality of the lower—none care to work now—they are fed while idle'. She welcomed the winding up of the government soup kitchens in August 1847, as there was apparently plenty of work available locally during the harvest season for those who could earn more; for those who were unable to work the workhouse beckoned. On the estate Elizabeth pinpointed a number of the tenants 'who must be forced into the Poor House for they cannot otherwise be supported', including the Doyles, the Widow Mulligan, the Widow Quin and 'fifty more'. What annoyed her most was not the acceptance of charity but people's reluctance to enter the workhouse, regardless of their destitute state.

When it came to those who defied Elizabeth's unshakeable logic, her humanitarian instincts deserted her. The reason these people refused to go to the workhouse was that it would remove them from their ancestral homesteads, however miserable these might have seemed to Elizabeth, and entering the workhouse most probably spelt illness in addition and even death. No wonder these poor people clung with whatever little energy they had to the land. An American evangelical, Asenath Nicholson, spent most of 1847 and 1848 working to assist the poor and wrote movingly of her experiences. She described the workhouses as 'little else than charnel houses', in which the 'living, shivering skeletons that squatted upon the floors, or stood with arms folded against the wall, half-clad, with hair uncombed, hands and faces unwashed, add a horror if not terror to the sight'.[37]

The slow disintegration of commercial life also troubled Elizabeth Smith. On a visit to Dublin she was shocked by the empty houses of tradesmen and the number of shops that were shut; those that were open were deserted. In October 1847 newspapers reported the bankruptcy of cattle dealers, merchants and brokers, and the local markets were very quiet. Yet when Elizabeth attended an auction at nearby Kilbride Manor there was a large crowd of farmers 'buying as fast as the articles were put up'. This class seemed not to be suffering. The Smiths' friend William Ogle Moore, Anglican rector of Blessington and Kilbride and a local landlord, was deeply indebted, and selling off his furniture was the only recourse to help meet his burgeoning bills.

The fragile state of the Smiths' own finances was given a boost by income from Elizabeth's writings. When an issue of the short-lived *Howitt's Journal* arrived in the post in July she took understandable pride in reading her article on Irish charity.[38] Her main preoccupation, however, was placing her writings with *Chambers's Edinburgh Journal*, and she devoted a considerable portion of her time to corresponding with the editor, Robert Chambers, and making revisions to take account of his suggestions. At this time she was working on an article on another subject she knew well, a thoughtful fictional account of the life of a Highland officer, which was published later that year.[39] It was not only for the extra money, however: her 'scribblings', as she called them, provided a connection to the world beyond the mundane daily existence of Baltiboys and indeed Ireland. She clearly enjoyed both reading and writing for these journals: 'They fill the mind, exercise it, occupy it', as she said. Much of her writing was derived from acute personal observation, even if it was couched in more tactful terms than the blunt assessments confided to her private diary.

Her interest in public affairs continued apace. She tracked the visits of Queen Victoria to her beloved Scottish Highlands in September and resented the fact that it was the Duchess of Bedford, now living at the Doune, who received her at Ardverikie, rather than her own father, the laird, who was still in India. 'I grieve over this importation of Southrons, who with their gold steal from us the hearts of our followers'—a reluctant acknowledgement that the days of the great Highland lairds were past. When the queen's second letter calling for donations for Irish and Scottish famine relief was issued and a national day of thanksgiving declared on 17 October 1847, Elizabeth reacted furiously.[40] Funds were to be collected at church doors in England, and both Trevelyan and Sir John Burgoyne, a cousin of Elizabeth's whom she disliked, took the unusual and counterproductive step of writing to the press to support the appeal.

> One would suppose stones were scarce in Ireland and her rivers dry when no one hoots such drivellers out of the country. We want no charity. We want a paternal government to look a little after our interests, to legislate for us *fairly*, to spend what we should have properly among us without jobbing, to teach us, and to keep a tight rein over idleness, recklessness, apathy. It is plain these people can't do it. We must all begin and call again for Sir Robert Peel as we did some years ago, for the state of the Empire is unpromising.

The Whig ministry, and especially Russell, were particular targets for her ire. When in August 1847 the general election resulted in losses for the Liberals and the creation of a weak minority government, Elizabeth was not surprised. Russell's ministry was unpopular, and 'he has very evidently not a large capacity for his position, honest and hard-working though he be'. In Ireland, repeal candidates fared well, leading Russell to see this as sheer ingratitude. 'The Irish seem always to act in the manner most opposite to that which is usual in other countries. The expenditure of ten millions to save the People from starving has thus raised a bitter spirit of hostility.'[41] Elizabeth interpreted the shifting political landscape, in which support for Radicals in Britain was growing, in an altogether different way. The days of the *ancien régime* were numbered, as education heightened expectations, and political power based on aristocratic privilege would no longer be accepted by the rising middle classes.

> Up is heaving a force our bulwarks of mere canvass can't resist. On will come the flood and unless we can absorb it as it spreads, it will rush through and overwhelm us. 'Tis folly not to see it, not to prepare for it. But the aristocracy is blind, as the French in 1780.

TREVELYAN'S CLAW

A revolution was also on John Mitchel's mind at this time. Despite attempts at reconciliation in December 1846, the Young Irelanders stayed outside the Repeal Association. Differences remained about such central issues as O'Connell's insistence on the rejection of violence, his hatred of slavery, freedom of discussion within the association and accepting government positions. Mitchel was pleased with this outcome. He triumphantly said to his friend John Martin, 'I hope we have done with Dan for ever'.[42] Once the unsuccessful negotiations were concluded he wrote to William Smith O'Brien, the member of Parliament who was the most prominent supporter of Young Ireland and a persistent critic of the government's Irish policy, to express his satisfaction.

> I am heartily glad, as I think most of us are, that the 'Reconciliation' is all over. I never for one moment believed the proposal to be *bona fide*, (nor conceived it possible even if it were *bona fide*) to make a sound safe working Association out of the present one. There are certainly surer and wider spheres of activity preparing for us and better elements gathering around us.[43]

At this time Mitchel was recovering from a very serious illness, inflammation of the lungs, related to his chronic asthma; for a couple of days during the previous October he had been in 'considerable danger'.[44]

In early 1847 the Young Irelanders formed a new association, the Irish Confederation, which held its first meeting in Dublin on 13 January. The objectives of the body were essentially those of O'Connell's Repeal Association, 'honestly and vigorously worked out,' as Duffy later put it—in other words, repeal of the Union and self-government for Ireland.[45] Mitchel saw the landlords and gentry as essential components of any widespread movement for repeal and felt that they could 'be brought to see the error of their ways and to take their stand on the national side as the natural leaders of their people'.[46] Promising signs of a fusion of such interests were evident, such as the large meeting held in Dublin on 14 January attended by landlords, gentry and Irish MPs which issued a series of resolutions critical of government relief policy and promised a new united stand in Parliament on issues relating to Ireland.[47] While the much-hoped-for unity of an Irish parliamentary party soon unravelled, it was a symbolic moment, indicative of the crisis that the country now faced.

Mitchel was soon casting around for more radical solutions to Ireland's difficulties. He was impressed with the ideas outlined in a series of letters by James Fintan Lalor published in the *Nation*. Lalor was the son of a strong farmer in Co. Laois and former O'Connellite MP (1832–5). Michael Doheny, another Young Irelander, referred to Lalor as a 'poor, distorted, ill-favoured, hunch-backed little creature'.[48] Duffy thought him a 'most original and intense' thinker, even if his schemes often faltered when it came to the practicalities of implementing them, not helped by his abrasive personality.[49] With Mitchel he shared similar views on the landlords and gentry being central to the regeneration of Ireland, and he was opposed to O'Connell's liberalism.[50] He saw the issue of land as the 'engine' for achieving revolutionary change. What he advocated was linking agitation for wholesale land reform to political reform. In his letters to the *Nation* he argued that the famine had led to a complete dissolution of the existing social order, out of which a new one would emerge. He directly addressed Irish landlords, urging them to reach an 'accommodation and arrangement' with the occupiers of the land rather than a 'struggle', which would destroy the landed classes.[51] Tenants should be granted the right of joint ownership with landlords, as what Lalor was advocating was the 'soil of Ireland for the people of Ireland', rather than legal titles derived from the Crown. By evicting large numbers of tenants the landed classes were sowing the seeds of their own destruction.

> The landowners have adopted the purpose of depopulating the island, and are pressing it forward to their own destruction, and to ours. They are declaring that they and we can no longer live together in this land. They are enforcing self-defence on us. They are, at least, forcing on us the question of submission or resistance; and I, for one, shall give my vote for resistance.[52]

Lalor's fusing of agrarian radicalism with nationalism was iconoclastic, not least because it was a strong rejection of all that the repeal movement stood for, especially the call to arms. More detailed statements were circulated to leading members of the Irish Confederation, and Mitchel pondered the implications of Lalor's radical programme over a couple of weeks. In the first half of 1847 he still believed that the landed classes could bring about substantive change and, in doing so, become the 'most powerful aristocracy in the world'.[53] To this end he was an active member of the Irish Council from June 1847. The council aimed to develop policies that would benefit Ireland as a whole and encourage unity of purpose among benevolent landlords and gentry.[54] It turned out to be a powerless body, and unrepresentative of the landed interest.

Over the summer of 1847 Mitchel, who had taken a house in Malahide, the pretty town on the north coast of Co. Dublin, was preoccupied with his work for the Irish Council as well as writing for the *Nation*. Family members, including his beloved mother, came down from Newry to stay, and prominent figures within Young Ireland visited also. Mitchel's other concern during the summer was the general election of August 1847, in which no Confederate went forward for election, though two MPs who were broadly supportive of their programme were elected.[55] He had opposed fighting the election, believing that parliamentary politics in London were redundant during a time of widespread famine.[56] The poor results meant that Ireland rather than London should be the focus of the Confederation's activities.

> On the whole, we are all, in great measure, out of Parliament. And I can't say that I am sorry. It will force us into the policy that I have often urged, to neglect Parliament and its proceedings, and work at home.[57]

The group suffered from a backlash in the wake of O'Connell's death, as the popular view was that the rash men of Young Ireland had hastened his demise. A tasteless letter written by the radical priest John Kenyon in June 1847, shortly after O'Connell's death, published in the *Nation* merely confirmed this impression, even if the paper repudiated his vitriolic views, including the assertion that the Liberator's death was 'no loss whatever to Ireland'.[58]

On a journey to Galway to campaign for a Repeal candidate in a by-election to be won by the government's solicitor-general six months earlier Mitchel had been visibly moved by the scenes he encountered, 'sights that will never wholly leave the eyes that beheld them'.[59] He described the poor women searching the fields for turnips, the families he met along the road 'with dim, patient eyes, gazing hopelessly into infinite darkness', and groups of young men with 'a fierce but vacant scowl'. As he passed the houses of the poor it was children who epitomised the destruction caused by the famine. When he wrote about this experience later Mitchel was in no doubt where the blame lay.

> Sometimes, I could see, in front of the cottages, little children leaning against a fence when the sun shone out,—for they could not stand,—their limbs fleshless, their bodies half-naked, their faces bloated yet wrinkled, and

of a pale, greenish hue,—children who would never, it was too plain, grow up to be men and women. I saw Trevelyan's claw in the vitals of those children: his red tape would draw them to death; in his Government laboratory he had prepared for them the typhus poison.[60]

Throughout the second half of 1847 Mitchel's views were increasingly radicalised by the events unfolding around him. His critique of government policy was slowly yet surely developed in uncompromising articles in the *Nation*, in which he deplored the continued export of food, lambasted official relief efforts, and viewed the destruction of the Irish poor through hunger, emigration and death as a deliberate and calculated policy on the part of the governing elite in London.

By September that year the timidity of the Irish Council—'a mere fraud and delusion'—and the limited involvement of Irish landlords in its activities led Mitchel to conclude that action of a different nature was required.[61] Writing to O'Brien, he observed that 'the time has nearly come when affairs must take a decisive turn, either in the one way or the other. I sincerely hope it will be in the moderate direction.'[62] His revolutionary call to arms in editorials in the *Nation* suggests that moderation was far from his mind. He was a strong supporter of Lalor's proposal for a rent strike and also urged tenant-farmers to withhold poor rates in what was a campaign of civil disobedience.

The Crime and Outrage (Ireland) Bill, introduced to deal with an upsurge in agrarian crime in parts of the south and midlands and debated in Parliament in late November 1847, was yet more evidence of the true intentions of the British government and their allies, the Irish landed classes. 'From this moment, all hope that the landed gentry would stand on the side of Ireland against England, utterly vanished', Mitchel was later to say.[63] As far as he was concerned this was the last stand for the Catholic Irish peasantry, who had been misled by O'Connell into accepting passively, and without a fight, their own annihilation.[64]

Mitchel's revolutionary rhetoric meant that Duffy had to censor his articles for the *Nation*. Matters came to a head in early December when they violently disagreed about a proposal to reinvigorate the campaign for repeal using constitutional methods. Many of the other members of the Irish Confederation were shocked by the tone and ferocity of Mitchel's statements. He formally ceased to have any connection with the *Nation*, though he remained at first on good terms with Duffy. In later years they would become bitter enemies. For Mitchel, if he could not write what he truly believed there was simply no point in writing at all. He later described the turning-point in self-sacrificial terms: 'A kind of sacred wrath took possession of a few Irishmen at this period. They could endure the horrible scene no longer, and resolved to cross the path of the British car of conquest, though it should crush them to atoms.'[65]

Though he had severed his connection with the *Nation*, Mitchel remained a member of the Irish Confederation. Whether he could continue to do so while advocating physical force was another matter.

'THE CRUEL AND MERCILESS THEORIES OF POLITICAL ECONOMY'

By 1847 Ireland's plight had become an international Catholic cause. In March, Pope Pius ix, who had previously donated a sum equivalent to approximately £800, devoted an encyclical letter to an appeal for three days of prayer and the collection of funds for famine relief. Catholic congregations in Europe, North and South America, India and South Africa responded with remarkable generosity to the appeal. One estimate puts the total in donations from Catholic sources outside the United Kingdom in the region of £400,000, of which Dr Daniel Murray, Archbishop of Dublin, handled roughly £150,000. English Catholics, spurred on by the exhortations of Frederick Lucas, editor of the Catholic journal *Tablet*, who was shocked by reports emanating from Ireland, also organised an effective campaign for funds. Irish bishops in the United States were particularly energetic and at the forefront of fund-raising efforts that raised thousands of dollars for the poor in Ireland.[66] These very considerable sums were then distributed by the bishops to the clergy, according to the relative needs of a parish.

John MacHale's daily life was dominated by the disbursement of funds sent to him by Catholics, especially in Britain and the United States. MacHale later told a biographer that he spent on average ten hours each weekday from October 1846 until the end of 1847 dealing with the money he received, writing acknowledgements and distributing the money to those most in need, without the assistance of a secretary.[67] Donations arrived at St Jarlath's in Tuam from around the world, each of which was acknowledged by MacHale in a series of letters to the *Freeman's Journal* throughout 1847.[68] They ranged from small amounts from private individuals to large donations from a committee formed in Liverpool for Irish famine relief, which sent more than £2,000. American Catholic bishops also sent large amounts of money, either directly to MacHale or by way of Archbishop Crolly of Armagh. In total he received roughly £40,000 in charitable donations in 1847 and 1848.[69] Characteristically, MacHale used the public acknowledgements of this charity as an opportunity to chastise the government for allowing such a state of affairs to develop.

> What a pity that such noble charity, which in other times and circumstances, would have afforded such vast relief, is rendered almost inoperative by the cruel and merciless theories of political economy, or, what is worse than theories, the cruel and merciless practical policy that has been adopted by our incapable rulers.[70]

His practice of writing public letters to the prime minister continued throughout 1847. He reminded Russell that it was the Catholic clergy who were working to prevent the outbreak of widespread disorder in the face of almost universal hunger and starvation, and after the passing of the Crime and Outrage (Ireland) Act he implored Russell to protect not only property but 'what is far more valuable—the lives of the people', who if left reliant on the provisions of the Poor Law would starve.[71]

In his persistent and vocal criticism of the Whig ministry's policy MacHale cut a lonely figure among the Irish Catholic bishops, no others openly criticising the government before the winter of 1847. Another powerful Catholic bishop, however, John Hughes, born in Clogher, Co. Tyrone, emigrant to the United States and now Archbishop of New York, denounced British policy in Ireland in a lecture given in March 1847. Having returned to his native land in 1846, he worked tirelessly in collecting funds for famine relief.[72] He placed the famine within the framework of British involvement in Ireland over the centuries and its upholding of the rights of property above all other considerations. Hughes was contemptuous of the principle of maintaining the free market at any cost and emphasised the responsibility of a state to protect the lives of its citizens.

> Let us be careful, then, not to blaspheme Providence by calling this God's famine. Society, that great civil corporation that we call the State, is bound so long as it has the power to do so, to guard the lives of its members against being sacrificed by famine from within, as much against their being slaughtered by the enemy from without.[73]

By the autumn of 1847 a growing number of the Irish bishops were concerned about the condition of the country and the calamitous effects of government policy. In mid-October the bishops met in Dublin and drew up a detailed memorial to be presented to Lord Clarendon, the lord lieutenant. Judging by its tone and context, MacHale exercised a strong hand in the drafting, as it was openly critical of the government's measures for relieving the poor.

MacHale was part of a delegation that went to meet Lord Clarendon in October 1847. Long vilified, Lord Clarendon found MacHale 'vain and turbulent' but 'not a bad man'.[74] He then tried to engage him in an exchange of letters in which MacHale pointed to the potential for large-scale disorder if more relief was not made available.[75] Lord Clarendon proudly told Russell some months later in December 1847: 'I have had a shot at the Lion in his den'.[76] He then tried, unsuccessfully, to gain additional funds for Ireland, but none were forthcoming. 'If I could assist MacHale in relieving the people of Tuam … and could continue to communicate confidentially with him I should not despair of making him an instrument of good'.[77] Subsequent events, however, put paid to this rare outbreak of cordiality.

By late December MacHale was writing another public condemnation of Russell. He chastised him for the lack of provision for the poor and emphasised how this had been predicted by the bishops' delegation. Urgent relief was required to 'avert from society the disorganisation with which it is menaced', yet Parliament chose instead to pass coercive legislation. Evictions and destitution meant that 'the cruelties committed in Ireland on the starving people are scarcely equalled under the sun'.[78]

CONCLUSION

There was a widespread feeling by the end of 1847 that the pauperisation of Ireland had resulted in a complete breakdown of society after successive years of hunger and destitution. Many smallholders who had managed to survive, albeit in precarious circumstances, were now paupers, reliant on official relief. The country as a whole was dependent on charity and the benevolence of the government, and this had a demoralising effect. The Archbishop of Cashel, Michael Slattery, wrote to the president of St Patrick's College, Maynooth, in June 1847, denouncing the effects of the famine on the attitudes of the people.

We are still struggling with famine and fever, and what is more than both, the demoralisation of our people consequent on the system of relief that this incapable Government has inflicted on the country. Every feeling of decent spirit and of truth has vanished, and instead there is created for us a cringing lying population, a Nation of Beggars.[79]

In a speech at a meeting of the Irish Confederation in December 1847 John Mitchel expressed a similar view.

This nation ... it is not to be concealed, is lying in a most helpless and degraded condition; we have neither moral force nor physical force wherewith to right our wrongs. Our moral force has turned out a humbug—our physical force is nothing but our naked hands. We can do little but remonstrate, and strive to keep alive what manly public opinion remains amongst us, which is our only weapon.[80]

The following year Mitchel sought to counter this despondent spirit.

PART IV

Legacies

Chapter 9 ⌐

VICTORIA'S SUBJECTS

A HERO OR A MARTYR

John Mitchel's departure from the *Nation* caused a controversy within the Irish Confederation, with both Mitchel and Charles Gavan Duffy publishing the reasons for the schism. Mitchel, whose supporters were mostly the young members of the Confederate Clubs, held to his view that the policy of the Confederation should be to promote an agrarian struggle, reflecting the continued influence of James Fintan Lalor's writings, which would inevitably involve conflict with the landlords and gentry. William Smith O'Brien and Duffy were wedded to a more moderate line of constitutional agitation. Mitchel and his intimates, especially a young fellow-journalist, Thomas Devin Reilly, rejected this approach; in his words, 'the country is actually in a state of war—a war of "property" against poverty—a war of "law" against life'.[1]

What followed was a three-day debate within the Irish Confederation in early February 1848 about the methods to be employed by the organisation. All the prominent leaders spoke against Mitchel's proposals. He was defeated, and a set of resolutions, advocating the co-operation of classes, ruling out the non-payment of rents and rates and stating that 'force of opinion' should be the principal means of achieving its goals, were adopted by a considerable majority. Throughout the debates Mitchel denied that he was advocating violence but rather using 'passive resistance' over constitutional means.[2] He later modified his stance to say that what he really intended was 'to offer a passive resistance universally; but, occasionally, when opportunity served, to try the steel'.[3]

Mitchel's advocacy of non-payment of poor rates would have had disastrous consequences for those struggling to survive with meagre rations from the workhouse, placing hard-pressed Poor Law unions in even further financial difficulties. Whether the government would have stepped in to meet the shortfall in the face of considerable public opposition in Britain for further funding for Ireland is very uncertain. This proposal underlines the essential shortcoming in Mitchel's vision, identified by his opponents in the Confederation debates. His policies were based on universal principles but, unlike Lalor, he knew relatively little about the rural economy of the south and west of Ireland, especially the lives of smallholders and middling tenant-farmers. Thomas Francis Meagher declared that 'the people of Munster ... know as little of Mitchel as of Mahomet'.[4]

The wisdom of urging a peasant rebellion when there was neither support nor arms was also questioned. Such an uprising during a time of hunger and starvation would be easily defeated by a vastly superior army, with more than thirty thousand soldiers stationed in the country at the time. Mitchel was vehement about what he disliked: British rule, capitalists, landlords, liberals, and the whole nineteenth-century world in which industrialisation and materialism dominated every aspect of life.[5] Where he was less convincing was on the means that could bring about the revolution that he so desired, a criticism that was levelled at him subsequently by his former associate and future bitter enemy Duffy: 'he was not a guide whom it was possible to follow; in the main he pointed to no road which led anywhere, but he was a constant trumpet of resistance to England, and this was enough.'[6]

Mitchel was one of the worst potential organisers of a revolution, communicating his thinking to as wide a newspaper readership as possible. He saw his role as essentially that of a 'herald', preparing the ground for revolution rather than actually planning and instigating one.[7] Mitchel was no leader of people, urging them to man the barricades: his strength lay in the power of his pen. An unnamed intimate who worked closely with him in 1848 saw his role rather differently.

> He could sow the seed, but not wait for it to grow; could rouse men to action, and point out the direction they should take, but to guide their actual steps was not given him. We used to laugh at the advice given him in that '48 time by a well-meaning friend—that he should 'allow his opinions to take root before he disseminated them.' But what the friend meant was true, and needed saying. He either did not know, or could not

sufficiently bear in mind what the mass of men are, and was subject to a perpetually recurrent surprise at finding that they were not of his temper,—recurrent despair of all parties, including his own, which in turn quickly gave way before the strong necessity of action.[8]

Mitchel remained within the Confederation but was preoccupied with his own efforts to bring about this revolution through exhortation. Despite earlier indications that he would not seek to compete with the *Nation* he founded his own paper, the *United Irishman*, in February 1848. Its first issue, with a print run of five thousand, sold out quickly. Other writers included his friends John Martin, Thomas Devin Reilly and Father John Kenyon and a little-known young poet, James Clarence Mangan—'Catholics, Protestants, and Pagans, but all resolute revolutionists', as Mitchel was subsequently to say.[9] Free from the restraints of Duffy's moderating censorship, Mitchel openly preached sedition and revolution in his typical seething prose. In his inaugural editorial he declared that the purpose of the *United Irishman* was to overthrow British rule. In the form of an open letter to the lord lieutenant, Lord Clarendon, it declared: 'To educate that holy Hatred [of foreign dominion], to make it know itself, and avow itself, and, at last, fill itself full, I hereby devote the columns of the *United Irishman*'.[10] He published articles on such topics as street fighting, making barricades and drilling, from an office in Trinity Street that was a stone's throw from Dublin Castle, the centre of the British administration in Ireland. The revolution in France of February 1848 and the abdication of the King prompted him to call on the small farmers in an open letter to engage likewise in open rebellion.

> Arise from the death-dust where you have long been lying, and let this light visit your eyes also, and touch your souls. Let your ears drink in the blessed words, 'Liberty! Fraternity! Equality!' which are soon to ring from pole to pole. Clear steel will, ere long, dawn upon you in your desolate darkness; and the rolling thunder of the people's cannon will drive before it many a heavy cloud that has long hidden from you the face of heaven. Pray for that day: and preserve life and health, that you may worthily meet it. Above all, let the man amongst you who has no gun, sell his garment and buy one.[11]

The 1848 revolutions in Europe completely changed the context in which Mitchel's views were seen, suggesting that the moment for change had dawned. When he returned to a meeting of the Irish Confederation in March

1848 he was loudly cheered, and a motion he proposed that Confederate Clubs should arm themselves was passed with almost universal approval.[12] These clubs, which contained the rank-and-file members of the confederation, were always more favourably disposed towards Mitchel than the leaders who constituted the Council.

A large demonstration was held in Dublin on 20 March 1848 expressing support for the revolution in France. A deputation including O'Brien and Meagher was despatched to Paris to present an address to the people of France and to secure 'a declaration of French sympathy for Irish national claims' but received a cool response from Alphonse de Lamartine, head of the Provisional Government.[13] Intensive diplomatic efforts by the British government ensured that no public support was given to Irish nationalists, as the Anglo-French relationship was considered of more importance. Mitchel remarked in the *United Irishman* that 'we are well pleased that M. Lamartine has let us know distinctly that we must rely on ourselves'.[14]

Mitchel was now continually followed by detectives and by March was convinced that he would be arrested. O'Brien, Meagher and Mitchel, who had spoken at the Dublin demonstration, were arrested a couple of days later and charged with sedition. The case against Mitchel was based on articles in the *United Irishman*, which 'were certainly about as seditious as it was possible for language to be.'[15] Mitchel had goaded the Irish administration into arresting him, and his ambition was realised.

Lord Clarendon was increasingly concerned with the upsurge in popular radicalism and urged the cabinet to give him additional legal powers, not least because, even though the agitation was a threat, he was alarmed at 'the distress which affects all classes and which must during the next few months become immeasurably greater'.[16] Russell, for his part, suggested in March 1848 that both restrictions on the power of landlords to evict tenants and a land tax to finance the salaries of Catholic clergy, together with the suspension of *habeas corpus*, would meet the immediate threat. His cabinet colleagues were less convinced, and two Irish landlords, Lord Lansdowne and Lord Palmerston, rejected these measures. A compromise was arrived at under which a new offence of treason-felony would be introduced, allowing for the prosecution not alone of those who engaged in treason but of those also who advocated treason in public speeches. Rushed through Parliament, it became law in late April.

The cases against O'Brien and Meagher collapsed, and Lord Clarendon decided that Mitchel's earlier charges would be dropped and that he would be prosecuted under the new Treason Felony Act. On 13 May 1848, after returning home from the offices of the *United Irishman*, Mitchel had sat down to dinner with his wife, his brother William and Thomas Devin Reilly when there was a knock on the door. Two detectives entered. On seeing that Mitchel was having his dinner they apologised and waited until he had finished his meal and then brought him away to be charged and installed in Newgate Jail.

Nearly two weeks later the case was heard, and with the jury packed with government supporters to ensure a successful outcome there was little doubt about the verdict. Mitchel had retained as his defence counsel Robert Holmes, the hero of the Duffy case two years earlier, now aged eighty-two. Holmes concentrated his case not on whether Mitchel had engaged in sedition but on the right of people to resist an unjust government, as was the case in Ireland.

On the way to the courthouse for sentencing he was passed a letter from Thomas Carlyle. He did not open it, fearing that the authorities would confiscate it, but passed it to his wife for safe keeping. When the couple were united three years later he finally read it, but the contents are unknown. Whatever it contained, he prized this letter.[17] When he came across it again in Paris eighteen years later he wrote a reply. His principal purpose was to offer his condolences on the death of Jane Welsh Carlyle, but he reminisced about the evening in Carlyle's house in May 1846. 'Words of consolation I have none', he told Carlyle, 'but you will take this bit of letter as at least a token of human sympathy, from one who also hath losses'.[18] By this time two of Mitchel's sons had been killed fighting for the Confederate forces in the American Civil War.

As Mitchel's trial continued, Carlyle also wrote to Lord Clarendon, whom he knew through common friends. Mitchel was 'enveloped in such frightful aberrations', he wrote, yet 'is nevertheless instrinically a gifted, brave, and even noble minded young man; whom indeed it has now grown absolutely indispensable to silence'.[19] He pleaded that if convicted he should not be treated as a common felon and that 'it might beseem the Lord Lieutenant's magnanimity to subdue this man by nobleness and clemency rather than by force and rigour'.

Lord Clarendon replied a couple of days later. While acknowledging Mitchel's obvious gifts, he said he believed he was not 'quite sane'—a frequent characterisation of such revolutionary spirits in Ireland in the late 1840s. He concluded that Mitchel's growing audience for his revolutionary writings made action necessary, and that his lack of remorse was because he 'must be a hero or a martyr, and if he cannot make himself President of the Irish Republic he will not move a finger to save himself from transportation'.[20]

After a trial lasting two days Mitchel was predictably convicted. The following day, 27 May, he was sentenced to fourteen years' transportation, widely regarded as a very harsh sentence, and the *United Irishman* appeared for the last time. Mitchel's oft-quoted speech after the sentencing was unrepentant and drew attention to the symbolic significance of his conviction.

> What I have now to add is simply this: I have acted all through this business, from the first, under a strong sense of duty. I do not repent anything I have done, and I believe that the course which I have opened is only commenced. The Roman who saw his hand burning to ashes before the tyrant promised that three hundred should follow out his enterprise. Can I not promise for one, for two, for three?

He indicated, as he spoke, Reilly, Martin and Meagher.

> 'Promise for me'—'and me'—'and me, Mitchel,' rose around him in commingled tones of earnest solemnity, passionate defiance, and fearless devotion, from his friends and followers; and, embracing the exciting scene in a glance, he cried with proud eagerness—'For one, for two, for three? Ay, for hundreds!'[21]

After a brief time with his wife and two eldest sons Mitchel was brought with a strong military escort to the steamer *Shearwater*, which conveyed him from the North Wall to Spike Island in Cork Harbour. On 1 June 1848 he boarded a ship destined for Bermuda. He had hoped that the Confederates might attempt to break him out of the jail, but this was ruled out, as it was too heavily guarded.

There was widespread discontent in Ireland at the severity of Mitchel's sentence. One of the most prominent martyrs for the cause of nationalist Ireland was beginning a new life as a felon. He was treated, however, with the respect due to a person of his standing by his jailers, in sharp contrast to the fate of Fenian prisoners seventeen years later. He would again set foot on his native soil only a quarter of a century later. As he left Dublin his thoughts naturally turned to his wife and five children, 'none of them old enough to understand the cruel blow that had fallen on them this day'.[22]

It was to Mitchel's credit that his revolutionary principles, stretched to their logical extremity, prevented him from either recanting or seeking to reach an arrangement with the authorities. Lord Clarendon was right, however: Mitchel did indeed become a martyr to Irish republicanism, and his integrity in accepting exile rather than compromising his principles ensured that almost immediately on his sentencing he emerged as a hero.

REBELLION

Mitchel's direct involvement in revolutionary intrigues ceased in June 1848. His transportation had a radicalising effect on his comrades in the Irish Confederation, who vowed as he was deported that an uprising should be organised.[23] As Duffy later noted, it was ironic that after Mitchel's transportation the leaders of the Irish Confederation should make plans for an insurrection: 'It amounts to an emphatic verdict on Mitchel's policy of no conspiracy, no preparation, and no leader, that the moment he was withdrawn from the arena his closest friends agreed without hesitation to pursue a directly opposite course'.[24] His close friends John Martin and Thomas Devin Reilly established a new radical newspaper, the *Irish Felon*, which preached similar sentiments to those espoused by Mitchel in the *United Irishman* and included articles by James Fintan Lalor. But it was short-lived, as the authorities suppressed it after five issues at the end of July.

During June and July 1848 new Confederate Clubs were established around the country, and by July they numbered 150, apparently representing some fifty thousand men.[25] The increasing militarisation of the country struck fear into the hearts of the authorities, especially Lord Clarendon, who anticipated a widespread revolution, as the clubs were procuring arms and openly drilling.[26] The first step taken was to suppress the radical newspapers, including the *Nation* and the *Irish Tribune*, and to arrest the publishers and editors, including Duffy. Other Young Ireland leaders, such as Meagher and Michael Doheny, now openly expressed the need for an insurrection. Taking fright at the deteriorating state of the country, Lord Clarendon, by now 'in a fever', pleaded with Russell for more effective legal measures.[27] After considerable discussion it was agreed that *habeas corpus* would be suspended on 25 July 1848: in other words, those suspected of treason could be imprisoned without a trial.

Elizabeth Smith noted how 'gallantly the Commons responded to Lord John, carrying his measure through all its stages by acclamation in a few minutes'.[28] Sensing that arrest was imminent, O'Brien and other Confederate leaders, including Meagher and Dillon, fled to the south of the country to avoid imprisonment. They had planned that the rising would take place in Co. Kilkenny, but the reluctance of local Confederates resulted in the action shifting to Co. Tipperary. Led by O'Brien, they gathered at the town of Ballingarry, prepared for a battle with police and soldiers. About two thousand turned out, but then the numbers began to dwindle. When the police from Callan arrived there was a stalemate when approximately a hundred Confederates faced about half that number of constabulary, who had taken refuge in the home of the widow Margaret McCormack and her five children. Reinforcements arrived, and many of the crowd fled, leaving O'Brien and other leaders no recourse but to go on the run.

The 'battle of Widow McCormack's cabbage-patch', as it came to be dubbed, was an inglorious affair. British conservative newspapers ridiculed the feeble attempt at revolution. Smaller uprisings took place later but were easily suppressed.

What had gone wrong? O'Brien was a talented politician and a person of integrity but no revolutionary leader. Duffy said of him that 'he was too cold and too scrupulous to be a leader in a revolution'.[29] His fatalistic attitude, presuming that the uprising would fail, and that he would lose his life in the process, was unlikely to inspire any fellow-insurrectionists. The lack of planning was equally fatal; the suspension of *habeas corpus* rushed the leaders into premature action, without any overall co-ordination.

Even more detrimental to any chance of a popular revolt was the opposition of the group who were the leaders of the people: the Catholic clergy. Priests counselled their flock against involvement and in Co. Tipperary persuaded would-be participants not to follow O'Brien.[30] They feared that an ill-conceived and poorly led uprising would result in wholesale slaughter, and they were probably right. When Dillon and Meagher called on Father John Kenyon, parish priest of Templederry on the Tipperary-Limerick border and a close friend of Mitchel, they were shocked to learn that he wished to have no part in the rebellion. Later this was justified by Kenyon as being due to an agreement by his bishop to lift a suspension of his clerical privileges if he would not 'take the initiative' in any uprising.[31] But Kenyon, like many other clerics, also realised that this haphazard effort was futile. In Ballingarry a young curate, Philip Fitzgerald, who spoke to O'Brien, later described what he saw as the dilemma of the situation.

On the one hand, a numerous army, well-appointed and disciplined and supplied with all the munitions of war, on the other, an undisciplined and unarmed peasantry, without leaders of any knowledge or experience and destitute of everything that could render success certain or even probable. This weighed also heavily with me ... for that there should be carnage at all, was much to be lamented, but that it should be entirely on one side, and especially on the side of a poor and oppressed population, with whom all my sympathies were enlisted, and with whom I in every way identified, was an idea from which I recoiled instinctively.[32]

After the event a number of the leaders, including O'Brien, who was a Protestant, attributed its failure to the opposition of the Catholic clergy. But this merely shows the gulf in understanding between the Young Irelanders, with their romantic middle-class urban outlook, and the majority of the people on whom they counted to join their ranks. After three years of hunger, mounting an insurrection was hopeless. A disillusioned O'Brien was later to say that 'it matters little whether the blame of failure lies on me or upon others; but the fact is recorded in our annals—that the people preferred to die of starvation at home, or to flee as voluntary exiles to other lands, rather than to fight for their lives and liberties'.[33]

After a couple of days evading the authorities O'Brien and the other rebels were arrested, tried for high treason, and convicted in September and October 1848. The sentence was that they should be hanged, drawn and quartered, though neither the government nor public opinion could countenance such actions. In June 1849 the sentences were commuted to transportation for life, and a month later O'Brien, Meagher, Terence Bellew McManus and P. J. O'Donohue joined Mitchel in Van Diemen's Land (Tasmania). Others, such as Thomas D'Arcy McGee and Michael Doheny, escaped to the United States, as did John Blake Dillon.

DEFENDER OF THE FAITH

John MacHale was in Rome when the rebellion took place. He had left Ireland in April and returned in December 1848, missing the tumultuous events. While acknowledging the frustrations that led to open revolt, MacHale would not countenance violence.[34] One of the reasons for his travelling to Rome was to challenge British accusations that the Irish Catholic clergy were fomenting disorder.[35] Such was the force of these allegations that when Pope Pius ix learnt of them from Lord Minto, the Lord Privy Seal and an experienced diplomat, he undertook to stamp out any such clerical involvement.

The specific charge arose from the murder of Major Denis Mahon, the landlord of Strokestown Park, Co. Roscommon, on 2 November 1847, and the role of the local parish priest, the Rev. Michael McDermott, in the whole affair. The attack on Mahon occurred at about the same time that a small number of other landlords were killed. When Mahon inherited the estate in 1845 he set about a vigorous scheme of 'improvement', with the encouragement of his agent, John Ross Mahon, offering to pay the fare of his tenants to Canada. Some seven hundred accepted his offer, but most did not.[36] More than three thousand tenants were then evicted. The motive for his murder, insofar as any motive has been positively identified, was the report circulating that the ship on which some of his tenants were travelling to Canada, the *Virginius*, had sunk, with all lives lost.[37] This turned out be untrue: the *Virginius* had made it to Canada, though roughly a third of the passengers had died at sea; of those still alive, most were in a terrible state of illness and disease when they landed at Grosse-Île, the quarantine station for the city of Québec about thirty miles down the Saint Lawrence River. Family and friends in Strokestown were later outraged that Mahon had sent his tenants on what was a cheap and unseaworthy vessel.

Two men were subsequently executed for their role in the conspiracy to murder Mahon; another two who had pleaded guilty were sentenced to death, later commuted to transportation for life.[38]

Lord Clarendon, always the alarmist and by now seeking refuge in the Viceregal Lodge more or less permanently, pleaded with Russell for more coercion measures, as a 'servile war against all landlords and English rule', fuelled by hunger and desperation, was looming. Russell's response was revealing.

It is quite true that landlords in England would not like to be shot like hares and partridges. But neither does any landlord in England turn out fifty persons at once, and burn their houses over their heads, giving them no provision for the future. The murders are atrocious, so are the ejectments.[39]

MacHale's role in the whole affair was as the defender of the Catholic priesthood. Long-held suspicions of the malevolent role of the Catholic clergy in encouraging their flock were fuelled by unsubstantiated reports that

McDermott had incited his parishioners to murder Mahon. It was charged that he had denounced him from the altar for his indiscriminate eviction of tenants. It was alleged that he had said in a sermon at Sunday mass, 'Major Mahon is worse than Cromwell, and still he lives'.[40] McDermott denied he had ever uttered these words.

The case received widespread publicity in the newspapers. Lord Farnham, a Cavan landlord and prominent Orangeman with evangelical sympathies, publicised McDermott's alleged role to the House of Lords, setting in train a bitter controversy that would last throughout much of 1848.

Prominent English Catholic aristocrats now became involved. The Earl of Arundel published private correspondence with MacHale about McDermott's alleged incitement to murder, though he was not named.[41] Then there appeared a famous attack on MacHale from Lord Shrewsbury, a prominent English Catholic peer and patron of Catholic revival in Britain at this time.[42] In the *Morning Chronicle*, responding to MacHale's most recent salvo at Russell in December 1848, he listed a catalogue of errors in MacHale's actions, such as his opposition to the national schools, which left the poor in his archdiocese without education, and more immediately questioned why McDermott was still continuing with his priestly duties.[43] He also pointed out that within Britain the Irish Catholic Church was described as 'an accessory to crime' and that there was a deep sense of the ingratitude of the Irish for the charitable offerings. On MacHale's criticisms of Russell, Lord Shrewsbury believed they showed 'a very unjust severity after an effort such as no nation has perhaps ever yet made—and made at *his* urgent solicitation to relieve the distresses of another'.[44] Adopting a providentialist viewpoint, he argued that no individual could undo the wrongs of centuries.

> I desire now only to protest against the injustice … of visiting the sins of a hundred successive ministers on the head of one, who has to work against the accumulated evil of ages. As it is not in the power of man to flee from the wrath of God in the day of visitation, so neither is it given to him to transform a country torn with intestine divisions, and sick with unnumbered ills, into a land of peace and prosperity in a single session; nor, indeed, can it ever be done at all, without the cordial co-operation of clergy, landlords, and people, with the government that undertakes the task.[45]

The rage of MacHale's reply was palpable. In a lengthy response he rejected all these charges, point by point, and, as if to remind the British public of the continuance of the famine, described the heart-rending scenes he encountered every day.[46] Famine for him was a reality on his doorstep, not a vague concern in a faraway land. Subsequent letters between MacHale and Lord Shrewsbury also received much newspaper comment.[47] Rather than weakening his position, the Shrewsbury controversy served to consolidate MacHale's public role as the defender of the Catholic faith in Ireland, not least because by sending copies to the *Freeman's Journal* he ensured that it would.[48]

This attack from a leading Catholic peer, together with intrigue in Rome by government representatives to secure more papal pressure on the Irish bishops, led to MacHale's trip to lobby directly and to counter accusations emanating from British sources that the Catholic clergy were inciting violence. Many bishops believed there was a conspiracy orchestrated by the government in London that sought to muzzle the hierarchy and make it more pliable from the Russell ministry's point of view. In return for this acquiescence the government would provide state aid to the Catholic Church—a long-time aim of Russell, despite Catholic bishops' hostility to the idea, as being bound to alienate them from their laity.

This all failed miserably. MacHale left Rome with a renewed condemnation of the 'godless colleges'; the diplomatic manoeuvres to censure the Irish bishops served only to cluster support around him; and the intrigue fuelled suspicion of the true motives of Russell's ministry.[49]

Nevertheless, these issues diverted MacHale's attention from Ireland for nearly eight months during a time of acute crisis when leadership was required. Undoubtedly his views on the government's responsibility had hardened by the time he returned. By 1848 he was unequivocal that evictions and mass starvation were the harsh reality of the policies that were promulgated through the alliance of the Russell ministry and the Irish landed elite. Interpretations in which the divine hand of Providence was at work were jettisoned by MacHale and other influential nationalists: the real purpose of government policy was to exterminate the Celt. An article in the *Nation* in April 1848 summed up this view.

> It is evident to all men that our foreign government is but a club of grave-diggers ... It is not Providence but provincialism that plays the thief; we are decimated not by the will of God but by the will of the Whigs.[50]

MacHale was the most vociferous and most well-known critic of government policy, and even if he was too ready to express his views in public, by virtue of his position and the respect he commanded these opinions were taken seriously. That he should place the protection of the Catholic faith in Ireland or, more precisely, the authority of the church above all other considerations was characteristic of his concern about principles over all other matters. In this respect he mirrored Trevelyan.

On his departure from Rome, MacHale had his own encounter with revolutionary zeal. Travelling with the Bishop of Ardagh, William O'Higgins, he was stopped by Italian revolutionaries who had orders to prevent any cleric leaving Rome. Fortunately they were not dressed in ecclesiastical garb, and O'Higgins demanded that they be let through as foreigners with a valid passport. The following day the pope's prime minister, Count Pellegrino Rossi, was killed. Later MacHale described his lucky escape.

Before the Revolution broke out, I had fortunately to return from the Eternal City. I awaited only the issuing of the decree which in spite of all the corruption that gives them a precarious support, has struck and blighted for ever the infidel colleges. On the very eve of the Revolution I took my departure from Rome in the last of the public vehicles of the Pope's government that was permitted to leave the city; and had I remained until the following morning, the fatal day on which Rossi fell by the hand of an assassin, I should have to sustain the shock of the Pope's flight, and to endure seven months of a dreary captivity; doomed to witness, perhaps to share, the constitutional blessings of the sanguinary reign of Garibaldi.[51]

When MacHale returned to Ireland he had to face another, more immediate threat: the proselytising activities of Protestant missionary societies within his archdiocese. 'Taking the soup'—converting to Protestantism to obtain education, food or other benefits—was the ultimate sign of desperation on the part of the hungry. Connemara and other parts of the west, but also Cos. Cork and Kerry, were the main areas selected by evangelicals for these activities. Schools for poor children were established, an effort given an impetus after the formation of the Society for the Irish Church Missions to Roman Catholics.[52] A famous settlement on Achill Island led by the Rev. Edward Nangle reported increases in conversions throughout 1848 and 1849.[53] Certainly conversions were exaggerated, but the accusation of 'souperism' is to this day one of the most controversial aspects of these missionary endeavours. Folklore accounts stress the temporary and opportunist nature of these supposed conversions and how within local communities 'taking the soup' was regarded as the ultimate betrayal of the Catholic faith. To be called a 'souper' was 'tantamount to the great taunt and insult'.[54]

THE WORTHY WILL RISE OUT OF THE MIRE

The clearances of smallholders continued at an accelerated pace throughout 1848 and into 1849. Now liable for rates for holdings valued at £4 or under, many landlords received from the revised Poor Law regulations the incentive to do what they had long wished to do: 'improve' their estates through wholesale evictions, creating bigger commercial holdings worked by strong farmers with teams of paid labourers, with ultimate control vested in the landlord. Ulick de Burgh, Lord Clanricarde, who had a large estate, wrote to Lord Clarendon in December 1848 acknowledging as much: 'The landlords are prevented from aiding or tolerating poor tenants. They are compelled to hunt out all such, to save their property from the £4 clause.'[55]

While formal ejectment procedures were time-consuming and costly, landlords and their agents sought to get 'voluntary surrender'. Tenants who gave up their holdings were financially compensated or, less frequently, offered a passage to North America.[56] It was not only individual landlords who took determined action: tenants on the Crown estate of Ballykilcline, near Strokestown, were offered passage to North America. By mid-1848 nearly five hundred had left and the land was more or less completely shorn of human beings, 'perfectly untenanted', as it was described in the prospectus when it went on the market for sale.[57] Around the country many of those who had attempted to cling to their smallholdings up to the winter of 1847/8, worn down by years of hunger and suffering, eventually surrendered their holdings.

The eviction of tenants, whether 'voluntarily' or by legal means, was long remembered for its inhumanity. From 1849 onwards, when statistics were first collected by the constabulary, the counties that had the highest rate of evictions were Clare, Mayo, Galway and Kerry. Stories tell of people dispossessed and forced to take to the road to beg. A woman from Mullingar, Co. Westmeath, born a quarter of a century after the famine remembered stories that her grandmother had recounted about the plight of the evicted.

I heard my grandmother saying that the poor people left their homes and started walking on and on along the roads, from one place to another. They would have been sitting on the sides of the roads and they would be begging a night's lodgings here and there, and a bit to eat. That left so many poor people on the roads. The homes were taken off some of them because they were unable to pay their rents, and more of them cleared out themselves.[58]

It is almost impossible to imagine the amount of movement 'on the roads' as the dispossessed made their way to an unknown destination. People walked into the towns and cities seeking refuge from the famine; others simply walked while they still had strength, not knowing what else to do. Contagious diseases were spread by this extraordinary degree of movement. During the famine and shortly thereafter roughly half a million people were put out of their homes, either through legal methods, illegal actions, inducements to quit or sometimes just brute force.[59]

'A PESTILENCE IN THIS DARKENED LAND'

As landlords go, Elizabeth Smith was more humane than most. But she was not beyond using the strong arm of compulsion when specific circumstances arose, such as attempting to force the labouring Doyle family into the workhouse. Their plight appeared hopeless to her. The husband was a 'cripple', the wife was blind, and their one daughter was 'hopelessly lazy'. Hal Smith even rented a cart to convey the family to the workhouse in Naas, but they refused to go and set upon the driver. Elizabeth maintained that, as her estate already paid heavy rates to support the poor, they should not help this wretched family. 'I told her that we could not help her nor the farmers either; she must go to the Poor House towards which this little estate pays ninety-six pounds a year and hitherto sends no paupers to it'.[60] The workhouse was no solution, however, and Elizabeth was angry that the family relied on a son in the United States to support them.

> As they can't earn and won't starve they will steal waiting an answer they have a hope of from the son in America, whose industry they are willing to tax for the support of their own idleness and meanness, for their low feelings and unprincipled selfishness prevent their seeing how utterly depraved is such conduct. I will not sanction such want of principles and have forbidden her applying again here. At the same time I hate the Poor House. A sink of vice: idleness finishing to corrupt the miserable inmates; but when people have brought themselves down to it, they must put up with it. I begin to think a pestilence in this darkened land would be a mercy to it.

A month later, however, she was observing that 'none of the lower orders need suffer for an hour, the poor house is open', even if she acknowledged that only in complete desperation did anyone enter it.

Earlier that year she had taken particular satisfaction in Lord Shrewsbury's letter about MacHale. His letter was

> really fine, utterly fearless, he tells them all their misdeeds … They never got such a castigation from an heretick as from this true son of their church.

On reading MacHale's response a couple of weeks later she was outraged by the abuse that was heaped on Lord Shrewsbury and described MacHale's letter as

> columns of rubbish, unreadable, no argument, no reply, coarse abuse from an ignorant, vulgar, low born, low bred, bigotted despot, of an accomplished nobleman.

The Irish clergy were lacking in education and breeding and misled their unquestioning flock. While MacHale was the principal target of her venom, no doubt she had in mind her local Catholic clergy, with whom she had a very tense relationship about the national school. She held St Patrick's College, Maynooth, in particular contempt, where MacHale was educated and had served as a professor but also where the three Catholic clerics she clashed with had trained to be priests. In 1841 she had concluded that Maynooth was a 'perfect pest to the country, a plague spot whose contamination is daily spreading … At present it is nursery for bigots.'[61] It seemed that all Ireland's ills could be attributed to Irish Catholicism. 'All reflecting persons' would recognise that

> the Roman Catholic Irish are inferior in morals, in principles, in conduct, in intelligence, and I trust that henceforth they will be left in the low estate suited to their low character, for it really endangers the country to put them on a par with their fellow subjects. The worthy will rise out of the mire, and be very easily distinguished. But that wretched priesthood should be silently kept down or educated.

This diatribe was written from Edinburgh, where Elizabeth spent much of the summer of 1848, after a few weeks in Dublin. She saw old friends, including Francis Lord Jeffrey, founder and former editor of the *Edinburgh Review*. Her time in Scotland provided a welcome break from Baltiboys, and she thrived on the literary and political intrigue. When away from Ireland her views invariably hardened and were more 'bigoted' (to use a term she frequently employed herself). The interactions with people who had relatively little interest in or understanding of Ireland seem to have influenced her thinking. In late July the talking-point was Ireland, and she watched events unfold with increasing incredulity. William Smith O'Brien was 'quite mad', but the 'Lancers headed by Habeas Corpus will soon end his crazy career'. She praised the Dublin administration for acting in the nick of time to avert a widespread rebellion, regardless of the fact that this involved the suspension of the basic rights afforded by habeas corpus.

During her time in Edinburgh she heard the news that her father, Sir John Grant, had died on board ship returning from India on 16 May 1848. Her sister Jane was the bearer of the bad news but could not face telling their mother, who had arrived back from India some months previously. Elizabeth was the only person strong enough to break the news to their mother that the ship had arrived without her husband. Her mother looked at her and said, 'My child, I never expected him', and it was the first time she had seen her mother weep openly. To make matters worse, he had been buried at sea, off the Cape of Good Hope. During his time in India, Elizabeth had rarely heard from her father, until near the time he was due to return. She was also heartbroken that her father died alone, 'in that solitary cabin on a stormy sea, feeble in body and depressed in mind'. But she cherished the childhood memories of her time with him. Clearly she had enjoyed a good relationship with her father, unlike her cold mother, notwithstanding his many faults.

At least, she concluded, he was spared the indignity of seeing his son William dismissed from his post as a judge in India. He was heavily implicated in a financial scandal as a director of the insolvent Union Bank of Calcutta that left him owing more than £70,000. Because of speculation he had accumulated huge debts, and even more perturbing from Elizabeth's point of view was that he had encouraged others to do so, including his sister Jane and her husband. She concluded that her brother was 'not a man I should like to have any dealings with—speculating, arrogant, and I am afraid selfish'. She was deeply embarrassed by the whole affair, as her family 'seems inclined to occupy the tongues of the world with the scandal of its affairs'.

While she blamed her brother, who—like her father—had a habit of accumulating massive debts, it was his education, at Eton College and the

University of Edinburgh, that she believed was really the source of his character flaws.

His education was thoroughly vicious. A spoiled childhood, a publick school, the low dissipation of college, a habit of debt, a scramble for money all round him, a very unhappy home, and the means not forthcoming to give him his profession.

Before he even left Eton he had a mountain of debts, to which he added during his time at Edinburgh.[62] He lost his home in Calcutta and a coffee plantation in Ceylon (Sri Lanka) but was later cleared of any wrongdoing. After his father's death he inherited the estate in Scotland in 1848. By other accounts he was a very successful Laird of Rothiemurchus, bringing about a substantial number of improvements in the estate throughout the 1850s and 1860s.[63]

From 1848 and into the following year Elizabeth's comments about the famine become more infrequent. After successive crop failures there was a sense that it was now expected that distress would occur after each failure. Unlike the previous years, when helping the poor dominated her thoughts, after 1847 there was a sense of resolution: those who could get by did so, those who could not should go to the workhouse. On hearing that the blight had re-emerged in 1849 she concluded that 'we have a poor look out for the winter I know'. Again in August 1850 she noted that the blight had ravaged some fields, yet others were left untouched. What was once exceptional was now regrettably routine.

'BEGINNING OF THE END'

1848 was a year of personal vindication for Charles Trevelyan. In May he was made a knight commander of the Order of the British Empire for his contribution to the relief efforts in Ireland. The previous year he had been given a bonus of a year's salary—£2,500—free of tax, as he was the 'key-stone of the whole', to quote Russell. After he was knighted the bonus was questioned in Parliament by Benjamin Disraeli, a protectionist Tory seeking to make trouble, and Trevelyan decided to return the gratuity, as it 'would be inconsistent with my sense of what is due to the public service and to myself to retain it'.[64]

His review of the official relief policies was published under his name in the same year. Such was his pride in this record of the measures that he sent an inscribed copy to Lord Minto in Rome, for presentation to the pope. The overt purpose was to counter the opinions of MacHale and other Catholic critics of government policy.[65] In his actions he was also reflecting a more general desire to ensure that on the international stage it would be widely known that the British government had responded effectively and energetically to the famine.

Prophetically, Trevelyan declared to Lord Clarendon in February 1849: 'I think we have come to the beginning of the end in Ireland'.[66] The much-hoped-for transformation of Irish society was taking shape, and he told Lord Clarendon later that month that 'I expect the foundation of a great change in the West of Ireland will be laid this summer, and that it will proceed with accumulated force for several years to come'.[67]

The winding down of the soup kitchens in September 1847 placed the responsibility for famine relief on the Poor Law administration. Trevelyan emphasised to his subordinates that the time had come to shut off any further aid from central government. Writing to Burgoyne, chairman of the Relief Commission, at the end of July 1847 he told him that 'whatever the difficulties and dangers may be … I am convinced that nothing but local self government and self-support … hold out any hope of improvement for Ireland.' He saw it as 'not merely a cessation but a transfer' to the Poor Law authorities.[68]

In August 1847 he went on holiday to France to rest after two years of hard work on behalf of the Irish poor. On his return he travelled to Dublin for his first and only visit to Ireland during the famine years to meet Burgoyne and other officials and to explain the new scheme. In Dublin he took the unusual step for a civil servant of writing a letter to the *Times* about famine relief, much to the irritation of Lord Clarendon, who felt it was not a proper course of action for someone in his position. Characteristically, in his letter Trevelyan left the readers of the *Times* in no doubt about who was the driving force behind the operation of Irish famine relief.[69]

The Poor Law, introduced in 1838, was never intended to deal with wholesale destitution, and within months the cracks were beginning to appear. Assistance for those most in need would become a local responsibility, financed by ratepayers within the Poor Law union. The collection of these rates, particularly in the west and south-west of the country, proved very difficult, though some unions were using more rigorous methods to ensure that ratepayers did not renege on payments. It soon became clear that what were officially termed 'distressed' unions required additional financial support from the Treasury to meet the high level of demand, both from within the workhouse and for outdoor relief. If the elected Poor Law guardians were unable to manage the finances, or failed to collect rates, the union was declared insolvent and paid officials were appointed to run it, as happened throughout the country during late 1847 and into 1848.[70] Such cases received extensive publicity in the newspapers.

Only the most desperate would enter the workhouses, which were often overcrowded, full of sick people, and often surviving on meagre rations. The outbreak of cholera in November 1848 placed extraordinary demands on the fever hospitals that were established and financed by the Poor Law unions, primarily to cater for victims of the famine. Kilrush workhouse had more than five thousand inmates in its main and auxiliary accommodation by June 1850, almost double the number who were housed there six months earlier.[71] The Skibbereen workhouse, designed for eight hundred inmates, contained a little less than three thousand in December 1848.[72]

One of the reasons for the rapid rise in numbers was that many boards of guardians were reluctant to grant outdoor relief, so the able-bodied poor were forced to enter the workhouse as a 'test of destitution', there to engage in such demeaning work as stone-breaking. By June 1848, 834,000 people were receiving outdoor relief. Of the 131 Poor Law unions, 71 were authorised to provide outdoor relief, and a similar number the following year.[73] Another quarter of a million people were incarcerated in the workhouses. Officials were very reluctant to give food to those beyond the workhouse, fearing that huge sections of the population would become dependent. So there was a concerted effort to provide additional places in the workhouses, and to limit outdoor relief wherever possible.

Any demands for additional funds for bankrupt or near-bankrupt unions had to be authorised by the Treasury. Charles Trevelyan was engaged in more or less constant vigilance to ensure that the resources of the exchequer were safeguarded, reminding officials in Ireland that the Poor Law system was essentially meant to be self-financing. 'Distressed' unions were eligible for exceptional loans, to be repaid when sufficient finances were available. Trevelyan favoured raising the rates to pay for the additional demands. But the general principle was clear, as he explained to Edward Twisleton, chairman of the Irish Poor Law Commission, in February 1848.

The state of the case is simply this: The only hope, not only for saving the whole Empire from Bankruptcy, but also of arriving at a satisfactory permanent settlement of Ireland is by making the support of the Irish Poor a local charge, and this cannot be done without much painful discipline of this kind. You will strive against it as far as you can, but where it cannot be avoided, it must be submitted to as a smaller evil by which a greater good is to be attained for Ireland and the whole British Nation.

The British Association for the Relief of the Extreme Distress was used by Trevelyan in 1847 and 1848 to funnel funds to the areas that were badly hit, so avoiding public scrutiny of the expenditure. There was considerable opposition to advancing additional sums to Ireland, which intensified after the 1848 Rebellion, when 'Irish ingratitude' became the standard refrain. Even Russell, who was more even-handed than most British politicians, remarked that the reluctance to provide additional funds was not due solely to the attitudes of Sir Charles Wood or Trevelyan but 'lies deep in the breasts of the British people'.

We have granted, lent, subscribed, worked, visited, clothed, the Irish millions of money, years of debate &c., &c.—the only return is calumny and rebellion. Let us not grant, lend, clothe &c., &c. any more, and see what that will do. Such is the result to which MacHale, J. O'Connell and S. O'Brien have brought us.[74]

The solution to the financial problems of the impoverished unions lay in levying a rate-in-aid on the more prosperous ones. A levy of 6 pence in the pound would be paid to support the 'distressed unions', and the Treasury would give advances against the total sum collected.

When this was proposed there was strong resistance, especially in Ulster.[75] Poor Law officials also had reservations, as had prominent Irish landowners. The chairman of the Poor Law Commission, Edward Twisleton, resigned in protest in March 1849 when the new policy was introduced in the House of Commons. For him this meant that no longer was the crisis a British one but merely an Irish one. Lord Clarendon told Russell that the 'destitution here is so horrible, and the indifference of the House of Commons to it is so manifest, that he was an unfit agent of a policy which must be one of extermination,' and that he was placed in a position 'which no man of honour and humanity can endure'.[76]

The legislation was passed in May 1849 and it was calculated that the total sum available for the distressed unions in the west and south-west was £322,552. As far as the government was concerned, the famine was over or, more accurately, it was now a local problem, and central resources could no longer be drawn upon. Placing the responsibility for the lives of the poor on such an ill-equipped and inadequately financed system was a fatal decision; and it also raised the question of the integrity of the Act of Union, as Ireland would henceforth have to rely on its own resources.

FAMINE QUEEN

Even though the harvest of 1849 was badly damaged by blight, it was decided that Queen Victoria should visit Ireland, for the first time, in August. This coincided with one of the worst years of the famine, as widespread deaths occurred throughout the country. Victoria was anxious about travelling to Ireland, given the unstable political situation, and had earlier indicated to Russell back in August 1846 that 'it should be a National thing, and the good it is to do must be a permanent and not a transitory advantage to a particular government'.[77] It was over a decade since her coronation and she had not visited her Irish subjects, which suggests reluctance to do so. It was considered inappropriate for it to be a state visit when the country was in the grip of such destitution, so it was described as a private one, albeit with the usual pomp. Russell was concerned about how the queen might be received, but the public message was that the famine was well and truly over. For Lord Clarendon, even if distress did exist in some districts this would allow the queen to 'do what is kind and considerate to those who are suffering'.[78] Russell, equally, was concerned about what response she might provoke; but Lord Palmerston, the foreign secretary and an Irish landowner, was sanguine. 'I shall be very much mistaken in Paddy's character, if the Queen is not satisfied with the demonstrations of Joy and Loyalty with which her arrival in Ireland will be greeted.'[79]

The visit was carefully choreographed. On 2 August 1849 the queen arrived on the royal yacht, *Victoria and Albert*, in Cóbh, which was renamed Queenstown in her honour. She then proceeded to Cork, where she received an enthusiastic response. Travelling by sea to Dublin, she attended receptions and levees and visited Carton House at Maynooth, seat of the Duke of Leinster, the most senior Irish aristocrat. From Dublin she sailed to Belfast, where the reception was equally warm, before leaving for the Scottish Highlands.[80] Her itinerary was carefully kept to the east coast, and within Dublin only the main thoroughfares were used, so that she would not see some of the least prosperous corners of her kingdom.

The visit was generally judged to be a success by the queen, and also especially by Lord Clarendon, who, writing to Sir George Grey immediately after her trip, believed that it marked a turning-point in relations with Ireland: 'The Queen's visit … will be associated with a turn in the tide of their affairs after four years' suffering, with an unprecedented influx of strangers and expenditure of money.'[81] The visit was also seen as a sustained demonstration of Irish loyalty less than twelve months since the 1848 Rebellion. While the welcome was warm, it was not as unequivocal as was judged by Lord Clarendon. One of the ballads sung by the welcoming crowds in Cork underlined the mixed views about her visit: 'Arise, you dead of Skibbereen, and come to Cork to see the Queen'.[82]

When it came to presenting an address of welcome to the queen, the divisions among the Catholic bishops soon came to the fore. Daniel Murray, Archbishop of Dublin, drafted an address, but both John MacHale and Michael Slattery, Archbishop of Cashel, refused to add their signatures. MacHale wanted the memorial to convey to the queen 'a knowledge which has, probably, been withheld from her, of the terrible sufferings of her subjects, as well as the cruel neglect with which they have been treated by her Ministers.'[83] He wrote his own address, in which he mentioned that royal visits to the country were regrettably rare. He reminded the queen of the tragic fate of many of her subjects.

> The painful ordeal which your people have been traversing, and out of which the surviving remnant are yet struggling to come in safety, has in several parts of Ireland diminished your Majesty's subjects by a fourth, and in some by a half, of their former numbers.[84]

MacHale and Slattery refused to attend, but eventually Murray managed to secure twelve signatures.[85]

What the address of welcome exposed was the different worlds Murray and MacHale inhabited. MacHale's archdiocese was devastated by the famine, whereas Murray sought to reach compromises with the government, believing that its intentions were noble. MacHale had no such illusions and was determined that he would not be obsequious to win the approval of the administration in Dublin or indeed of the monarch herself.

One of Queen Victoria's most rebellious subjects, John Mitchel, was sitting on a ship waiting to be transferred to a convict settlement at the Cape of Good Hope, where he had been transferred from Bermuda, as his health was failing. Reading newspaper reports of the royal visit, he poured scorn on it and the queen in October 1849. The expression of loyalty that cheered the British press 'consists in a willingness to come out into the street to see a pageant pass'. He sardonically remarked on the places chosen for her to see:

> Her majesty did not visit Skibbereen, Westport or Schull; neither did she 'drop in' (as sometimes in Scotland) to dine with any of her peasantry on their 'homely fare'. After a few years, however, it is understood that her majesty will visit the West—the human inhabitants are expected by that time to have been sufficiently thinned, and the deer and other game to have proportionately multiplied. The Prince Albert will then take a hunting-lodge in Connemara.[86]

Chapter 10 ~

EXILES

MAY THE MERCIFUL GOD BLESS, PROTECT AND PRESERVE YE
Michael Prendergast departed from his home in Milltown, Co. Kerry, to board
a ship at Cork destined for Saint John, New Brunswick, in late March 1847.
He left behind his wife, Ellen, and four young children. He had two brothers
and a sister already living in Boston. By late July his elderly parents had heard
nothing about his fate. They were increasingly agitated about him, 'really
alarmed on his account'.[1] The newspaper reports of large numbers of deaths
on the ships crossing the Atlantic to Canada in the summer of 1847 added to
their understandable anxiety.

Though not destitute, Prendergast's parents were reliant on their children
in America to send home remittances, without which help they would not
have survived. James Prendergast wrote to his children to say that their 'filial
care has placed your aged parents beyond the reach of distress for the ensuing
summer notwithstanding the extreme dearness of every article of food'.[2] Each
sum was conscientiously acknowledged by their father in a series of letters
until his death in 1848 and thereafter by their mother, Elizabeth. Most of the
letters were written by professional scribes, such as priests and school-masters,
even though James had basic writing competence.

Eventually Michael turned up at Saint John in June, whence he wrote to
his brothers. They sent him $10 and told him to make his way to Boston
without delay.[3] His ship had docked in May but, like many other Irish
immigrants, he had to stay on Partridge Island, the quarantine station for
New Brunswick.[4] When, two months later, his parents heard that he was safe

they were overjoyed, as they had given up hope that he had survived the voyage. His departure had left his wife reliant on her own family and the elderly Prendergasts for food for herself and her children. The local relief committee refused to give meal to any family on learning that the husband had left for America.

A couple of months later Michael sent his first instalment of money orders for the support of his family, who would eventually join him in Boston a few years later. He was not the most dutiful of husbands. His mother was ashamed at the infrequency of his letters to his wife, and the money he sent was not nearly enough to support his young family.[5]

Those left behind—the elderly parents, Michael's wife and children and his brother Maurice and his wife—were completely reliant on the flow of American money for their survival. Another brother, John, had died in April 1847, leaving a widow and a young daughter, Elizabeth. The circumstances of John's death are not entirely clear, but it seems it was famine-related, as all the girls' dresses were pawned, suggesting that the family were in financial trouble. The descriptions they sent of conditions in Ireland at the time underlined this dependence. In October 1848, shortly before his death, their father described the state of the country:

Ye desired [us] to let you know the state of the country. It is bad in one respect. Distress is very great. The blight swept off the potatoe crop and this left provision short here. We have no sort of employment for the poor, and the workhouses are scarcely sufft [sufficient] to receive them. Farmers are oppressed with poor rates and other charges. Many are deserting their farms and flying to America as fast as they can. Destitution is seen almost everywhere.[6]

This was not an exaggeration. Elizabeth Smith also recounted tales of farmers who sold their livestock and simply disappeared to America without a trace, leaving the landlord short on rent. 'The runaway farmers have learned the trick of thrashing out their corn by night, leaving the straw neatly cocked, selling off stock and furniture and bolting, with heavy arrears due to the ruined landlords.'[7]

In December 1848 James Prendergast died. Two years later his widow, Elizabeth, left Ireland with her now orphaned granddaughter, also called Elizabeth. When her daughter Julia had suggested joining her children in Boston she at first refused reluctantly, saying that she had a few years left and wished to be buried with her late husband. Within a matter of months she had changed her mind and explained that her son Maurice now seemed to be doing better, especially after his own eldest son had gone to America and was now regularly sending back money. But she also admitted to being evasive with the truth about her promise to her late husband.

> I pretended that I promised your father to be buried with him, but now I must tell the truth, he never desired it. His last words to me were that he would wish I should go to my children and be under the eye of daughter if I thought I could ensure the fatigue of the Voyage, but if I did not go he desired I should be buried in Keel. I am sure I am strong and healthy enough and I am I would get better from the thought of being going to my children. Therefore I hope and request ye will send for me as soon as possible while I have the fair weather and I go without delay.[8]

In September 1850 Elizabeth set sail on the *Niobe* from Liverpool, accompanied by her granddaughter. Before she left she wrote to her son Thomas saying: 'Figure to yourself what comforts I anticipate at the thoughts of embracing each and every of you so long parted from me'.[9] Though she had turned eighty, she made it safely to Boston, lived with her children and died seven years later and was buried there. Her other son, Maurice, eventually emigrated to Boston in the 1870s. All the surviving children of James and Elizabeth Prendergast had ended up living far from Milltown.

In Boston, members of the Prendergast family had settled first in the poor district of Fort Hill along the waterfront. They worked in various jobs associated with horses—as coachmen, stablers and harness-cleaners. In the 1850s they moved to the South Cove district and purchased buildings in South Street, close to the railway terminals, and servicing the railways proved profitable. The second generation of Prendergasts achieved remarkable success in property and other fields and established themselves as scions of Catholic Boston society. In particular, James Maurice Prendergast (1851–1920) was a prominent businessman who served on numerous public bodies and spent his holidays at Hyannis Port, where he owned a substantial house, the true sign of acceptance and recognition among the Boston elite.[10]

A DOOMED AND STARVING ISLAND[11]

In the decade after 1845 more than 2 million people—a quarter of the country's population in 1841—left in what was one of the largest population movements in recorded history. 1851 was the worst year, when almost a quarter of a million people emigrated. Contrary to conventional wisdom, the crisis of the late 1840s did not initiate emigration from Ireland—people had been leaving in significant numbers since the 1820s and 1830s for North America and Britain—but the scale, background, language, class and impact were entirely on a different level.

The famine exodus began in earnest after the failure of the potato crop in August 1846.[12] For the first time, emigrants decided to face the hazardous winter crossing, sometimes with little by way of provisions for the long voyage. Such was the panic that detailed preparations were rarely made: this was a flight of the frightened. One woman from Ardnaglass, Co. Sligo, Mary Rush, wrote in September 1846 to her parents, who had settled in Québec, pleading with them to send the money for a passage for her family.

> Now, my dear father and mother if you knew what danger we and our fellow countrymen are suffering, if you were ever so much distressed, you would take us out of this poverty isle ... If you don't endeavour to take us out of it, it will be the next news you will hear by some friend of me and my little family to be lost by hunger, and there are thousands dread they will share the same fate.[13]

At the end of the letter she wrote a stark message: 'For God's sake take us out of poverty, and don't let us die with the hunger'. Her earnest wish was granted, and in May 1847 Mary and Michael Rush, along with other family members, left Liverpool on the *Garrick*, destined for New York.

Yet it was only a prelude to what would occur the following year. The spring of 1847 witnessed a desperate exodus of unimaginable proportions, as cottiers and smallholders flocked to Liverpool seeking a passage to North America. It was the un-coordinated nature of the flow that alarmed contemporaries, and newspapers published numerous stories that emphasised the panic behind these departures. One group of emigrants, on being questioned, responded that they had no fixed plan and that all they wanted was 'to get out of Ireland ... We must be better anywhere than here.'[14] Many of those who left took cheap passage from Irish ports, such as Cork or Sligo, or travelled first to Liverpool. The least expensive fares were to Canada, landing in ports in Québec and New Brunswick on ships that were poorly regulated and whose passengers experienced atrocious conditions, while those with more resources could travel directly to New York or Boston.

The flight from famine in 1847 had an air of desperation about it as whole communities became increasingly despondent about their future. The historian Oliver MacDonagh has described this as the outbreak of an element of mass hysteria.[15] Jonathan Pim, the Dublin Quaker philanthropist, reckoned that emigration in 1847 would be 'enormous'; he was told by one man that 'every one who can make out the money will go'. He observed the departure of an emigrant ship at Sligo just before Christmas, 1846, and was struck by the expressions of those who were leaving. They were overjoyed to be escaping. 'A ship left Sligo before Christmas, and instead of the sorrow usual on leaving their native country, there was nothing but joy at their escape, as from a doomed land.'[16]

Often seen by unfriendly eyes as a mass of poor people, in fact the stream in 1847 included middling farmers, members of the urban middle classes and workers. Newspapers were full of accounts of the departure of the 'better' type of individuals.[17] Leaving the country required resources or capital in some form to pay for the passage, and many of the poor had no access to such money. The option for these people was to tramp across the country to Dublin or other ports and to cross the Irish Sea in steamers destined for Liverpool. Nevertheless Ireland never lost nor the United States received paupers in such numbers.

The regions with the highest rates of emigration were not necessarily those where most people died.[18] Farmers had access to savings and therefore could leave in the early years of the crisis. The poorest people had none and had to endure hunger and starvation until relatives could send them money for their passage.

The numbers leaving slackened in late 1847 and continued to do so until the complete failure of the potato crop in the summer of 1848. A massive surge occurred in the autumn of 1848 as widespread despondency about the future set in throughout the country. Large numbers of small farmers, especially along the western seaboard, simply gave up their farms and left. What also emerged in 1848–9 was emigration paid for with the remittances of those who had left in previous years in the form of pre-paid passage. This enabled the poor to obtain a passage that otherwise they could not afford.

Complete families left as well as individuals—husbands, sons and brothers—who intended to pay the fares of those left behind once a job was secured.

Up to the mid-1850s this massive exodus continued. Emigration became a normal and routine matter in post-famine Ireland, a rite of passage for those coming of age, especially in Munster and Connacht, the provinces that supplied the largest number of emigrants. These refugees from the famine mostly sought to travel to North America, where opportunities were perceived to exist in abundance. For the poorest among them this could be achieved only by getting to Liverpool and then hoping to save for the passage to America. The great majority of famine emigrants went to the United States, even if a sizeable number had to take the circuitous route via Canada.

After 1848 mass emigration showed that a 'deep mood of staleness and defeat' took hold from the successive failures of the potato crop. The atmosphere throughout the country was 'marked by a note of doom, an air of finality, a sense that a chapter in history has come decisively to its close'.[19]

ASSISTED EMIGRATION

For most people, emigration was privately organised and either financed with their own money or paid for by relatives already living overseas. For landlords, providing the means for impoverished tenants to quit their holdings to facilitate the 'improvement' of estates made economic and political sense and was preferable to large-scale evictions. Many prominent landowners—such as Lord Fitzwilliam (owner of the Powerscourt estate at Enniskerry, Co. Wicklow), Sir Robert Gore Booth, Lord Palmerston and Lord Lansdowne— offered subsidies to their tenants.[20] Smaller landlords, including the Smiths, would assist a troublesome tenant to leave, calculating that it was better to be rid of such individuals, whatever the cost. As well as the passage money, would-be emigrants were given clothing, some provisions and landing money, though the details depended on the generosity of the particular landlord. Landlords sending large numbers of former tenants, such as Gore Booth at Drumcliff and Mahon at Strokestown, clubbed together to charter a ship or to negotiate reductions in fares to keep the costs down.

As a result of the changes in the Poor Law whereby landlords were responsible for the rates on holdings valued at £4 or less, and of the non-payment or arrears in rental income, there was an opportunity to consolidate holdings and to get a 'better class of tenants'. When seeking to persuade Lord Palmerston that assisted emigration from his Sligo estates would make economic sense in April 1847 his agent told him that he made the recommendation 'on the principle of profit and economy'.[21] While economic concerns were the principal driving force behind such assisted emigration schemes, there was in some instances a genuine benevolent concern for the welfare of tenants. In June 1848 Gore Booth, speaking before a select committee of the House of Lords on colonisation, stated that he could have simply evicted his tenants but that if he had followed that course of action he 'would have been throwing them on the world and leaving them to beg'.[22] Tenants to be given assistance with emigration were selected by landlords, or their agents in the case of large absentee estates, and there was invariably an insistence on whole families leaving, so that the cabin could be levelled.[23] The total number of people who left under these schemes is not known, as the activities of many smaller landlords did not attract public attention, but at least fifty thousand and perhaps even twice that number left with some form of assistance.[24]

Direct state assistance for emigration came in the form of schemes operated on Crown estates, the most well known being the Ballykilcline estate in Co. Roscommon. The troublesome tenants on this estate had a tense relationship with the authorities, having withheld rent for years and engaged in a series of violent and legal confrontations with the Crown's commissioners. By 1847 the resolve to resist eviction had weakened in the face of increasing destitution, and many tenants took advantage of the offer of free passage to North America between September 1847 and April 1848, ensuring that the commissioners achieved their ultimate objective: clearing the estate of its troublesome tenants.[25] Tenants on the Crown estates of Irvilloughter (Ervallagh Oughter) and Boughil, Co. Galway, and the Kilconcouse estate at Kinnitty, Co. Offaly, as well as other properties in Cos. Cork and Kerry, were assisted to leave. More than 1,100 people left these estates for a new life in Canada or the United States with passage paid for by the state.[26] These emigrants were more fortunate than most, as detailed preparations were made by Crown officials for their travel and subsequent landing. One assisted emigrant from the Boughil estate wrote from Vermont to the Crown agent in Galway who oversaw the emigration scheme to thank him.

> Every promises that ever your Honour made to us was performed & Sir I have to let your Honour know that we had a safe and speedy passage which is A Consolation to you and which I am bound to pray for you during my Days ... I am employed in the rail road line earning 5s. a day of your Irish money. And instead of being chained with poverty in Boughill I am crowned with glory and so I bless the day that you had come to Boughill.[27]

A less desirable form of state aid for emigration was the assistance offered by Poor Law unions to 'paupers' to move to the British colonies after 1849. Only relatively small numbers were helped to emigrate under this scheme. In

1848 a separate scheme was established to send orphan girls to the colonies, and more than four thousand girls and young women from workhouses around the country had travelled to Australia by 1850, when the scheme was wound up.

There was much debate about the potential Irish role in 'peopling' the colonies throughout the late 1840s, but in the end proposals for widespread official support came to nothing. The purpose was to remove Ireland's 'surplus' population and transfer it to the colonies, where people were needed to develop the economy and populate the land. In the end these proposals faltered because colonial governments in Canada, Australia and New Zealand were not keen on financing large numbers of poor Catholic Irish, who were not exactly the type of settlers they envisaged. There was also resistance within Russell's ministry on ideological and financial grounds, not least as state assistance went against the moralist agenda of promoting self-help in Ireland.[28] When Charles Trevelyan considered the role of the state in promoting emigration he argued strongly against any form of intervention, believing that emigration should be financed by those most directly affected: the people leaving and the landlords who benefited from their departure.[29] He was not against using the 'surplus population' of Ireland for schemes of colonisation *per se* but thought it should be financed by private sources or colonial governments rather than the Treasury.

But landlord-assisted and state-assisted emigration accounted for only a tiny fraction of the exodus. Most refugees from the famine left Ireland on the strength of their own resources or those of other family members living overseas. Accounts abound of large withdrawals from savings banks in the early years of the crisis, which, together with the selling of livestock to finance the passage, or money derived from dowries, gifts and loans, made up the necessary fares. By the later years family members and other relatives who had left earlier were often in a position to send home the passage money for the New World. In 1848 the remittances amounted to half a million pounds; the following year this doubled and it continued to rise until the mid-1850s. Extraordinary sacrifices made by the early emigrants ensured that siblings, wives, children and other relatives could escape the hunger. It was not unusual for a husband to leave first and hope to earn enough money to pay for his wife and children to join him a few years later. No wonder officials termed the flow of money back to Ireland the 'stream of gold'.[30] Not all this money paid for passage tickets, which accounted for roughly two-fifths of the total remitted to Ireland: the remainder, termed 'American money', was used to support families like the Prendergasts by paying the rent, paying bills or simply surviving.[31]

'A CROWDED CEMETERY'

Even when the passage money arrived, or enough resources were pieced together to buy a fare, the first challenge most emigrants faced was getting to the port. For those whose intention was to make it to Liverpool this involved a long journey across the country, perhaps on foot, to Dublin or Cork and then securing a place on one of the many ships that plied the Irish Sea. Depending on the vessel, it usually took a day to get to Liverpool by steamer, but older sailing-ships could take up to three days to convey hundreds of emigrants crammed together in often horrendous conditions. The great surge in emigration after 1847 ensured that the owners and masters made huge profits from the emigrant trade.[32]

Liverpool was one of the great European ports for travel to North America, with thousands of people waiting to board ships to the United States and Canada. Such an environment was disconcerting for the Irish people who arrived; and, as with any port, there was a fair share of tricksters and crooks (sometimes Irish) seeking to get the naïve emigrant to part with any items of value, including cash.

Ships also sailed directly from Irish ports or called to them for passengers. Sligo, Derry, Limerick and New Ross, as well as Cork and Dublin, handled huge numbers of emigrants in what was, financially at least, a thriving business. The price of passage to Canada was always cheaper than to the American ports, not least because the route was less well regulated and vessels were poorly equipped for the long voyage across the Atlantic.

Facing a transatlantic voyage before the advent of regular steam services in the 1850s was a harrowing experience. Depending on sailing conditions, the journey could take any time up to six weeks. A crossing in the winter months was even more fraught with danger, given the uncertainties of the weather. In a time of famine and the consequent widespread malnutrition this natural anxiety was heightened by fear that fellow-passengers could have contagious diseases, which would rarely be noticed in the cursory medical examination before embarkation. Overcrowded, lacking in provisions and water and sometimes ancient in construction, these unworthy ships soon earned the designation 'coffin ships'.[33] Many were designed to carry goods rather than people, and in bad weather the emigrants were confined below deck or in the hold. Access to food and water was largely dependent on the ship's crew, who could be extremely harsh, caring little for the human cargoes they conveyed. The conditions were very cramped, and when typhus broke out among passengers the results were disastrous.

Stephen de Vere's account of his voyage from Ireland to Canada in steerage (the lowest deck, for third-class passengers) in May and June 1847 publicised the terrible conditions the emigrants had to endure. De Vere, from the prominent Limerick landowning family—his uncle was Lord Monteagle— was a philanthropist who sought to promote emigration as a means of alleviating Ireland's overpopulation. He wrote a long letter to the colonial secretary, Earl Grey, in November 1847 describing problems with the shipping regulations and equally the difficulties in enforcing them. It was the dehumanising aspect of the conditions that troubled him most.

> Before the Emigrant has been a week at sea he is an altered man. How can it be otherwise? Hundreds of poor people, men, women, and children; of all years from the drivelling idiot of 90 to the babe just born; huddled together without light; without air; wallowing in filth and breathing a foetid atmosphere; sick in body; dispirited in heart;—the fevered Patients lying between the Sound, in sleeping places so narrow as almost to deny them the power of indulging by a change of position the natural restlessness of the disease; by their agonized ravings disturbing those around, & predisposing them through the Effects of the imagination, to imbibe the contagion; living without food or medicine except as Administered by the hand of Casual charity; dying without the voice of Spiritual Consolation; and buried in the deep—without the rites of the Church.[34]

Drunkenness was common, fuelled by the sale of 'grog' by the captain, who also rationed the water by using a false measure. According to de Vere, this ship apparently 'was better regulated and more comfortable than many that reach Canada'.[35]

The facilities at Grosse-Île were wholly inadequate in his view for the enormous number of ill and dying people who arrived there from mid-1847. Travellers were housed in sheds, the fit mixing with the ill, and were required to sleep on straw that had been used by previous occupants; many families preferred 'to burrow under heaps of loose stones which happened to be piled up near the shore, rather than accept the shelter of the infected Sheds'.[36]

Grosse-Île became synonymous with death and disease in the summer of 1847, when the huge influx of ships carrying diseased and malnourished refugees from Ireland completely overwhelmed the meagre medical staff on the island. The medical superintendent of the station, Dr George Mellis Douglas, was shocked at the state of the arrivals in May 1847; he had 'never contemplated the possibility of every vessel arriving with fever as they do now.'[37] Ship after ship waited for inspection, with people dying on board or soon after they landed. Throughout the summer of 1847 the deaths mounted. Best estimates suggest that at least twelve thousand people were interred there, with many more buried at sea.

When the Anglican Bishop of Montréal visited Grosse-Île in August he was shocked by the plight of the emigrants, with people dying in front of him, 'ships that had not one really healthy person on board', and the sad sight of the body of a boy who had been walking with friends and then sat down under a tree and died.[38] At that time more than 2,500 people were admitted to the poorly equipped hospital, with fever rampant. Many arrived in a state of starvation, as the inadequate provision of food had left them malnourished and susceptible to disease. Arrivals who went to the quarantine station at Partridge Island in New Brunswick faced similar fates, though the numbers were smaller.

The fact that the tenants of the foreign secretary, Lord Palmerston, were part of this ill-fated exodus added to the public outcry in Canada about the appalling state of the arrivals, who were barely clothed. Lord Palmerston left the details to his agents, who were called to account for their actions in front of a House of Lords committee in 1848.[39] For a landlord who sought to exemplify how humanely he treated his tenants, the succession of ships that arrived late in the 1847 season packed full of ill, malnourished and almost naked emigrants from his own Sligo estate was a shocking indictment of the disregard of a basic duty of care.

Approximately one out of every twenty people who left Ireland or Liverpool for North America during the late 1840s died on board the ship.[40] In 1847 nearly a third of the 100,000 people who departed for Canada perished in what was a tragedy of staggering proportions. One American official involved with regulating immigration later observed that 'if crosses and tombs could be erected on the water the whole route of the emigrant vessels from Europe to America would long since have assumed the appearance of a crowded cemetery'.[41] Canadian officials blamed the huge loss of life on the conditions on board the ships, and the greed of owners and captains who sought to profit from the panic to escape Ireland that took hold in 1847. The weak enforcement of shipping regulations played a large part in allowing this to occur.

Because of the imposition of more rigorous regulations, this catastrophe was not repeated in subsequent years.[42]

A PERFECT HIVE OF HUMAN BEINGS

For those who did survive the crossing and the quarantine stations, the next step was to get to a city or town. From Grosse-Île, steamers departed along the Saint Lawrence River to Québec and Montréal. Both cities experienced outbreaks of typhus. In Montréal those with fever were housed in sheds at Pointe-Saint-Charles, which soon became another Grosse-Île. Up to six thousand Irish emigrants died here. The typhus took its toll on those who visited the sheds: eight Catholic priests and the mayor of the city died after contracting fever during mercy visits. From Montréal, barges carried people upriver to the cities of Toronto and Kingston, where the streets were 'crowded with emaciated, destitute Irish emigrants, many actually in fever', causing widespread panic about contagion.[43]

Roughly half those who landed in Canada made immediately for the United States, as relatives and friends already living there could offer much-needed financial support, as was the case with Michael Prendergast. Despite the best efforts of officials to turn back Irish immigrants at the border, most made it to the 'land of liberty', where they gravitated towards the big East Coast cities. There they joined the large numbers who had arrived at American ports, such as New York, Boston, Philadelphia and New Orleans. Unlike the Canadian passage, ships landing at American ports were subject to stringent regulation and heavy fines, and the system of regulation was further tightened in the spring of 1847 under the Passenger Acts after a significant number of deaths on ships arriving the previous summer. Both New York and Boston had quarantine stations outside the city at which passengers were inspected.[44] Ships that were suspected of carrying passengers who were ill with fever were turned away from Boston in 1847. Between 1847 and 1851 roughly 850,000 Irish people landed at New York. Many left immediately for other cities and towns, joining family members, but others stayed, most often those with fewest resources. By 1855 people born in Ireland accounted for a third of New York's expanding population.[45] Wards in Lower Manhattan, where cheap accommodation was available in cellars and boarding-houses, were attractive to the poorest, and significant numbers ended up in the Five Points district, including some of Lord Palmerston's tenants from Co. Sligo and those assisted to leave the Lansdowne estate in Kenmare.[46]

In Boston similarly the Irish arrivals crowded into the poor districts of the city, including Fort Hill, where the Prendergasts first settled. One report from August 1847 described houses in North Square where nine people shared a single room and another where fifteen people shared two attics.[47] Cellars without light or air housed large numbers of people, sometimes up to fifteen people sharing these confined spaces. The outbreak of cholera in 1849 prompted investigations into the conditions of the famine Irish living in the city, and the members of the Committee on Internal Health were shocked by what they discovered in Ward 8, the Irish district.

> During the visits last summer your Committee were witnesses of scenes too painful to be forgotten and yet too disgusting to be related here. It is sufficient to say that this whole district is a perfect hive of human beings, without comforts and mostly without common necessaries; in many cases huddled together like brutes, without regard to age or sex or sense of decency; grown men and women sleeping together in the same apartment and sometimes wife and husband, brothers and sisters in the same bed. Under such circumstances self-respect, forethought, all the high and noble values soon die out, and sullen indifference and despair or disorder, intemperance and utter degradation reign supreme.[48]

In all the American cities the famine refugees posed what was essentially a massive public-health challenge. On arrival, the diseased and destitute needed to be cared for, preferably with no contact with others, in fever hospitals. In Philadelphia, where more than 75,000 Irish arrivals landed, the municipal authorities sought to cope with a range of issues arising from the influx, including destitution, medical care, sanitation and then a cholera epidemic in 1849.[49] Cramped housing bred disease, and the famine Irish were often confined to poor-quality accommodation for the first few years after settling in towns and cities, by virtue of their poverty.

Lastly, a whole range of social problems emerged, though not exclusive to the Irish, associated with any group of poor and vulnerable people: criminality, a propensity to violence, and drunkenness.

'IRISH FEVER'

The great majority of refugees opted for North America, but a significant share also travelled across the Irish Sea to Britain in the 1840s and early 1850s. The number of Irish people living in Britain nearly doubled during the 1840s, and it is estimated that up to 300,000 people settled there. Those with fewest resources could usually scrape enough for the fare on the steamers that connected Ireland with ports in England, Wales and Scotland. Newport, Cardiff, Swansea, Whitehaven and London all received arrivals from Ireland, but it is Liverpool that is most associated with the famine influx. After arriving, many radiated out of the ports to other towns and cities. Nearly 300,000 people arrived from Ireland in 1847 alone, most of whom then booked transatlantic voyages.[50] Many of those who came to Liverpool intended saving the fare to make the transatlantic passage, a forlorn hope given their circumstances. Scotland, especially Glasgow, was also an important destination, especially for emigrants from the north of Ireland.

A Liverpool magistrate, Edward Rushton, writing in 1849, feared that the city had become a dumping-ground for the Irish poor.

> Beyond all doubt, the towns on the seacoast in Ireland and many of landed proprietors in Ireland furnish the wretched Irish with the means of coming to Liverpool. I have often discovered this from the examination of the poor and only the other day an Irish offender, when asked where he came from, said he was sent with one shilling from the Irish workhouse to Liverpool.[51]

Unlike the Poor Law in Ireland, under the English system the destitute had to be provided with food. The influx of poor Irish people in 1847 placed a huge burden on the authorities, who struggled to cope, while pleas for assistance from the government in London fell on deaf ears.

By far the more potent threat was from fever—'Irish fever', as it was called. A typhus epidemic broke out in March 1847, and this was attributed to the Irish. Typhus spreads in unsanitary and overcrowded conditions, and many of the Irish people lived in the cellars of poor districts. The medical officer for the city, Dr W. H. Duncan, described Liverpool as a 'city of plague' in 1847. By May urgent action was required, and the government set aside two ships as hospitals for Irish arrivals. Altogether about five thousand Irish people died in the city from fever in 1847, earning it the description of the 'hospital and cemetery of Ireland'.[52] From late 1847 onwards the flow from Ireland to Liverpool slowed down, much to the relief of hard-pressed medical and Poor Law officials.

Irish people also went in large numbers to ports in south Wales, posing similar problems for the authorities.[53] The west of Scotland, and especially Glasgow, was also an important destination. Like Liverpool, Glasgow was a port from which transatlantic passengers left for the New World, and it also experienced an outbreak of famine fever in 1847. The Irish were pinpointed as the source. Unlike Liverpool, however, Highlanders seeking to escape the Great Highland Famine also travelled to the city, adding to the demand for poor relief and medical care. In March 1847, just as the epidemic was beginning to take hold, the *Glasgow Herald* declared that the 'great majority of cases of typhus which occurred may be traced to the masses of diseased and famished Irish which have been thrown amongst us'.[54]

Through efforts to isolate fever victims in hospitals and to fumigate their houses, undertaken vigorously from July 1847, the outbreak was contained. The total number of Irish people who died from fever is estimated at just over two thousand. An outbreak of cholera the following year was also attributed to the Irish. Some refugees made their way to Edinburgh, attracted by the possibility of employment, and settled in the Irish districts of the city, around the Cowgate and Grassmarket, and also in Leith.[55] When a medical officer compiled a report on sanitary conditions in the city in 1849 he argued that only a restriction on Irish immigration would solve the problem.

> By far the greatest proportion of the lowest class in Edinburgh is now composed of Irish; and the state of overcrowding, filth, and want of the necessaries of life amid which they live makes it surprising that typhus fever should ever leave their dwellings ... It is true that the measures now needed [for sanitary improvements] would require to be somewhat different from those in former times; but it is to be feared that nothing will be effectual till a stop is put to the now regular immigration and settlement of the low Irish in all our towns.[56]

Restrictions on Irish immigration were discussed openly from 1847 onwards, but any such barriers on movement flew in the face of the Act of Union. What the authorities could do was to remove the Irish people who were dependent on poor relief back to Ireland, to stop them becoming a permanent charge on the poor rates. About fifteen thousand Irish paupers were removed from Liverpool in 1847, along with ten thousand more from Scottish ports in both 1847 and 1848, at the expense of the Poor Law authorities.[57]

There was little to stop those removed from heading back on the next ship going across the Irish Sea. Few people left Ireland to take advantage of the poor relief or charity available in England, Scotland and Wales. Dire circumstances dictated that they had to leave in order to survive.

LEGACIES

The great exodus from Ireland from 1847 onwards had a lasting legacy. The immediate effect, however, was to bring the destruction of the famine to the attention of American and British people in the stark reality of destitute, malnourished and often desperately ill people. These images of the poor Irish who arrived in the 1840s and early 1850s proved to be enduring stereotypes in Britain, the United States and Canada.[58] The constant stream of 'wretched' Irish people arriving in Britain hardened attitudes both towards Irish landlords—who it was widely perceived had sent them—and towards the Irish poor themselves. The amendments made to the Irish Poor Law in 1847 were partly an effort to contain the poor within that country, with Irish rather than British ratepayers footing the bill.

The long-term consequence was that every generation that grew up in Ireland in the wake of the famine sent a vast number of people to live overseas—in the United States, Canada, Australia and New Zealand as well as Britain—causing a sharp decline in population that was reversed only in the last quarter of the twentieth century and that in the process created a massive global diaspora.

The image of the 'coffin ship' was seared into memory and is one that endures even to the present day. The success of a fictional account written in the 1890s that purported to be the diary of Gerald Keegan shows how the Canadian voyages in 1847 are regarded as symbolic of the experience of refugees from the famine. Another evocative account was supposedly written by Robert Whyte, who apparently joined a ship in Dublin bound for Québec in May 1847. He allegedly kept a diary of his experiences: the document recounts in graphic detail how the ship was overrun by fever and was then held at Grosse-Île, where many of the passengers perished. Who the author was, and whether he was indeed on a ship that left Ireland for Québec in that year, are uncertain.[59]

For the famine Irish, the experience of leaving in an atmosphere of panic and basic struggle for survival created a bitter memory that fuelled later nationalist sentiment in the United States. The sense of exile that was created had far-reaching consequences, particularly as a central grievance of nationalists was the negligent role of the British government during the famine, which led to these forced departures. Most never returned and spent their lives in distant places far from Ireland. But for them home was always the country that they were forced to leave in those years of hunger. Such sentiments of exile, revenge and ultimately the redemptive return are captured ironically in the words of George Bernard Shaw's Irish-American character, Hector Malone, in *Man and Superman* (1903):

Malone   He will get over it all right enough. Men thrive better on disappointments in love then on disappointments in money. I daresay you think that sordid; but I know what I'm talking about. Me father died of starvation in Ireland in the black 47. Maybe you've heard of it.

Violent   The Famine?

Malone   [*with smouldering passion*] No, the starvation. When a country is full o food, and exporting it, there can be no famine. Me father was starved dead: and I was starved out to America in me mother's arms. English rule drove me and mine out of Ireland. Well, you can keep Ireland. Me and me like are coming back to buy England; and we'll buy the best of it.

EPILOGUE
The death of Martin Collins

On 23 November 1850 Martin Collins, aged fifty, died at the side of the road in Co. Clare. There was nothing exceptional about his death: in fact such personal tragedies had become commonplace. He was found dying on the roadside and brought into a house, and a priest was sent for. The priest gave the old woman living in the house money to get milk and some meal, which she did. Collins lay down on the stone floor of her cabin and died.

At the inquest his son testified that he had gone to the local Poor Law official seeking relief and was given permission to get some meal, but when he went to collect it it was all gone. As Lord Sidney Godolphin Osborne wrote, this 'is only the routine end of such folk in that part of the world'. When he was buried the following day there was no coffin or shroud, and his body was merely 'rolled up in straw'.[1] When the readers of the *Times* saw this account they were perhaps by this time inured to accounts of Irish suffering. It served to remind them, however, that the famine in Ireland was not over.

Outbreaks of potato blight continued to occur in parts the country until the early 1850s. Only in 1852 did the workhouse population begin to decrease gradually from its peak of more than 800,000 in July 1848, and outdoor relief was still needed in parts of Munster and Connacht to feed local populations.[2] When the cost was counted it was estimated in 1850 that £8.1 million was spent from central government funds in Ireland—a modest amount by any standards, given the scale of suffering, and much of which was to be repaid. In the event, many of the debts were written off, as no repayments could be made.[3]

The Great Irish Famine was the world's first modern famine, in that it was widely reported in the international press and documented by a state. Ironically, responsibility for dealing with it lay with the state that documented it. British politicians and officials controlled the most developed state system in the world. It had sophisticated systems of governance and, possessed of a vast empire and immense financial reserves, had the capacity to mitigate the worst effects of the destruction of the potato crop. The politicians who governed this state were self-consciously 'enlightened' men: strict disciples of the equally potent values of Christian conviction and rationalist thought, who saw in the famine an opportunity to initiate lasting change. On 31 March 1848 Lord Palmerston, more rationalist than Christian, identified what he saw as the essential change needed in Ireland:

> It is useless to disguise the truth that any great improvement in the social system of Ireland must be founded upon an extensive change in the present state of agrarian occupation, and that this change necessarily implies a long continued and systematic ejectment of Small Holders and Squatting Cottiers.[4]

Such views were shared by other politicians, officials, leader-writers and many other powerful contemporaries.

The fact that the word 'famine' was rarely used by ministers or officials, in public at least, indicates a deep reluctance to confront fully the human consequence of the failure of the potato crop. Acknowledging the existence of a famine placed these responsibilities on an altogether different level. 'Distress', 'crisis', 'destitution', or similar terms combined with such adjectives as 'severe' or 'extreme', were widely used, even in the title of the British Association for the Relief of the Extreme Distress in Ireland and Scotland.[5] There was also an element of double-speak. On the one hand in the early years the Whig government and its supporters in the newspapers denied that the conditions in Ireland constituted a famine; yet by 1847 they were pointing out that the Irish poor lived constantly in a state of near-famine and that this was the explanation why no government could ever deal with such a level of suffering.[6]

The Irish rural economy confounded reason, so rationality must then be imposed. The body of thought on which contemporaries drew consisted of variations of classical political economy.[7] This led to a number of fatal decisions. The first was to use public works as the principal means of relief when a starving population was unable to work. This was such a cumbersome and blunt instrument for helping the poor that it could not fulfil its stated objective—providing the means to buy food—while at the same time ensuring that dependence was not created. It became a tried and trusted element of famine relief policy in Ireland but worked only in isolated incidences of food shortages of limited duration.

The stated policy of not interfering with the food supply in the winter of 1846/7 was also in line with the doctrines of free trade. When the government did seek to purchase quantities of corn on the international market it was too little and too late. By restricting the activities of the relief measures to the western part of the country, and then imposing a strict embargo on when food could be sold at cost price, it created severe hardship and caused many deaths from October 1846. The powerful and possessing elites worried that the poor would become debased by the absence of work and self-reliance.

Arguably most lethal in the great loss of life was the ending of temporary relief measures in the autumn of 1847, and making the Irish Poor Law the principal mechanism for helping the poor, destitute and dying. At the heart of this decision was the imperative to reduce the exposure of the exchequer to the continuing costs of relief during a financial crisis in Britain. Ireland would be made to rely on its own resources. A secondary aim was to ensure that relief was given in the harsh conditions of the workhouse, distinguishing the needy from the indolent. This made a mockery of the Act of Union, as it emphasised Ireland's separateness.

Declaring the crisis to be coming to an end in 1847—or at least winding up the main activities of central government—meant that millions of people were forced to rely on the wholly inadequate Poor Law system from August 1847. Thousands of the now enlarged ranks of the poor were destined for a long, slow and painful death in the years up to the early 1850s, whether this was at home, in the workhouse or, like Martin Collins, at the side of the road.

Can this be explained by inadequate information or knowledge? If anything, politicians had an excess of information—though not necessarily understanding—about the unfolding crisis, as the huge volumes of official correspondence from various arms of the Irish executive in Dublin Castle and reports from relief workers, landlords and clergy from around the country demonstrate.

Underlying each individual decision was a more insidious objective: the wholesale transformation of Irish society. The 'Irish problem', as identified by a plethora of observers in the 1830s and 1840s, centred on two related aspects: the dehumanising poverty of much of the rural population and the system of land tenure. The Irish rural economy was perceived to be anachronistic, a relic of an old world that was sustained by an indifferent class of landlords, who had little interest in improving their estates and who simply extracted the rental income. Even though there were regions in the north, east and south where commercialised farming was the norm, it was widely perceived that the root cause of Irish poverty was this form of 'primitive' agriculture. The aim was to make labourers and smallholders into wage workers employed by large farmers on commercial holdings that would use the most up-to-date agricultural techniques to maximise production and profit. Land, together with labour, was a commodity from which the maximum return should be squeezed. Any 'surplus' population would be encouraged to emigrate to the colonies, which were badly in need of Anglophone settlers.

Central to this regeneration was the removal of the worst landlords and their replacement with a new class of capitalists, encouraged to purchase debt-ridden estates under the Encumbered Estates Act, and bringing about similar transformations on a smaller scale. The parallel here was with Scotland, where new landowners who had recently purchased Highland estates with commercial wealth proved effective in the face of similar failures of the potato crop. The Great Highland Famine of the 1840s was nowhere near as widespread as the Irish one, but it is telling that the loss of life was minimal, largely because of the activities of energetic landlords and the Free Church of Scotland.[8]

Leaving aside the disastrous human consequences of this radical remaking of Irish society, promoting changes towards this end during a time of acute crisis was the most brutal aspect of policy in Ireland in the late 1840s. Charles Trevelyan's vision of regeneration through forced change was forged in his experiences in India in the 1830s, where he actively promoted the adoption of European languages to impose European civilisation on an inferior culture. It was not coincidental that when a famine broke out in Orissa in the mid-1860s, officials in India cited Trevelyan's policy in Ireland in the 1840s as justification for not interfering with the market.[9]

Nowhere are such views more evident than in Trevelyan's self-satisfied review of government policy, first published anonymously in January 1848. By then it was declared that the famine had passed, notwithstanding the fact that many more people would die. Trevelyan wrote that 'although the process by which long-established habits are changed, and society is reconstructed on a new basis, must necessarily be slow, there are not wanting signs that we are advancing by sure steps towards the desired end'.[10] History would judge that the famine had initiated a 'salutary revolution in the habits of a nation long singularly unfortunate' and would 'acknowledge that on this, as on many other occasions, Supreme Wisdom has educed permanent good out of transient evil'.[11]

Trevelyan took a perverse pride in the 'sure steps': the demise of the potato and the increasing cultivation of corn, the reduction in competition for small plots of land, the deserted farms, and the consolidation of holdings. For him 'the large quantity of land left uncultivated in some of the western districts is a painful but decisive proof of the extent to which this change is taking place', and he was convinced that 'the appointed time of Ireland's regeneration is at last come'.[12] His concluding statement fused providentialism—the belief that events were divinely predestined—with lofty aspirations in one of the most revealing insights into the world view of the most influential civil servant in charge of Irish famine relief.

> The deep and inveterate root of social evil remained, and this has been laid bare by a direct stroke of an all-wise and all-merciful Providence, as if this part of the case were beyond the unassisted power of man. Innumerable had been the specifics [remedies] which the wit of man had devised; but even the idea of the sharp but effectual, remedy by which the cure is likely to be effected had never occurred to any one. God grant that the generation to which this great opportunity has been offered, may rightly perform its part, and that we may not relax our efforts until Ireland fully participates in the social health and physical prosperity of Great Britain, which will be the true consummation of their union.[13]

While the openly providential element was certainly characteristic of Trevelyan, British ministers, including Lord John Russell, the Liberal prime minister, shared his assessment that the famine was an opportunity to bring about real and lasting change in Ireland.[14] These were an incremental, constantly evolving and opportunist set of policies that were implemented over the famine years in response to specific circumstances, but the general effect amounted to the destruction of the culture of smallholders, cottiers and landless labourers, with great loss of life.

Trevelyan was right, however. The transformation for which he longed was set in train as hundreds of thousands of labourers and smallholders were removed from the landscape by eviction, emigration and death. Large tenant-farmers, many of whom consolidated and extended their holdings, dominated the economic, political and social life of post-famine Ireland. The remaining smallholders who managed to cling to their parcels of land were marginalised and mostly clustered in the poorer regions along the western and north-western coast. Landless labourers fared even worse.[15]

Such changes might have occurred gradually anyway, as agriculture became an increasingly commercial activity over the course of the nineteenth century; it is impossible to know. A review of the 'progress of Ireland' a decade later declared with some satisfaction that a 'social revolution' had occurred, comprising the sale of indebted estates, the transfer of the land from 'pauper cottiers to real farmers', and the growth in pastoral farming. According to William O'Connor Morris, an Irish barrister and noted historian, while the country's 'strange regeneration is, in some respects, owing to a power above that of man, we should not forget how greatly human wisdom has contributed to it'.[16]

If the ideology of the free market were not lethal enough, there was also a racist element in many of the public discussions in Britain about the proper relief policies to be pursued in Ireland. The Irish 'national character' was deemed to be debased and the Celts were an altogether inferior race, whose culture and ways of life were simply not worth preserving. This culture was seen as inimical to economic development, and its eradication was crucial to Ireland's prosperity.

These views were given particular prominence in the *Times*, especially from 1847 onwards. The editor, John Thadeus Delane, was descended from the Delaneys of Queen's County but was no friend of Ireland. The role of the *Times* in shaping public opinion on the deficiencies of the Irish national character should not be underestimated.[17] Ministers were acutely sensitive to any criticism that could be directed at policies by this influential organ of public opinion. The degree to which individual politicians fully subscribed to this racist interpretation is difficult to judge with precision. One powerful figure, Lord Clarendon, who became lord lieutenant of Ireland in 1847, did seem to have some sympathy with such views. On 10 June 1848 he observed that Ireland's ills were due to its deficient national character: 'The real Celt is … almost incapable … of foreseeing the consequences of his own acts … He will … rather plot than work … sooner starve … than prosper by industry.'[18] Writing shortly after his appointment to his friend Henry Reeve, who worked at the *Times*, Clarendon declared that the 'real difficulty lies, however, with the people themselves. They are always in the mud … Their idleness and helplessness can hardly be believed.'[19]

Why was this not more aggressively challenged within Ireland? After the death of Daniel O'Connell in May 1847 and the forced exile of the Young Ireland leaders there was a lack of political leadership. If Archbishop MacHale had not been so preoccupied with defending Irish Catholicism in Rome in 1848 he might have played a more active role, though the papacy was notoriously uneasy at Catholic prelates adopting a political function. In any event, MacHale's record of open criticism of the government on a range of policies from the 1830s militated against this, as he was seen to be simply opposed to almost every important policy and particularly viewed as anxious to keep Catholics uneducated at a level where they could not challenge clerical teaching.

If the church's silence was noticeable, the Irish middle classes were equally muted. A number of Irish MPs cheerfully voting for the Gregory clause in March 1847, including the Liberator's nephew, Morgan John O'Connell, spoke volumes about the concern of the elite for the Irish poor.[20] There was no doubt that some restriction on relief from the Poor Law would be introduced; the question was at what level. Morgan John O'Connell viewed the clause 'as a valuable alteration. It might not give complete satisfaction at first; but I am sure that before many years it will be found most useful.'[21] The only sustained opposition in the House of Commons came from the English radical MP and champion of the smallholder George Poulett Scrope.[22] Scrope accurately predicted the effects of this measure:

> Its consequence would be a complete clearance of the small farmers in Ireland—a change which would amount to a perfect social revolution in the state of things in that country. Such a change might be desirable, if effected by degrees; but to introduce it at once would have the effect of turning great masses of pauperism adrift on the community—a catastrophe which would undoubtedly not be without its effects in this country.[23]

A handful of MPs, seven in total, including Scrope and the radical Ulster reformer William Sharman Crawford, opposed the Gregory clause.

Strong farmers had much to gain from this transformation, in their capacity as ratepayers and also when more land became available and they could adopt ranching practices, based on the profitable rearing of livestock. Living standards rose in the wake of the famine as millions of people left the country, drawn primarily from the lower classes. The 'problem' of Irish poverty so often described to account for the country's 'backwardness' was largely solved. The nostrums advocated by the disciples of reason and free trade in the 1830s and 1840s, such as the promotion of commercialised farming and the displacement of large numbers of cottiers, smallholders and labourers, were achieved in practice by the brutal mechanisms of death and emigration.

One of the ironies is that the middle classes who benefited from these changes in the reshaping of post-famine Ireland would later blame the British government for the disaster of the 1840s. As the nationalist critiques of British rule evolved in the 1870s and 1880s, the inadequate response of the government to the Great Irish Famine was seen as a major grievance. When it came to the question of the very survival of the poor they were themselves largely powerless and had few defenders to moderate or resist the effects of the omnipotent state.

Trevelyan went on to jointly write the famous Northcote-Trevelyan Report in 1854, which established the principle of open competition and promotion by merit within the British civil service. He was appointed governor of Madras in 1859 but recalled after a dispute that involved passing a document to a newspaper. Subsequently vindicated, he was made a minister of finance in India in 1862 and returned to Britain in 1865. After his retirement he wrote about a number of social problems, such as poverty. He was created a baronet in 1874, inherited his cousin's estate at Wallington, Northumberland, in 1879, and died in London in 1886.

The ascendancy of Paul Cullen as Archbishop of Armagh and then of Dublin meant that from the early 1850s John MacHale was effectually sidelined within the ranks of the Irish Catholic bishops; his 'influence was waning so fast that it came to nothing'.[24] After a series of controversies with powerful figures in Rome in the 1850s his once-potent connections there fell away. With the emergence of the home rule movement in the 1870s, which he supported, he consolidated his image as the patriot bishop.[25] An unseemly attempt in 1875 to have his nephew, Thomas MacHale, named coadjutor bishop with the right to succeed him ended in ignominious failure. He died in November 1881 and was buried in his cathedral in Tuam.

John Mitchel escaped from Van Diemen's Land in 1853 and eventually reached San Francisco, where he received a hero's welcome. He then moved to New York, where he started a newspaper, the *Irish Citizen*, in which he defended slavery in the United States, most notoriously arguing in 1854 that slavery 'is good in itself, good in its relations with other countries, good in every way'.[26] In this he was echoing his hero Thomas Carlyle, with all the racist underpinnings.

In 1855 Mitchel left New York for East Tennessee, where he bought a large farm and edited a newspaper, the *Southern Citizen*, that strongly supported slavery. During this time he wrote his famous books about Ireland, including *The Last Conquest of Ireland (Perhaps)* (1861) and *The History of Ireland* (1867), which achieved remarkable success and helped foster Irish-American nationalist sentiment. After a brief period in Paris he returned to the United

States on the outbreak of the Civil War in 1861, in which his three sons fought on the Confederate side, two being killed. In the mid-1860s he worked as a Fenian agent in Paris but soon returned to the United States. By the early 1870s he was a revered figure within Irish-American nationalist circles. In 1875 he was elected a member of parliament for Tipperary in a by-election but as a runaway felon was disqualified. He returned to Ireland that year but was seriously ill. He died on 20 March 1875 and was buried with his parents in the Unitarian cemetery in Newry.

Elizabeth and Hal Smith moved from Baltiboys, Co. Wicklow, to a house in Lower Leeson Street, Dublin, in 1850 when their daughter Annie married James King, and the young couple took over the running of the estate. Their management was not successful, however, and Elizabeth returned to run the estate after Hal's death in December 1862. A decade later, in 1873, their son Jack, an army officer, contracted sunstroke and died. He left a young wife and a baby girl, and Elizabeth saw it as her duty to maintain the estate for her granddaughter, resolving to 'become a tenant where I had been so long, nearly fifty years, as mistress'.[27] She spent the rest of her long life in Baltiboys, dying in November 1885. Shortly before her death she confided to her diary that 'I am happy still, remembering the past fondly and looking cheerfully forward for a space that won't be long'.[28]

As for the country itself, the traumatic events of the Great Irish Famine were etched into the consciousness, shaping the Irish psyche for generations to come. A natural disaster became a human one over the course of the late 1840s. Universal systems of thought derived from Enlightenment concern with reason were translated in Ireland into rigid adherence to the ideologies of free trade and the protection of the rights of property over and above that of human life. Notwithstanding the different inflexions within these ideological outlooks, be they of a moralist or rationalist bent, the cumulative effect was a brutal logic. No doubt for these politicians and officials this mass suffering was regrettable, but it was seen as a necessary stage in the imposition of reason on a society and culture that was steeped in archaic ways of life. Only regeneration could bring about the complete transformation of the country. The violence of this process compressed within seven short years confounds present-day sensibilities. The results were just as horrific: at least a million people perished, and another two million left the country within a decade. Reason exacted an apocalyptic toll.

NOTES

Prologue (pp. 1–5)

Full bibliographical details for printed items can be found in the list of references.

1. *Illustrated London News*, 22 December 1849.
2. House of Commons, *Report of the Select Committee into the Administration of the Poor Law in Kilrush Union*, P.P 1850 [613], XI, p. 248. This data was compiled by Francis Coffee, a civil engineer living in Kilrush.
3. Quoted by Murphy in *A Starving People*, p. 53.
4. Ciarán Ó Murchadha, '"The Exterminator General of Clare": Marcus Keane of Beech Park (1815–1883)', in Ciarán Ó Murchadha (ed.), *County Clare Studies: Essays in Memory of Gerald O'Connell, Seán Ó Murchadha, Thomas Coffey and Pat Flynn* (Ennis: Clare Archaeological and Historical Society, 2000), pp. 169–200.
5. A revealing indication of his approach to ejecting tenants is contained in his evidence to the select committee: see *Report of the Select Committee into the Administration of the Poor Law in Kilrush Union*, pp. 86–104.
6. Donnelly, *The Great Irish Potato Famine*, pp. 144–6.
7. *Illustrated London News*, 22 December 1849.
8. Quoted in Ó Murchadha, *The Great Famine*, pp. 125–6.
9. *Times*, 17 December 1850; see also his account of evictions in Sidney Godolphin Osborne, *Gleanings in the West of Ireland* (London: T. and W. Boone, 1850), based on his visits to Ireland in the summers of 1849 and 1850.

Chapter 1 (pp. 8–27)

1. O'Reilly, *John MacHale, Archbishop of Tuam*, vol. I, p. 25.
2. This account is based on Richard Musgrave, *Memoirs of the Different Rebellions in Ireland …* (3rd ed., Dublin: J. Archer, 1802), vol. II, pp. 135–6; Thomas Pakenham, *The Year of Liberty: The History of the Great Irish Rebellion of 1798* (rev. ed., London: Phoenix, 1992), pp. 308–11; James Quinn, 'John Denis Browne, 3rd Earl of Altamont', in McGuire and Quinn, *Dictionary of Irish Biography*; Guy Beiner, *Remembering the Year of the French: Irish Folk History and Social Memory* (Madison: University of Wisconsin Press, 2007), pp. 217–19, 262.

3. O'Reilly, *John MacHale, Archbishop of Tuam*, vol. I, p. 28.
4. Quoted in Katherine Prior, Lance Brennan and Robin Haines, 'Bad Language: The Role of English, Persian and other Esoteric Tongues in the Dismissal of Sir Edward Colebrooke as Resident of Delhi in 1829', *Modern Asian Studies*, 35, no. 1 (2001), p. 75.
5. Frederick Charles Danvers et al., *Memorials of Old Haileybury College* (London: A. Constable, 1894), p. 374; Keith Tribe, 'Professors Malthus and Jones: Political Economy at the East India College, 1806–1858', *European Journal of the History of Economic Thought*, 2, no. 2 (1995), pp. 327–54; S. Ambirajan, *Classical Political Economy and British Policy in India* (Cambridge South Asian Studies, 21) (New York and London: Cambridge University Press, 1978), pp. 9–17; Haines, *Charles Trevelyan and the Great Irish Famine*, pp. 33–4.
6. Quoted in Prior et al., 'Bad Language', p. 105.
7. Haines, *Charles Trevelyan and the Great Irish Famine*, p. 35.
8. Details from Roger T. Stearn, 'Sir John Peter Grant of Rothiemurchus (1774–1848)', in *Oxford Dictionary of National Biography*.
9. Grant, *Memoirs of a Highland Lady*, vol. I, p. 200, 213.
10. *Blackwood's Edinburgh Magazine*, 163, no. 990 (April 1898), p. 537. For unflattering assessments of his career in the House of Commons see R. G. Thorne, *The House of Commons, 1790–1820* (London: Secker and Warburg, 1986), vol. V, pp. 68–70, and D. R. Fisher, *The History of Parliament: The House of Commons, 1820–1832* (Cambridge: Cambridge University Press, 1989), vol. V, pp. 379–83.
11. T. C. Smout, 'The Grant Lairds of Rothiemurchus', in Smout and Lambert, *Rothiemurchus*, p. 16.
12. Dillon, *The Life of John Mitchel*, vol. I, p. 25. All subsequent quotations in this section are from this work unless otherwise indicated.
13. *Times*, 25 January 1871. The Orange Order, founded in September 1795 at Loughgall, Co. Armagh, sought to defend Protestantism through commemorating the victory of William of Orange over the forces led by King James II at the Battle of the Boyne on 1 July 1690. In its early years its support was mostly from lower-class Anglicans and relatively few Presbyterians.
14. Thomas Carlyle's note, Jane Welsh Carlyle to Thomas Carlyle, 23 August 1846, in Kenneth J. Fielding and Clyde De L. Ryals (eds.), *The Collected Letters of Thomas and Jane Welsh Carlyle* (Durham, NC, and London: Duke University Press, 1995), vol. 21, p. 25.
15. The Society of United Irishmen, founded in 1791, was a middle-class non-denominational radical organisation with Presbyterian, Catholic and Anglican members that evolved into a revolutionary republican movement

which initiated the 1798 Rebellion to overthrow British rule and establish an Irish republic. It had a disproportionate appeal to Presbyterians, particularly in Cos. Antrim and Down, where the numbers of Catholics were small and unthreatening.

16. Robert Mahony, "'New Light': Ulster Presbyterianism and the Nationalist Rhetoric of John Mitchel', in Lawrence M. Geary (ed.), *Rebellion and Remembrance in Modern Ireland* (Dublin: Four Courts Press, 2001), pp. 148–58.

17. Biographical details are taken from Colin Barr, 'John MacHale', in McGuire and Quinn, *Dictionary of Irish Biography*; Bourke, *The Life and Times of the Most Rev. John MacHale*; Emmet Larkin, 'John MacHale', in *Oxford Dictionary of National Biography*; O'Reilly, *John MacHale, Archbishop of Tuam*, vol. I, pp. 13–92.

18. Caesar Otway, *Sketches in Erris and Tyrawly* (Dublin: W. Curry, 1841), p. 8.

19. O'Reilly, *John MacHale, Archbishop of Tuam*, vol. I, p. 43.

20. Costello, *John MacHale*, p. 20.

21. Ibid.

22. Hierophilos [John MacHale], *Letters to the English People: On the Moral and Political State of Ireland* (London: Keating and Brown, 1822), p. vii.

23. Quoted in Costello, *John MacHale*, p. 30.

24. *Eighth Report of the Commissioners of Irish Education Inquiry, dated London 2 June 1827: Roman Catholic College of Maynooth*, P.P. 1826–7 (509), XIII, p. 831.

25. O'Reilly, *John MacHale, Archbishop of Tuam*, vol. I, p. 161.

26. Quoted in Kerr, *Peel, Priests and Politics*, p. 24.

27. Quoted in John F. Broderick, *The Holy See and the Irish Movement for the Repeal of the Union with England, 1829–1847* (Rome: Universitas Gregoriana, 1951), p. 91.

28. Daniel O'Connell to John MacHale, 10 December 1834, in W. J. Fitzpatrick (ed.), *Correspondence of Daniel O'Connell, the Liberator* (2 vols., London: John Murray, 1888), vol. I, p. 509.

29. Broderick, *The Holy See and the Irish Movement for the Repeal of the Union*, p. 96.

30. Quoted in Quinn, *John Mitchel*, p. 6.

31. Dillon, *The Life of John Mitchel*, vol. I, p. 41.

32. John Clive, *Thomas Babington Macaulay: The Shaping of the Historian* (London: Secker and Warburg, 1973), pp. 256–88.

33. John Rosselli, *Lord William Bentinck: The Making of a Liberal Imperialist, 1774–1839* (London: Chatto and Windus, for Sussex University Press, 1974), p. 188.

34. All quotations in this section unless otherwise indicated are from T. B. Macaulay to Mrs Edward Cropper [Margaret Macaulay], 7 December 1834, in Thomas Pinney (ed.), *The Letters of Thomas Babington Macaulay* (Cambridge: Cambridge University Press, 1976), vol. III, pp. 99–107. Margaret never saw this letter, as she died before it arrived.

35. Robert E. Sullivan, *Macaulay: The Tragedy of Power* (Cambridge, Mass., and London: Belknap Press, 2009), p. 150.

36. This tragedy is recounted in Macaulay's letters to Zachary Macaulay, 8 May 1837, and to William Empson, 19 June 1837, in Pinney (ed.), *The Letters of Thomas Babington Macaulay*, vol. III, p. 214, 218–19.

37. Grant, *Memoirs of a Highland Lady*, vol. I, p. 222. All subsequent quotations are from this source unless indicated otherwise.

38. John William Kaye, *The Life and Correspondence of Major-General Sir John Malcolm* … (2 vols., London: Smith, Elder, 1856), vol. II, p. 505.

39. Tod, 'The Smiths of Baltiboys', p. 40.

40. Malcolm McRae, 'Sir Charles Trevelyan's Indian Letters, 1859–1865', *English Historical Review*, 77, no. 305 (1962), p. 707.

Chapter 2 (pp. 28–47)

1. *The Census of Ireland for the Year 1851, Part v: Tables of Deaths, Vol. 1: Containing the Report, Table of Pestilences, and Analysis of the Tables of Death*, P.P. 1856 [2087–I], XXIX, p. 261.

2. Peter Carr, *The Night of the Big Wind* (Belfast: White Row Press, 1993), p. 17; Kevin Danaher, 'The Night of the Big Wind', *Biatas*, 17, part 5 (1963), pp. 311–12.

3. Quoted in *The Census of Ireland for the Year 1851, Part v: Tables of Deaths…*, p. 221.

4. *Dublin Evening Post*, 11 January 1839, quoted in Lisa Shields and Denis Fitzgerald, 'The "Night of the Big Wind" in Ireland, 6–7 January 1839', *Irish Geography*, 22 (1989), p. 33.

5. P. W. Joyce, 'Recollections of Two Great Storms', *Catholic Bulletin*, 2 (1912), p. 15.

6. Shields and Fitzgerald, 'The "Night of the Big Wind"', p. 33; Carr, *The Night of the Big Wind*, p. 39.

7. Danaher, 'The Night of the Big Wind', p. 310; Cormac Ó Gráda, '"The Greatest Blessing of All": The Old Age Pension in Ireland', *Past and Present*, no. 175 (2002), p. 134.

8. See Shields and Fitzgerald, 'The "Night of the Big Wind"', pp. 38–41, and Hubert Lamb, *Historic Storms of the North Sea, British Isles and Northwest Europe* (Cambridge: Cambridge University Press, 1991), pp. 132–3.

9.   Lady Wilde, *Ancient Legends, Mystic Charms, and Superstitions of Ireland* (2 vols., London: Chatto and Windus, 1887), vol. I, p. 154.

10. Seán Ó Súilleabháin, *A Handbook of Irish Folklore* (Dublin: Educational Company of Ireland, for Folklore of Ireland Society, 1942), p. 356.

11. S. J. Connolly, 'The "Blessed Turf": Cholera and Popular Panic in Ireland, June 1832', *Irish Historical Studies*, 23, no. 91 (1983), pp. 214–32; Patrick O'Farrell, 'Millennialism, Messianism and Utopianism in Irish History', *Anglo-Irish Studies*, 2 (1976), p. 47.

12. *Freeman's Journal*, 20 July 1844; *Times*, 22 July 1844. I am very grateful to Dr Ciarán Reilly of NUI, Maynooth, for advice on this murder.

13. Michael Beames, 'Rural Conflict in pre-Famine Ireland: Peasant Assassinations in Tipperary, 1837–1847', *Past and Present*, no. 81 (1978), p. 75. A large and impressive literature exists on the subject of rural unrest in pre-Famine Ireland. The most important contributions are Samuel Clark and James S. Donnelly, Jr. (eds.), *Irish Peasants: Violence and Political Unrest, 1780–1914* (Manchester: Manchester University Press, 1983); David Fitzpatrick, 'Class, Family and Unrest in Nineteenth-Century Ireland', in P. J. Drudy (ed.), *Ireland: Land, Politics and People* (Cambridge: Cambridge University Press, 1985), pp. 37–75; J. J. Lee, 'Patterns of Rural Unrest in Nineteenth Century Ireland', in L. M. Cullen and F. Furet (eds.), *Ireland and France, 17th–20th Centuries: Towards a Comparative Study of Rural History* (Proceedings of the First Franco-Irish Symposium on Social and Economic History, Dublin) (Paris: UMI Monograph Publishing, 1980), pp. 223–37.

14. George Cornewall Lewis, *On Local Disturbances in Ireland, and on the Irish Church Question* (London: B. Fellowes, 1836), p. 319, 324.

15. Sydney Smith, *A Fragment on the Irish Roman Catholic Church* (7th ed., London: Longman, Brown, Green, and Longmans, 1845), p. 7.

16. G. Locker Lampson, *A Consideration of the State of Ireland in the Nineteenth Century* (London: Constable, 1907), p. 165.

17. M. A. G. Ó Tuathaigh, *Thomas Drummond and the Government of Ireland, 1835–41* (Dublin: National University of Ireland, 1978), pp. 20–21.

18. This account is based largely on the classic studies of James S. Donnelly, Jr., *The Land and the People of Nineteenth-Century Cork*, chap. 1, T. W. Freeman, *Pre-Famine Ireland*, pp. 139–47, and K. T. Hoppen, *Elections, Politics and Society in Ireland*, chap. 2.

19. T. W. Freeman, 'Land and people c. 1841', in Vaughan (ed.), *A New History of Ireland*, v, p. 255.

20. Donnelly, *The Land and the People of Nineteenth-Century Cork*, pp. 11–14.

21. Connolly, *Priests and People in Pre-Famine Ireland*, p. 23.

22. *Digest of Evidence Taken before Her Majesty's Commissioners of Inquiry into the State of the Law and Practice in Respect to the Occupation of Land in Ireland by J. P. Kennedy* (2 vols., London and Dublin, 1847–8), vol. II, p. 1116.

23. Quoted in Hoppen, *Elections, Politics and Society in Ireland*, p. 95

24. J. E. Bicheno, *Ireland and its Economy: Being the Result of Observations Made in a Tour through the Country in the Autumn of 1829* (London: John Murray, 1830), pp. 251–2, quoted in Timothy P. O'Neill, 'The Catholic Church and Relief of the Poor, 1815–1845', *Archivium Hibernicum*, 31 (1973), p. 134.

25. Quoted in Hoppen, *Elections, Politics and Society in Ireland*, p. 95.

26. Thomson and McGusty, *The Irish Journals of Elizabeth Smith*, p. xvi.

27. Grant, *The Highland Lady in Ireland*, p. 294.

28. Matthew Stout, 'The Geography and Implications of Post-Famine Population Decline in Baltyboys, County Wicklow', in Morash and Hayes (eds.), *Fearful Realities*, pp. 16–24.

29. Thomson and McGusty, *The Irish Journals of Elizabeth Smith*, p. xviii.

30. For its application to her native Scotland see T. M. Devine, *Clearance and Improvement: Land, Power and People in Scotland, 1700–1900* (Edinburgh: John Donald, 2006).

31. Grant, *The Highland Lady in Ireland*, p. 150. For more on this see Tod, 'The Smiths of Baltiboys', pp. 165–71.

32. Henry Heaney (ed.), *A Scottish Whig in Ireland, 1835–1838: The Irish Journals of Robert Graham of Redgorton* (Dublin: Four Courts Press, 1999), pp. 98–102.

33. This description is based on the account of the famous ballerina Ninette de Valois (Edris Stannus), a great-granddaughter of Elizabeth Smith who was raised at Baltiboys House in the early twentieth century: Ninette de Valois, *Come Dance with Me: A Memoir, 1898–1956* (rev. ed., Dublin: Lilliput Press, 1992), pp. 4–8.

34. All quotations unless indicated otherwise are from Thomson and McGusty, *The Irish Journals of Elizabeth Smith*, pp. xvi–xvii.

35. Jonathan Binns, *Miseries and Beauties of Ireland* (2 vols., London: Longman, Orme, Brown, 1837), vol. II, p. 413, 414, 416.

36. Thomas Reid, *Travels in Ireland in the Year 1822 …* (London: Longman, Hurst, Rees, Orme, and Brown, 1823), p. 276.

37. Gustave de Beaumont, *Ireland: Social, Political, and Religious* [1839], ed. W. C. Taylor (Cambridge, Mass.: Belknap Press, 2006), p. 130.

38. J. G. Kohl, *Travels in Ireland* (London: Bruce and Wyld, 1844), p. 19.

39. Hooper, *The Tourist's Gaze*, pp. 2–75.

40. Williams, *Tourism, Landscape, and the Irish Character*, pp. 107–14.

41. Henry D. Inglis, *Ireland in 1834* (2 vols., London: Whittaker, 1834), vol. I, p. 10, 30.

42. M. A. Titmarsh [W. M. Thackeray], *The Irish Sketch Book, 1842* (London: Chapman and Hall, 1843), quoted in Hooper, *The Tourist's Gaze*, p. 67.

43. Quoted in Williams, *Tourism, Landscape, and the Irish Character*, p. 152.

44. Joel Mokyr and Cormac Ó Gráda, 'Poor and Getting Poorer?: Living Standards in Ireland before the Famine', *Economic History Review*, 41, no. 2 (1988), pp. 229–31.

45. *Second Report of the Commissioners Appointed to Consider and Recommend a General System of Railways for Ireland*, P.P. 1837-38 [145], xxxv, p. 533.

46. John MacHale, *The Letters of the Most Rev. John MacHale, D.D.* (2 vols., Dublin: M. H. Gill and Son, 1888), vol. I, p. 265.

47. Timothy P. O'Neill, 'The Catholic Church and Relief of the Poor', pp. 135–6; Connolly, *Priests and People in Pre-Famine Ireland*, pp. 53–8; John A. Murphy, 'Priests and People in Modern Irish History', *Christus Rex*, 23, no. 4 (1969), pp. 235–59.

48. O'Neill, 'The Charities and Famine in Mid-Nineteenth Century Ireland', in Jacqueline Hill and Colm Lennon (eds.), *Luxury and Austerity: Papers Read before the 23rd Irish Conference of Historians* (Dublin: UCD Press, 1999), p. 140.

49. O'Reilly, *John MacHale, Archbishop of Tuam*, vol. I, p. 153.

50. Ibid., vol. I, p. 269.

51. *Census of Ireland for the Year 1851: Part V, Table of Deaths…*, pp. 305–597; see also Peter Gray, 'Accounting for Catastrophe: William Wilde, the 1851 Irish Census and the Great Famine', in Michael de Nie and Seán Farrell (eds.), *Power and Popular Culture in Modern Ireland: Essays in Honour of James S. Donnelly, Jr.* (Dublin: Irish Academic Press, 2010), pp. 50–66.

52. Dickson, *Arctic Ireland*, p. 69.

53. Ó Gráda, *The Great Irish Famine*, pp. 19–22.

54. S. A. Royle, 'Irish Famine Relief in the Early 19th Century: The 1822 Famine on the Aran Islands', *Irish Economic and Social History*, 11 (1984), pp. 44–59; O'Neill, 'The Catholic Church and Relief of the Poor', pp. 136–7.

55. Quoted in Bourke, *'The Visitation of God'?* p. 22.

56. Ó Gráda, *The Great Irish Famine*, pp. 24–5; Clarkson and Crawford, *Feast and Famine*, pp. 59–87.

57. Quoted in Ó Gráda, *The Great Irish Famine*, p. 33.

58. Mokyr, *Why Ireland Starved*, p. 43.

59. Quoted in ibid.

60. T. R. Malthus, 'Newenham and Others on the State of Ireland', *Edinburgh Review*, 12, no. 24 (1808), pp. 336–55.

61. Mokyr, *Why Ireland Starved*, p. 64.

62. O'Farrell, *England and Ireland since 1800*, p. 85.

63. Ibid., pp. 130–31.

Chapter 3 (pp. 48–74)

1. Mitchel, *The History of Ireland*, vol. II, p. 218. See Thomas A. Boylan and Timothy P. Foley, 'A Nation Perishing of Political Economy', in Morash and Hayes (eds.), *Fearful Realities*, pp. 138–50.

2. MacDonagh, *O'Connell*, p. 309.

3. See Joseph Lee, 'The Social and Economic Ideas of O'Connell', in Kevin B. Nowlan and Maurice R. O'Connell (eds.), *Daniel O'Connell: Portrait of a Radical* (Belfast: Appletree Press, 1984), pp. 70–86.

4. S. Ambirajan, *Classical Political Economy and British Policy in India* (Cambridge South Asian Studies, 21) (New York and London: Cambridge University Press, 1978), pp. 59–63.

5. Both quotations are from Thomas Pinney (ed.), *The Letters of Thomas Babington Macaulay* (6 vols., Cambridge: Cambridge University Press, 1974–81), vol. III, p. 317, n. 2.

6. Quoted in Haines, *Charles Trevelyan and the Great Irish Famine*, p. 37.

7. N. G. Annan, 'The Intellectual Aristocracy', in J. H. Plumb (ed.), *Studies in Social History: A Tribute to G. M. Trevelyan* (London: Longmans, Green, 1955), pp. 243–87.

8. Haines, *Charles Trevelyan and the Great Irish Famine*, p. 58.

9. Jenifer Hart, 'Sir Charles Trevelyan at the Treasury', *English Historical Review*, 75, no. 294 (1960), pp. 97–8.

10. *Morning Chronicle* (London), 14, 16 October 1843; *Times*, 16, 17 October 1843.

11. Quoted in Woodham-Smith, *The Great Hunger*, p. 60.

12. Haines, *Charles Trevelyan and the Great Irish Famine*, p. 53.

13. McDowell, *Public Opinion and Government Policy in Ireland*, p. 14.

14. MacDonagh, *Ireland*, p. 33. This section draws on MacDonagh's stimulating work, along with O'Farrell, *England and Ireland since 1800*, pp. 67–76, and K. Theodore Hoppen, 'An Incorporating Union?: British Politicians and Ireland, 1800–1830', *English Historical Review*, 123, no. 501 (2008), pp. 328–50.

15. Black, *Economic Thought and the Irish Question*, pp. 86–99.

16. O'Reilly, *John MacHale, Archbishop of Tuam*, vol. I, p. 139.

17. Hoppen, 'An Incorporating Union?' p. 344.

18. Roberto Romani, 'British Views on Irish National Character, 1800–1846: An Intellectual History', *History of European Ideas*, 23, no. 5–6 (1997), pp. 193–219.

19. Quoted in O'Farrell, *England and Ireland since 1800*, p. 15.

20. G. Locker Lampson, *A Consideration of the State of Ireland in the Nineteenth Century* (London: Constable, 1907), p. 160.

21. Quoted in Hoppen, 'An Incorporating Union?' p. 348.

22. MacDonagh, *O'Connell*, pp. 526–7.

23. Ó Tuathaigh, *Ireland Before the Famine*, p. 81.

24. Quoted in MacDonagh, *O'Connell*, p. 113.

25. Ibid., p. 138.

26. Woodham-Smith, *The Great Hunger*, p. 42.

27. MacDonagh, *O'Connell*, p. 599.

28. Karl Marx and Frederick Engels, *Ireland and the Irish Question* (Moscow: Progress Publishers, 1971), p. 35.

29. Ibid., pp. 35–6.

30. W. J. Fitzpatrick (ed.), *Correspondence of Daniel O'Connell, the Liberator* (2 vols., London: John Murray, 1888), vol. ii, pp. 307–10.

31. MacIntyre, *The Liberator*, p. 296; Nowlan, *The Politics of Repeal*, pp. 7–8.

32. Tod, 'The Smiths of Baltiboys', p. 321.

33. Quoted in 'Introducing Elizabeth Smith', in James and Ó Maitiú, *The Wicklow World of Elizabeth Smith*, p. 10.

34. Donald H. Akenson, *The Irish Education Experiment: The National System of Education in the Nineteenth Century* (Studies in Irish History) (London: Routledge and Kegan Paul, 1970), pp. 57–8.

35. David Kennedy, 'Education and the People', in R. B. McDowell (ed.), *Social Life in Ireland, 1800–45* (Dublin: Three Candles, for the Cultural Relations Committee of Ireland, in association with Radio Éireann, 1957), p. 69.

36. *Freeman's Journal*, 13 February 1838; see Akenson, *The Irish Education Experiment*, pp. 207–13.

37. Kerr, *Peel, Priests and Politics*, pp. 58–64.

38. Ignatius Murphy, 'Primary Education', in Patrick J. Corish (ed.), *A History of Irish Catholicism, Vol. v: The Church Since Emancipation* (Dublin: Gill and Macmillan, 1971), fasc. 6, p. 21.

39. Colin Barr, 'John MacHale', in McGuire and Quinn (eds.), *Dictionary of Irish Biography*; Pius Devine, 'John MacHale, Archbishop of Tuam', *Dublin Review*, 26, no. 1 (1891), pp. 33–4.

40. J. F. Hilliker, 'Charles Edward Trevelyan as an Educational Reformer in India, 1827–1838', *Canadian Journal of History*, 9, no. 3 (1974), p. 282.

41. Quoted in John Rosselli, *Lord William Bentinck: The Making of a Liberal Imperialist, 1774–1839* (London: Chatto and Windus, for Sussex University Press, 1974), p. 183.

42. *The Application of the Roman Alphabet to All the Oriental Languages, Contained in a Series of Papers Written by Messrs. Trevelyan, J. Prinsep, and Tytler, Rev. A. Duff, and Mr. H. T. Prinsep, and Published in Various Calcutta Periodicals in the Year 1834* (Calcutta: Serampore Press, 1834), p. 21.

43. Ibid., p. 26.

44. Thomas Babington Macaulay, 'Minute on Indian Education', 2 February 1835, reproduced in John Clive and Thomas Pinney (eds.), *Selected Writings of*

Thomas Babington Macaulay (Chicago: University of Chicago Press, 1972), p. 241, 242–3.

45. Charles E. Trevelyan, *On the Education of the People of India* (London: Longman, Orme, Brown, Green, and Longmans, 1838), p. 78, 81–94.

46. All quotations are from John Clive, *Macaulay: The Shaping of the Historian* (London: Secker and Warburg, 1973), pp. 360–61.

47. Macaulay, 'Minute on Indian Education', p. 249.

48. Hilliker, 'Charles Edward Trevelyan as an Educational Reformer in India', p. 28.

49. George Smith, *The Life of Alexander Duff*, D.D., LL.D. (2 vols., London: Hodder and Stoughton, 1879), vol. I, p. 183–4.

50. W. G. Blaikie, 'Alexander Duff (1806–1878)', rev. David W. Savage, in *Oxford Dictionary of National Biography*.

51. Smith, *The Life of Alexander Duff*, vol. I, p. 224.

52. Nowlan, *The Politics of Repeal*, p. 7.

53. Fitzpatrick (ed.), *Correspondence of Daniel O'Connell*, vol. II, p. 17; Virginia Crossman, 'Constantine Henry Phipps, 1st Marquis of Normanby', in McGuire and Quinn (eds.), *Dictionary of Irish Biography*.

54. MacDonagh, *O'Connell*, p. 409.

55. M. A. G. Ó Tuathaigh, *Thomas Drummond and the Government of Ireland, 1835–41* (Dublin: National University of Ireland, 1978).

56. R. Barry O'Brien, *Thomas Drummond, Under-Secretary in Ireland, 1835–40: Life and Letters* (London: Kegan Paul, Trench, 1889), p. 284. For the provenance of the famous aphorism see J. F. M'Lennan, *Memoir of Thomas Drummond, R.E., F.R.A.S., Under Secretary to the Lord Lieutenant of Ireland, 1835–1840* (Edinburgh: Edmonston and Douglas, 1867), pp. 325–39.

57. *Times*, 15 January 1839.

58. *Report of the Select Committee on the State of Crime in Ireland since 1845*, P.P. 1839 [486], XI, p. 1.

59. O'Brien, *Thomas Drummond*, p. 354.

60. *Freeman's Journal*, 16 April 1840.

61. M'Lennan, *Memoir of Thomas Drummond*, p. 426, 429 (Larcom quotation).

62. Stanley H. Palmer, 'Thomas Drummond (1797–1840)', in *Oxford Dictionary of National Biography*.

63. Jackson, *Ireland*, p. 63.

64. Seán Farrell, *Rituals and Riots: Sectarian Violence and Political Culture in Ulster, 1784–1886* (Lexington: University Press of Kentucky, 2000), pp. 44–5. For a partisan yet detailed listing of such cases see O'Brien, *Thomas Drummond*, pp. 116–23.

65. Quoted in O'Brien, *Thomas Drummond*, p. 122.

246 NOTES TO PAGES 68–78

66. Ó Tuathaigh, *Thomas Drummond and the Government of Ireland*, pp. 12–14.
67. Hereward Senior, *Orangeism in Ireland and Britain, 1795–1836* (London and Toronto: Routledge and Kegan Paul, 1966), pp. 270–1. Senior casts serious doubt on this supposed conspiracy.
68. *Hansard* (Commons), 39, col. 630–87 (5 December 1837).
69. M'Lennan, *Memoir of Thomas Drummond*, pp. 296–303.
70. Charles Gavan Duffy, *Young Ireland: A Fragment of Irish History, 1840–1850* (London: T. Fisher Unwin, 1880), pp. 730–31.
71. Dillon, *The Life of John Mitchel*, vol. 1, p. 48; MacCall, *Irish Mitchel*, p. 57.
72. Dillon, *The Life of John Mitchel*, vol. 1, p. 49. Emphasis as in original.
73. Ibid., vol. 1, p. 55.
74. Quoted in Black, *Economic Thought and the Irish Question*, p. 107; see also Gray, *The Making of the Irish Poor Law*.
75. *Report of Geo. Nicholls, Esq., to His Majesty's Principal Secretary of State for the Home Department, on Poor Laws*, P.P. 1837 [69], LI, p. 201, 207.
76. Ibid., p. 223.
77. Grant, *The Highland Lady in Ireland*, p. 80.
78. J. G. Kohl, *Travels in Ireland* (London: Bruce and Wyld, 1844), p. 278.
79. Tod, 'The Smiths of Baltiboys', pp. 136–8.
80. Grant, *The Highland Lady in Ireland*, p. 18.
81. *Freeman's Journal*, 23 February 1838.

Chapter 4 (pp. 76–95)
1. Éamonn Mac Dhuirnín (b. 1878), quoted in Póirtéir, *Famine Echoes*, p. 35.
2. John Reader, *The Untold History of the Potato* (London: Vintage Books, 2008), p. 195.
3. Quoted in Murphy, *A Starving People*, p. 11.
4. *Freeman's Journal*, 23 July 1845.
5. *Gardeners' Chronicle* (London), 13 September 1845. On Lindley's career see Richard Drayton, 'John Lindley (1799–1865)', in *Oxford Dictionary of National Biography*.
6. Quoted in Bourke, 'The Visitation of God'? p. 171.
7. For a contemporary account of the 'abundance' of the early crop see Thomas Campbell Foster, *Letters on the Condition of the People of Ireland* (London: Chapman and Hall, 1846), pp. 438–9.
8. Daly, *The Famine in Ireland*, pp. 53–4.
9. Her experiences are recounted with typical élan in Patricia Pelly and Andrew Tod (eds.), *A Highland Lady in France, 1843–1845* (East Linton, East Lothian: Tuckwell Press 1996).

10. As with so much else about her life, I am indebted to Andrew Tod, 'The Smiths of Baltiboys', pp. 383–7, for details on Elizabeth's health. Emphasis as in original.

11. Quoted in Tod, 'The Smiths of Baltiboys', p. 387.

12. Thomson and McGusty, *The Irish Journals of Elizabeth Smith*, pp. 71–2.

13. Grant, *The Highland Lady in Ireland*, p. 208. All subsequent quotations are from this edition unless otherwise indicated.

14. For Elizabeth's complex relationship with Tom Darker see Tod, 'The Smiths of Baltiboys', pp. 141–59.

15. Thomson and McGusty, *The Irish Journals of Elizabeth Smith*, p. 69.

16. J. A. Bennett, 'William Parsons, third Earl of Rosse (1800–1867)', in *Oxford Dictionary of National Biography*.

17. Thomson and McGusty, *The Irish Journals of Elizabeth Smith*, p. 74. Emphasis as in original.

18. Trevelyan, *The Irish Crisis*, p. 34.

19. Sir Robert Peel, *Memoirs* (ed. Lord Mahon and Edward Cardwell, 2 vols., London: John Murray, 1856–7), vol. II, pp. 118–19; Gash, *Sir Robert Peel*, p. 536; Donnelly, *The Great Irish Potato Famine*, p. 44; E. C. Large, *The Advance of the Fungi* (London: Jonathan Cape, 1940), p. 26.

20. Peel, *Memoirs*, vol. II, p. 117–18.

21. T. P. O'Neill, 'The Scientific Investigation of the Failure of the Potato Crop in Ireland, 1845–6', *Irish Historical Studies*, 5, no. 18 (1946), p. 126. This section relies heavily on that account, but for subsequent clarifications see Bourke, 'The Visitation of God'? pp. 129–58.

22. Charles Stuart Parker (ed.), *Sir Robert Peel: From His Private Papers* (3 vols., London: John Murray, 1899), vol. III, p. 223.

23. *Copy of the Report of Dr. Playfair and of Mr. Lindley on the Present State of the Irish Potato Crop, and on the Prospect of Approaching Scarcity, 15 November 1845*, P.P. 1846 [28], XXVII, p. 1.

24. Foster, *Letters on the Condition of the People of Ireland*, p. 439. For an example of such guidance see *Freeman's Journal*, 5 November 1845.

25. Quoted in Donnelly, *The Great Irish Potato Famine*, p. 46.

26. John Mitchel, *An Apology for the British Government in Ireland* (Dublin: O'Donoghue, 1905), p. 23, quoted in O'Neill, 'The Scientific Investigation of the Failure of the Potato Crop', p. 131.

27. Ibid.

28. Large, *The Advance of the Fungi*, p. 27.

29. Bourke, 'The Visitation of God'? p. 200, n. 17.

30. This account draws heavily on Bourke, 'The Visitation of God'? pp. 150–54; Woodham-Smith, *The Great Hunger*, pp. 94–102; Ó Gráda, *The Great Irish*

Famine, pp. 39–40; O'Neill, 'The Scientific Investigation of the Failure of the Potato Crop'.

31. O'Neill, 'The Scientific Investigation of the Failure of the Potato Crop', p. 136.

32. Bourke, *'The Visitation of God'?* p. 152.

33. Large, *The Advance of the Fungi*, pp. 225–39; Bourke, *'The Visitation of God'?* p. 150, 153–4.

34. This anonymous individual is quoted in O'Reilly, *John MacHale, Archbishop of Tuam*, vol. I, p. 609.

35. O'Rourke, *The History of the Great Irish Famine of 1847*, p. 52.

36. Roger McHugh, 'The Famine in Irish Oral Tradition', in Edwards and Williams (eds.), *The Great Famine*, p. 396.

37. Ibid.

38. Quoted in Gray, *Famine, Land and Politics*, p. 99.

39. Peter Gray, '"Potatoes and Providence": British Government Responses to the Great Famine', *Bullán: An Irish Studies Journal*, 1, no. 1 (1994), p. 76.

40. Ibid., p. 79.

41. Donald M. MacRaild, *Irish Migrants in Modern Britain, 1750–1922* (Basingstoke, Hants: Macmillan, 1999), pp. 169–74. For more details see E. R. Norman, *Anti-Catholicism in Victorian England* (London: Allen and Unwin, 1968) and D. G. Paz, *Popular Anti-Catholicism in Mid-Victorian England* (Stanford, Conn.: Stanford University Press, 1992).

42. Kerr, *'A Nation of Beggars'?* pp. 241–81.

43. Patrick O'Farrell, *Ireland's English Question: Anglo-Irish Relations, 1534–1970* (London: B. T. Batsford, 1971), p. 112.

44. William (Bill) Powell (b. 1869), quoted in Póirtéir, *Famine Echoes*, p. 40.

45. Cathal Póirtéir, 'Folk memory and the Famine', in Póirtéir (ed.), *The Great Irish Famine*, p. 221. This was in fact a commonplace dictum in Victorian England.

46. McHugh, 'The Famine in Irish Oral Tradition', p. 395.

47. MacIntyre, *The Liberator*, pp. 280–81; Kerr, *Peel, Priests and Politics*, p. 21.

48. MacDonagh, *O'Connell*, pp. 541–2.

49. Quoted in Kerr, *Peel, Priests and Politics*, p. 224.

50. Oliver MacDonagh, 'Politics, 1830–45', in Vaughan (ed.), *A New History of Ireland*, v, part 1, p. 186; Kerr, *Peel, Priests and Politics*, pp. 224–89.

51. Anthony Trollope, *The Three Clerks* (Oxford: Oxford University Press, 1989 [1857]), p. 58.

52. Haines, *Charles Trevelyan and the Great Irish Famine*, p. 129.

53. Quoted in Bourke, *'The Visitation of God'?* p. 173.

54. Apparently he had extremely short legs.

55. *Times*, 8 November 1845.

56. Foster, *Letters on the Condition of the People of Ireland*, p. 397; MacDonagh, *O'Connell*, pp. 563–4.

57. Foster, *Letters on the Condition of the People of Ireland*, pp. 442–3. (Emphasis in original.)

58. MacCall, *Irish Mitchel*, p. 101.

59. Dillon, *The Life of John Mitchel*, vol. I, p. 63, 70.

60. Ibid., vol. I, p. 112.

61. Ibid.

62. Dillon, *The Life of John Mitchel*, vol. I, p. 35, 86–7, 134.

63. *Nation*, 25 October 1845.

64. *Nation*, 1 November 1845.

65. Davis, *The Young Ireland Movement*, p. 86; Quinn, *John Mitchel*, p. 10.

66. *Nation*, 22 November 1845.

67. MacDonagh, *O'Connell*, p. 563; Davis, *The Young Ireland Movement*, p. 86; *Nation*, 29 November 1845.

68. Gwynn, *Young Ireland and 1848*, p. 58; Dillon, *The Life of John Mitchel*, vol. I, p. 95.

69. Hilton, *A Mad, Bad, and Dangerous People?* p. 554.

Chapter 5 (pp. 96–116)

1. W. E. Gladstone to Catherine Glynne Gladstone, 12 October 1845, reproduced in A. Tilney Bassett (ed.), *Gladstone to his Wife* (London: Methuen, 1936), p. 64.

2. Gladstone was in Baden at the request of his father, trying to help his sister, Helen Gladstone, who had become a Catholic and was also addicted to laudanum (a tincture of opium): M. R. D. Foot and H. C. G. Matthew (eds.), *The Gladstone Diaries*, vol. 3, 1840–1847 (Oxford: Clarendon Press, 1974), pp. xliii, 488.

3. Graham to Peel, 13 October 1845, Charles Stuart Parker (ed.), *Sir Robert Peel: From His Private Papers* (3 vols., London: John Murray, 1899), vol. III, p. 223.

4. Graham to Peel, 13 October 1845, Charles Stuart Parker (ed.), *Sir Robert Peel: From His Private Papers* (3 vols., London: John Murray, 1899), vol. III, p. 223; Gash, *Sir Robert Peel*, p. 535.

5. O'Rourke, *The History of the Great Irish Famine of 1847*, p. 55, 56; T. P. O'Neill, 'The Administration of Relief', in Edwards and Williams (eds.), *The Great Famine*, p. 211.

6. *Freeman's Journal*, 4 November 1845. Emphasis as in original.

7. *Freeman's Journal*, 4 November 1845.

8. Gray, *Famine, Land and Politics*, p. 113.

9. *Freeman's Journal*, 4 November 1845. Emphasis as in original. Peel did occasionally suffer from gout: Gash, *Sir Robert Peel*, p. 538.

10. Dillon, *The Life of John Mitchel*, vol. I, p. 82.

11. Ibid., p. 123.

12. Dillon, *The Life of John Mitchel*, vol. I, pp. 82–4; Duffy, *Four Years of Irish History*, p. 501.

13. Duffy, *Four Years of Irish History*, p. 12.

14. *Freeman's Journal*, 18 June 1846.

15. Davis, *The Young Ireland Movement*, p. 32; Quinn, *John Mitchel*, pp. 12–13.

16. Owen Dudley Edwards, '"True Thomas": Carlyle, Young Ireland, and the Legacy of Millennialism', in David R. Sorensen and Rodger L. Tarr (eds.), *The Carlyles at Home and Abroad: Essays in Honour of Kenneth J. Fielding* (Aldershot: Ashgate, 2004), pp. 65–70.

17. Dillon, *The Life of John Mitchel*, vol. I, p. 82–4.

18. K. J. Fielding, 'Ireland, John Mitchel and his "Sarcastic Friend" Thomas Carlyle', in Joachim Schwend, Susanne Hagemann and Hermann Völkel (eds.), *Literatur im Kontext / Lierature in Context: Festschrift für Horst W. Drescher* (New York: Peter Lang, 1992), pp. 131–43; see also John Morrow, 'Thomas Carlyle, Young Ireland and the "Condition of Ireland Question"', *Historical Journal*, 51, no. 3 (2008), pp.643–67.

19. I owe this illustration and much of the following three paragraphs to Gray, *Famine, Land and Politics*, pp. 107–19.

20. Peel to Heytesbury, 15 October 1845, Sir Robert Peel, *Memoirs* (ed. Lord Mahon and Edward Cardwell, 2 vols., London: John Murray, 1856–7), vol. II, p. 121.

21. Routh to Trevelyan, 6 April 1846, *Correspondence Explanatory of the Measures Adopted by Her Majesty's Government for the Relief of Distress Arising from the Failure of the Potato Crop in Ireland*, P.P. 1846 [735], XXXVII, p. 143.

22. See Hilton, *A Mad, Bad, and Dangerous People?* pp. 551–8.

23. Trevelyan, *The Irish Crisis*, p. 33.

24. From February 1846 it became known as the Relief Commission: Haines, *Charles Trevelyan and the Great Irish Famine*, p. 123.

25. Gash, *Sir Robert Peel*, p. 570.

26. Grant, *The Highland Lady in Ireland*, p. 213.

27. *Freeman's Journal*, 2 March 1846. All subsequent quotations in this paragraph are from this source unless otherwise indicated.

28. The definitive account is Kerr, *Peel, Priests and Politics*.

29. *Hansard* (Commons), 83, col. 1050 (17 February 1846).

30. *Hansard* (Commons), 83, col. 1066–7 (17 February 1846).

31. Coffin to Archer, 30 March 1846, *Correspondence Explanatory of the Measures Adopted by Her Majesty's Government for the Relief of Distress Arising from the Failure of the Potato Crop in Ireland*, p. 137.

32. Ó Cathaoir, *Famine Diary*, pp. 35–48.

33. Timothy P. O'Neill, 'The Catholic Church and Relief of the Poor, 1815–1845', *Archivium Hibernicum*, 31 (1973), pp. 133–4.

34. Grant, *The Highland Lady in Ireland*, pp. 215–16.

35. *Nation*, 7 March 1846. Emphasis as in original.

36. Bourke, 'The Visitation of God'? pp. 159–69, which broadly confirms an earlier paper by T. P. O'Neill, 'Food problems during the Great Irish Famine', *Journal of the Royal Society of Antiquaries of Ireland*, LXXXII (1952), pp. 99–108. For considered assessments see Donnelly, *The Great Irish Potato Famine*, pp. 209–21, and Peter Solar, 'The Great Famine Was No Ordinary Subsistence Crisis', in Crawford (ed.), *Famine*, pp. 112–31.

37. O'Rourke, *The History of the Great Irish Famine of 1847*, p. 107.

38. Peter Gray, 'Famine Relief Policy in Comparative Perspective: Ireland, Scotland and Northwestern Europe, 1845–1849', *Éire-Ireland*, 32, no. 1 (1997), p. 98; Peter Gray, 'The European Food Crisis and the Relief of the Irish Famine, 1845–1850', in Ó Gráda et al. (eds.), *When the Potato Failed*, pp. 95–107.

39. Trevelyan to Hewetson, 3 September 1845, quoted in Gray, 'Famine Relief Policy in Comparative Perspective', p. 97.

40. Woodham-Smith, *The Great Hunger*, pp. 72–3.

41. Gray, *Famine, Land and Politics*, pp. 120–21.

42. Quoted in Woodham-Smith, *The Great Hunger*, p. 77.

43. Kinealy, *The Great Irish Famine*, pp. 141–2.

44. This account is drawn from Woodham-Smith, *The Great Hunger*, p. 72.

45. Woodham-Smith, *The Great Hunger*, p. 72.

46. Ibid., p. 58.

47. Quoted in Kinealy, *This Great Calamity*, p. 39.

48. Trevelyan, *The Irish Crisis*, p. 34.

49. Trevelyan to Routh, 3 February 1846, *Correspondence Explanatory of the Measures Adopted by Her Majesty's Government for the Relief of Distress Arising from the Failure of the Potato Crop in Ireland*, p. 77.

50. Trevelyan to Routh, 29 April 1846, *Correspondence Explanatory of the Measures Adopted by Her Majesty's Government for the Relief of Distress Arising from the Failure of the Potato Crop in Ireland*, p. 125.

51. Murphy, *A Starving People*, pp. 16–17.

52. Documented in detail in Haines, *Charles Trevelyan and the Great Irish Famine*, pp. 53–72.

53. Routh to Trevelyan, 28 May 1846, *Correspondence Explanatory of the Measures Adopted by Her Majesty's Government for the Relief of Distress Arising from the Failure of the Potato Crop in Ireland*, p. 143.
54. Haines, *Charles Trevelyan and the Great Irish Famine*, p. 177.
55. This section draws on Ó Gráda, *Black '47 and Beyond*, p. 48; Woodham-Smith, *The Great Hunger*, p. 81; Donnelly, *The Great Irish Potato Famine*, pp. 54–6.
56. O'Neill, 'The Administration of Relief', p. 221.
57. Quoted in Woodham-Smith, *The Great Hunger*, p. 67.
58. O'Neill, 'The Administration of Relief', p. 215.
59. Pole to Trevelyan, [10] April 1846, *Correspondence Explanatory of the Measures Adopted by Her Majesty's Government for the Relief of Distress Arising from the Failure of the Potato Crop in Ireland*, p. 147.
60. *Illustrated London News*, 4 April 1846.
61. E. M. Crawford, 'Indian Meal and Pellagra in Nineteenth-Century Ireland', in J. M. Goldstrom and L. A. Clarkson (eds.), *Irish Population, Economy, and Society: Essays in Honour of the Late K. H. Connell* (Oxford and New York: Clarendon Press, 1981), p. 120; Clarkson and Crawford, *Feast and Famine*, pp. 80–81.
62. Kinealy, *This Great Calamity*, p. 48.
63. Trevelyan, *The Irish Crisis*, p. 34, n. 1.
64. Haines, *Charles Trevelyan and the Great Irish Famine*, pp. 182–3.
65. Quoted in Woodham-Smith, *The Great Hunger*, p. 74.
66. Quoted in Haines, *Charles Trevelyan and the Great Irish Famine*, p. 95.
67. Trevelyan, *The Irish Crisis*, p. 38.
68. Haines, *Charles Trevelyan and the Great Irish Famine*, p. 185; Gray, *Famine, Land and Politics*, p. 125, n. 145.
69. Quoted in Arnold, *Famine*, p. 43.
70. Trevelyan to Routh, 24 July 1846, *Correspondence Explanatory of the Measures Adopted by Her Majesty's Government for the Relief of Distress Arising from the Failure of the Potato Crop in Ireland*, p. 266.
72. Woodham-Smith, *The Great Hunger*, p. 92.
72. Quoted in Kerr, *'A Nation of Beggars'?* p. 34.

Chapter 6 (pp. 118–43)
1. [Central Relief Committee], *Transactions of the Central Relief Committee*, extracts from James H. Tuke's report, pp. 150–51.
2. [Central Relief Committee], *Transactions of the Central Relief Committee*, p. 146.
3. O'Rourke, *The History of the Great Irish Famine of 1847*, p. 260.

4. *Times*, 24 December 1846.
5. Bourke, '*The Visitation of God*'? p. 178.
6. This section is based on Davis, *The Young Ireland Movement*; Geoghegan, *Liberator*, pp. 224-7; Gwynn, *Young Ireland and 1848*, pp. 67–78; MacDonagh, *O'Connell*, pp. 553–78; MacIntyre, *The Liberator*, pp. 284–98; Nowlan, *The Politics of Repeal*, pp. 108–11; Quinn, *John Mitchel*, pp. 13–17.
7. Duffy, *Four Years of Irish History*, p. 227.
8. Ibid., p. 232.
9. Ibid., p. 233.
10. Dillon, *The Life of John Mitchel*, vol. I, pp. 120–21.
11. Quoted in Nowlan, *The Politics of Repeal*, p. 110.
12. Thomas Carlyle's note, Jane Welsh Carlyle to Thomas Carlyle, 23 August 1846, in Kenneth J. Fielding and Clyde De L. Ryals (eds.), *The Collected Letters of Thomas and Jane Welsh Carlyle* (Durham, NC, and London: Duke University Press, 1995), vol. 21, p. 25. On Carlyle's views of O'Connell see Owen Dudley Edwards, '"True Thomas": Carlyle, Young Ireland, and the Legacy of Millennialism', in David R. Sorensen and Rodger L. Tarr (eds.), *The Carlyles at Home and Abroad: Essays in Honour of Kenneth J. Fielding* (Aldershot: Ashgate, 2004), p. 71.
13. Dillon, *The Life of John Mitchel*, vol. I, p. 129.
14. Thomas Carlyle's note, Jane Welsh Carlyle to Thomas Carlyle, 23 August 1846, in Kenneth J. Fielding and Clyde De L. Ryals (eds.), *The Collected Letters of Thomas and Jane Welsh Carlyle* (Durham, NC, and London: Duke University Press, 1995), vol. 21, p. 25.
15. Dillon, *The Life of John Mitchel*, vol. I, p. 129.
16. Ibid., p. 134.
17. Prest, *Lord John Russell*, pp. 234–5.
18. Quoted in T. P. O'Neill, 'The Administration of Relief', in Edwards and Williams (eds.), *The Great Famine*, p. 223.
19. *Correspondence from July 1846 to January 1847 Relating to the Measures Adopted for the Relief of the Distress in Ireland: Board of Works Series, Part I*, P.P. 1847 [764], L, p. 90.
20. See Ó Gráda et al. (eds.), *When the Potato Failed*.
21. M. Bergman, 'The Potato Blight in the Netherlands and its Social Consequences, 1845–47', *International Review of Social History*, 12, no. 3 (1967), p. 417.
22. Eric Vanhaute, Richard Paping and Cormac Ó Gráda, 'The European Subsistence Crisis of 1845–1850: A Comparative Perspective', in Ó Gráda et al. (eds.), *When the Potato Failed*, p. 32.

23. Peter Gray, 'Famine Relief Policy in Comparative Perspective: Ireland, Scotland and Northwestern Europe, 1845–1849', *Éire-Ireland*, 32, no. 1 (1997), p. 89.
24. Eric Vanhaute, '"So Worthy an Example to Ireland": The Subsistence and Industrial Crisis of 1845–1850 in Flanders', in Ó Gráda et al. (eds.), *When the Potato Failed*, p. 130.
25. Quoted in Gray, 'Famine Relief Policy in Comparative Perspective', p. 98.
26. Vanhaute, Paping and Ó Gráda, 'The European Subsistence Crisis of 1845–1850: A Comparative Perspective', in Ó Gráda et al. (eds.), *When the Potato Failed*, pp. 28–33.
27. Roger Price, 'Poor Relief and Social Crisis in Mid-Nineteenth-Century France', *European Studies Review*, 13 (1983), pp. 423–54; Manfred Gailus, 'Food Riots in Germany in the Late 1840s', *Past and Present*, no. 145 (1994), pp. 157–93; Bergman, 'The Potato Blight in the Netherlands'.
28. Gailus, 'Food Riots in Germany', p. 193.
29. *Correspondence from July 1846 to January 1847 Relating to the Measures Adopted for the Relief of the Distress in Ireland: Board of Works Series, Part I*, P.P. 1847 [764], L, p. 87.
30. Trevelyan, *The Irish Crisis*, p. 61.
31. Quoted in Gray, *Famine, Land and Politics*, p. 243.
32. Quoted in ibid., p. 230. Emphasis added.
33. This section relies on ibid., pp. 228–39.
34. Trevelyan, *The Irish Crisis*, p. 2.
35. Quoted in Gray, *Famine, Land and Politics*, p. 232.
36. Prest, *Lord John Russell*, p. 236.
37. James S. Donnelly, Jr., '"Irish Property Must Pay for Irish Poverty": British Public Opinion and the Great Irish Famine', in Morash and Hayes (eds.), *Fearful Realities*, pp. 60–76, and more generally Lengel, *The Irish through British Eyes*, pp. 97–127.
38. A. R. G. Griffiths, 'The Irish Board of Works during the Famine Years', *Historical Journal*, XIII, no. 4 (1970), p. 643.
39. Brian MacDonald, 'A Time of Desolation: Clones Poor Law Union', *Clogher Record*, XVII (2000), p. 49.
40. Murphy, *A Starving People*, p. 32.
41. Quoted in Woodham-Smith, *The Great Hunger*, p. 126.
42. Haines, *Charles Trevelyan and the Great Irish Famine*, p. 265.
43. This account draws on David Fitzpatrick, 'Famine, Entitlements and Seduction: Captain Edmond Wynne in Ireland, 1845–1851', *English Historical Review*, 110, no. 437 (1995), pp. 596–619.
44. Quoted in ibid., p. 603. Emphasis as in original.
45. Quoted in ibid.

46. Woodham-Smith, *The Great Hunger*, p. 129.

47. William Henry Smith, *A Twelve Months' Residence in Ireland, During the Famine and the Public Works, 1846 and 1847 …* (London: Longman, Brown, Green and Longmans, 1848), p. 50.

48. Gray, *Famine, Land and Politics*, pp. 241–4; Woodham-Smith, *The Great Hunger*, p. 130; Trevelyan, *The Irish Crisis*, p. 68.

49. Woodham-Smith, *The Great Hunger*, pp. 148–9.

50. Ibid., p. 150.

51. *Fermanagh Reporter*, 10 December 1846, cited in MacDonald, 'A Time of Desolation', p. 50.

52. O'Neill, 'The Administration of Relief', p. 229.

53. For Co. Clare see Murphy, *A Starving People*, p. 32.

54. Trevelyan, *The Irish Crisis*, p. 84.

55. Robert Huston, *The Earnest Minister: Exemplified in the Life and Labours of the Rev. Fossey Tackaberry* (London and Dublin: J. Mason Robertson, 1853), p. 280.

56. Ibid.

57. Fitzpatrick, 'Famine, Entitlements and Seduction', p. 606.

58. Woodham-Smith, *The Great Hunger*, pp. 125–6.

59. *Freeman's Journal*, 2 October 1846.

60. *Freeman's Journal*, 30 October 1846.

61. Ibid.

62. Ibid.

63. *Pictorial Times* (London), 10 October 1846.

64. Kerr, 'A Nation of Beggars'? p. 35.

65. Ibid.

66. Quoted in MacDonald, 'A Time of Desolation', p. 45.

67. Christine Kinealy and Gerard Mac Atasney, *The Hidden Famine: Hunger, Poverty and Sectarianism in Belfast, 1840–50* (London: Pluto Press, 2000), pp. 62–3.

68. Andrés Eiríksson, 'Food Supply and Food Riots', in Ó Gráda (ed.), *Famine 150*, p. 68.

69. Hewetson to Trevelyan, 21 September 1846, *Correspondence from July 1846 to January 1847 Relating to the Measures Adopted for the Relief of the Distress in Ireland: Commissariat Series*, P.P. 1847 [761] LI, p. 105.

70. Eiríksson, 'Food Supply and Food Riots', p. 83.

71. Ibid., p. 80.

72. Bourke, 'The Visitation of God'? p. 165.

73. Quoted in Donnelly, *The Great Irish Potato Famine*, p. 69. Emphasis as in original.

74. Trevelyan to Hewetson, 29 September 1846, *Correspondence from July 1846 to January 1847 Relating to the Measures Adopted for the Relief of the Distress in Ireland: Commissariat Series*, p. 121.
75. *Freeman's Journal*, 5 August 1846.
76. *Freeman's Journal*, 19 December 1846.
77. Prest, *Lord John Russell*, p. 271.
78. *Freeman's Journal*, 19 December 1846.
79. Grant, *The Highland Lady in Ireland*, p. 234. All subsequent quotations are from this source unless otherwise indicated.
80. Tod, 'The Smiths of Baltiboys', p. 419.
81. O'Rourke, *The History of the Great Irish Famine of 1847*, p. 272.
82. Quoted in Woodham-Smith, *The Great Hunger*, p. 163.

Chapter 7 (pp. 144–65)

1. *News Letter* (Belfast), 2 April 1847. Attention was first drawn to this account by David Miller, 'Irish Presbyterians and the Great Famine', in Jacqueline Hill and Colm Lennon (eds.), *Luxury and Austerity: Papers Read before the 23rd Irish Conference of Historians* (Dublin: UCD Press, 1999), p. 165.
2. For a series of valuable studies that contradict this view, see Christine Kinealy and Trevor Parkhill (eds.), *The Famine in Ulster: The Regional Impact* (Belfast: Ulster Historical Foundation, 1997).
3. Karl Marx, *Capital*, vol. 1 [1887] (London: Lawrence and Wishart, 1970), vol. 1, p. 704.
4. Matthew Stout, 'The Geography and Implications of Post-Famine Population Decline in Baltyboys, County Wicklow', in Morash and Hayes (eds.), *Fearful Realities*, p. 21.
5. Ibid., p. 22.
6. Bourke, *The Life and Times of the Most Rev. John MacHale*, p. 149.
7. Quoted in MacDonagh, *O'Connell*, p. 595.
8. R. V. Comerford, 'Daniel O'Connell', in *Oxford Dictionary of National Biography*.
9. O'Reilly, *John MacHale, Archbishop of Tuam*, vol. II, p. 8.
10. Joseph Spence, 'Isaac Butt, Irish Nationality and the Conditional Defence of the Union, 1833–70', in D. George Boyce and Alan O'Day (eds.), *Defenders of the Union: A Survey of British and Irish Unionism since 1801* (London: Routledge, 2001), pp. 74–5. See also David Thornley, *Isaac Butt and Home Rule* (London: MacGibbon and Kee, 1964), pp. 16–18.
11. Isaac Butt, 'The Famine in the Land', *Dublin University Magazine*, 29, no. 172 (1847), p. 514, published as a pamphlet later the same year.
12. Ibid., p. 503.

13. Ibid., pp. 514–15. The use of Cornwall may have been sharpened by the Cornish name of the relevant civil servant, Charles Trevelyan.

14. O'Reilly, *John MacHale, Archbishop of Tuam*, vol. II, p. 9. Emphasis as in original.

15. For more details of the work of the Quakers see Hatton, *The Largest Amount of Good*, and Goodbody, *A Suitable Channel*. Older but still containing useful information is Thomas P. O'Neill, 'The Society of Friends and the Great Famine,' *Studies*, 39, no. 154 (1950), pp. 203–13. For a wider assessment of private relief efforts see Christine Kinealy, 'Potatoes, Providence and Philanthropy: The Role of Private Charity during the Irish Famine', in Patrick O'Sullivan (ed.), *The Meaning of the Famine* (London: Leicester University Press, 1997), pp. 140–71.

16. [Central Relief Committee], *Transactions of the Central Relief Committee*, pp. 38–41. Forster's son, William Edward Forster (1818–86), accompanied him on part of the tour. Later to become chief secretary for Ireland in the early 1880s, his experiences during the 1840s had a profound impact on his views.

17. William Bennett, *Narrative of a Recent Journey of Six Weeks in Ireland, in Connexion with the Subject of Supplying Small Seed to Some of the Remoter Districts …* (London: Charles Gilpin, 1847), pp. 138–9.

18. Ibid., p. 138. Emphasis as in original.

19. R. Barclay Fox, *Distress in Ireland: Narrative of R. Barclay Fox's Visit to Some Parts of the West of Ireland* (London: Society of Friends, 1847), p. 2.

20. Ibid., p. 4.

21. Ibid., pp. 5–6.

22. [Central Relief Committee], *Transactions of the Central Relief Committee*, p. 50. What follows is largely based on this valuable source.

23. [Central Relief Committee], *Transactions of the Central Relief Committee*, p. 49; Timothy Jerome Sarbaugh, 'A Moral Spectacle: American Relief and the Famine, 1845–1849', *Éire-Ireland*, 15, no. 4 (1980), p. 9.

24. [Central Relief Committee], *Transactions of the Central Relief Committee*, p. iv.

25. Quoted in Kinealy, 'Potatoes, Providence and Philanthropy', p. 146.

26. British Association for the Relief of the Extreme Distress in Ireland and Scotland, *Report: With Correspondence of the Agents, Tables, &c.* (London: British Association for the Relief of the Extreme Distress in Ireland and Scotland, 1849), p. 193.

27. Thomas P. O'Neill, 'The Queen and the Famine', *Threshold*, 1, no. 2 (1957), p. 62. O'Neill, it should be added, was sceptical about the provenance of this story. Charles Stewart Parnell cited it in a tour of the United States in 1880.

28. Kinealy, 'Potatoes, Providence and Philanthropy', p. 151.

29. Peter Gray, 'National Humiliation and the Great Hunger: Fast and Famine in 1847', *Irish Historical Studies*, 32, no. 126 (2000), p. 209.
30. British Association, *Report*, p. 92.
31. Alan E. J. Andrews, 'Sir Paul Edmund de Strzelecki', in *Oxford Dictionary of National Biography*.
32. British Association, *Report*, p. 92.
33. Ibid., p. 97.
34. Ibid., p. 101.
35. Trevelyan, *The Irish Crisis*, pp. 126–8.
36. British Association, *Report*, p. 114–15.
37. Quoted in Sarbaugh, 'A Moral Spectacle', p. 11.
38. Ibid., p. 13.
39. Haines, *Charles Trevelyan and the Great Irish Famine*, p. 273.
40. Ibid., pp. 287–90.
41. O'Rourke, *The History of the Great Irish Famine of 1847*, pp. 337–8.
42. Haines, *Charles Trevelyan and the Great Irish Famine*, p. 300.
43. Routh to Trevelyan, 3 February 1847, *Correspondence from July 1846 to January 1847 Relating to the Measures Adopted for the Relief of the Distress in Ireland: Commissariat Series, Second Part*, P.P. 1847 [796], LII, p. 64.
44. Quoted in Haines, *Charles Trevelyan and the Great Irish Famine*, p. 281.
45. Ibid.
46. Quoted in Nowlan, *The Politics of Repeal*, p. 165.
47. Trevelyan to Routh, 18 February 1847, *Correspondence Explanatory of the Measures Adopted by Her Majesty's Government for the Relief of Distress Arising from the Failure of the Potato Crop in Ireland*, P.P. 1846 [735], XXXVII, p. 149. Emphasis as in original.
48. Ibid.
49. Gray, *Famine, Land and Politics*, p. 257.
50. Quoted in ibid.
51. O'Rourke, *The History of the Great Irish Famine of 1847*, pp. 301–2.
52. Woodham-Smith, *The Great Hunger*, pp. 180–81. For a commendatory account see O'Rourke, *The History of the Great Irish Famine of 1847*, pp. 335–63.
53. George L. Bernstein, 'Liberals, the Irish Famine and the Role of the State', *Irish Historical Studies*, 39, no. 116 (1995), pp. 519–22.
54. Gray, *Famine, Land and Politics*, pp. 227–39.
55. Prest, *Lord John Russell*, p. 237. Monteagle was a former Whig chancellor of the exchequer but neither he nor Clanricarde were in Russell's cabinet.
56. Bernstein, 'Liberals, the Irish Famine and the Role of the State', pp. 522–3; Prest, *Lord John Russell*, pp. 234–5.
57. Gray, *Famine, Land and Politics*, p. 234.

58. Donnelly, *The Great Irish Potato Famine*, p. 72. The multiplier used by Donnelly is four dependants for every person employed.

59. Trevelyan to the Commissioners under the New Relief Act, 10 February 1847, *Correspondence Explanatory of the Measures Adopted by Her Majesty's Government for the Relief of Distress Arising from the Failure of the Potato Crop in Ireland*, P.P. 1846 [735], XXXVII, p. 106.

60. Trevelyan, *The Irish Crisis*, p. 90.

61. Trevelyan to Routh, 23 January 1847, *Correspondence Explanatory of the Measures Adopted by Her Majesty's Government for the Relief of Distress Arising from the Failure of the Potato Crop in Ireland*, P.P. 1846 [735], XXXVII, p. 38.

62. O'Neill, 'The Administration of Relief', in Edwards and Williams (eds.), *The Great Famine*, p. 241.

63. Joel Mokyr and Cormac Ó Gráda, 'What Do People Die of During Famines? The Great Irish Famine in Comparative Perspective', *European Review of Economic History*, 6 (2002), pp. 339–63.

64. Clarkson and Crawford, *Feast and Famine*, pp. 144–5.

65. Ibid., pp. 152–63.

66. Ibid., p. 354, n. 9.

67. *Hansard* (Commons), 89, col. 439 (25 January 1847).

68. Ibid.

Chapter 8 (pp. 166–84)

1. Quoted in Devine, *The Great Highland Famine*, p. 91.

2. Ibid.

3. Caffon to Hamilton, 15 February 1847, *Correspondence from July 1846 to January 1847 Relating to the Measures Adopted for the Relief of the Distress in Ireland: Commissariat Series, Second Part*, P.P. 1847 [796], LII, p. 162.

4. Caffon to Hamilton, 15 February 1847, *Correspondence from July 1846 to January 1847 Relating to the Measures Adopted for the Relief of the Distress in Ireland: Commissariat Series, Second Part*, P.P. 1847 [796], LII, p. 163.

5. Quoted in Donnelly, *The Land and the People of Nineteenth-Century Cork*, p. 86.

6. Elihu Burritt, *A Journal of a Visit of Three Days to Skibbereen, and its Neighbourhood* (London: Charles Gilpin, 1847), pp. 12–13.

7. Copy of letter sent by Rev. Richard Francis Webb, Rector of Caheragh, to the editor of the *Southern Reporter*, n.d. [February 1847], *Correspondence Explanatory of the Measures Adopted by Her Majesty's Government for the Relief of Distress Arising from the Failure of the Potato Crop in Ireland*, P.P. 1846 [735], XXXVII, p. 164.

8. Treasury Minute, 23 February 1847, *Correspondence Explanatory of the Measures Adopted by Her Majesty's Government for the Relief of Distress Arising from the Failure of the Potato Crop in Ireland*, P.P. 1846 [735], xxxvii, p. 165.

9. See Patrick Hickey, 'Famine, Mortality and Emigration: A Profile of Six Parishes in the Poor Law Union of Skibbereen, 1846–7', in Patrick O'Flanagan and Cornelius G. Buttimer (eds.), *Cork: History and Society* (Dublin: Geography Publications, 1993), pp. 873–918.

10. Gerard P. Moran, *Sir Robert Gore Booth and his Landed Estate in County Sligo, 1814–1876* (Maynooth Studies in Local History, 70) (Dublin: Four Courts Press, 2006), pp. 22–32.

11. Norton, *Landlords, Tenants, Famine*, pp. 45–9.

12. Quoted in Moran, *Sir Robert Gore Booth*, p. 32.

13. John Hamilton (ed. H. C. White), *Sixty Years' Experience as an Irish Landlord: Memoirs of John Hamilton, D.L., of St Ernan's, Donegal* (London: Digby, Long, [1894]).

14. R. Barclay Fox, *Distress in Ireland: Narrative of R. Barclay Fox's Visit to Some Parts of the West of Ireland* (London: Society of Friends, 1847), p. 2.

15. Joe Walsh, 'The Butlers of Ballyslatten: Two Famine Notebooks', *Tipperary Historical Journal* (1997), pp. 174–7.

16. See for example, Séamus O'Brien, *Famine and Community in Mullingar Poor Law Union, 1845–1849: Mud Cabins and Fat Bullocks* (Maynooth Studies in Local History, 21) (Dublin: Irish Academic Press, 1999), especially pp. 17–19, 22–7.

17. British Association for the Relief of the Extreme Distress in Ireland and Scotland, *Report: With Correspondence of the Agents, Tables, &c.* (London: British Association for the Relief of the Extreme Distress in Ireland and Scotland, 1849), pp. 82, 88, 92, 96.

18. Kinealy, *This Great Calamity*, p. 107.

19. Quoted in Gray, *Famine, Land and Politics*, p. 283.

20. See Kinealy, *This Great Calamity*, pp. 175–85, Donnelly, *The Great Irish Potato Famine*, pp. 92–102, and Gray, *Famine, Land and Politics*, pp. 269–83, for fuller accounts.

21. Quoted in James S. Donnelly, Jr., '"Irish Property Must Pay for Irish Poverty": British Public Opinion and the Great Irish Famine', in Morash and Hayes (eds.), *Fearful Realities*, p. 62. This section relies heavily on this work.

22. Quoted in Gray, *Famine, Land and Politics*, p. 277.

23. Donnelly, '"Irish Property Must Pay for Irish Poverty"', p. 62.

24. See below, pp. 222–4, for more details.

25. Prest, *Lord John Russell*, p. 251.

26. Gerard J. Lyne, *The Lansdowne Estate in Kerry under the Agency of William Steuart Trench, 1849–72* (Dublin: Geography Publications, 2001), p. xxxvii. Lord Lansdowne's personal contribution to Irish famine relief amounted to the princely sum of £100.

27. T. P. O'Neill, 'The Administration of Relief', in Edwards and Williams (eds.), *The Great Famine*, p. 247.

28. Donnelly, *The Great Irish Potato Famine*, p. 258, n. 5.

29. O'Rourke, *The History of the Great Irish Famine of 1847*, p. 333.

30. Ibid., p. 331.

31. Ibid., p. 333.

32. Colm Tóibín, 'The Irish Famine', in Tóibín and Ferriter, *The Irish Famine*, pp. 3–4; see also Eagleton, *Heathcliff and the Great Hunger*, pp. 251–2.

33. Prest, *Lord John Russell*, p. 270.

34. Gray, *Famine, Land and Politics*, pp. 222–4; Prest, *Lord John Russell*, pp. 236–7.

35. Donnelly, *The Great Irish Potato Famine*, pp. 164–8.

36. Grant, *The Highland Lady in Ireland*, p. 334. All subsequent quotations are from this source unless otherwise indicated.

37. Nicholson, *Annals of the Famine in Ireland*, p. 108.

38. Anonymous [Elizabeth Smith], 'Thoughts on the Present System of Irish Charities', *Howitt's Journal of Literature and Popular Progress* (London), 1, no. 27 (1847), pp. 362–3.

39. Anonymous [Elizabeth Smith], 'A Highlander of the Last Age', *Chambers's Edinburgh Journal*, new series, 9, no. 198 (1847), pp. 241–4.

40. Peter Gray, 'National Humiliation and the Great Hunger: Fast and Famine in 1847', *Irish Historical Studies*, 32, no. 126 (2000), pp. 211–13.

41. Quoted in Prest, *Lord John Russell*, p. 263.

42. Dillon, *The Life of John Mitchel*, vol. I, p. 141.

43. Quoted in Gwynn, *Young Ireland and 1848*, p. 92.

44. Dillon, *The Life of John Mitchel*, vol. I, p. 140.

45. Duffy, *Four Years of Irish History*, p. 129.

46. Dillon, *The Life of John Mitchel*, vol. I, p. 143.

47. For details see Nowlan, *The Politics of Repeal*, pp. 126–8.

48. Duffy, *Four Years of Irish History*, p. 473.

49. Ibid., p. 465.

50. Mary E. Daly, 'James Fintan Lalor', in McGuire and Quinn (eds.), *Dictionary of Irish Biography*, R. V. Comerford, 'James Fintan Lalor', in *Oxford Dictionary of National Biography*, and at greater length Mary E. Daly, 'James Fintan Lalor (1807–1849) and Rural Revolution', in Ciarán Brady (ed.), *Worsted in the Game: Losers in Irish History* (Dublin: Lilliput Press, 1989), pp. 111–19.

51. L. Fogarty, *James Fintan Lalor: Patriot and Political Essayist (1807–1849)* (Dublin: Talbot Press, 1918), p. 25.

52. Ibid., p. 37.

53. Duffy, *Four Years of Irish History*, p. 472.

54. Nowlan, *The Politics of Repeal*, p. 152.

55. Davis, *The Young Ireland Movement*, p. 133.

56. Quinn, *John Mitchel*, p. 23.

57. Dillon, *The Life of John Mitchel*, vol. I, p. 166.

58. Quinn, *John Mitchel*, p. 129–31. The *Nation* quotation (5 June 1847) is from Desmond McCabe and James Quinn, 'John Kenyon', in McGuire and Quinn (eds.), *Dictionary of Irish Biography*.

59. Mitchel, *The Last Conquest of Ireland (Perhaps)*, p. 148. First published in Dublin by James Duffy in 1861.

60. Mitchel, *The Last Conquest of Ireland (Perhaps)*, p. 148.

61. Mitchel to Lalor, 4 January 1848, in Fogarty, *James Fintan Lalor*, p. 120.

62. Dillon, *The Life of John Mitchel*, vol. I, p. 169.

63. Mitchel, *The Last Conquest of Ireland*, p. 143.

64. Quinn, *John Mitchel*, pp. 21–2.

65. Mitchel, *The Last Conquest of Ireland*, p. 143.

66. This section draws heavily on Kerr, '*A Nation of Beggars*'? pp. 51–60.

67. Bourke, *The Life and Times of the Most Rev. John MacHale*, pp. 146–7. See also O'Reilly, *John MacHale, Archbishop of Tuam*, vol. I, pp. 652–4.

68. *Freeman's Journal*, 13 February, 3 March, 21 April, 21 July and 17 November 1847.

69. Bourke, *The Life and Times of the Most Rev. John MacHale*, p. 146.

70. *Freeman's Journal*, 3 March 1847.

71. *Freeman's Journal*, 2 December 1847.

72. On his visit to Ireland see Brian MacDonald, 'A Time of Desolation: Clones Poor Law Union', *Clogher Record*, XVII (2000), p. 68.

73. John Hughes, *A Lecture on the Antecedent Causes of the Irish Famine in 1847: Delivered under the Auspices of the General Committee for the Relief of the Suffering Poor of Ireland* (New York: E. Dunigan, 1847), p. 22.

74. Quoted in Kerr, '*A Nation of Beggars*'? p. 83.

75. This correspondence is reproduced in O'Reilly, *John MacHale, Archbishop of Tuam*, vol. II, pp. 32–6.

76. Quoted in Kerr, '*A Nation of Beggars*'? p. 85.

77. Ibid.

78. *Freeman's Journal*, 20 December 1847.

79. Quoted in Kerr, '*A Nation of Beggars*'? p. 41.

80. Dillon, *The Life of John Mitchel*, vol. I, p. 220.

Chapter 9 (pp. 186–209)

1. Nowlan, *The Politics of Repeal*, p. 175.
2. Davis, *The Young Ireland Movement*, pp. 143–4.
3. Mitchel, *The Last Conquest of Ireland*, p. 157.
4. Quoted in Duffy, *Four Years of Irish History*, p. 494.
5. See Quinn, *John Mitchel*, pp. 27–39.
6. Duffy, *Four Years of Irish History*, p. 587.
7. John Newsinger, 'John Mitchel and Irish Nationalism', *Literature and History*, 6, no. 2 (1980), pp. 189–90.
8. Dillon, *The Life of John Mitchel*, vol. 1, p. 199.
9. Mitchel, *The Last Conquest of Ireland*, p. 159.
10. *United Irishman*, 12 February 1848.
11. *United Irishman*, 4 March 1848. Emphasis as in original.
12. Quinn, *John Mitchel*, p. 30.
13. Nowlan, *The Politics of Repeal*, p. 190.
14. Quoted in ibid., p. 192.
15. Dillon, *The Life of John Mitchel*, vol. 1, p. 222.
16. Ibid., vol. 1, pp. 196–9.
17. Ibid., vol. 1, p. 127–8.
18. Quoted in K. J. Fielding, 'Ireland, John Mitchel and His "Sarcastic Friend" Thomas Carlyle', in Joachim Schwend, Susanne Hagemann and Hermann Völkel (eds.), *Literatur im Kontext / Lierature in Context: Festschrift für Horst W. Drescher* (New York: Peter Lang, 1992), p. 140.
19. Thomas Carlyle to Clarendon, 26 May 1848, in Clyde de L. Ryals and Kenneth J. Fielding (eds.), *The Collected Letters of Thomas and Jane Welsh Carlyle* (Durham, NC, and London: Duke University Press, 1995), vol. 23, p. 35.
20. Clarendon to Carlyle, 30 May 1848, in ibid., p. 36.
21. This account of the trial and subsequent events relies on Dillon, *The Life of John Mitchel*, vol. 1, pp. 237–48.
22. Mitchel, *Jail Journal*, p. 28.
23. This account relies on Gwynn, *Young Ireland and 1848*; Davis, *The Young Ireland Movement*; Kinealy, *Repeal and Revolution*; and Nowlan, *The Politics of Repeal*. Many biographies of the principal leaders are also available, including Ó Cathaoir, *John Blake Dillon*, and Sloan, *William Smith O'Brien and the Young Irelander Rebellion of 1848*.
24. Duffy, *Four Years of Irish History*, p. 608.
25. Ibid., p. 632.
26. Nowlan, *The Politics of Repeal*, p. 210.
27. Prest, *Lord John Russell*, p. 286.
28. Grant, *The Highland Lady in Ireland*, p. 398.

29. Duffy, *Four Years of Irish History*, p. 691.

30. For a first-hand account see Michael Doheny, *The Felon's Track, or History of the Late Attempted Outbreak in Ireland* ... [1849] (Dublin: Gill, 1918).

31. Duffy, *Four Years of Irish History*, p. 670.

32. Quoted in Kerr, *'A Nation of Beggars'?* p. 161.

33. Quoted in Gwynn, *Young Ireland and 1848*, p. 269.

34. O'Reilly, *John MacHale, Archbishop of Tuam*, vol. II, p. 163.

35. This section relies heavily on Kerr, *'A Nation of Beggars'?* pp. 88–121.

36. For the background see Stephen J. Campbell, *The Great Irish Famine: Words and Images from the Famine Museum, Strokestown Park, County Roscommon* (Strokestown: Famine Museum, 1994), pp. 40–41.

37. For a recent account see Peter Duffy, *The Killing of Major Denis Mahon: A Mystery of Old Ireland* (New York: Harper-Collins, 2007). See also Scally, *The End of Hidden Ireland*, pp. 38–40, and Woodham-Smith, *The Great Hunger*, pp. 324–5.

38. The trials are painstakingly reconstructed in Duffy, *The Killing of Major Denis Mahon*, pp. 237–302. It should be pointed out that local folklore casts doubt on the soundness of these convictions.

39. Quoted in Kerr, *'A Nation of Beggars'?* p. 93.

40. Quoted in ibid., p. 92.

41. *Morning Chronicle* (London), 22 December 1847.

42. E. B. Stuart, 'John Talbot (1791–1852)', rev. G. Martin Murphy, in *Oxford Dictionary of National Biography*.

43. See *Freeman's Journal*, 20 December 1847.

44. *Morning Chronicle* (London), 4 January 1848.

45. Ibid.

46. First published in *Freeman's Journal*, 22 January 1848, but also in *Morning Chronicle* (London), 24 and 25 January 1848.

47. *Freeman's Journal*, 12 and 19 February 1848.

48. See, for example, the editorial in the *Freeman's Journal*, 1 February 1848.

49. Kerr, *'A Nation of Beggars'?* pp. 119–21.

50. Quoted in James S. Donnelly, Jr., 'Mass Evictions and the Great Famine', in Póirtéir (ed.), *The Great Irish Famine*, p. 173.

51. Bourke, *The Life and Times of the Most Rev. John MacHale*, p. 154.

52. See Miriam Moffitt, *The Society for Irish Church Missions to the Roman Catholics, 1849–1950* (Manchester: Manchester University Press, 2010).

53. Donnelly, *The Great Irish Potato Famine*, p. 234; Irene Whelan, 'The Stigma of Souperism', in Póirtéir (ed.), *The Great Irish Famine*, pp. 146–50.

54. Seán Ó Domhnaill (b. 1873), in Póirtéir (ed.), *Famine Echoes*, p. 170.

55. Quoted in Woodham-Smith, *The Great Hunger*, p. 364.

56. Norton, *Landlords, Tenants, Famine*, pp. 300–301.

57. Scally, *The End of Hidden Ireland*, p. 115.

58. Kate O'Carroll (b. 1877), in Póirtéir (ed.), *Famine Echoes*, p. 232.

59. Donnelly, 'Mass Evictions and the Great Famine', p. 156. See also Tim P. O'Neill, 'Famine Evictions', in Carla King (ed.), *Famine, Land, and Culture in Ireland* (Dublin: UCD Press, 2000), pp. 29–70.

60. Grant, *The Highland Lady in Ireland*, p. 428. All subsequent quotations in this section are from this edition unless otherwise indicated.

61. For her views on the Irish Catholic Church see Tod, 'The Smiths of Baltiboys', pp. 292–315.

62. Grant, *Memoirs of a Highland Lady*, vol. 1, p. 301.

63. T. C. Smout, 'The Grant Lairds of Rothiemurchus', in Smout and Lambert (eds.), *Rothiemurchus*, p. 18.

64. Both quotations are from Haines, *Charles Trevelyan and the Great Irish Famine*, p. 549, 550–51.

65. Ibid., p. 407.

66. Ibid., p. 515.

67. Ibid.

68. Both quotations are from Woodham-Smith, *The Great Hunger*, pp. 302–3.

69. Ibid., p. 309.

70. This section relies heavily on Kinealy, *This Great Calamity*, pp. 175–231, and Christine Kinealy, 'The Poor Law during the Great Famine: An Administration in Crisis', in Crawford (ed.), *Famine*, pp. 157–75.

71. Murphy, *A Starving People*, p. 74.

72. Donnelly, *The Great Irish Potato Famine*, p. 104.

73. Ibid., pp. 106–7.

74. Prest, *Lord John Russell*, p. 289.

75. See James Grant, 'The Great Famine and the Poor Law in Ulster: the Rate-In-Aid Issue of 1849', *Irish Historical Studies*, 27, no. 105 (1990), pp. 30–47,

76. Quoted in Woodham-Smith, *The Great Hunger*, p. 380.

77. Quoted in Christine Kinealy, 'Famine Queen or Faery? Queen Victoria and Ireland', in Roger Swift and Christine Kinealy (eds.), *Politics and Power in Victorian Ireland* (Dublin: Four Courts Press, 2006), p. 24.

78. James Loughlin, 'Allegiance and Illusion: Queen Victoria's Irish Visit of 1849', *History*, 87, no. 288 (2002), p. 499.

79. Prest, *Lord John Russell*, p. 300.

80. See Loughlin, 'Allegiance and Illusion', pp. 501–4.

81. Quoted in Kinealy, 'Famine Queen or Faery?' p. 31.

82. Quoted in Thomas P. O'Neill, 'The Queen and the Famine', *Threshold*, 1, no. 2 (1957), p. 63.

83. MacHale to Murray, 24 July 1849, in O'Reilly, *John MacHale, Archbishop of Tuam*, vol. II, p. 189.
84. O'Reilly, *John MacHale, Archbishop of Tuam*, vol. II, p. 193.
85. Kerr, '*A Nation of Beggars*'? p. 204. The letters were published later as *Correspondence between the Most Rev. Dr. MacHale … and Most Rev. Dr. Murray … Relative to an Address to be Presented to Her Majesty Queen Victoria, on the Occasion of her Visit to Ireland in 1849* (Dublin: M. H. Gill and Son, 1885).
86. Mitchel, *Jail Journal*, p. 217.

Chapter 10 (pp. 210–26)

1. James Prendergast to his children in Boston, 25 July 1847, in Shelley Barber (ed.), *The Prendergast Letters: Correspondence from Famine-Era Ireland, 1840–1850* (Amherst, Mass.: University of Massachusetts Press, 2006), p. 106.
2. James Prendergast to his children in Boston, 21 April 1847, in ibid., p. 101.
3. Michael Prendergast [probably written by his brother Thomas], 14 June 1847, in ibid., pp. 103–4.
4. For conditions there see Oliver MacDonagh, 'Irish Overseas Emigration during the Famine', in Edwards and Williams (eds.), *The Great Famine*, p. 373.
5. Elizabeth Prendergast to her daughter Julia and to her son Thomas, 23 February 1850, in Barber (ed.), *The Prendergast Letters*, p. 152.
6. James Prendergast to his children in Boston, 29 October 1848, in ibid., p. 138.
7. Grant, *The Highland Lady in Ireland*, p. 428.
8. Elizabeth Prendergast to her children, 14 July 1850, in Barber (ed.), *The Prendergast Letters*, p. 155.
9. Elizabeth Prendergast to her children, 19 August 1850, in ibid., p. 163.
10. Marie E. Daly, 'The Prendergast Family in America', in ibid., pp. 171–90.
11. Quoted in Miller, *Emigrants and Exiles*, p. 292.
12. This account is largely based on David Fitzpatrick, 'Emigration, 1801–70', in Vaughan (ed.), *A New History of Ireland, v*, part 1, pp. 562–622 Miller, *Emigrants and Exiles*, pp. 291–300, and MacDonagh, 'Irish Overseas Emigration during the Famine'.
13. Michael and Mary Rush to Thomas Barrett, 6 September 1846, reproduced in Kerby A. Miller and Bruce D. Boling, 'The Pauper and the Politician: A Tale of Two Immigrants and the Construction of Irish-American Society', in Gribben (ed.), *The Great Famine and the Irish Diaspora in America*, p. 201.
14. Quoted in MacDonagh, 'Irish Overseas Emigration during the Famine', p. 321.

15. Quoted in ibid., p. 321.
16. [Central Relief Committee], *Transactions of the Central Relief Committee*, p. 255.
17. Miller, *Emigrants and Exiles*, p. 294.
18. See Donnelly, *The Great Irish Potato Famine*, pp. 182–5.
19. Both quotations are from MacDonagh, 'Irish Overseas Emigration during the Famine', p. 325, 329.
20. See Tyler Anbinder, 'Lord Palmerston and Irish Famine Emigration', *Historical Journal*, 44, no. 2 (2001), pp. 441–69; Patrick J. Duffy, 'Assisted Emigration from the Shirley Estate, 1843–54', *Clogher Record*, 14, no. 2 (1992), pp. 7–62; Gerard J. Lyne, *The Lansdowne Estate in Kerry under the Agency of William Steuart Trench, 1849–72* (Dublin: Geography Publications, 2001), pp. 35–87; Gerard J. Lyne, 'William Steuart Trench and Post-Famine Emigration from Kenmare to America, 1850–55', *Kerry Archaeological and Historical Society Journal*, 25 (1992), pp. 51–137; Gerard P. Moran, *Sir Robert Gore Booth and his Landed Estate in County Sligo, 1814–1876* (Maynooth Studies in Local History, 70) (Dublin: Four Courts Press, 2006), pp. 33–48; Gerard P. Moran, *Sending Out Ireland's Poor: Assisted Emigration to North America in the Nineteenth Century* (Dublin: Four Courts Press, 2004); Jim Rees, *Surplus People: The Fitzwilliam Clearances, 1847–1856* (Cork: Collins Press, 2000).
21. Both quotations are from Anbinder, 'Lord Palmerston and Irish Famine Emigration', p. 456.
22. Quoted in Moran, *Sir Robert Gore Booth*, p. 33.
23. Fitzpatrick, *Irish Emigration*, p. 594.
24. Moran, *Sending Out Ireland's Poor*, p. 36.
25. See Scally, *The End of Hidden Ireland*.
26. Eilish Ellis, 'State-aided Emigration Schemes from Crown Estates in Ireland, c. 1850', *Analecta Hibernica*, 22 (1960), p. 334.
27. Michael Byrne to Golding Bird, Collector of Excise, Galway, 13 September 1848, quoted in ibid., p. 394.
28. Fitzpatrick, *Irish Emigration*, pp. 585–7; MacDonagh, 'Irish Overseas Emigration during the Famine', pp. 340–52; Peter Grey, '"Shovelling Out Your Paupers": The British State and Irish Famine Migration, 1846–50', *Patterns of Prejudice*, 33, no. 4 (1999), pp. 47–65.
29. Trevelyan, *The Irish Crisis*, pp. 131–3. See Haines, *Charles Trevelyan and the Great Irish Famine*, pp. 402–3, for the background to the drafting of this section.
30. Fitzpatrick, *Irish Emigration*, p. 601.
31. Arnold Schrier, *Ireland and the American Emigration, 1850–1900* (Minneapolis: University of Minnesota Press, 1958), pp. 104–14.

32. Scally, *The End of Hidden Ireland*, pp. 177–8.
33. Woodham-Smith, *The Great Hunger*, p. 216.
34. Stephen E. de Vere to T. F. Elliott, 30 November 1847, in *The Elgin-Grey Papers, 1846–1852* (ed. Arthur G. Doughty, 4 vols., Ottawa: J. O. Patenaude, 1937), vol. 4, p. 1341–2.
35. Ibid., p. 1343.
36. Ibid., p. 1344.
37. Quoted in Michael Quigley, 'Grosse Île: Canada's Famine Memorial', in Gribben (ed.), *The Great Famine and the Irish Diaspora in America*, p. 136.
38. Woodham-Smith, *The Great Hunger*, p. 222.
39. Anbinder, 'Lord Palmerston and Irish Famine Emigration', pp. 460–63.
40. MacDonagh, 'Irish Overseas Emigration during the Famine', p. 366.
41. Quoted in Woodham-Smith, *The Great Hunger*, p. 238.
42. See Coleman, *Passage to America*, pp. 205–9.
43. Woodham-Smith, *The Great Hunger*, p. 235.
44. MacDonagh, 'Irish Overseas Emigration during the Famine', p. 377.
45. Hasia R. Diner, '"The Most Irish City in the Union": The Era of the Great Migration', in Ronald H. Bayor and Timothy J. Meagher (eds.), *The New York Irish* (Baltimore, Md: Johns Hopkins University Press, 1996), p. 91.
46. Kevin Kenny, *The American Irish: A History* (Harlow, Middx: Longman, 2000), p. 107; Anbinder, *Five Points*, pp. 93–6, 111, 135–6.
47. Woodham-Smith, *The Great Hunger*, p. 249.
48. Quoted in ibid., p. 251.
49. See J. Mathew Gallman, *Receiving Erin's Children: Philadelphia, Liverpool and the Irish Famine, 1845–1855* (Chapel Hill, 2000).
50. Neal, *Black '47*, p. 62.
51. Ibid., p. 64.
52. Quoted in John Belchem, *Irish, Catholic and Scouse: The History of the Liverpool Irish, 1800–1939* (Liverpool: Liverpool University Press, 2007), p. 60.
53. See Paul O'Leary, 'A Regional Perspective: The Famine Irish in South Wales', in Roger Swift and Sheridan Gilley (eds.), *The Irish in Victorian Britain: The Local Dimension* (Dublin: Four Courts Press, 1999), pp. 14–30.
54. Quoted in Neal, *Black '47*, p. 161,
55. James Edmund Handley, *The Irish in Modern Scotland* (Cork: Cork University Press, 1947), pp. 37–40.
56. Quoted in ibid., p. 40.
57. David Fitzpatrick, '"A Peculiar Tramping People": The Irish in Britain, 1801–70,' in Vaughan (ed.), *A New History of Ireland, v*, part i, p. 638.
58. T. M. Devine, 'The Great Irish Famine and Scottish History', in Martin J. Mitchell (ed.), *New Perspectives on the Irish in Scotland* (Edinburgh:

John Donald, 2008), pp. 20–30; Dale T. Knobel, '"Celtic Exodus": The Famine Irish, Ethnic Stereotypes, and the Cultivation of American Racial Nationalism', in Mulrooney (ed.), *Fleeing the Famine*, pp. 79–96; Donald M. MacRaild, *Irish Migrants in Modern Britain, 1750–1922* (Basingstoke, Hants: Macmillan, 1999),pp. 58–65.

59. Gerald Keegan, *Famine Diary: Journey to a New World* (ed. James J. Mangan) (Dublin: Wolfhound Press, 1991); A Cabin Passenger [Robert Whyte?], *The Ocean Plague: or, A Voyage to Quebec in an Irish Emigrant Vessel* (Boston: Coolidge and Wiley, 1848); Jim Jackson, 'Famine Diary: The Making of a Best Seller', *Irish Review*, 11 (1991), pp. 1–8; Mark McGowan, 'Famine, Facts and Fabrication: An Examination of the Diaries from the Irish Famine Migration to Canada', *Canadian Journal of Irish Studies*, 33, no. 2 (2007), pp. 48–55.

Epilogue (pp. 227–35)

1. *Times*, 17 December 1850.

2. T. P. O'Neill, 'The Organisation and Administration of Relief, 1845–52', in Edwards and Williams (eds.), *The Great Famine*, p. 254.

3. Donnelly, *The Great Irish Potato Famine*, pp. 118–19.

4. Quoted in Gray, *Famine, Land and Politics*, p. 192.

5. I owe this point to O'Rourke, *The History of the Great Irish Famine of 1847*, p. 371.

6. Ibid., pp. 229–300.

7. For more details see Gray, *Famine, Land and Politics*, p. 192; Peter Gray, 'Ideology and the Famine', in Póirtéir (ed.), *The Great Irish Famine*, pp. 86–103, and most recently David P. Nally, *Human Encumbrances: Political Violence and the Great Irish Famine* (Notre Dame, Ind.: University of Notre Dame Press, 2011). For a valuable comparison with Indian famine policy see S. Ambirajan, *Classical Political Economy and British Policy in India* (Cambridge South Asian Studies, 21) (New York and London: Cambridge University Press, 1978), pp. 59–100.

8. Devine, *The Great Highland Famine*.

9. Ambirajan, *Classical Political Economy and British Policy in India*, p. 79.

10. Trevelyan, *The Irish Crisis*, p. 194. This was first published in the *Edinburgh Review*, 87, no. 175 (1848), pp. 229–320.

11. Ibid., p. 1.

12. Ibid., p. 196, 199.

13 Ibid., p. 201.

14. Prest, *Lord John Russell*, p. 236; Gray, *Famine, Land and Politics*, pp. 244–6; Peter Gray, '"Potatoes and Providence": British Government Responses to the Great Famine', *Bullán: An Irish Studies Journal*, 1, no. 1 (1994), pp. 75–90.

15. See David Fitzpatrick, 'The Disappearance of the Irish Agricultural Labourer, 1841–1912', *Irish Economic and Social History*, 7 (1980), pp. 66–92.

16. [William O'Connor Morris], 'Social Progress of Ireland', *Edinburgh Review*, 106, no. 215 (1857), p. 121, 122. This article was first cited by Peter Gray, 'The Making of Mid-Victorian Ireland?: Political Economy and the Memory of the Great Famine', in Peter Gray (ed.), *Victoria's Ireland?: Irishness and Britishness, 1837–1901* (Dublin: Four Courts Press, 2004), p. 158.

17. Quoted in Donnelly, *The Great Irish Potato Famine*, 166. For more details see James S. Donnelly, Jr., '"Irish Property Must Pay for Irish Poverty": British Public Opinion and the Great Irish Famine', in Morash and Hayes (eds.), *Fearful Realities*, pp. 60–76, and more generally Lengel, *The Irish through British Eyes*, pp. 97–127, and Michael de Nie, *The Eternal Paddy: Irish Identity and the British Press, 1798–1882* (Madison, Wis., 2004).

18. Quoted in David Steele, 'George William Frederick Villiers, fourth Earl of Clarendon (1800–1870)', in *Oxford Dictionary of National Biography*.

19. Herbert Maxwell (ed.), *The Life and Letters of George William Frederick Fourth Earl of Clarendon K.G., G.C.B.* (2 vols., London: Edward Arnold, 1913), vol. I, p. 281.

20. See Donnelly, *The Great Irish Potato Famine*, p. 102.

21. *Hansard* (Commons), 91, col. 590 (29 March 1847).

22. On Scrope, see Gray, *Famine, Land and Politics*, 13–14; Black, *Economic Thought and the Irish Question*, pp. 96–7.

23. *Hansard* (Commons), 91, col. 588–9 (29 March 1847).

24. Pius Devine, 'John MacHale, Archbishop of Tuam', *Dublin Review*, 26, no. 1 (1891), p. 36.

25. Emmet Larkin, 'John MacHale (1791–1881)', in *Oxford Dictionary of National Biography*.

26. Quoted in Quinn, *John Mitchel*, p. 57.

27. Quoted in Tod, 'The Smiths of Baltiboys', p. 576.

28. Ibid., p. 577.

BIBLIOGRAPHICAL NOTE

The historical literature on the Great Irish Famine is vast. No attempt is made here to list every item: it is necessarily a highly selective and personal choice, and it excludes individual chapters or articles in journals. Many of these studies are referred to in the notes to individual chapters, and only items of particular importance are identified.

GENERAL WORKS

The Great Irish Famine has generated a raft of single-volume accounts. In no particular order, the most accessible are Mary E. Daly, *The Famine in Ireland*, James S. Donnelly, Jr., *The Great Irish Potato Famine*, Austin Bourke, *'The Visitation of God'?*, Peter Gray, *The Irish Famine* (which contains an impressive collection of illustrations), Ciarán Ó Murchadha, *The Great Famine*, Christine Kinealy, *This Great Calamity*, and also two shorter accounts by the same author, *A Death-Dealing Famine* and *The Great Irish Famine*. Cormac Ó Gráda has raised the study of the topic to a new level of sophistication through his studies, *The Great Irish Famine, Black '47 and Beyond*, and more recently *Ireland's Great Famine*. Still retaining its appeal more than fifty years after its first publication, Cecil Woodham-Smith's *The Great Hunger* is a compelling narrative history written with style, even if it places too much emphasis on the personalities involved over broader structural issues.

The Famine's first major history by Canon John O'Rourke, *The History of the Great Irish Famine of 1847* (1875) (available on line in various editions), is a goldmine of information on the early years, but the coverage peters out after 1847. Two very important interpretative accounts are Peter Gray, *Famine, Land and Politics*, and David P. Nally, *Human Encumbrances: Political Violence and the Great Irish Famine*. For the literary representations see Christopher Morash, *Writing the Irish Famine*, Margaret Kelleher, *The Feminization of Famine*, Melissa Fegan, *Literature and the Irish Famine*, and—more idiosyncratically—Terry Eagleton, *Heathcliff and the Great Hunger*.

Before the 1980s the only collaborative collection was R. Dudley Edwards and T. Desmond Williams (eds.), *The Great Famine*. The essays by Kevin B. Nowlan, Sir William MacArthur, Oliver MacDonagh and T. P. O'Neill remain important treatments of their respective subjects. E. M. Crawford (ed.), *Famine: The Irish Experience*, contains much of relevance to the 1840s. The 150th commemoration of the outbreak of the Famine generated a number of important collections, including Cathal Póirtéir (ed.), *The Great Irish Famine*, Chris Morash and Richard Hayes (eds.), *Fearful Realities: New Perspectives on the Famine*, and Cormac Ó Gráda (ed.), *Famine 150*. A unique day-by-day record can be found in Brendan Ó Cathaoir, *Famine Diary*.

There are many general surveys of nineteenth-century Ireland, but authoritative coverage can be found in W. E. Vaughan (ed.), *A New History of Ireland, Vol. v: Ireland under the Union, 1801–70*, recently reissued in paperback. Two valuable bibliographical resources were used extensively for information on individuals: the *Dictionary of Irish Biography*, edited by James McGuire and James Quinn, available on line in many libraries, and the *Oxford Dictionary of National Biography*, again available on line. Both works are indispensable to anyone interested in modern Irish history.

For a flavour of the contemporary documents that constitute the building-blocks of any study see Noel Kissane (ed.), *The Irish Famine: A Documentary History*, Colm Tóibín and Diarmaid Ferriter, *The Irish Famine: A Documentary*, Ken Hannigan (ed.), *The Famine, Ireland, 1845–51*, John Killen (ed.), *The Famine Decade: Contemporary Accounts*, L. A. Clarkson and E. Margaret Crawford (eds.), *Famine and Disease in Ireland*, Public Record Office of Northern Ireland, *The Great Famine, 1845–1852*, and Liam Swords, *In Their Own Words: The Famine in North Connacht, 1845–1849*. Cathal Póirtéir (ed.), *Famine Echoes*, is a fascinating account based on folk memories collected by the Irish Folklore Commission. Another unique body of material can be found in Christopher Morash (ed.), *The Hungry Voice: The Poetry of the Irish Famine*.

For geographical viewpoints on both the course and the consequences of the Famine with perceptive accompanying commentaries see Liam Kennedy et al., *Mapping the Great Irish Famine*, and the encyclopaedic John Crowley et al., *Atlas of the Great Irish Famine*.

The remarkable growth in local history has generated hundreds of studies of the famine in districts, Poor Law unions and counties, many of which are published in the journals of local history societies. The excellent History and Society series published by Geography Publications is the first port of call, as each volume dealing with a county has a chapter on the Famine. At present there are twenty-one county histories, with additional volumes in progress.

An abundance of material is available on the internet, of varying quality and provenance. Two excellent web sites are the Cork Multitext Project, hosted by the National University of Ireland, Cork (http://multitext.ucc.ie/d/Famine), and Views of the Famine (http://adminstaff.vassar.edu/sttaylor/FAMINE/).

PART 1

The best introductory survey to pre-Famine Ireland is Gearóid Ó Tuathaigh, *Ireland Before the Famine*, which, even though published forty years ago, still manages to raise all the most interesting issues about the nature of Irish society. The chapters in *A New History of Ireland, v*, by S. J. Connolly, T. W. Freeman, Oliver MacDonagh and Cormac Ó Gráda establish the context for what unfolds in the late 1840s. T. W. Freeman, *Pre-Famine Ireland*, is a classic study by a historical geographer. Cormac Ó Gráda's *Ireland: A New Economic History* and *Ireland Before and After the Famine* (2nd ed., 1993), are indispensable for the economy, as is Joel Mokyr, *Why Ireland Starved* (2nd ed., 1985), where general statements about the nature of the pre-Famine economy and society are tested with all the powerful techniques of sophisticated economic history.

K. H. Connell, *The Population of Ireland, 1750–1845*, remains the starting-point on population growth, even if many of its conclusions have been challenged. Daniel O'Connell has been well served by high-quality biographies covering the period after 1830, including the brilliant work of Oliver MacDonagh, *O'Connell: The Life of Daniel O'Connell, 1775–1847*, Fergus O'Ferrall, *Daniel O'Connell*, and most recently Patrick M. Geoghegan, *Liberator: The Life and Death of Daniel O'Connell, 1830–1847*. O'Connell's campaign for repeal of the Act of Union is covered in Angus MacIntyre, *The Liberator: Daniel O'Connell and the Irish Party*, and Kevin B. Nowlan, *The Politics of Repeal: A Study in the Relations between Great Britain and Ireland*. Wide-ranging interpretations of political relationships after the Union can be found in Oliver MacDonagh, *Ireland: The Union and its Aftermath*, and Patrick O'Farrell, *England and Ireland since 1800*. R. B. McDowell, *Public Opinion and Government Policy in Ireland, 1801–1846*, describes the various efforts to reform the governance of Ireland, even if 'public opinion' is narrowly interpreted, and see for the early years Brian Jenkins, *Era of Emancipation: British Government of Ireland, 1812–1830*. For the inherent instabilities of the rural economy see the essays in Samuel Clark and James S. Donnelly, Jr. (eds.), *Irish Peasants: Violence and Political Unrest in Ireland, 1780–1914*, and James S. Donnelly, Jr., *The Land and People of Nineteenth-Century Cork*, a model study of rural history that says more about Ireland as a whole than the title might suggest. On popular Catholicism, S. J. Connolly, *Priests and People in Pre-Famine Ireland*, is by far the most original treatment. For the machinations of the relationship between the Catholic Church and the British state in the early 1840s see Donal A. Kerr, *Peel, Priests and Politics: Sir Robert Peel's Administration and the Roman Catholic Church in Ireland, 1841–1846*, the first chapter of which is a valuable survey of the position of the Catholic Church by the middle of the nineteenth century. R. D. Collison Black, *Economic Thought and the Irish Question, 1817–1870*, was a pioneering study of the history of economic thought; the sections on the

Poor Law have been superseded by Peter Gray, *The Making of the Irish Poor Law, 1815–1843*. For the British context, accessible and illuminating accounts can be found in Boyd Hilton, *A Mad, Bad, and Dangerous People?: England, 1783–1846*, and K. T. Hoppen, *The Mid-Victorian Generation, 1846–1886*.

For the principal individuals covered, Elizabeth Smith's early life is recounted in her own *Memoirs of a Highland Lady*, ed. Andrew Tod. On the Scottish background see T. C. Smout and R. A. Lambert (eds.), *Rothiemurchus: Nature and People on a Highland Estate, 1500–2000*. A valuable unpublished study by the leading expert on her life is Andrew Tod, 'The Smiths of Baltiboys: A Co. Wicklow Family and their Estate in the 1840s' (PhD thesis, University of Edinburgh, 1978). The absence of a critical biography of John MacHale means that the hagiographical work of Bernard O'Reilly, *John MacHale, Archbishop of Tuam: His Life, Times, and Correspondence* (2 vols., 1890), remains of critical importance, as his letters and papers, on which O'Reilly's account was based, were apparently lost. Nuala Costello's brief biography, *John MacHale: Archbishop of Tuam* (1939) is equally uncritical yet still useful, and Ulick Bourke, *The Life and Times of the Most Rev. John MacHale* (1882) is a sympathetic life written by a contemporary. Robin Haines's massive biography, *Charles Trevelyan and the Great Irish Famine*, covers his family background and time in India briefly, albeit as a secondary concern to her Irish focus, which is based on an exhaustive range of source materials, including twenty volumes of private letterbooks relating to the Great Famine. An affectionate portrait is provided by his great-grandnephew Humphrey Trevelyan, who also began his career as a civil servant in India, in The *India We Left*. Laura Trevelyan traces her distinguished ancestors, including Charles, in *A Very British Family: The Trevelyans and Their World*.

John Mitchel has been the subject of numerous biographies, mostly admiring. William Dillon, *The Life of John Mitchel* (1888), is the most detailed, and the author had access to family members and friends as well as papers, yet Dillon (son of the Young Irelander John Blake Dillon) retains a degree of critical detachment from his subject. James Quinn, *John Mitchel*, is a concise recent treatment and full of insight. Séamus MacCall, *Irish Mitchel* (1938), and Bryan McGovern, *John Mitchel: Irish Nationalist, Southern Secessionist*, cover the Irish and American dimensions, respectively.

PART II

Most of the studies listed above have considerable coverage of the Peel government's handling of the partial failure in late 1845. The Young Ireland movement is examined in Richard Davis, *The Young Ireland Movement*, and the older yet nevertheless useful Denis Gwynn, *Young Ireland and 1848*. Norman Gash, *Sir Robert Peel: The Life of Sir Robert Peel after 1830*, is helpful on the wider context of Peel's actions in 1845–6. For the Irish diet (and the famous Indian meal) see L. A. Clarkson and E. M. Crawford, *Feast and Famine: A History of Food and Nutrition in Ireland, 1500–1920*. Elizabeth Smith's years in Co. Wicklow are recorded in Elizabeth Grant, *The Highland Lady in Ireland: Journals, 1840–50*, which is a fuller edition than David Thomson and Moyra McGusty (eds.), *The Irish Journals of Elizabeth Smith, 1840–1850*, though the masterful introduction by Thomson makes this an important volume in its own right. Dermot James and Séamus Ó Maitiú (eds.), *The Wicklow World of Elizabeth Smith*, places Elizabeth within her west Wicklow context.

PART III

Eye-witness accounts of the unfolding tragedy from late 1846 onwards are especially vivid and graphic. A superb guide may be found in C. J. Woods, *Travellers' Accounts as Source-Materials for Irish Historians*, and a number of important accounts are anthologised in Glenn Hooper (ed.), *The Tourist's Gaze: Travellers to Ireland, 1800–2000*. For their interpretation see Glenn Hooper, *Travel Writing and Ireland, 1760–1860*, and W. H. A. Williams, *Tourism, Landscape and the Irish Character: British Travel Writers in Pre-Famine Ireland*. A number of well-known accounts have recently been republished, including Alexander Somerville, *Letters from Ireland During the Famine of 1847*, and Asenath Nicholson, *Annals of the Famine in Ireland* (1851). Kerr's *A Nation of Beggars?* is a fascinating and richly-documented account of both the responses of the Irish Catholic Church to the famine and the complex relations between the church and the Russell administration. Lord John Russell's life, with good coverage of Irish affairs, is recounted in John Prest, *Lord John Russell*. On the Society of Friends see Helen E. Hatton, *The Largest Amount of Good: Quaker Relief in Ireland, 1654–1921*, and Rob Goodbody, *A Suitable Channel: Quaker Relief in the Great Famine*. The records of the Quaker effort have been republished as *Transactions of the Central Relief Committee of the Society of Friends during the Famine in Ireland in 1846 and 1847*. The changes within British public opinion are charted in Edward G. Lengel, *The Irish through British Eyes: Perceptions of Ireland in the Famine Era*, and in a broader context by Michael de Nie, *The Eternal Paddy: Irish Identity and the British Press, 1798–1882*. On landlords and the crisis an important book that challenges much of the conventional wisdom is Desmond Norton, *Landlords, Tenants, Famine: The Business of an Irish Land Agency in the 1840s*.

PART IV

The background to the 1848 Rebellion is traced in the work of Davis and Gwynn referred to in part II; see, however, the recent re-evaluation by Christine Kinealy, *Repeal and Revolution: 1848 in Ireland*. A number of biographies are also helpful, including Brendan Ó Cathaoir, *John Blake Dillon: Young Irelander*, Robert Sloan, *William Smith O'Brien and the Young Ireland Rebellion of 1848*, Richard Davis, *William Smith O'Brien: Ireland—1848—Tasmania*, and David A. Wilson, *Thomas D'Arcy McGee, I: Passion, Reason, and Politics, 1825–1857*. Queen Victoria's visit to Ireland is covered in James Loughlin, *The British Monarchy and Ireland: 1800 to the Present*, and James H. Murphy, *Abject Loyalty: Nationalism and Monarchy in Ireland during the Reign of Queen Victoria*.

There is a huge literature on the Famine exodus. The most authoritative treatment may be found in Kerby A. Miller, *Emigrants and Exiles: Ireland and the Irish Exodus to North America*, but see also the micro-studies of Robert James Scally, *The End of Hidden Ireland: Rebellion, Famine, Emigration*, and Mary Lee Dunn, *Ballykilcline Rising: From Famine Ireland to Immigrant America*. A useful collection of essays is E. Margaret Crawford (ed.), *The Hungry Stream: Essays on Emigration and Famine*. On the horrors of the voyage and subsequent reception, Terry Coleman, *Passage to America*, is illuminating. On the Famine Irish in Britain the definitive account is Frank Neal, *Black '47: Britain and the Famine Irish*. Aspects of the experience in North America are examined in Arthur Gribben (ed.), *The Great Famine and the Irish Diaspora in America*, and Margaret M. Mulrooney (ed.), *Fleeing the Famine: North America and Irish Refugees, 1845–1851*. One admittedly unique place of settlement, the notorious Five Points district in New York, is explored with imagination in Tyler Anbinder, *Five Points: The 19th-Century New York Neighborhood that Invented Tap Dance, Stole Elections, and Became the World's Most Notorious Slum*.

The consequences for emigration and population change are charted by David Fitzpatrick in *Irish Emigration, 1801–1921*, and Timothy J. Guinnane in *The Vanishing Irish: Households, Migration, and the Rural Economy in Ireland, 1850–1914*. There is a very large literature on post-Famine Ireland. On the economy the relevant chapters of Ó Gráda's *Ireland: A New Economic History* are the standard work. For politics see K. T. Hoppen, *Elections, Politics and Society in Ireland, 1832–85*, a classic of Irish historical scholarship. J. J. Lee's *The Modernisation of Irish Society, 1848–1918* (2nd ed., 1989) is full of challenging interpretations. All the major surveys, including R. F. Foster, *Modern Ireland, 1600–1972*, K. T. Hoppen, *Ireland since 1800* (2nd ed., 1999), Alvin Jackson, *Ireland, 1798–1998* (2nd ed., 2010) and Paul Bew, *Ireland: The Politics of Enmity, 1789–2006*, treat the changes that occurred in the wake of the Great Irish Famine. Still the best introduction is F. S. L. Lyons, *Ireland since the Famine* (1973). Many of the chapters in W. E. Vaughan (ed.), *A New History of Ireland, Vol. v: Ireland under the Union, 1801–70*, and *Vol. vi: Ireland Under the Union, 1870–1921*, are especially instructive on Ireland between the 1840s and the First World War, especially those by R. V. Comerford, L. P. Curtis, David Noel Doyle, David Fitzpatrick, H. D. Gribbon and Patrick O'Farrell.

For a sense of how the Irish Famine compares with other historical famines see Cormac Ó Gráda, *Famine: A Short History*, David Arnold, *Famine: Social Crisis and Historical Change*, and the penetrating interpretations offered in Mike Davis, *Late Victorian Holocausts: El Niño Famines and the Making of the Modern World*. For the 'forgotten' Irish famine of 1740–41 see David Dickson, *Arctic Ireland: The Extraordinary Story of the Great Frost and Forgotten Famine of 1740–41*. For the effect of the potato failure of the late 1840s elsewhere see especially T. M. Devine, *The Great Highland Famine*, and Cormac Ó Gráda, Richard Paping and Eric Vanhaute (eds.), *When the Potato Failed: Causes and Effects of the Last Great European Subsistence Crisis, 1845–1850*.

The works listed here represent only a small fraction of studies of the Great Irish Famine. For further studies, readers should consult the comprehensive database *Irish History Online* at www.irishhistoryonline.ie.

REFERENCES

Anbinder, Tyler, *Five Points: The 19th-Century New York City Neighborhood That Invented Tap Dance, Stole Elections, and Became the World's Most Notorious Slum*, New York: Free Press, 2001.

Arnold, David, *Famine: Social Crisis and Historical Change*, Oxford: Basil Blackwell, 1988.

Bew, Paul, *Ireland: The Politics of Enmity, 1789–2006*, Oxford: Oxford University Press, 2007.

Black, R. D. C., *Economic Thought and the Irish Question, 1817–1870*, Cambridge: Cambridge University Press, 1960.

Bourke, Austin (ed. Jacqueline Hill and Cormac Ó Gráda), *'The Visitation of God'?, The Potato and the Great Irish Famine*, Dublin: Lilliput Press, 1993.

Bourke, Ulick J., *The Life and Times of the Most Rev. John MacHale, Archbishop of Tuam*, Dublin: Gill and Son, 1882.

[Central Relief Committee], *Transactions of the Central Relief Committee of the Society of Friends during the Famine in Ireland, in 1846 and 1847* [1852], Dublin: Edmund Burke, 1996.

Clark, Samuel, and Donnelly, James S., Jr. (eds.), *Irish Peasants: Violence and Political Unrest, 1780–1914*, Manchester: Manchester University Press, 1983.

Clarkson, Leslie A., and Crawford, E. Margaret (eds.), *Famine and Disease in Ireland* (5 vols.), London: Pickering and Chatto, 2005.

Clarkson, L. A., and Crawford, E. Margaret, *Feast and Famine: A History of Food and Nutrition in Ireland, 1500–1920*, Oxford: Oxford University Press, 2001.

Coleman, Terry, *Passage to America: A History of Emigrants from Great Britain and Ireland to America in the Mid-Nineteenth Century*, London: Hutchinson, 1972.

Connell, K. H., *The Population of Ireland, 1750–1845*, Oxford: Clarendon Press, 1950.

Connolly, S. J., *Priests and People in Pre-Famine Ireland, 1780–1845*, Dublin: Gill & Macmillan, 1982.

Costello, Nuala, *John MacHale, Archbishop of Tuam*, Dublin: Talbot Press, 1939.

Crawford, E. Margaret (ed.), *Famine: The Irish Experience, 900–1900: Subsistence Crises and Famines in Ireland*, Edinburgh: John Donald, 1989.

Crawford, E. Margaret (ed.), *The Hungry Stream: Essays on Emigration and Famine* (proceedings of the conference held at the Ulster-American Folk Park, 1995), Belfast: Institute of Irish Studies, Queen's University, and Centre for Emigration Studies, Ulster-American Folk Park, 1997.

Crowley, John, et al. (eds.), *Atlas of the Great Irish Famine*, Cork: Cork University Press, 2012.

Daly, Mary E., *The Famine in Ireland*, Dundalk: Dundalgan Press, for Dublin Historical Association, 1986.

Davis, Mike, *Late Victorian Holocausts: El Niño Famines and the Making of the Modern World*, London: Verso, 2001.

Davis, Richard, *The Young Ireland Movement*, Dublin: Gill & Macmillan, 1987.

Davis, Richard, *William Smith O'Brien: Ireland—1848—Tasmania*, Dublin: Geography Publications, 1989.

de Nie, Michael, *The Eternal Paddy: Irish Identity and the British Press, 1798–1882*, Madison: University of Wisconsin Press, 2004.

Devine, T. M., *The Great Highland Famine: Hunger, Emigration and the Scottish Highlands in the Nineteenth Century*, Edinburgh: John Donald, 1988.

Dickson, David, *Arctic Ireland: The Extraordinary Story of the Great Frost and Forgotten Famine of 1740–41*, Belfast: White Row Press, 1997.

Dillon, William, *The Life of John Mitchel* (2 vols.), London: Kegan Paul, Trench, 1888.

Donnelly, James S., Jr., *The Great Irish Potato Famine*, Stroud (Glos.): Sutton, 2001.

Donnelly, James S., Jr., *The Land and the People of Nineteenth-Century Cork: The Rural Economy and the Land Question* (Studies in Irish History, 2nd series, vol. 9), London: Routledge and Kegan Paul, 1975.

Dudley Edwards, R., and Williams, T. Desmond (eds.), *The Great Famine: Studies in Irish History, 1845–52*, Dublin: Browne and Nolan, for the Irish Committee of Historical Sciences, 1956.

Duffy, Charles Gavan, *Four Years of Irish History, 1845–1849: A Sequel to 'Young Ireland'*, London, Paris and New York: Cassell, Petter, Galpin, 1883.

Dunn, Mary Lee, *Ballykilcline Rising: From Famine Ireland to Immigrant America*, Amherst (Mass.): University of Massachusetts Press, 2008.

Eagleton, Terry, *Heathcliff and the Great Hunger: Studies in Irish Culture*, London: Verso, 1995.

Fegan, Melissa, *Literature and the Irish Famine, 1845–1919*, Oxford: Clarendon Press, 2002.

Fitzpatrick, David, *Irish Emigration, 1801–1921* (Studies in Irish Economic and Social History, 1), Dublin: Economic and Social History Society of Ireland, 1984.

Foster, R. F., *Modern Ireland, 1600–1972*, London: Allen Lane, 1988.

Freeman, Thomas Walter, *Pre-Famine Ireland: A Study in Historical Geography*, Manchester: Manchester University Press, 1957.

Gash, Norman, *Sir Robert Peel: The Life of Sir Robert Peel after 1830*, London: Longman, 1972.

Geoghegan, Patrick M., *Liberator: The Life and Death of Daniel O'Connell, 1830–1847*, Dublin: Gill & Macmillan, 2010.

Goodbody, Rob, *A Suitable Channel: Quaker Relief in the Great Famine*, Bray: Pale Publishing, 1995.

Grant, Elizabeth (ed. Andrew Tod), *Memoirs of a Highland Lady: Elizabeth Grant of Rothiemurchus*, Edinburgh: Canongate, 1988.

Grant, Elizabeth, *The Highland Lady in Ireland: Journals, 1840–50: Elizabeth Grant of Rothiemurchus* (ed. Patricia Pelly and Andrew Tod), Edinburgh: Canongate Classics, 1991.

Gray, Peter, *Famine, Land and Politics: British Government and Irish Society, 1843–1850*, Dublin: Irish Academic Press, 1999.

Gray, Peter, *The Irish Famine*, London: Thames and Hudson, 1995.

Gray, Peter, *The Making of the Irish Poor Law, 1815–43*, Manchester: Manchester University Press, 2009.

Gribben, Arthur (ed.), *The Great Famine and the Irish Diaspora in America*, Amherst (Mass.): University of Massachusetts Press, 1999.

Guinnane, Timothy W., *The Vanishing Irish: Households, Migration, and the Rural Economy in Ireland, 1850–1914*, Princeton: Princeton University Press, 1997.

Gwynn, Denis, *Young Ireland and 1848*, Cork: Cork University Press, 1949.

Haines, Robin F., *Charles Trevelyan and the Great Irish Famine*, Dublin: Four Courts Press, 2004.

Hannigan, K. (ed.), *The Famine: Ireland, 1845–51* (Facsimile Documents Series), Dublin: Public Record Office, 1982.

Hatton, Helen E., *The Largest Amount of Good: Quaker Relief in Ireland, 1654–1921*, Kingston and Montréal: McGill-Queen's University Press, 1993.

Hilton, Boyd, *A Mad, Bad, and Dangerous People?: England, 1783–1846*, Oxford: Oxford University Press, 2006.

Hooper, Glenn, *Travel Writing and Ireland, 1760–1860: Culture, History, Politics*, Basingstoke (Hants): Palgrave Macmillan, 2005.

Hooper, Glenn (ed.), *The Tourist's Gaze: Travellers to Ireland, 1800–2000*, Cork: Cork University Press, 2001.

Hoppen, K. Theodore, *Elections, Politics and Society in Ireland, 1832–1885*, Oxford: Oxford University Press, 1984.

Hoppen, K. Theodore, *Ireland Since 1800: Conflict and Conformity* (2nd ed.), London: Longman, 1999.

Hoppen, K. Theodore, *The Mid-Victorian Generation, 1846–1886*, Oxford: Oxford University Press, 1998.

Jackson, Alvin, *Ireland, 1798–1998: War, Peace and Beyond* (2nd ed.), Oxford: Wiley-Blackwell, 2010.

James, Dermot, and Ó Maitiú, Séamas (eds.), *The Wicklow World of Elizabeth Smith, 1840–1850*, Dublin: Woodfield Press, 1996.

Jenkins, Brian, *Era of Emancipation: British Government of Ireland, 1812–1830*, Kingston and Montréal: McGill-Queen's University Press, 1988.

Kelleher, Margaret, *The Feminization of Famine: Expressions of the Inexpressible?*, Cork: Cork University Press, 1997.

Kennedy, Liam, et al., *Mapping the Great Irish Famine: A Survey of the Famine Decades*, Dublin: Four Courts Press, 1999.

Kerr, Donal A., *'A Nation of Beggars'?, Priests, People, and Politics in Famine Ireland, 1846–1852*, Oxford: Clarendon Press, 1994.

Kerr, Donal A., *Peel, Priests and Politics: Sir Robert Peel's Administration and the Roman Catholic Church in Ireland, 1841–1846*, Oxford: Oxford University Press, 1982.

Killen, John (ed.), *The Famine Decade: Contemporary Accounts, 1841–1851*, Belfast: Blackstaff Press, 1995.

Kinealy, Christine, *A Death-Dealing Famine: The Great Hunger in Ireland*, London: Pluto Press, 1997.

Kinealy, Christine, *Repeal and Revolution: 1848 in Ireland*, Manchester: Manchester University Press, 2009.

Kinealy, Christine, *The Great Irish Famine: Impact, Ideology and Rebellion*, Basingstoke (Hants): Palgrave, 2002.

Kinealy, Christine, *This Great Calamity: The Irish Famine, 1845–52*, Dublin: Gill & Macmillan, 1994.

Kissane, Noel (ed.), *The Irish Famine: A Documentary History*, Dublin: National Library of Ireland, 1995.

Lee, Joseph, *The Modernisation of Irish Society, 1848–1918* (2nd ed.), Dublin: Gill & Macmillan, 1989.

Lengel, Edward G., *The Irish through British Eyes: Perceptions of Ireland in the Famine Era*, Westport (Conn.): Praeger, 2002.

Loughlin, James, *The British Monarchy and Ireland: 1800 to the Present*, Cambridge: Cambridge University Press, 2007.

Lyons, F. S. L., *Ireland since the Famine*, London: Weidenfeld and Nicolson, 1971.

MacCall, Séamus, *Irish Mitchel: A Biography*, London: Thomas Nelson, 1938.

MacDonagh, Oliver, *Ireland: The Union and its Aftermath*, London: George Allen and Unwin, 1977.

MacDonagh, Oliver, *O'Connell: The Life of Daniel O'Connell, 1775–1847*, London: Weidenfeld and Nicolson, 1991.

McDowell, R. B., *Public Opinion and Government Policy in Ireland, 1801–1846*, London: Faber and Faber, 1952.

McGovern, Bryan P., *John Mitchel: Irish Nationalist, Southern Secessionist*, Knoxville: University of Tennessee Press, 2009.

McGuire, James, and Quinn, James (eds.), *Dictionary of Irish Biography: From the Earliest Times to the Year 2002* (9 vols.), Cambridge: Cambridge University Press, 2009.

MacIntyre, Angus, *The Liberator: Daniel O'Connell and the Irish Party, 1830–1847*, London: Hamish Hamilton, 1965.

Miller, Kerby A., *Emigrants and Exiles: Ireland and the Irish Exodus to North America*, New York: Oxford University Press, 1985.

Mitchel, John, *Jail Journal, or Five Years in British Prisons …* New York: P. M. Haverty, 1854.

Mitchel, John, *The History of Ireland: From the Treaty of Limerick to the Present Time* (2 vols.), Dublin: James Duffy, 1869.

Mitchel, John, *The Last Conquest of Ireland (Perhaps)* [1861] (Author's Edition), Glasgow: R. and T. Washbourne, n.d. [1883].

Mokyr, Joel, *Why Ireland Starved: A Quantitative and Analytical History of the Irish Economy, 1800–1850* (2nd ed.), London: Allen and Unwin, 1985.

Morash, Chris, and Hayes, Richard (eds.), *Fearful Realities: New Perspectives on the Famine*, Dublin: Irish Academic Press, 1996.

Morash, Christopher, *Writing the Irish Famine*, Oxford: Clarendon Press, 1995.

Morash, Christopher (ed.), *The Hungry Voice: The Poetry of the Irish Famine* (2nd ed.), Dublin: Irish Academic Press, 2009.

Mulroney, Margaret M. (ed.), *Fleeing the Famine: North America and Irish Refugees, 1845–1851*, Westport (Conn.): Praeger, 2003.

Murphy, Ignatius, *A Starving People: Life and Death in West Clare, 1841–1851*, Dublin: Irish Academic Press, 1996.

Murphy, James H., *Abject Loyalty: Nationalism and Monarchy in Ireland during the Reign of Queen Victoria*, Cork: Cork University Press, 2007.

Nally, David P., *Human Encumbrances: Political Violence and the Great Irish Famine*, Notre Dame (Ind.): University of Notre Dame Press, 2011.

Neal, Frank, *Black '47: Britain and the Famine Irish*, Basingstoke (Hants): Macmillan, 1998.

Nicholson, Asenath (ed. Maureen Murphy), *Annals of the Famine in Ireland* [1851], Dublin: Lilliput Press, 1998.

Norton, Desmond, *Landlords, Tenants, Famine: The Business of an Irish Land Agency in the 1840s*, Dublin: UCD Press, 2006.

Nowlan, Kevin B., *The Politics of Repeal: A Study in the Relations between Great Britain and Ireland, 1841–50* (Studies in Irish History, 3), London: Routledge and Kegan Paul, 1965.

Ó Cathaoir, Brendan, *Famine Diary*, Dublin: Irish Academic Press, 1999.

Ó Cathaoir, Brendan, *John Blake Dillon: Young Irelander*, Dublin: Irish Academic Press, 1990.

O'Farrell, Patrick, *England and Ireland since 1800*, London: Oxford University Press, 1975.

O'Ferrall, Fergus, *Daniel O'Connell* (Gill Irish Lives), Dublin: Gill & Macmillan, 1981.

Ó Gráda, Cormac, *Black '47 and Beyond: The Great Irish Famine in History, Economy, and Memory*, Princeton (NJ): Princeton University Press, 1999.

Ó Gráda, Cormac, *Famine: A Short History*, Princeton (NJ): Princeton University Press, 2009.

Ó Gráda, Cormac, *Ireland: A New Economic History, 1780–1939*, Oxford: Clarendon Press, 1994.

Ó Gráda, Cormac, *Ireland Before and After the Famine: Explorations in Economic History, 1800–1925* (2nd ed.), Manchester: Manchester University Press, 1993.

Ó Gráda, Cormac, *Ireland's Great Famine: Interdisciplinary Perspectives*, Dublin: UCD Press, 2006.

Ó Gráda, Cormac, *The Great Irish Famine*, London: Macmillan, 1989.

Ó Gráda, Cormac (ed.), *Famine 150: Commemorative Lecture Series*, Dublin: Teagasc, 1997.

Ó Gráda, Cormac, et al. (eds.), *When the Potato Failed: Causes and Effects of the 'Last' European Subsistence Crisis, 1845–1850*, Turnhout: Brepols, 2007.

Ó Murchadha, Ciarán, *The Great Famine: Ireland's Agony, 1845–1852*, London and New York: Continuum, 2011.

O'Reilly, Bernard, *John MacHale, Archbishop of Tuam: His Life, Times, and Correspondence* (2 vols.), New York and Cincinnati: F. Pustet and Co., 1890.

O'Rourke, John, *The History of the Great Irish Famine of 1847: With Notices of Earlier Irish Famines* (3rd ed.), Dublin: James Duffy, 1902.

Ó Tuathaigh, Gearóid, *Ireland Before the Famine, 1798–1848* (Gill History of Ireland, 9), Dublin: Gill & Macmillan, 1972.

Oxford Dictionary of National Biography: From the Earliest Times to the Year 2000 (60 vols.), Oxford: Oxford University Press, 2004.

Póirtéir, Cathal (ed.), *Famine Echoes*, Dublin: Gill & Macmillan, 1995.

Póirtéir, Cathal (ed.), *The Great Irish Famine* (Thomas Davis Lecture Series), Cork and Dublin: Mercier Press, in association with Raidió-Teilifís Éireann, 1995.

Prest, John M., *Lord John Russell*, London: Macmillan, 1972.

Public Record Office of Northern Ireland, *The Great Famine, 1845–1852*, Belfast: PRONI, 1970.

Quinn, James, *John Mitchel*, Dublin: UCD Press, for Historical Association of Ireland, 2008.

Scally, Robert James, *The End of Hidden Ireland: Rebellion, Famine, and Emigration*, New York: Oxford University Press, 1995.

Sloan, Robert, *William Smith O'Brien and the Young Irelander Rebellion of 1848: The Road to Ballingarry*, Dublin: Four Courts Press, 2000.

Smout, T. C., and Lambert, R. A. (eds.), *Rothiemurchus: Nature and People on a Highland Estate, 1500–2000*, Dalkeith: Scottish Cultural Press, 1999.

Somerville, Alexander (ed. K. D. M. Snell), *Letters from Ireland During the Famine of 1847* [1852], Dublin: Irish Academic Press, 1994.

Swords, Liam (ed.), *In Their Own Words: The Famine in North Connacht, 1845–1849*, Dublin: Columba Press, 1998.

Thomson, David, and McGusty, Moyra (eds.), *The Irish Journals of Elizabeth Smith, 1840–1850*, Oxford: Clarendon Press, 1980.

Tod, Andrew, 'The Smiths of Baltiboys: A Co. Wicklow Family and their Estate in the 1840s' (PhD thesis, University of Edinburgh, 1978).

Tóibín, Colm, and Ferriter, Diarmaid, *The Irish Famine: A Documentary*, London: Profile Books, in association with London Review of Books, 2001.

Trevelyan, C. E., *The Irish Crisis*, London: Longman, Brown, Green and Longmans, 1848.

Trevelyan, Humphrey, *The India We Left: Charles Trevelyan, 1826-65*, Humphrey Trevelyan, 1929–47, London: Macmillan, 1972.

Trevelyan, Laura, *A Very British Family: The Trevelyans and Their World*, London: I. B. Tauris, 2006.

Vaughan, W. E. (ed.), *A New History of Ireland, Vol. v: Ireland under the Union, i: 1801–70*, Oxford: Clarendon Press, 1989.

Vaughan, W. E. (ed.), *A New History of Ireland, Vol. vi: Ireland under the Union, ii: 1870–1921*, Oxford: Clarendon Press, 1996.

Williams, W. H. A., *Tourism, Landscape, and the Irish Character: British Travel Writers in Pre-Famine Ireland*, Madison (Wis.): University of Wisconsin Press, 2008.

Wilson, David A., *Thomas D'Arcy McGee, Vol. 1: Passion, Reason, and Politics, 1825–1857*, Montréal: McGill-Queen's University Press, 2008.

Woodham-Smith, Cecil, *The Great Hunger: Ireland, 1845–9*, London: Hamish Hamilton, 1962.

Woods, C. J., *Travellers' Accounts as Source-Materials for Irish Historians* (Maynooth Research Guides for Irish Local History), Dublin: Four Courts Press, 2009.

INDEX

ent3ning

INDEX 287

Delany family, 106
Dempsey, Bryan, 146
Denmark, 108
Denvir, Cornelius, Bishop of Down and Connor, 87
de Rothschild, Lionel, 155
Derry, County, 15, 123, 218
de Strzelecki, Paul Edmund, 156–7
de Tocqueville, Alexis, 40
de Vere, Stephen, 219
Devon Commission, 34–5
Dillon, John Blake, 99, 193, 194
Dilworth, John, 144
Disraeli, Benjamin, 203
Doheny, Michael, 178, 192–4
Donegal, County, 40, 118, 119, 156, 169
Donoughmore, Earl of, 37, 65
Douglas, Dr George Mellis, 220
Down, County, 14–16, 21, 69, 77
Downshire, Marquess of, 33, 80
Doyle, Garrett, 146
Doyle, Michael, 146
Doyle family, 174, 200
Drummond, Thomas, 65–8, 73
Drummond Commission, 41
Drummond-Stewart, John A., Laird of Murthly, 140
Dublin, 15, 28–9, 40, 46, 92–4, 155, 157, 175, 190–91, 204, 207, 218
Dublin, County, 77, 134
Dublin Castle, 42, 52–3, 55, 64–8, 73, 111, 125, 134, 188, 229
Dublin Evening Mail, 28–9
Dublin Metropolitan Police (DMP), 65
Duff, Rev. Alexander, 63–4
Duffy, Charles Gavan, 68–9, 93–4, 99–100, 121, 177, 180–81, 186–7, 190, 192–3
Duncan, Dr W.H., 223

East India Company, 10, 26
Ecclesiastical Titles Act (1851), 86
Edinburgh Review, 202
education, 58–63, 86–7, 90–91, 103–4, 120, 149, 150, 176, 196
emigration, 169, 195, 199, 210–26
'coffin ships', 218–19
remittances, 217–18
Emmet, Robert, 100
Encumbered Estates Act (1848), 173–4, 230
Engels, Frederick, 57–8
evictions, 1–3, 106, 109, 170–71, 174, 183, 195, 197, 199–200

Farnham, Lord, 196
Feeney, Patrick, 132
Fenianism, 73, 191, 236
Fitzgerald, Garrett Hugh, 83
Fitzgerald, Rev. Philip, 193–4
Fitzwilliam, Earl, 33, 215
food exports, 107–8, 135–6
Forster, William, 153
Forster, William E., 118
Foster, T.C., 91–2
Fox, R. Barclay, 153, 170
France, 76, 78–9, 83, 124, 204, 235–6
revolution, 188–9
Fraser, Samuel, 22
Free Church of Scotland, 166, 230
Freeman's Journal, 19, 67, 77, 82, 98–9, 133, 181, 197
Fremantle, Sir Thomas, 111

Galway, County, 40, 42, 78, 109, 153, 172, 179–80, 198–9, 216
Gardeners' Chronicle, 77, 83
Gardiner, Charles, 25
Gardiner, Mary, 78
Garvey, George, 31